STUDIES IN INTERNATIONAL LAW AND HISTORY
AN ASIAN PERSPECTIVE

Developments in International Law

VOLUME 49

R.P. ANAND

Studies in International Law and History

An Asian Perspective

SPRINGER-SCIENCE+BUSINESS MEDIA, B.V.

A C.I.P. Catalogue record for this book is available from the Library of Congress.

Printed on acid-free paper.

ISBN 978-90-04-13859-9 ISBN 978-94-017-5600-6 (eBook)
DOI 10.1007/978-94-017-5600-6

Originally published by Martinus Nijhoff Publishers in 2004
Softcover reprint of the hardcover 1st edition 2004

To

My Students

For

Their Love and Affection

R.P. Anand

Professor Emeritus at present in the Division of International Legal Studies of the Jawaharlal Nehru University in New Delhi, India, Professor Anand retired from the University in 1998 after serving there for nearly 33 years as Professor and Head of that Division. Anand is a well-known scholar in the field of International Law and widely recognized as a spokesman of the Third World views on the subject. Member of the prestigious *Instiut de Droit International*, Professor Anand has been recipient of a number of awards and honours in the field, Visiting Professor or Scholar in several universities and institutes of higher learning in the United States and Europe, Lecturer at the Hague Academy of International Law, U.G.C. National Lecturer in Law in India, and has served as Legal Consultant to the UN Secretary-General on Law of the Sea. Author or Editor of 18 books, Professor Anand has published more than one hundred articles in professional journals in Canada, Europe, India, Japan, and the United States.

By the Same Author

BOOKS

New Law of the Sea: Emergent Norms and Institutions, Lectures delivered at the Institute of International Public Law and International relations, Aristotle University, Thessaloniki, Greece 1996;

The United Nations and the Gulf Crisis (Published under the auspices of the International Legal Studies Division of the Jawaharlal Nehru University) (New Delhi, 1994);

South Asia: In Search of a Regional Identity (Banyan Publications, New Delhi, 1991).

Confrontation or Co-operation: International Law and the Developing Countries (Banyan Publications, New Delhi; Martinus Nijhoff. The Hague, 1987), pp. 267.

Sovereign Equality of States in International Law, Lectures at the Hague Academy of International Law (*Extract from Recueil des Cours,* vol. 197, 1986-III 9 Martinus Nijhoff, The Hague, 1986.

Origin and Development of the Law of the Sea: History of International Law Revisited (Martinus Nijhoff, The Hague, 1983), pp. 287,

International Courts and Contemporary Conflicts (Published under the auspices of the Indian School of International Studies) (Asia Publishing House, New York, London, Bombay 1974), pp. 479.

New States and International Law, Lectures delivered under the University Grants Commission's National Lecturership scheme) (Vikas Publications, Delhi, 1972), pp. 119.

Studies in International Adjudication (Vikas Publications, Delhi: Oceana Publications, Dobbs Ferry, N.Y. 1969), pp. 298.

Compulsory Jurisdiction of the International Court of Justice (Published under the auspices of the Indian School of International Studies) (Asia Publishing House, New York, London, Bombay, 1961) pp. 342.

Salient Documents in International Law (Editor), (New Delhi, 1994).

Recent Developments in Civil Aviation in India (Co-editor) (Lacers Books, New Delhi, 1987).

Law, Science and Environment (Co-editor) (Lancers Books, New D 1987).

ASEAN; Identity, Development and Change (Co-editor) (Published u the auspices of the University of Philippines Law Center and East- Center Culture Learning Institute, Honolulu, Hawaii) (Quezon City, 19 pp. 411.

Cultural factors in International Relations (Editor) (Published unde auspices of the East-West Center Culture Learning Institute, Hono Hawaii) (Abhinav Publications, New Delhi, 1981), pp. 291.

Law of the Sea: Caracas and Beyond (Editor) (Radiant Publishers, Delhi, 1978), pp. 380.

Asian States and the Development of a Universal International Law (E (Vikas Publications, New Delhi, 1972), pp. 245.

Contents

Preface

International law is understood to be a law applicable among all the states in equal measure in their relations with each other. It is generally defined "as the body of rules which are legally binding on states in their intercourse with each other."[1] It is "composed for its greater part of the principles and rules of conduct which states feel bound to observe, and therefore, do observe in their relations with each other."[2] It is defined and described by scholars and statesmen alike as a law which makes no distinction between nations, large or small, east or west, north or south. As Oppenheim, in its latest edition, declares: "International law does not recognize any distinctions in the membership of the international community based on religious, geographical or cultural differences."[3] Moreover, sovereign equality of states is a well-recognized and fundamental principle of international law which is said to be "absolute" and "unquestionable".[4] Proclaiming its faith "in the equal rights of men and women and nations large and small", the Charter of the United Nations clearly and boldly declares in Article 2, paragrah 1, that "the Organization is based on the principle of sovereign equality of all its Members."

But although modern international law is now recognized as universally applicable to all the states and all new entities, as soon as they emerge as independent states, whether members of the United Nations or not, are accepted as members of the ever-expanding international society and are bound by its rules and seek its protection, this is only a recent phenomenon not older than the United Nations itself. Before that modern international law was supposed to be merely a product of the Western European Christian states, or states of European origin, and applicable only between them. As Oppenheim points out:

> "The old Christian states of Western Europe constituted the original international community within which international law grew up gradually through custom and treaty. Whenever a new Christian state made its appearance in Europe, it was

[1] *Oppenheim's International Law*, vol. I, *Peace* (Edited by Sir Robert Jennings and Sir Arthur Watts), 9th editon (London, 1997), p. 4.

[2] *Starke's International Law*, Eleventh Edition by I. A. Shearer (London, 1994), pp. 104-105.

[3] Oppenheim, note 1, p. 87.

[4] See R.P. Anand, "Sovereign Equaltiy of States in International Law", *Recueil des Cours*, Vol. 197 (1986-II), p. 53.

> received into the existing European community of states. But, during its formative period, this international law was confined to those states. In former times European states had only very limited intercourse with states outside Europe, and even that was not always regarded as being governed by the same rules of international conduct as prevailed between European states."[5]

Gradually, as Oppenheim goes on to explain, the international community expanded by the inclusion of Christian states outside Europe, such as the United States, which became independent in 1776, and later by inclusion of non-Christian states, like Turkey, which was admitted as a member of the international community by the Peace Treaty of Paris in 1856. But "there were numerous states outside the international community" and "international law was not as such regarded as containing rules concerning relations with such states, although it was accepted that those relations should be regulated by the principles of morality."[6] As late as the First World War, we are told, "the position of such states as Persia, Siam, China, Abyssinia, and the like was to some extent anomalous". Although there was considerable international intercourse between these states and states of Western civilization — treaties had been concluded, full diplomatic relations had been established, China, Japan, Persia and Siam, had even taken part in the Hague Peace Conferences—, since they belonged to "ancient but different civilizations there was a question how far relations with their governments could usefully be based upon the rules of international society."[7]

As we study and look at international law from historical perspective, especially in the context of the role of Asian and even African countries in its origin and development, there are several questions which have been raised but not satisfactorily answered. After the fifteenth century, Europeans went to Asian countries for their own needs and developed not only active trade and commercial relations, but intimate political relations as well with these independent Asian communities, especially in India and the East Indies. What rules of inter-state conduct applied between these European countries and Asian states? Without some common rules of international law, Europeans could not have survived in Asian countries. And if some rules of international law and comity did apply between them and their relations, a question may be raised if these rules had no influence whatsoever on the emerging international law among European countries during this period?

After a few centuries of trade, commercial and political relations, European countries defeated Asian rulers and became dominant. Most of the European international lawyers talk about the development of international law without any reference to Asian states or their role in its development. There are a few further questions which need answers. When did European international

[5] Oppenheim, note 1, pp. 87-88.
[6] Oppenheim, ibid, p. 88.
[7] Oppenheim, ibid, p. 89.

law become universally binding? Can states which did not, could not, were not permitted to, participate in its origin and development question some of its rules which are inimical to their interests or very survival? How can and does this law change, or be modified, in the absence of any supra-national legislature or other authority? Has the present system of international law, which was nothing but European law writ large until the Second World War, changed or is changing from the European law of nations to a common law of mankind?

We have tried to deal with, though not satisfactorily answer, some of these questions in the following nine papers published at different times. As we shall see, despite the Eurocentric nature of contemporary international law, which was developed largely by and for the benefit of the rich, industrial and powerful states of Western Europe and the United States, newly-independent states and new members of the international society have never questioned or denied the binding force of international law and they accept a large part of it without any question. Certain differences with the Western Powers in regard to codification and progressive development of international law should not be understood as rejection of the present system. They only indicate conflicts of interests between the developed and the developing states and attempts on the part of the latter to exert their influence in reformulation of international law. We shall see that their attitude towards international law has been respectful rather than disdainful. They have used principles of international law for or against their international claims, with an underlying assumption that these principles are binding. They have submitted their disputes to international arbitration or the International Court of Justice which are bound to apply international legal rules. Far from rejecting the tenets of international law, most of the new states of Asia and Africa claim to be scrupulous adherents of those principles and are quite conservative and traditionalist in their approach.

I am grateful to the editors and publishers of the following journals and books for permission to include them in this book:

1. "Jawaharlal Nehru and International Law", *Indian Journal of International Law*, Vol. 42, No. 1 (January-March, 2002), pp. 5-29.
2. "Family of 'Civilized' States and Japan: A Story of Humiliation, Assimilation, Defiance and Confrontation", *Journal of the History of International Law* (Kluwer Law International), Vol. 5 (2003), pp. 1-75.
3. "Status of Tibet in International Law", *International Studies* (New Delhi) (April, 1969), pp. 401-445.
4. "Enhancing the Effectiveness of Compulsory Procedures of International Dispute Settlement" , Paper presented at the Inauguration of the Law of the Sea Tribunal at Hamburg, Germany, September 14, 2000 . *Max Planck Yearbook of United Nations Law,* Volume 5 (2001), pp. 1-20.(Kluwer Law International The Hague, The Netherlands.)

5. "The World Court on Trial" in R.S. Pathak and R.P. Dhokalia, *International Law in Transition: Essays in Honour of Judge Nagendra Singh) Lancer's Books New Delhi in Cooperation with Martinus Nijhoff, Dordrecht, 1992), pp. 245-66.*
6. "Common Heritage of Mankind: Mutilation of an Ideal", *Indian Journal of International Law*, Vol. 37, No. 1., (*January –March 1997), pp. 1-18.*
7. "Navigation through Territorial Sea and Straits" *Indian Journal of International Law*, Vol. 36, no. 4 (October – December, 1996), pp. 13-38.
8. "South Asia and the Law of the Sea: Problems and Prospects" in Thomas A. Mensah (editor), *Ocean Governance: Strategies and Approaches for the 21st Century* (Law of the Sea Institute, Honolulu, Hawaii, 1996), pp. 331-353.
9. "A New International Economic Order for Sustainable Development?, Najeeb Al-Nauimi and R. Meese (Editors) *Proceedings of the International Conference on Sustainable Development held under the auspices of the Asian African Legal Consultative Committee in Doha* (Qatar) (1995) pp.1209-1247

Though one of the papers is rather old, we feel that it has not lost its relevance. Some papers overlap each other, but we have left them as they were published originally to maintain their integrity.

I am grateful to Mr. S. Kumar of Lancers Books for taking the onerous responsibility of publishing the book.

Last, but not least, I must thank my wife for her confidence, continued support and encouragement.

R.P. ANAND

Jawaharlal Nehru and International Law and Relations

Jawaharlal Nehru: Epoch-Maker and Architect of Modern India

There are some people who leave an indelible mark on history. Jawaharlal Nehru, the first Prime Minister of independent India, was such a great leader. He was not only the architect of independent India's destiny during the first seventeen years he was its undisputed leader and the prime minister, but he "played a decisive role in the history of the twentieth century—as a leader of the Indian people, as a representative of the new mood of Asia, and as a spokesman of the international conscience."[1] As Michael Brecher, his political biographer, said:

> "Few statesmen in the twentieth century have attained the stature of Jawaharlal Nehru. As the pre-eminent figure in India's era of transition he bears comparison with Roosevelt and Churchill, Lenin and Mao, men who towered above their colleagues and guided their people through a period of national crisis. Only Gandhi inspired greater faith and adoration among the masses. Only Stalin, perhaps, had greater power. Like these outstanding men of the age he has also imposed his personality on a wider canvas. He is for many a symbol of Asia's political awakening and the outstanding spokesman of 'the middle way' in a world of ideological crusades. His name conjures up a host of associations, some praiseworthy, some critical... Yet friends and foes alike recognize him as a leading actor on the stage of contemporary history."[2]

Although he was not specifically trained as an international lawyer, as a keen student and practitioner of international affairs, as the Foreign Minister of India and chief spokesman of the newly independent Asian countries, he influenced the development of international law in no uncertain terms. There is no doubt about his tremendous influence on the formulation of India's foreign policy. To quote Brecher again,

The article is based on a paper presented as an address at the Nehru Centre, Mumbai, on May 11,2001. The author is grateful to the Nehru Centre for all their help in giving him an opportunity to present his views on the subject.

[1] Sarvepalli Gopal, *Jawaharlal Nehru: A Biography*, vol. 1 (1889-1947), (Bombay,1976), p. 5.

[2] Michael Brecher, *Nehru—A Political Biography*" (London, 1959), p. 595.

> "In no other state does one man dominate foreign policy as does Nehru in India. Indeed so overwhelming is his influence that India's policy has come to mean in the minds of people everywhere the personal policy of Pandit Nehru. And justifiably so, for Nehru is the philosopher, the architect, the engineer and voice of his country's policy towards the outside world."[3]

Educated and trained in Europe, Pandit Nehru (as he was known) well understood the European mind and policies, their culture and history. But as a freedom-fighter and leader of the people in subservient India, an ardent student of the Indian history and culture, well-trained in the Indian ethos by his political guru, Mahatma Gandhi, he was well-equipped to play a very important role in the re-emergence and re-awakening of India and Asia and taking their rightful position in international relations.

Second World War and the Collapse of Colonialism

There is little doubt that until the Second World War international law was largely European law writ large. With the sole exception of Japan, which had learned European ways soon after it was forced to open its doors to the United States in 1854 and later to other European powers, and "Europeanized" itself to take benefit of the European international law,[4] it was a law made by Europeans, for Europeans and for the protection of European interests. It was only after the Second World War that Western Europe lost its primacy. It must be mentioned, however, that European peoples and countries were not a unified group living at peace with each other and exploiting the other parts of the world. In fact lop-sided developments in some parts of Europe, German ambitions for a place in the Asian sun, mutual jealousies amongst European countries for the distribution and exploitation of colonies, and strain of a double attack by the newcomers among the imperialists, Germany and Japan, led to a major "civil war" in Europe called the First World War from 1914 to 1919.[5] Europe had hardly recovered from the vast devastation when it drifted towards the second holocaust from 1939 to 1945.

If a divided Asia could not withstand the European onslaught, a divided, warring, and weakened Europe could not permanently dominate Asia. The world as it emerged from the Second World War was a different world altogether. The whole balance of forces had changed and Western Europe had ceased to be the pivot of power. The European powers, which had dominated the world scene for nearly three hundred years, had been pushed aside and were no longer at the centre of the world stage. Out of the ruins of

[3] Brecher, ibid., p. 564.

[4] See R. P. Anand, "Japan and International Law in Historical Perspective", Paper presented at the Centenary Symposium of the Japanese Association of International Law (Kyoto, 1997).

[5] K.M. Panikkar, *Asia and Western Dominance* (London, 1954) pp. 197, 199.

the world holocaust of 1939-45 emerged the United States and the Soviet Union with enough strength to dominate the international scene and seriously challenge each other. Since then the world divided into two groups or blocs plunged into a bitter cold war and a most dangerous armament race.

There was another phenomenal change. Shocked by the significant Japanese military sweep in early forties in East and South-East Asia,[6] and the general weakening of Europe, colonialism collapsed and there emerged numerous independent countries in Asia and Africa which for a long time had had no status and played no role in the formulation and development of international law for they were considered as no more than its objects.

Nehru's Perception of India

It is interesting to note that Asia and later Africa lost their independence and importance once India was defeated, occupied and colonized in the nineteenth century. As India got out of the shackles of colonialism and became independent, it gave impetus and momentum to the collapse of colonialism and reawakening of Asia and Africa. As Brecher said, "with the loss of its imperial bastion England could no longer retain its paramount influence in the Arab world" of the Middle East.[7] India, under the dynamic and progressive leadership of Jawaharlal Nehru and other enlightened leaders, like Mahatma Gandhi, Sardar Vallabhbhai Patel, Maulana Abul Kalam Azad and others, played an important role in the process. Nehru was "the most articulate spokesman for a deep-seated urge to reassert Asia's rightful place in the world community."[8] Although he repeatedly denied any claim to leadership for India, he was acutely aware of the 'special position', which made India pre-eminently fitted to play this role. In a speech in the Constituent Assembly of India on March 8, 1949, he said:

> "When we talk of Asia, remember that India, not because of any ambition of hers, but because of the force of circumstances, because of geography, because of history and because of so many other things, inevitably has to play a very important part in Asia. And not only that; India becomes a kind of meeting ground for various trends and forces and meeting ground between what might roughly be called the East and the West".[9]

[6] According to Professor Brecher, "Japan's military sweep of 1941—2 had shattered the foundations of the colonial order. In the aftermath of the Second World War a dozen states acquired independence in the region..." Michael Brecher, *The New States of Asia: A Political Analysis* (London, 1963), p. 155.

[7] Brecher, n. 2, p. 592.

[8] Brecher, ibid., p. 593.

[9] Jawaharlal Nehru, "Meeting ground of East and West", Speech in the Constituent Assembly, New Delhi, March 8, 1949, in *Jawaharlal Nehru's Speeches*, vol. One, (Delhi, 1949), pp. 232-33.

In one of his speeches during the 1949 American tour he said:

> "India's pivotal position between Western Asia, South-East Asia and the Far East made it the crossroads of that part of the world. India is central point of the Asian picture... India's role of leadership may not be so welcome to others although it may satisfy our vanity. We cannot escape the various responsibilities that arise out of our geography and history."[10]

Nehru calls Asian Relations Conference

Even before India became formally independent, he called the Asian Relations Conference to emphasize that "imperialism" of Europe was over and "as that domination goes, the walls that surrounded us fall down and we look at one another again and meet as old friends long parted."[11] He asserted:

> "For too long have we of Asia been petitioners in Western courts and chancelleries. The story must now belong to the past. We propose to stand on our own legs and to co-operate with all others who are prepared to co-operate with us. We do not intend to be the playthings of the others...The countries of Asia can no longer be used as pawns by others; they are bound to have their own policies in world affairs."[12]

He further stressed that India and Asia must help others to get the political freedom they deserve:

> "We of Asia have a special responsibility to the people of Africa. We must help them to their rightful place in human family. The freedom that we envisage is not to be confined to this nation or that or to a particular people, but must spread out over the whole human race."[13]

Two years later, he organized another emergency Conference of Asian States in Delhi to bring pressure to bear upon the Dutch and the United Nations and champion the independence of Indonesia which was sought to be re-occupied and re-colonized by the Netherlands after the war. He called it,

> "A challenge to a newly awakened Asia which has so long suffered under various forms of colonialism. It is also a challenge to the spirit of man and to all the progressive forces of a divided and distracted world."[14]

[10] To the Overseas Club in New York on 19 October 1949, quoted in Brecher, n. 2, p. 593.

[11] Jawaharlal Nehru, "Asia finds herself again", Inaugural speech at Asian Relations Conference, New Delhi, March 23, 1947, vol. I, n. 9, p. 300.

[12] Nehru, ibid., p. 301.

[13] Ibid., p. 303.

[14] Nehru, "Crisis in Indonesia", Presidential speech delivered in New Delhi inaugurating the 18-nation conference on Indonesia, January 20, 1949, ibid., p. 324.

He warned the international community that "Asia, too long submissive and dependent and a plaything of other countries, will no longer brook any interference with her freedom."[15]

In fact acting as a representative of the newly-independent Asian countries, he was determined to speed up the end of colonialism and left no one in doubt that Asia was wide awake and could no longer be taken for granted. End of colonialism was his goal because he and India deemed colonialism as a permanent form of aggression under international law, which could no longer be tolerated. Law must change with the changing circumstances and could not remain static. But although India considered colonialism not merely as illegal in an age of freedom under the United Nations Charter, but immoral, Nehru was very much against the use of force for the achievement of freedom for the colonized countries unless there was absolutely no other choice.

Liberation of Goa

The small Portuguese colony of Goa on the West Coast of India was a test case for Nehru and India's patience. While France agreed to hand over Pondicherry and other small French possessions in 1954, Portuguese had no such intention and refused to see reason. Although Nehru strongly felt that "there is nothing more scandalous on God's earth today than the Portuguese occupation of Goa, historically, factually, religiously if you like or from any point of view"[16], and there was a lot of internal pressure on him to use military force which would be the easiest and fastest solution, Nehru was strongly against the use of force as a matter of policy. He argued for patience and "was not to be stampeded into forgetting or bypassing" India's basic principles of foreign policy.[17] He admitted that "Goa continues to be a headache" and "it is natural for people to demand strong action" but stressed that "we should not, in the excitement of the moment or because of anger and resentment, undertake any action without thinking out all the consequences."[18] Pressed even more, he made it clear:

> "If you are under the impression that the Government will take police action or use force to liberate Goa from Portuguese domination, you are entirely mistaken. I am not going to do any such thing...Wars and armed actions have never solved any problem anywhere in the world."[19]

[15] Nehru, ibid., p 325. in *Jawaharlal Nehru's Speeches*, vol. One, (Delhi, 1949), p. 300.

[16] Nehru, Press conference 19 July 1955, quoted in Sarvepalli Gopal, *Jawaharlal Nehru: A Biography, vol. Two 1947-1956* (Delhi, 1979). p. 217.

[17] Gopal, ibid., p. 217.

[18] Nehru's communication to Chief Ministers, 20 May 1955, quoted in Gopal, ibid., p. 216.

[19] Nehru, speech at Poona, 4 June 1955, quoted in Gopal, ibid., p. 217.

He insisted that "we have set our face against the solution of problems by warlike methods, and we intend to adhere to that decision. Once the necessity of war on some occasions was accepted, who was to define the occasion? Every country would decide for itself, and floodgates would be opened."[20] He honestly felt that if the Government of India were to use force, they would be regarded as "deceitful hypocrites" and "opportunists" with no principle.[21]

Idealist as Nehru was, he waited for fourteen long years and more in the hope that Portugal would accept the spirit of the time and leave peacefully. Or perhaps, other Western countries would put pressure on Portugal to see reason. But that was not to be. On the contrary, Nehru's policy was regarded as a weakness.[22] Ultimately when there was no choice left, India used minimal force on 17 December 1961 to throw out the Portuguese. There was practically no resistance, no casualty, and the whole 'action' was over in 24 or at the most 36 hours. Lack of action on the part of India would have led to "terrible repression" of the people of Goa who wanted to join India and resulted in "absolute chaos in Goa". [23] Besides solid support of all sections of the society in India and Goa itself, all the countries in Asia and Africa "rejoiced at this action" of India.[24] But some of the Western powers, which, despite realizing the gravity of the situation, had done nothing all these years to solve the issue, now criticized India's action as "aggression" and a gross violation of the United Nations Charter. They contended that the merits of the dispute over Goa were not the issue, but the issue was the use of force forbidden by the Charter. As Stevenson of the United States, discounting the problem of colonialism altogether, said:

> What is at stake today is not colonialism; it is a bold violation of one of the most basic principles in the United Nations Charter."[25]

He went on to give the grim warning:

> "Tonight we are witnessing the first act in a drama which could end with the death of the organization. The League of Nations died, I remind you, when its Members no longer resisted the use of aggressive force... we have witnessed tonight an effort to rewrite the Charter, to sanction the use of force when it suits one's own purposes."[26]

[20] Nehru, address to U.P.P.C.C. at Sitapur 21 August 1955, quoted in Gopal, ibid.

[21] Nehru, speech in Lok Sabha, 17 September, 1955,quoted in Gopal, ibid.

[22] Gopal, ibid., pp. 217-18.

[23] See Jawaharlal Nehru, "Background to the Liberation", in *Jawaharlal Nehru's Speeches*, Vol. 4 (Sept. 1957—April 1963), (Delhi, 1964), p. 36. It may be noted that the Portuguese authorities threatened to "blow up most of the important institutes, buildings etc. in Goa." Nehru, ibid., p. 39.

[24] Nehru, ibid. p.36.

[25] *Security Council Official Records, 16th year* 987th meeting, 18 December 1961, para 75.

[26] ibid. 988th meeting, paras 130-31.

Apart from the fact that such a warning did not sound very convincing in a world where countries, especially the big powers, give little heed to the principles of the Charter when their own interests are involved, the newly-independent states were more inclined to agree with Soviet Ambassador Zorin, who said:

> "If the United Nations does not defend the colonial countries and peoples, but tries to defend the colonial system and the most reactionary representative of that system, then this indeed may mean the collapse of the United Nations."[27]

India refused to accept the Western contention that the use of force in Goa by India was an "aggression" under the Charter and claimed that it had acted only in self-defense against the long-standing 'aggression' of Portugal against India and its people. As India's ambassador, C. S. Jha, trying to drive home the real issue, said:

> "It must be realized that this is a colonial question. It is a question of getting rid of the last vestige of colonialism in India. That is a matter of faith with us. Whatever anyone else may think... that is our basic faith which we cannot afford to give up at any cost".[28]

The newly independent Asian-African states, comprising a vast majority of the new international community, have made it clear beyond doubt that whatever the legal validity of colonialism under traditional European international law supporting imperialism, it can no longer be accepted as valid. At the first Asian-African Conference at Bandung in 1953 they declared that "colonialism in all its manifestations is an evil which should speedily be brought to an end".[29] In 1960 the General Assembly of the United Nations declared, without a dissenting note, that "all peoples have an inalienable right to complete freedom" and solemnly proclaimed "the necessity of bringing to a speedy and unconditional end of colonialism in all its forms and manifestations."[30] In 1963, the Charter of Organization of African Unity declared as one of the objectives of the Organization the eradication of "all forms of colonialism from Africa" and the member states solemnly declared their "absolute dedication to total emancipation of the African territories which are still dependent".{Art. 3(5)} Asian and African states believe that even the use of force, if other means fail, for the elimination of colonialism is an act of "self-defense" and, being in accordance with the declared

[27] Ibid. para 140. But see Quincy Wright, "The Goa Incident", *American Journal of International Law*, vol. 56 (1962), p. 617.

[28] Ibid, 987th Meeting, 18 December 1961, para 40.

[29] *Selected Documents of the Bandung Conference* (Institute of Public Relations) (New York, 1955), p. 34.

[30] Declaration on granting of Independence to Colonial Countries and Peoples, Res. 1514 (XV) 14 December 1960. *United Nations Review* (January 1961), p. 6.

objectives of the United Nations, is not prohibited under the UN Charter.[31] There is, or should be, no doubt that old European law has come to be modified and India under Nehru played no mean role in this modification.

Racialism Decried

If new India and Nehru, as its representative, could not tolerate colonialism any more, they abhorred racialism even more which had been the basis of much of modern international law during the nineteenth and the first half of the twentieth centuries. European civilization not only provided legal title to the position of dominating power, but also determined the circle within which the law of nations applied because it did not apply to 'uncivilized' and 'semi-civilized' nations of Asia and Africa.. Unfortunately, racialism continued even after the independence of numerous Asian and African states in the worldwide community of states in the form of *apartheid* in a few countries like South Africa and Rhodesia. Nehru condemned this practice in unmistakable terms, especially the treatment of Indians and black people as second-class citizens in South Africa. He said:

> "It is a matter which concerns us all. It is not merely a question of Indians or South Africans, but it is a matter of vital significance to the world. If that is to continue in the world, then there is bound to be conflict and conflict on a big scale, because it is a continuous challenge to the self-respect of a vast number of people in the world and they will not put up with it. The matter is thus before the United Nations and I hope the United Nations will help in its solution...there cannot be a shadow of doubt that if such a policy is continued, it will breed conflict. And that conflict will not be confined to particular areas in South Africa or elsewhere; it will affect peoples in vast continents."[32]

India's positive role in the development of international law in this respect should certainly be recognized.

Nehru accepted and Followed International Law Rules

Despite the clear bias of numerous international law rules because it was largely a "ruler's law" during its formative years, Nehru was all in favour of accepting its tenets. In fact none of the newly independent countries rejected

[31] See report of the Special Committee on principles of International Law Concerning Friendly Relations and Cooperation among States, *General Assembly Official Records, 23rd Session* (New York, 1968), pp. 37-8,53,63. The Friendly Relations Declaration was later adopted by the General Assembly by consensus on 24 October, 1970. For a doctrinal study of the Declaration see V.S. Mani, *Basic Principles of International Law: A Study of the United Nations Debates on the Principles of International Law concerning Friendly Relations and Cooperation among States* (New Delhi, 1993).

[32] Nehru, "Our Objectives", in Nehru, vol. I, n. 9, p. 265.

international law on the ground that it was European in its origin and bias. India and other newly independent countries mostly accepted the treaties concluded by the European countries on their behalf and before their independence. All they wanted and demanded was that international law, like all laws, must change with the changing circumstances. For one thing, what has been called the "geography" of international law has changed. International law is "no longer the almost exclusive preserve of the peoples of European blood"[33] by whose consent, it used to be said, "it exists and for the settlement of whose differences it is applied or at least invoked."[34] As it must now be assumed to embrace other peoples, it clearly requires their consent no less. The creation of international law is no more "the prerogative of countries bearing the cultural heritage of the west but the common task of all members of the international community."[35] The new majority has naturally new needs and new demands and they want international law to serve their needs and heed to their demands. The alteration in the sociological structure of the international society, it is stressed, must be accompanied by an alteration in law.[36] "International law, if it is to be effective", said Nehru, "has to be related to the realities of international life; otherwise it becomes merely an academic exercise of some professor or pandit sitting in an university." Referring to the phenomenal developments in political, economic, scientific and technological fields, Nehru felt:

> "It may be said that international organization and international law have not kept pace with this advance which is posing many problems before us. We have to catch up before the gap widens, and there is always a possibility of cracking up, of disaster. This aspect of the matter is of vital significance in that the effectiveness of international law is of concern to every single individual."[37]

The Constitution of India, in Part IV relating to the Directive Principles of State Policy, which may be considered "as a commandment to the Union of India",[38] provides in Article 51:

"The State shall endeavour to—

(a) promote international peace and security;
(b) maintain just and honourable relations between nations;

[33] R. B. Pal, *Yearbook of the International Law Commission* (1957), vol. 1, p. 158.

[34] Westlake, quoted in Pal, ibid.

[35] R.B. Pal, "Future Role of the International Law Commission in the Changing World", *United Nations Review* vol. 9 (September 1962), p. 31.

[36] See R.P. Anand, *New States and International Law* (New Delhi, 1972) pp. 45ff.

[37] Nehru, Inaugural Address at the Indian Society of International Law, *Indian Journal of International Law,* vol. 1 (1960), p. 6.

[38] P. Chandrasekhara Rao, *The Indian Constitution and International Law* (New Delhi, 1993), p. 5.

(c) foster respect for international law and treaty obligations in the dealings of organized peoples with one another; and
(d) encourage settlement of international disputes by arbitration."

Nehru pleads for Peace and condemns Nuclear Weapons and Tests

Although he was not a pacifist, and nascent India had to use force several times for the protection of its interests, as the case of Goa discussed above shows, Nehru believed in peace and peaceful settlement of international disputes and wanted to avoid war as far as possible. He made it clear:

> "The objectives of our foreign policy are the preservation of world peace and enlargement of human freedom. Two tragic wars have demonstrated the futility of warfare. Victory without the will to peace achieves no lasting result and victor and the vanquished alike suffer from deep and grievous wounds and a common fear of the future."

He went on to say:

> "India may be new to world politics and her military strength insignificant in comparison with that of giants of our epoch. But India is old in thought and experience and has travelled through trackless centuries in the adventure of life. Throughout her long history she has stood for peace and every prayer that an Indian raises ends with an invocation to peace".[39]

Nehru was particularly against war in the atomic age, which could bring unimaginable destruction. He said:

> "This age we live in has been called the atomic age. Vast new sources of energy are being tapped but instead of thinking of them in terms of service and betterment of mankind, men's thoughts turn to destructive purposes. Destruction by these new and terrible weapons of war can only lead to unparalleled disaster for all concerned and yet people talk lightly of war and bend their energies to prepare for it. A very distinguished American said the other day that the use of atom bomb might well be likened to setting a house on fire in order to rid it of some insects and termites."[40]

Calling the atom bomb "a symbol of evil," he earnestly hoped that there would "be no question now or hereafter of the use of the atom bomb."[41]

He appealed to the leaders of America and Russia "to stop all nuclear test explosions and thus to show to the world that they are determined to end this

[39] Nehru, "Discovery of America", Address to the East and West Association, New York, October 10, 1949, in Nehru, *Jawaharlal Nehru Speeches 1949-1953* (New Delhi, 1954), pp. 124-25.

[40] Nehru, "Asia is Renascent", Speech delivered in Canadian Parliament, October 24, 1949, ibid., p. 129.

[41] Nehru, "Peace or War", Speech in Parliament on December 6, 1950, in Nehru, vol. II, n. 69, p. 173.

menace, and to proceed also to bring about effective disarmament."[42] That was, of course, not to be and nobody listened to his sane voice with the result that it has become so much more difficult to control the proliferation of these ultimate weapons of destruction. He was afraid:

> "Asia has been and will continue to be the scene of hydrogen bomb experiments and of war in which Asians are made to fight Asians. It may be that it will be Asians again who will have the unfortunate privilege of experiencing the effects of atomic bombing."[43]

Judicial Settlement of International Disputes

Although Article 51(d) of the Constitution of India directed the state to "encourage settlement of international disputes by arbitration", India has never been an enthusiastic supporter of arbitration or adjudication as a means for the settlement of its international disputes. This clause was included in the Constitution, according to Dr. P. C. Rao, Law Secretary to the Government of India, on the basis of a couple of statements made in the Constituent Assembly which "did not display adequate understanding of the system of settlement of international disputes".[44] Rao also points out that, "in practice, India has never advocated, and rightly so, the cause of arbitration as the preferred plank of its foreign policy."[45] There are not more than a couple of cases in which India agreed to submit its disputes to international arbitration courts and even in those cases it did not feel much satisfied with the resulting settlements.[46]

If India has been reluctant to accept arbitration, it has accepted the jurisdiction of the International Court of Justice more or less as a formality without any real intention to appear before the World Court. India was caught off-guard when Portugal suddenly accepted the compulsory jurisdiction of the International Court and brought a case against India on 22 December 1955 in regard to the *Right of Passage over Indian Territory* on the basis of British India's declaration accepting compulsory jurisdiction of the ICJ made in 1929, which was still binding on India. India immediately withdrew its

[42] Nehru, "Appeal to the USA and the USSR", New Delhi December 27, 1957, in Jawaharlal Nehru's Speeches 1957-1963, vol. 4, (New Delhi, 1964), pp. 308-309.

[43] Nehru in a communication to the Chief Ministers of States in India 14 April, 1954, quoted in Gopal, n. 16, p. 191.

[44] Rao, n. 38, p. 6.

[45] Rao, ibid., p. 7.

[46] The case concerning Gujarat-West Pakistan boundary dispute between India and Pakistan was submitted to Pakistan Western Boundary Case Tribunal which gave its award , known as the Kutch Award on 19 February 1968.The award created a lot of controversy in India and was strongly criticized. R. P. Anand, "The Kutch Award", in his *Studies in International Adjudication* (New Delhi, 1969), pp. 218-49. See also Rao, ibid.

1929 declaration but had to appear before the Court in that case which related to right of passage claimed by Portugal on the basis of a treaty concluded with a Maratha ruler in 1779. Portugal wanted right of passage for its armed forces and civilian authorities between Goa and two of its enclaves, Dadra and Nagar- Aveli, which had already been merged into the Indian Union. India was lucky in the case because the Court declared that Portugal did not have the right of passage for its armed forces and the right of passage for its civil officials and goods had already become fruitless.[47]

India filed on 9 January 1956, a new declaration under optional clause or Article 36, paragraph 2 of the Statute of the International Court of Justice accepting compulsory jurisdiction of the Court but with wide-ranging reservations. Still not satisfied, it again withdrew its declaration after one year and filed another declaration in September 1959. A close look at this declaration makes it clear, as we have noted at another place,

> "that there has been left wide freedom in the hands of the Government of India to refuse to submit to the Court any dispute arising in the future, and her most important existing disputes have specifically been excluded from any such jurisdiction."[48]

We must hasten to add, however, India, or for that matter most of the Asian-African states, as well as the old European and American states, are all generally reluctant to accept the compulsory jurisdiction of the International Court. In 1998, out of 187 members of the international judicial community, including 185 members of the United Nations and 2 non-members (Switzerland and Nauru), only 60 States, or less than one-third, had accepted the jurisdiction of the Court under Article 36(2) of its Statute. Since 1951, 12 other declarations under the optional clause have expired, been withdrawn or been terminated without being subsequently replaced. Not only do most of these declarations which are still valid contain far-reaching reservations, but nearly 50 per cent of them may be terminated by a simple notice which may take effect immediately or in some cases after a specified time

Power Blocs and India's Policy of Non-alignment

As we have mentioned above, ever since the Second World War, the world had been deeply divided into two power blocs, led by the United States and the Soviet Union, preparing for war which they knew and admitted no combatant could win. Claiming to be "driven by the needs of self-defense, by noble intentions, by fear of ignoble aggression of the other", the two super antagonists, even as they talked of peace, were engaged in the

[47] See *ICJ Reports, 1960, p. 6.*

[48] Anand, "India and the World Court", in his *Studies in International Adjudication (New Delhi, 1972)*, p.52.

preparations for war.[49] Throughout the 1950's and 1960's, both the power groups concluded numerous collective "self-defense" alliances relying more on their ideological allies than on the United Nations' "collective security" system. Even more than that, having acquired the most fearful weapons, they were engaged in frightening each other and themselves as well. As in all wars, small newly independent states and international law itself could not but helplessly watch this new "cold war" being waged with increasing ferocity.

But Jawaharlal Nehru, even at the risk of annoying the two super-powers, refused to leave and abandon India's newly won independence and join any of the power groups and become their "camp followers in the hope that some crumbs might fall from their table". Declaring that such a policy would be "a bad and harmful policy", he said:

> "I can understand some of the smaller countries of Europe or some of the smaller countries of Asia being forced by circumstances to bow down before some to the great powers and becoming practically satellites of those powers, because they cannot help it. The power opposed to them is so great and they have nowhere to turn. But I do not think that consideration applies to India.
>
> We are not citizens of a weak or mean country and I think it is foolish for us to get frightened, even from a military point of view, of the greatest powers today."[50]

Insisting that India need not be afraid of great powers, he said, "our policy is not a passive policy and negative policy."[51] Moreover, "even in getting economic help, or in getting political help, it is not a wise policy to put all our eggs in one basket...Therefore, purely from the point of view of opportunism, if you like, a straightforward, honest policy, an independent policy, is the best."[52] Non-alignment did not mean 'neutrality', because "neutrality has little meaning except in times of war".[53] The purpose of the policy, in his view, was to—

> "help as best as it [India] can to maintain world peace and also avoid, as far as possible, entanglements in world conflicts. Whether that is possible or not is another question; how far our influence can make a difference to world forces is still another question. I do not pretend to say that India, as she is, can make a vital difference in world affairs."[54]

[49] C. Wright Mills, *The Causes of World War III* (New York, 1960, p. 18.

[50] Nehru, "Non-alignment with Blocs", Speech in the Constituent Assembly, New Delhi, March 8, 1948, in Nehru, vol. I, n. 9, pp. 214-15.

[51] Ibid, p 215.

[52] Nehru, ibid., p. 219.

[53] Nehru, speech in Parliament June 12, 1952, in Nehru, vol. II, n. 41, pp. 116-17.

[54] Nehru, "Our policy is positive", Speech in Parliament on March 17, 1950, ibid., p. 144.

Despite its political and economic weaknesses, uncommitted India could still play a necessary and very useful role of "building a bridge which otherwise would not exist between the two blocs." In doing so, it would not only serve "its own vital interests, but also the vital interest of all states."[55] India did play a very important and helpful role in the crises in Korea and Indo- China.

Therefore, he was against India "lining up with this or that forces but try to maintain a certain friendliness and spirit of cooperation with both the great and small countries of the world."[56] He said:

> "If we did align ourselves we would only fall between two stools. We will neither be following the policy based on our ideals inherited from our past or the one indicated by our present nor will we be able easily to adapt ourselves to the new policy consequent on such alignment. Our present policy flows from what we thought and said in the past, while incidentally it also helps in the maintenance of peace and the avoidance of war in the world today."[57]

"Essentially", Nehru further clarified, non-alignment "is freedom of action which is a part of independence". It implied basically, he said, "a conviction that good and evil are mixed up in the world, that the nations cannot be divided into sheep and goats to be condemned or approved accordingly, and that if we were to join one military group or the other it was liable to increase and not diminish the risk of a major clash between them." In fact, he noted, perhaps influenced by India to some extent, a large number of countries, including most of the newly independent states of Asia and Africa, "have adopted a similar outlook on international affairs."[58]

Nehru opposed to Military Alliances

Nehru was very much against military alliances and the armament race, which it entailed among the two blocs in the age of atom and hydrogen bombs. He was strongly opposed to the western-sponsored alliances, such as SEATO (1954) and the Baghdad Pact (1955), because by including Pakistan as member of both the treaties, "they brought the cold war to the very borders of India...and thereby endangered India's security." In fact he believed that "these military pacts represented an indirect return of Western power to an area from which it had retreated".[59]

Suggesting that these military alliances had returned to some extent the

[55] Brecher, n. 2, p. 559.

[56] Nehru, n. 54, p. 144.

[57] Nehru, "We will not compromise", Speech in Parliament on March 28, 1951, in Nehru, vol. II, n. 41, pp. 192-93.

[58] Nehru, "Changing India", *Foreign Affairs* (New York, April 1963) in Nehru, vol. 4, p. 407.

[59] Brecher, n. 2, p. 555.

idea of "old holy alliance", backed by military pacts and economic measures, they had made the world more dangerous. This was, he felt, really against the spirit of international law which "is meant primarily to prevent war. Its purpose is to settle problems and disputes by methods other than war. War is an absence of law."[60] It might be desirable, therefore, for these countries to consider, "whether and how far these preparations for nuclear warfare or test explosions are in keeping with any conception of international or moral law."[61]

Principles of Peaceful Co-existence or *Panch Sheel*

Nehru not only emphasized the importance of peaceful settlement of international disputes, but formulated along with China in a treaty on Tibet signed in 1954, five principles of peaceful co-existence or *Panch Sheel,* as they were called. Based on Article 2 of the United Nations Charter, these "wholesome principles", in Nehru's words, as laid down in the bilateral treaty provided:

(i) Mutual respect for each other's territorial integrity and sovereignty;
(ii) Mutual non-aggression;
(iii) Mutual non-interference in each other's internal affairs;
(iv) Equality and mutual benefit; and
(v) Peaceful coexistence.

If these principles were followed amongst states, he believed, "a great deal of the trouble of the present-day world would disappear."[62] If you want peace in the world, said Nehru,

> "It cannot be done through threats. Once you recognize...that war is no solution, and that the two major protagonists are too powerful to be dismissed one by the other, then you have to coexist, you have to understand, you have to be restrained and you have to deal with each other. If you reject coexistence, the alternative is war and mutual destruction."[63]

In Support of the United Nations

Nehru had tremendous faith, at least in the early years of India's independence, in the United Nations. He considered it "a great and powerful organization and it has a Charter that lays down its ideals and objectives in language so impressive that it can hardly be bettered."

[60] Nehru, "Effective International Law", in *Nehru's Speeches*, vol. III, p. 510.
[61] Nehru, ibid., p 511.
[62] Nehru, "Agreement on Tibet", *Nehru's Speeches*, vol. III, pp. 262-63.
[63] Nehru, "The South-East Asia Treaty Organization", ibid., p. 273.

He said:

> "Towards the UN, India's attitude is that of wholehearted cooperation and unreserved adherence, in both spirit and letter to the Charter governing it. To that end, India will participate fully in its various activities and endeavour to play that role in its councils to which her geographical position, population and contribution towards peaceful progress entitle her."
>
> We have always been a staunch supporter of the United Nations. As a member of that august body, India has undertaken its full measure of responsibility in all aspects of UN activities. The UN is the one hope of the world for bringing peace and freedom to humanity."[64]

The world organization had been founded, he believed, "for the great nations as well as the small."[65] It might not be "a perfect organization but ...it was a step in the right direction, because ...its objectives were right." It might have made mistakes, and it was distressing to see that it moved away from its ideals, but that could not prove "the need for such an organization". He felt that,

> "if the UNO ceased to function today, it would be a disaster for the world. For the world cannot afford to do without some such organization."[66]

It could not be denied that the UN was "dominated more or less" by certain nations of Europe and the United States with the result that the main problems discussed there were the problems of Europe and America while the other parts of the world and their concerns were generally ignored.[67] In his address to the United Nations General Assembly on November 3, 1948, he therefore said:

> "May I say, as a representative from Asia, that we honour Europe for its culture and for the great advance in human civilization which it represents? May I say that we are equally interested in the solution of European problems; but may I also say that the world is something bigger than Europe, and you will not solve your problems by thinking that the problems of world are mainly European problems. There are vast tracts of the world, which may not in the past, for a few generations, have taken much part in world affairs. But they are awake, their people are moving and they have no intention whatever of being ignored or being passed by."

He went on tell the UN delegates:

> "Today I do venture to submit that Asia counts in world affairs. Tomorrow it will count much more than today."[68]

[64] Nehru, "United Nations in India", *World Focus* (New Delhi, Oct.-Dec. 1997), p. 59.

[65] Nehru, "Peace or War", *Nehru's Speeches*, vol. II, p. 169.

[66] Nehru, "We will not compromise", ibid. p. 199.

[67] Nehru, "Our objectives", *Nehru's Speeches*, vol. I, p. 257.

[68] Nehru, "To the United Nations", ibid., pp. 317-18.

India's Policy on Recognition of States and Governments

Realizing how Asian countries had suffered during the nineteenth century and later because of non-recognition of Asian states as members of the international community, Nehru was very much in favour of independence of the Asian and African countries and their recognition as independent states or governments as soon as it became clear that they had emerged as independent entities and were viable and effective. India therefore subscribed "to the principle of *de factoism*, even if it was at the risk of some misunderstanding or alienating the sympathies of her best friends".[69] India recognized Communist Chinese Government as soon as became clear that "the new Chinese Government was in possession of practically the entire mainland of China, when it was quite clear that this Government was stable, and that there was no force which was likely to supplant it or push it away."[70] Similarly, once Israel had emerged as an independent state, even at the risk of annoying its best friends among Arab states, Nehru recognized it as an independent state though he deferred the establishment of diplomatic relations with the new state.[71]

Nehru Supports Communist China's Recognition and Representation in the United Nations

Nehru was the foremost champion of the recognition of the Communist Chinese Government and its representation in the United Nations. The emergence of a united and forceful China free from Western domination was a matter of satisfaction and pleasure for Nehru. India was the second non-Communist state to recognize the government of Mao Tse-Tung.[72] Nehru was the most vociferous critic of the United States' policy of non-recognition and urged the West time and again to accept the 'facts of political life' in East Asia.[73] He helped China, supported by Chou En-Lai's charm and skilful diplomacy, to emerge as an important and respected member of the Asian-African group at Bandung.[74]

In fact one may surmise that in blindly cultivating China's friendship, he sacrificed India's interests and Tibet's independence. In the famous India-China treaty on Tibet concluded in 1954, he not only gave up India's largely

[69] K. P. Misra, "India's policy of recognition of states and governments", *American Journal of International Law*, vol. 55 (1961), p. 408.

[70] Nehru in a speech in Parliament on March 17, 1950, quoted in Misra, ibid., p. 401.

[71] See for a discussion on Nehru's policy, Misra, ibid., pp. 404-408.

[72] Burma was the first. See Brecher, n. 2, p. 588

[73] Brecher, ibid.

[74] See also Brecher, ibid., p. 588.

commercial and cultural rights and interests[75] in Tibet, inherited from the British, but accepted Tibet as a part of China, or rather under the 'suzerainty' of China, in the vain hope that China would decide the problem peacefully and would not forcibly trample Tibet's autonomy and way of life.[76] In the process, not only millions of Tibetans lost their independence and homeland, but it created a lot of problem for India as well because Indo-Tibetan border came to be accepted as Indo-Chinese border.[77] For several years, China's ambivalent attitude towards the border lulled India into believing that China had no objection to Indo-Tibetan border being recognized as the Indo-Chinese border. As Nehru thought and said soon after the Indo-Chinese Treaty on Tibet was signed:

> "We have only given up what in fact we could not hold and what in fact had in reality gone. We have given up certain rights that we exercised internally in Tibet. Obviously, we cannot do that. We have gained instead something that is very important, i.e., a frontier and an implicit acceptance of that frontier."[78]

Within a few years, China attacked and occupied Tibet and the Dalai Lama had no choice but to leave Tibet in 1959 and take refuge in India. China also began to question the legal validity of the Indo-Chinese border and began showing, in some of its maps, parts of Indian territory as part of China.[79]

Asylum given by India to the Dalai Lama made Communist China angry at India. Forgetting all the promises of friendship and cooperation since its emergence, it attacked India and occupied a large chunk of the Indian territory. Nehru was left aghast, and India had no choice but to defend itself as best as it could. But it is interesting to note that even after China changed its policy and attacked India, Nehru continued to support Communist Chinese representation in the United Nations.

Reference of Kashmir Dispute to the United Nations

Impressed by the ideals expressed in the UN Charter and its provisions to control aggression and punish the aggressors, even against the advice of some of his senior colleagues in the Government, Nehru, persuaded by Lord

[75] India had post office, telegraph office, some soldiers, trade and commercial rights, and some pilgrim routes. See Nehru, "India's border with China". Nehru's Speeches, vol. IV, p. 210.

[76] See Nehru, "Peace or War",*Jawaharlal Nehru's Speeches*, vol. II, pp. 173-74.

[77] See for a detailed discussion about Tibet's de facto independence which was not formally 'recognized' by any state, R.P. Anand, "The Status of Tibet in International law", *International Studies* (New Delhi), vol.10 (1968-69), pp.401-445

[78] Nehru, Letter to G. L. Mehta, quoted in Gopal, n. 16, p. 181.

[79] See Gopal, ibid., pp.175-81. Even when Nehru pointed out about the mistakes in Chinese maps, Chinese leaders avoided the issue. See Gopal' ibid., pp. 228-29.

Mountbatten, the last British Governor-General of independent India, referred the case of Kashmir to the Security Council of the United Nations.[80] It is well known that soon after India and Pakistan's emergence as independent states in August 1947, a large number of infiltrators equipped with all sorts of guns and weapons, and supported by the Pakistan's armed forces, attacked the state of Kashmir to force it to join Pakistan. On receiving an urgent message from the Maharaja of Kashmir, after the latter unconditionally signed an accession instrument joining the Union of India, India sent its troops to fight the invaders on 27 October 1947. Although the accession of Kashmir with India was complete according to law, as in the cases of all other independent princely states which had joined India, on the suggestion of Lord Mountbatten,[81] Nehru and his Government gave an undertaking that once the invaders were cleared from India's soil and law and order was established, the question of the accession of Kashmir would be settled by reference to its people by a plebiscite.[82] Such a condition was neither necessary nor required under the instrument of accession. But "the Government of India unilaterally announced it" and declared that the accession of Kashmir would be "subject to the proviso that a plebiscite would be held in the state when the law and order situation allowed."[83]

Nehru was utterly disappointed when he found that instead of dealing with the problem of Pakistan's aggression, the UN Security Council tried to put India and Pakistan on an equal footing and Pakistan received unexpected support. Britain and the United States, as Permanent Members of the Security Council, took extremely partisan and anti-India attitude. Some of the proposals put forward by these countries in the Security Council seemed to Nehru "monstrous",[84] Rather than "surrender either to the gangster tactics of Pakistan and the raiders or to attempts at bullying by Britain and the United States", Nehru was willing to consider defiance of the United Nations, to which he had personally taken the initiative in appealing.[85] Nehru was angry:

> "I must say that prepared as I was for untoward happenings, I could not imagine that the Security Council could possibly behave in the trivial and partisan manner in which it functioned. These people are supposed to keep the world in order. It is not surprising that the world is going to pieces. The United States and Britain have played a dirty role, Britain probably being the chief actor behind the scenes. I have expressed myself strongly to the (British Prime Minister) Attlee about it

[80] V. P. Menon, *The Story of the Integration of the Indian States* (Calcutta, 1956), p. 410.

[81] Menon, ibid. p. 399; see also Gopal, n. 16, p. 20.

[82] Nehru, "The State's Accession", vol. I, ibid., 162 ff.

[83] See Menon, n. 80, pp. 400, 413.

[84] See Gopal, n. 16, p. 27.

[85] Nehru Letter to Krishna Menon, 20 February, 1948, quoted in Gopal, ibid.

and I propose to make it perfectly clear to the British Government what we think about it. The time for soft and meaningless talk has passed."[86]

But despite India's unhappiness and frustration, which India expressed several times in no uncertain terms, the United Nations continued to act in a very partisan manner. United Nations' handling, or rather mishandling, of the Kashmir dispute left India in a very difficult situation and many people blame Nehru for this mess. India had to fight three wars with Pakistan on Kashmir and the problem is far from being solved. From hindsight it is felt that India would have been far better of if it had never referred the dispute to the United Nations. But despite all the hostility India had to face, Nehru did not want to withdraw from the United Nations. That would be "immaturity", he said. Rejecting any such suggestion, he pointed out:

> "One cannot run away like this from a problem. The United Nations, inspite of all its failings—and there are many—is a great world organization. It does contain within it the seeds of hope and peace, and it would be rather perverse for any country to try to destroy this structure because it is not to its entire liking. If a country does that, I have no doubt that it is that country which will suffer more than the organization. We cannot remain isolated in the world, cut off from everything and living our life in our limited sphere... Therefore, to talk of getting out of the United Nations or of otherwise keeping apart from all these problems is not to take cognizance of the realities of the situation."[87]

India acts as a bridge between the power blocs in the United Nations

But although India was totally dissatisfied with the UN role in Kashmir dispute, it did not run away from the world body. On the contrary, it played a very active and positive role in the United Nations. Non-aligned to any of the power blocs, and claiming to be on good terms with all of them, it acted as a mediator and helped reach agreements in several disputes, such as Korea, Suez crisis, Congo and Rhodesia. Even more important, for the first time in history, independent India sent its armed forces out of the country to various trouble spots not to fight any body or conquer other states,[88] but as messengers of peace, to restore peace and help the United Nations and the international community in the establishment of peace and security.

[86] Nehru, Letter to Vijayalakshmi, 16 February 1948, quoted in Gopal, ibid., pp. 27-28.

[87] Nehru, Speech in Lok Sabha, September 17, 1953, *Nehru"s Speeches,* vol. III, pp. 243-44.

[88] See how British sent Indian armed forces "to conquer and suppress other peoples", Nehru, *The Discovery of India,* Bombay, 1961, p. 448.

'Group of 77' in the United Nations

In many a situation India acted more or less as a spokesman of the newly independent countries. With the collapse of colonialism, as more and more Asian and African states became independent they all wanted to join the United Nations as sovereign and equal members of the international community. But in the Cold War tension, both the power blocs used veto to stop the entry of numerous states to the United Nations suspecting their affiliations and there was an impassé. Nehru believed in universal membership of the United Nations. In 1955, during the visit in India of Chairman Khrushchev and Prime Minister Bulganin of the Soviet Union, Nehru raised the question of the Soviet veto on the admission of eighteen countries to the United Nations. As a parting gift to their host, recognizing "India's importance and of Nehru's role in the world", the Soviet leaders agreed to withdraw the Soviet veto and permit the entry of all except Mongolia and Japan.[89] Once the ice was broken, almost a floodgate opened and many more Asian and African states joined the world organization. Although in 1945, of the 51 original members of the UN there were only 13 Asian-African states, it was not long after 1955 that Europe became a small minority of UN membership and the vast majority consisted of the thus far neglected and dominated countries of Asia, Africa and other parts of the world. Non-aligned as most of them were, they aligned themselves to play an important role in the international structure to get their fair share, dignity and responsibility. They formed a consortium within the United Nations, called the 'Group of 77', which actually had more than 120 members. The existence of an international forum where they had scope for concerted action, enhanced their power and helped them in pursuing their purposes. They were further helped by the rivalry between the big powers. As the work of the Security Council got frozen in the chilling atmosphere of the cold war, and with the persistent use and abuse of veto its authority as well as prestige declined, the power and influence of the General Assembly began to rise. After the passage of the Uniting for Peace Resolution in 1950 it began to deal with the most serious matters of peace and security which earlier were supposed to be barred from its consideration and beyond its power.[90] With the increase in the powers of the General Assembly, the United Nations changed from an instrument of the great powers to a forum for the smaller states to press their claims.

This is a phenomenon of tremendous significance in international law. Enjoying formal legal equality with the big powers in the new "Parliament of Mankind", and of course numerical superiority, the 'new' Asian-African

[89] Gopal, n. 16, p. 254

[90] This *de facto* amendment of the Charter got a powerful legal support from the Intrnaitional Court of Justice in its advisory opinion in *Certain Expenses of the United Nations case,* See *ICJ Reports,*1962, p. 163.

states, along with the equally disgruntled Latin American states—the so-called third World as they came to be called—acquired a new influence in the post-war divided world society. They joined hands together to play an important role in the international legal structure in pursuance of their interests. It was only to be expected that the new majority should try to mould the law according to their own views and for the protection of their interests. Not only colonialism, but also several parts of international law of the colonial period were challenged, modified and codified either through the UN General Assembly resolutions or various UN sponsored conferences.[91]

"Light of Asia"

Jawaharlal Nehru was a great statesman and able spokesman of the newly independent Asian and African countries whose cause he espoused throughout his long innings as Prime Minister and Foreign Minister of India. It has been correctly pointed out that "no single individual has done more, in the years since the Second World War, to project Asia on to the world stage."[92] Even Churchill, despite all his bias and bitterness against India, grasped the pre-eminence of India's Prime Minister and wanted him to play a crucial role:

> "I hope you will think of the phrase 'The Light of Asia'. It seems to me that you might be able to do what no other human being could in giving India the lead, at least in the realm of thought, throughout Asia, with the freedom and dignity of the individual as the ideal ..."[93]

Nehru was the proponent, architect and founder of the famous policy of non-alignment which most of the Asian and African countries accepted and on the basis of which they formed a strong pressure group in the United Nations and outside. He was a great advocate of the freedom of Asian and African states from colonialism and racialism and believed in their close friendship and cooperation. He was, therefore, very disappointed when China, whose friendship he cultivated for many years, broke his trust, deceived him and India by its very unexpected attack and occupation of a large chunk of India's territory. He was very disheartened at China's behaviour which he could not expect. He was a gentleman, a sincere friend, and innocent of diplomacy's duality and cunning moves. He failed in some of his policies because of his tremendous faith in democracy and people's right of self-determination (for example in Kashmir and Tibet), and sometimes misled by

[91] See R. P. Anand, "Influence of History on the literature of international law", in his *Confrontation or Cooperation: International Law and the Developing Countries* (New Delhi, 1986), pp. 34-36.

[92] Gopal, n. 16, p. 236.

[93] Churchill to Nehru, 21 February 1955. Quoted in Gopal, ibid., p. 236. Churchill again repeated this phrase in his letter to Nehru on 30 June 1955. Quoted in Gopal, ibid., p. 237.

his own friends, or whom he believed to be his friends. In Kashmir he trusted the United Nations and its ideals and was utterly disgusted at the behaviour of some of the Western states in the Security Council. His personal trust in the United Nations led India in a quagmire in the Kashmir case. So also his faith in China and its friendship landed him and his country in a difficult and bad situation and he died as a very disappointed and disheartened man. But despite all his failures as a statesman and the problems which emerged for India in Kashmir, Tibet, or India's border with China, no body can deny his sincerity and tremendous faith in India and its people. He was honest to the core in any thing he did and a legacy which India will cherish for a long time to come.

Jawaharlal Nehru was a lawyer by training but had little to do with international law. But as an architect of India's foreign policy and one of the foremost spokesman of the Third World he helped in the tremendous development of international law from a law made by and for the European countries to a common law of mankind applicable to the world-wide community of states. Asian-African countries, whom he so ably represented, have been playing an increasingly important role in the United Nations and outside in the development, modification and codification of international law for the twenty-first century. India has played a very active role in these developments and Nehru deserves most of the credit for giving India its importance and influence in bringing about these changes.

Family of "Civilized" States and Japan: A Story of Humiliation, Assimilation, Defiance and Confrontation

Modern Universal International Law

Modern international law is understood to be a law applicable among all the States in equal measure in their relations with each other. It is defined as "the body of rules which are legally binding on states in their intercourse with each other."[1] It contains "principles and rules of conduct which states feel themselves bound to observe, and therefore, do commonly observe in their relations with each other."[2] It is defined by scholars as a law, which makes no distinction between large and small States, east or west, north or south countries. As Oppenheim's latest edition declares: "International law does not recognize any distinctions in the membership of the international community based on religious, geographical or cultural differences."[3] Despite all the differences in their size and economic strength, political orientation or religious and cultural identity, they are all bound by its rules and are supposed to conduct their international relations on the basis of its tenets. Indeed, sovereign equality of States is supposed to be a fundamental principle of international law. In spite of wide and glaring inequalities amongst States, the equality of States is one of the most familiar and frequently reiterated principles of modern international law. Indeed, equality is traditionally accepted, along with sovereignty and independence, as an "absolute" and "unquestionable" principle upon which international law is based. As Vattel, in his classical exposition, declared:

* The author gratefully acknowledges his deep appreciation and indebtedness to the Max Planck Institute for Comparative Public Law and International Law, especially to its Directors, Professor Doctor Jochen Abr. Frowein and Professor Doctor Rudiger Wolfrum for all their help in providing him with a scholarship and an opportunity to work at the Institute in the summer of 2001, and collect material for this paper which is part of his project on "A Fresh Look at the History of International Law: Asian Perspective."

[1] *Oppenheim's International Law*, Vol. I, *Peace* (edited by Sir Robert Jennings and Sir Arthur Watts), 9th edn. (London, 1997), p. 4.

[2] *Starke's International Law*, (edited by I. A. Shearer) 11th edn., (London, 1994), p. 4.

[3] Oppenheim, note 1, p. 87.

> "Strength or weakness, in this case, counts for nothing. A dwarf is as much a man as a giant is; a small republic is no less a sovereign state than the most powerful kingdom.
>
> From this equality it necessarily follows that what is lawful or unlawful for one nation is equally lawful or unlawful for every other nation."[4]

Similarly, Chief Justice John Marshall of the United States Supreme Court declared in the *Antelope* case in 1825 in an oft-repeated dictum:

> "No principle of general law is more universally acknowledged than the perfect equality of nations. Russia and Geneva have equal rights. It results from this equality that no one can impose a rule on another."[5]

Proclaiming its faith "in the equal rights of men and women and nations large and small", the Charter of the United Nations declares in unambiguous terms in Article 2, paragraph 1, that "the Organization is based on the principle of sovereign equality of all its members". This is further reiterated in Article 78, which says that the relationship among members of the United Nations "shall be based on respect for the principle of sovereign equality".

Universality of International Law: A Recent Phenomenon

But while there is no question that modern international law is now recognized as universally applicable to all the States and all new entities, as soon as they emerge as independent States, whether members of the United Nations or not, they are members of the ever-expanding international society and are bound by its rules and can seek its protection, this is only a recent phenomenon not older than the United Nations itself. Before that modern international law was supposed to be merely a product of the Western European Christian States or States of European origin, and applicable only between them. As Oppenheim points out, "whenever a new Christian state made its appearance in Europe, it was received into the existing European community of states", but during that formative period "international law was confined to those states" only.[6] States outside this charmed circle were not accepted as members of their international society and relations with them were not "governed by rules of international conduct as prevailed between European states."[7]

Emergence of Modern International Law

Modern international law is believed to have emerged only after the disintegration of the Roman empire when numerous small States emerged in

[4] *See* quoted in R. P. Anand, "Sovereign Equality of States in International Law", *Recueil des cours*, vol.197 (1986-II), p. 53.

[5] Quoted in Anand, pp. 53-54.

[6] Oppenheim, note 1, p. 87.

[7] Ibid., pp. 87-88. R.P. Anand, p. 3.

Europe each competing with the other and is a product of no more than, "roughly speaking", 400 years. It grew "out of the usages and practices of modern European states in their intercourse and communications, while it still bears witness to the influence of writers and jurists of the sixteenth, seventeenth and eighteenth centuries, who first formulated some of its most fundamental tenets. Moreover, it remains tinged with concepts such as national and territorial sovereignty, and the perfect equality and independence of states, that owe their force to political theories underlying the modern European state system, although, curiously enough, some of these concepts have commanded the support of the newly emerged non-European states."[8]

Historically, in the period of antiquity before the dawn of Christianity, in ancient India and Egypt or China, there might have been and were rules of conduct to regulate the relations between independent communities, like treaties, the immunities of ambassadors, and certain laws and usages of war, or even historical cases of recourse to arbitration in ancient China and the early Islamic world. But it would be entirely wrong, it is pointed out, "to regard these early instances as representing any serious contribution towards the evolution of modern system of international law."[9] Even the contributions of rules of conduct among the Greek City States, because of the religious nature of their customs, and inter-State rules in the Roman period, because of Rome's dominance over the ancient world, are rather meagre. In fact, it is suggested, that "conditions favorable to the growth of a modern law of nations did not really come into being until the fifteenth century, when in Europe there began to evolve a number of independent civilized states." During the Roman period, the Roman Empire dominated the entire Western world, which did not let independent States emerge. After the fall of Rome for a long time the conditions in Europe "were so chaotic as to make impossible any ordered rules of conduct between nations."[10]

European Trade with Asia

It is important to note that while Europe was passing through its own turbulent period and engaged in its religious wars with the Muslims, who had got entrenched in west Asia or Arabia and what Europeans called the Middle East, Asian peoples and countries were fairly well developed and were engaged in a lot of intra-continental, interregional and maritime trade for centuries.[11] Although Asians had commercial and cultural contacts with

[8] *See* Starke, note 2, p. 7.

[9] Ibid., pp. 7-8.

[10] Ibid., p. 8.

[11] *See* R.P. Anand, *Origin and Development of the Law of the Sea: History of International Law Revisited*, (The Hague, 1983), Chapter 2 on "Freedom of the Sea and commercial shipping in the Indian Ocean", pp. 10-39.

Greece long before Alexander reached the Indian frontiers, and later active trade flourished between Indian States and the Roman Empire, during the socalled "Dark Ages" of Europe, the contacts were neither so regular nor so intimate. After the early crusade, Europe's interest in Asia increased and during the thirteenth century several European travellers, Marco Polo, Friar, Odoric and Monte Carvino, to name only a few, visited India and the other parts of Asia. However, ever since the twelfth century, Islam based in Egypt had been organized as a powerful barrier between Asia and Europe. Even after 200 years of efforts by the unified forces of Christendom, Syrian and Egyptian coasts remained firmly in Muslim hands.[12]

While Asian peoples were engaged in flourishing trade among themselves and did not particularly miss their trade with Europe, the European world had been possessed with the splendour of the East, ever since Rome had made Eastern products fashionable and her Egyptian subjects had gone to seek them in the Indies. When the Arabs shut off all access to the Indian Ocean, Europe continued to receive their supplies from the Asian markets through the caravan routes of the Levant. But even this was becoming increasingly more difficult in the fourteenth and the fifteenth centuries because of religious wars between the Muslims and the Christians. Aromatic spices from India and the East Indies had been and were in great demand and yielded large profits to merchants. Even during the Roman period, pepper was sold against the weight of gold.[13] "The scarcity of fresh meat", wrote Trevelyan, "in winter before the era of roots and artificial grasses was a chief reason why our ancestors craved for spices; they were used both to preserve meat, and to season it highly when it had little else to recommend it."[14] The supply was never sufficient and the prices charged by the middlemen, whether Arabs or Venetians, were exorbitant.[15]

The Europeans were more than eager to go to Asia and trade with the Asian countries, especially in spices which Europeans desperately needed and had been importing since time immemorial. Besides, taking Christendom directly to the Indian Ocean and trying to find some allies against the Muslims amongst the non-Muslim rulers of Asia was considered a religious duty and a patriotic necessity by some of the frontline States, like Portugal and Spain, which had been fighting the Muslims ("Moors", as they called them) for

[12] *See* K. M. Panikkar, *Asia and Western dominance* (London, 1954), pp. 24-25.

[13] In the ancient world India was the only pepper producing country and had no rivals. It was only in later centuries that Indonesian Islands became famous as pepper-producing regions. *See* O. W. Wolfers, *Early Indonesian Commerce* (Ithaca, N.Y., 1967), p. 66.

[14] *See* quoted in J. A. E. Morley, "The Arabs and the Eastern Trade", *Journal of the Royal Asiatic Society*, Singapore Branch, vol. 22, part I (March 1949), p. 146.

[15] *See* for details Anand, note 11, Chapter 3, pp. 40 *et seq.*

centuries.[16] This combination of greed and godliness—lust for riches and passion for God—led the Portuguese and the Spanish, and later, to a lesser extent, the British, the Dutch and the French, to relentlessly find a sea route to the dream land of India.[17] Once the Portuguese found a sea route to India, bypassing the Muslim world of the Middle East, Europeans started directly trading with India and the other Asian countries. Competing and fighting among themselves in Europe and struggling and competing for larger trading rights in Asian countries, slowly they came to have more and more influence and later even dominance over some areas of Asia and the Asian peoples. By the nineteenth century, after defeating and displacing the Portuguese, the Dutch and the French not only in Europe but also in Africa and the Americas, Britain not only got a foothold in India, but came to occupy large parts of it. With the expulsion of other European companies, especially French ones from India, the British Government was drawn increasingly into a policy of territorial occupation. Eventually a British "paramount power" empire emerged in place of the last major Indian empire of the Moguls. Once installed in Delhi, with almost unlimited human and material resources, the British were encouraged and empowered to expand into the rest of South and South-east Asia and beyond to East Asia.[18] This also encouraged other European countries to follow the British lead and expand to other areas or dominate other countries of Asia.

Europeans Go to East Asia

It was during this period of European expansion and Asian decline that the British and other western traders made up their minds to push towards East Asia to trade with China and Japan. It is important to note that compared to Asians, Europeans were much better sailors, were adept at maritime warfare with strong gunboats equipped with heavy guns, while Asian States were generally land powers who had never used warships or guns on the ships and were unable to compete with them on the sea. Several attempts had been made earlier by Western countries like Russia, Portugal, Holland, and Britain to open their trading posts in China but these had failed.[19] As a dominant

[16] *See* Auguste Toussaint, *History of the Indian Ocean* (Trans. by June Guicharnaud) (Chicago, 1966), p. 98; *see also* Panikkar, note 12, p. 28.

[17] *See* for a detailed discussion of the European motives and efforts to reach India Anand, note 11, chapter 3, pp. 40-50.

[18] *See* for more details about the struggles and fighting amongst the European countries for domination in Europe and Asia, Anand, note 11, Chapter 4, pp. 72 *et seq*.

[19] *See* Gerrit W. Gong, *The Standard of 'Civilization' in International Society* (Oxford, 1984), pp. 130 *et seq*.; see how the Portuguese went to China but could not settle there and were thrown out in G. B. Sansom, *The Western World and Japan* (New York, 1951), pp. 99-105.

European power, the British were particularly irked by the Chinese reluctance to trade with Europeans except on their own terms which were considered humiliating by the Europeans. They had developed a craving for Chinese tea and also wanted other Chinese products like silks, porcelain, and objects d'art of China. The tea trade caused a serious drain of gold and silver to China and the British had little else to offer, for China was more or less economically self-sufficient. Rebuffed by the Chinese in their attempts to settle in China and to establish trade relations with them, the British forced China to open its doors by attacking her in what is known as the Opium War in 1839 and concluding the Treaty of Nanking in 1842, coercing China to accept contraband opium as a legitimate item of trade. Several other European countries and the United States followed Britain and signed numerous treaties with China settling themselves in what were known as treaty ports and started their trade relations.[20]

Japan's Distinct Development before the Nineteenth Century

Geography has played a leading part in Japanese history. Lying off the mainland of Asia, the geographical isolation of the Japanese archipelago produced an early delineation of its frontiers and boundaries, thereby protecting and nurturing a distinct Japanese identity. Japan is separated from the southern tip of Korea by over a hundred miles of rough water. Japan was, therefore, always protected from armed invasion by her distance from the continental seats of power in China. All through its recorded history until modern times it was never seriously threatened so long as the Western maritime powers did not reach East Asia. The Chinese were usually preoccupied with their land frontiers and never persisted in a policy of expansion across water.[21] Thus the civilization of Japan was formed and developed in comparative seclusion and this has given it a special character.

But from the earliest times, Japan's relationships with China and Korea, sometimes peaceful, sometimes hostile, were continuous. Though the Japanese civilization owes a great deal to China, they contracted and adopted it willingly and under no pressure. To China they turned for the very foundations of their organized national life, adopted the Chinese written language and studied Chinese method of government. They welcomed Chinese teachers who brought to them the treasures of learning and religion. Chinese monks, doctors and craftsmen came in large numbers and were treated with distinction and respect and given special privileges.[22] For centuries they looked up to

[20] Gong, ibid., pp. 136 *et seq.*; *see also* Daniel R. Headrick, *The Tools of Empire: Technology and European Imperialism in the Nineteenth Century* (Oxford, 1981), pp. 43 *et seq.*

[21] *See* Sansom, note 19, p. 168. Twice, in 1274 and 1281, the Mongol Emperor tried to invade Japan but failed for want of naval competence.

[22] Sansom, at p. 106.

China for new ideas in religion and philosophy and revered Chinese classics.[23] But the Japanese also preserved much of their native quality. It has been pointed out that "no nation has been more ready to consider new teaching, and yet none has been more tenacious of its own tradition."[24] As a leading Japanese comparative lawyer, Yohiyuki Nodo, points out:

> "The Japanese from the early days of their history have come under the influence of, and benefited from, foreign cultures. They gluttonised with gusto whatever they thought to be beneficial and good for them. They have a gargantuan appetite for foreign culture and not inconsiderable power of digestion, though material was often impaired by swallowing it unmasticated."[25]

A few castaway Portuguese were the first to reach Japan in 1542 and were received in a friendly manner by the Japanese. It was not long before the first arrivals were followed by missionaries and traders who had little difficulty in establishing friendly relations with the people and their rulers. In 1549 Francis Xavier with several of his companions landed in Japan (at Kagoshima) where he was well received and given permission to preach. By the year 1600, the amount of Christian converts had risen to 300,000 and promised further increase.[26]

It is important to mention that Japan was ruled at that time by the Tokugawa family which had succeeded, after a long period of war, in reducing to submission the powerful feudal lords who had become his vassals or 'Daimyo', as they were called. The central administration of Japan, called the 'Bakufu', was headed by a 'Shogun', which in the ancient times was the title of the Emperor's *ad hoc* military deputy, but which had come to mean the supreme feudal lord formally authorized by the Emperor to rule Japan. The office of Shogun was hereditary in the House of Tokugawa which had its central administration in Edo, renamed Tokyo in 1868, and the period when the Tokugawa Family ruled from 1603 to 1868 is known in Japanese history as the Edo Period.[27] The Shogunate, or Bakufu as known in Japanese, was essentially a military dictatorship exercising powers delegated to them by the throne over which it had no choice, and these powers were assumed by each successive Shogun. The Emperor was given fairly adequate revenues but no administrative function was left to him. Powerful Bakufu officers and a suitable garrison were assigned to the capital (at Kyoto) to supervise the

[23] Ibid., pp. 106-107.

[24] Ibid., p. 169.

[25] *See* Yohiyuki Noda quoted in A. J. G. M. Sanders, "The reception of western law in Japan", *The Comparative and International Journal of Southern Africa*, vol. XXVIII, No. 2 (March 1995), pp. 286-287.

[26] *See* Sansom, note 19, pp. 106, 171.

[27] *See* Hidemi Suganami, "Japan's entry into international society", in Hedley Bull and Adam Watson, *The Expansion of International Society* (Oxford, 1984); p. 186.

Emperor and to acquaint him with the Shogun's policy. The Shogun never attempted to claim the throne and the fiction of the ultimate authority of the Emperor was scrupulously observed and the military dictators always submitted advice or request to him in the humble language of a loyal subject addressing his sovereign.[28]

Period of Isolation in Japan

It may be noted that besides the Portuguese and the Spaniards, the Dutch and the English were given trade facilities in Japan in the early 1600s and they were all competing and quarreling with each other. But as the number of Christian converts increased, the missionary activities of Catholic States, like Spain and Portugal, provoked hostility and there were isolated persecutions in different parts of Japan. Fearing the sinister designs of the Christian missionaries and their countries, the Tokugawa authorities decided to expel the dangerous aliens and exterminate native Christians. The Dutch were allowed to remain because they were clearly hostile to the Spaniards and the Portuguese and, since they eschewed all missionary activity, were thought by the Japanese not to be Christians at all.[29] In 1638, the Tokugawa regime adopted a policy of national seclusion and decided not only to exclude aliens but prohibit the Japanese from going abroad or building ships capable of making long voyages. The main purpose of this self-imposed seclusion was primarily to eliminate the effect of Christian missionaries.[30]

At the beginning of the seventeenth century, there were four European nations which had relations with Japan: the Portuguese, the Spanish, the English, and the Dutch. The first two were expelled by the Tokugawa seclusion edicts, while the third temporarily withdrew on account of lack of profit. When in 1673 the English attempted to resume trade, the Bakufu's seclusion policy had become too rigid to allow them to return.[31] Various attempts by France, Russia and also the United States to persuade Japan to reopen commercial relations, all proved fruitless until 1853, as we shall discuss later.[32]

For more than 200 years, while Japan remained outside the growing Western influence, it was never completely cut off from the so-called outside world. The Dutch and the Chinese had been granted an exemption from the prohibition on foreign contacts. They were both allowed to continue very restricted trade at Nagasaki port, and this also provided the Japanese with a

[28] *See* Sansom, note 19, pp. 172-173.

[29] *See* F. C. Jones, *Extraterritoriality in Japan and the Diplomatic Relations resulting in its Abolition 1853-1899* (New York, 1970), p. 6; Sansom, note 19, pp. 171-172.

[30] *See* Sansom, note 19, p. 171.

[31] *See* Suganami, note 27, p. 186.

[32] *See* Jones, note 29, pp. 6-7.

valuable window on what was happening in the outside world. From the little Dutch colony on the artificial island of Deshima in Nagasaki harbour, which the Japanese kept isolated, information about the inventions and affairs of Europe, Asia and elsewhere filtered into Japan to be analyzed and absorbed by the Japanese.[33] While there were no official relations with the Dutch and the Chinese and only merchants were permitted to visit Japan for trading, there were several official missions from Korea, and even some sporadic contacts with merchants and sailors from Russia, Britain and America. Japanese policy of seclusion and unconditional repulsion of foreigners did cause hardship and problems for the Western sailors, particularly the Americans, who were the most frequent victims.[34]

The United States Takes the Initiative to Open Japan

The United States, after the acquisition of the Pacific seaboard, felt that there might be great economic opportunities for trade between California and China. Already substantial American trade with Canton was being conducted from the East Coast via the Indian Ocean which the Americans wanted to expand. Moreover, after about 1820, a large number of American whaling vessels had started appearing off the coast of Japan. But these ships could not call at the Japanese ports for water, coal and other supplies because of Japanese isolation laws. Further, occasional Japanese ill treatment of the shipwrecked sailors caused resentment in the United States which wanted to put some pressure on Japan to overcome these difficulties.[35]

The Opium War with China and the more extensive opening of China ports seemed to the Americans and the British to make the opening of Japan both inevitable and easier. In 1846 an American naval officer, Biddle, was sent to Edo Bay to test the waters, but the Japanese firmly rejected his overtures, reaffirming their policy of national isolation, and he withdrew frustrated. The Americans were determined, however, to take benefit of the opening of the Pacific route to them and to increase their China trade. Japan was directly on line from San Francisco to Shanghai and had supplies of coal, mined near Nagasaki. In 1851 they decided to send a naval commander, with a letter from President Millard Fillmore addressed to the Emperor of Japan, to secure for the Americans the right to buy coal for steamers on the passage between California and China; proper protection for shipwrecked sailors; and permission for ships to dispose of cargo at one or more Japanese

[33] *See* Suganami, note 27, pp. 186-187; J. E. Hoare, *Japan's Treaty Ports and Foreign Settlements: The Uninvited Guests 1858-1899* (Kent, 1994), p. 1.

[34] *See* Suganami, note 27, pp. 187-189.

[35] *See* W. G. Beasley, "The foreign threat and the opening of the ports", Chapter 4 in Marius B. Jansen (ed.), *The Cambridge History of Japan*, vol. 5, *The Nineteenth Century*, (Cambridge, 1989), pp. 267-268.

ports of call. The President of the United States stated that the object in sending his officer was to propose that the United States and Japan "should live in friendship and have commercial intercourse with each other" and assured them that "the constitution and laws of the United States forbid all interference with the religions or political concerns of other nations."[36]

Commodore Matthew C. Perry with his squadron of four warships reached the Edo Bay on 8 July 1853. As we have noted earlier, although the *de jure* sovereign of Japan was the Emperor, or Mikado, the descendant of gods, for centuries *de facto* sovereignty was exercised by the Shoguns, the military leaders. In theory, the Emperors remained the ultimate sovereigns, who had delegated executive and administrative power to the Shoguns. In practice, they were mere puppets in the hands of their over-mighty vassals. This state of affairs was not understood by foreigners at the time of Commodore Perry's mission. The prevalent view, taken by the Dutch, was that there were two Emperors in Japan, one supreme in matters spiritual, the other in temporal affairs. Perry and subsequent Western envoys supposed that the potentate at Yedo, whom they knew as the Tycoon, was equivalent to an Emperor or King, whose decision would be final in all ordinary matters of State. They knew vaguely of a second ruler in the interior, but his power, so it was assumed, was limited to things ecclesiastical and they thought little of him.[37]

It is also pertinent to note that even the Tokugawa ruler, or Shogun, was, due to decline in his personal authority, losing his power and had become a tool in the hands of his feudal nobles. Commodore Perry insisted on handing over the President's letter at Kurihama with all appropriate formality and under the guns of his anchored ships. He refused to go to Nagasaki to receive a reply, as the Japanese urged. In a letter of his own he told the Japanese that although "as an evidence of his friendly intention" he had brought only a small squadron on this occasion, he intended, "should it become necessary, to return to Yedo in the ensuing spring with a much larger force."[38] There was no open threat but he left the Japanese under no illusion that he was prepared to use force. He decided it would be wiser to withdraw to the China coast for a while, rather than give the Japanese a chance to keep him waiting for their reply, and sailed for the Luchu Islands. On 12 February 1854, he reappeared, this time with six ships, and moved up the Bay of Yedo to Kanagawa. His mission was already causing a new orientation in the internal politics of Japan causing a civil strife in the country. For all its power, the Bakufu was helpless before the "black ships of the barbarians". That it knew, yet dared not openly acknowledge. Shogunate realized that to reverse the policy of exclusion at the bidding of the foreigner

[36] *See* President Fillmore's letter in Jones, note 29, pp. 7-8; *see also* Jansen, note 35, p. 269.

[37] *See* Jones, note 29, pp. 8-9.

[38] *See* Beasley, note 35, pp. 269-270.

would mean a fatal loss of prestige at home. But to refuse might mean the destruction of Yedo by the United States' fleet against which no effective defense could be provided.

The Yedo Government tried to get out of the dilemma by trying to shift the responsibility of a decision by asking the advice of the Court of the Mikado at Kyoto. This was a policy as dangerous as it was futile. The Emperor did not know the real power of the foreigner and did not realize that Japan was practically defenseless before him. The Emperor quite naturally declared that he should be driven away. But this was just what the Shogunate could not do and knew it could not do. The only result of the appeal was that the Shogun received instructions from the Emperor, the representative of the gods, to expel the barbarian, which it could not dare to act upon. When it made treaties with him instead, the Yedo administration put itself in the fatal position of appearing to act unpatriotically and in a manner prejudicial to the safety of the country. But they had no choice. Publicly announcing the Emperor's wish to have the foreigners driven away, the Bakufu proceeded to conclude a "Treaty of Peace, Amity and Commerce" with Commodore Perry on 31 March 1854, that gave Perry the substance of what he sought.[39] The ports of Shimoda and Hakodate were to be opened to American ships to replenish their stocks of coal and provisions; arrangements were made for the just treatment of shipwrecked sailors; a provision was made for the appointment of a United States consul at Shimoda, and an ill-defined right was given to US traders to purchase goods at open ports. There was no provision for the permanent residence of US citizens but a most-favoured-nation clause was included which secured to the United States any future privileges granted to other nations.[40] Although it was not in the full sense a commercial treaty, it was the beginning and, as Perry said in his report, Japan was "opened to the nations of the West".[41]

The Japanese are said to have congratulated themselves for conceding so little by this Treaty of Kanagawa, but did not realize they had opened the door for foreign penetration. Britain followed closely behind and Admiral Sir James Stirling arrived in Nagasaki on 14 September 1854, and negotiated a convention with the Japanese authorities to prevent the Russian warships from using the ports of Japan as bases for raids on British shipping during the ensuing Crimean War. The ports of Nagasaki and Hakodate were opened to the British ships for repairs and securing supplies, but no reference was made to trade or residence of British nationals. But the agreement included a most-favoured-nation clause.[42]

[39] *See* Jones, note 29, pp. 10-11.
[40] *See* Beasley, note 35, p. 270.
[41] Quoted in ibid., p. 270.
[42] *See* Jones, note 29, pp. 12-13.

Four months later, Russian Admiral Poutiatine concluded a treaty at Shimoda by which three Japanese ports were opened to Russian ships for repairs and supplies, Russians were given the right to trade at some of the ports, were given the right to station a consul, and for the first time the principle of extraterritoriality was clearly stated and the Russian consul given jurisdiction over Russian nationals living in Japan. The next agreement was concluded with the Dutch by which the latter secured full personal freedom, the privileges of extraterritoriality, and were to share in whatever privileges might be accorded to other nations in the future.[43] Copies of all these treaties were submitted to the Emperor by the Shogun's deputy in Kyoto, with a quite untruthful explanation that the negotiations had made no concessions of importance. In February 1855 His Majesty gave them his approval with thanks to the Shogun.[44]

The US Consul Arrives

The first treaties had given only very limited rights to foreign commerce and the Japanese hoped and wished that the foreigners would not come back with new demands. There was one uncomfortable clause in the 1854 US-Japan Treaty, providing that the United States might appoint agents to reside at an open port if either government deemed such an arrangement necessary, although the Japanese authorities, relying on the Japanese text, thought that this meant "if the Japanese Government thought it necessary".[45] In August 1856, the Japanese were taken by surprise when an American warship brought an unassuming but determined American consul, Townsend Harris, who carried a letter from the President, which he intended to present to the Shogun in person, with a purpose to extend the scope of the 1854 Treaty. The Japanese authorities implored him to go away urging that there was no need for his services, and if he stayed, other foreign consuls would also come. He encountered baffling obstructions and could not fulfil his objective until 1857 when the Japanese heard from interpreters in Nagasaki that, because the Chinese Government had failed to carry out treaty obligations, a British squadron, with assistance from French and Americans, had attacked and burned Canton. The Dutch Commissioner in Nagasaki, quoting the example of China, also sent a warning against the evasive and dilatory behaviour of the Japanese officials. Through persistence, and by playing on Japanese fears of British and other Europeans' actions in China, Harris secured a convention on 17 June 1857, which opened Nagasaki to the United States, provided for full diplomatic and consular privileges, permanent residence of Americans at Shimoda and Hakodate, permitted the appointment

[43] Ibid., p. 14.
[44] *See* Sansom, note 19, pp. 282-283.
[45] *See* ibid., p. 283.

of an American Vice-Consul at Hakodate, private import and export transactions, subject to an agreed tariff, and freedom of religion and extraterritorial jurisdiction. He was also received for a personal audience with the Shogun on 7 December 1857, and thereafter negotiated a formal Treaty of Amity and Commerce which was duly signed on 29 July 1858, on board the USS Pawhattan. The 1858 Treaty also included:

> "the provision for the United States to mediate any difficulties between Japan and the European powers;
> the option to revise the treaty, on the desire of either party and on one year's notice, after 4 July, 1872;
> various other provisions concerning the prohibition on importing opium, the right to freedom of religion, the right to circulate foreign coins in Japan, and the regulation of exchange at a specified rate."[46]

Unequal Treaties

The Netherlands, Russia, Great Britain and France followed the American lead and signed new treaties within a few months. Shortly thereafter, Portugal, Prussia, Sweden, Norway, Spain, Austria-Hungary, Hawaii and Peru joined in signing treaties with Japan.[47] Either specifically or by virtue of a most-favoured-nation clause, all these treaties provided for appointment of diplomatic agents, consuls-general, consuls, and for the exercise of extraterritorial rights in criminal and civil matters, along with a fixed custom tariffs at very low rates. These provisions and the fact that none of the treaties were for a specified duration, caused a lot of heart-burning in Japan within a few years and led to an outburst of anti-foreign sentiment in Japan. No wonder the Japanese perceived the treaty powers to be "foxes of the same hole" and were concerned that they would subjugate Japan, as they had China, by means of "unequal treaties."[48]

In the capital Kyoto, there was a widespread anti-foreign feeling and much hostility against the Bakufu Government which had signed these conventions. The Shogun was faced not only with the disagreeable problem of dealing with foreign envoys but also with the growing opposition among his own countrymen. Some were animated by blind hatred of the "ugly foreign barbarians" and angry because the Shogun had timidly abandoned the seclusion policy at their bidding. Others feared the renewed influence of Christianity. The Emperor and the nobles around him were genuinely alarmed at the prospect of foreigners living and trading near the capital and entirely

[46] *See* for a detailed and interesting account of Townsend Harris negotiations with the Japanese, Sansom, note 19, pp. 283-292; Gong, note 19, pp. 168-169; Jones, note 29, pp. 15-19.

[47] *See* Gong, note 19, pp. 169; Sansom, note 19, p. 300-301.

[48] *See* Gong, note 19, p. 169.

blamed Tokugawa for this state of affairs.[49] The only express wish of the throne was that the foreigners should be kept as far away as possible and not be allowed in the provinces near the capital. But while maintaining his objections, the Emperor gave an ambiguous and qualified consent to the treaties which came into force in July 1859. Foreign diplomatic envoys at once took up residence in Yedo and several ports were opened to foreign trade and residence.[50]

With all these treaties in place and the arrival of foreign envoys there was tension in the air. The Shogunate was openly committed to one policy, the Emperor to another, and the opinion in the country was bitter and divided. A clash was inevitable because evasion and concealment was no longer possible. The foreigners were present on the Japanese soil, the ships were there in the harbours, and it could not be pretended that they had not come to stay.[51] In this atmosphere of hostility there were several attacks with swords on foreigners and even some murders between 1860 to 1863. The secretary of the US legation was murdered in Yedo, the British legation was attacked twice, and the menace of assassination hung over every foreigner in the country.[52] With its rapidly declining power, the Shogunate was helpless in preventing these outrages. In 1862, the British Government demanded indemnity for attack on a British party of four resulting in grave injuries to some and the death of one of them. On the non-fulfillment of its demands a British squadron bombarded and destroyed the town of Kagoshima on 11 August 1863.[53]

The Emperor was extremely unhappy with this state of affairs and, in March 1863, felt strong enough to summon the Shogun to Kyoto and fix a date, 24 June 1863, for the expulsion of foreigners. The harassed Shogun was forced to give an outward consent to this impossible demand. All he could do was timidly approach the foreign ministers with the expulsion notice of the Emperor from whom he received the response that the foreign interests would be protected by the powers themselves. Afraid to arouse the ire of the foreign powers by the Emperor's notice, he sent a message to the court that it was not possible as yet to execute the Imperial command, to which the court reluctantly agreed and left the date for the expulsion of foreigners to the Shogun.[54] But as the Shogun's arrogant and powerful vassal, Daimyo of Choshiu, began to enforce the imperial edict by firing at foreign ships passing through the Straits of Shimonosoeki, an allied squadron of 17 vessels (nine British, four Dutch, three French and one American) destroyed

[49] *See* Jones, note 29, p. 21; Sansom, note 19, p. 292.
[50] Sansom, note 19, p. 295.
[51] *See* ibid., p. 297.
[52] *See* ibid., pp. 298-299.
[53] *See* Jones, note 29, pp. 23-24.
[54] Sansom, note 19, pp. 299-300

the fortifications and batteries the daimyo had erected at Shimonoseki on 5 and 6 September 1864.[55] While superior military force had not played a major role prior to the signing of the treaties, it was clearly available and could be used at the discretion of the Western powers.[56]

The Meiji Restoration

It was clear by now that the foreigners could not be expelled and the expulsion policy was futile. The foreign powers for long suspected the dual authority in Japan but did not understand the relationship between the court and the Shogunate. They were now realizing that the centre of power was moving to Kyoto. Although the Emperor had ratified the treaties, the court was not happy at the turn of events. The Shogunate was losing its face and power and, after a brief civil war, the whole country submitted to the Emperor's rule without delay. The Meiji era began on 25 January 1868. The name of Yedo was changed to Tokyo (Eastern capital) and in that city the Emperor's residence and the seat of government was established in March 1869. The new government no longer encouraged or tolerated anti-foreign activities, but the sentiment of hatred did not go away immediately.[57]

Period of Humiliation

This was a period of utter humiliation for the Japanese. The Tokugawas were shown to be unable to govern Japan because they failed to protect Japan from encroachment of the "barbarians". The power was restored to the Emperor and the anti-Tokugawa factions rallied round the slogan, "Revere the Emperor; Expel the Barbarians". It was argued that only through unification of the country under the leadership of the Emperor could Japan rebuild her strength to repel the Western powers.

The foreigners, of course, could not be expelled. In fact they were beginning to exercise privileges much beyond what the Japanese thought was necessary or reasonable. Japan's inability to protect foreigners led to deployment of British and French detachments. These brought new problems and resentments. Various ports, e.g. Kanagawa, Nagasaki and Hakodate had been opened to foreign residence since 1858-1859. Edo, renamed Tokyo, and Osaka were opened between 1859 and 1863. Western men – Europeans and Americans – who came to Japan in 1859, drew their experience from China and thought themselves of superior societies. Though the Japanese were still strongly opposed to Christianity, the Christian missionaries came with the foreign communities and, by the early 1870s, all the major

[55] *See* Jones, note 29, p. 24.
[56] *See* Gong, note 19, p. 172.
[57] Sansom, note 19, p. 307.

denominations had their churches and chapels. The Treaty Powers were exercising wide privileges of extraterritorial jurisdiction not only based on the terms of their own treaties, but, relying on the mostfavoured- nation clause, they could claim to possess all the rights enjoyed by another power. Thus, even Austria-Hungary, with quite minor interests in Japan, claimed the following privileges:

> "All questions, in regard to rights, whether of property or of person, arising between Austro-Hungarian citizens residing in Japan, shall be subject to the jurisdiction of the Imperial and royal authorities. In like manner the Japanese shall not interfere in any question which may arise between Austro-Hungarian citizens and the subjects of any other Treaty Power.
>
> Austro-Hungarian citizens, who may commit any crime against Japanese subjects, or the subjects of any other nation, shall be brought before the Imperial and Royal Consular officers and punished according to the laws of their country."[58]

Unequal provisions and superior military capability reflected in unequal elements in these treaties, led to a strong feeling in Japan that these were unjust treaties. These unjust and unequal treaties created a deep-seated "feeling that they (the Japanese) were dishonoured as a nation so long as they permitted the [extraterritorial] system to continue".[59] As a Japanese statesman, Iwakura, warned in 1869:

> "We must guard our country's independence. Foreign troops have been stationed in our open ports, and even when foreigners who live in our country violate our laws, we are forced to stand by while agents of their governments exercise jurisdiction over them. Our country has never before known such shame and disgrace."[60]

The "unequal treaties" also led to feelings of injustice and inferiority. Feeling of racial inequality to a proud people, who always had a certain self-imputed feeling of racial superiority, was "resented bitterly". The Japanese felt that this could be the only reason "behind the insistence of the occidental powers" to claim "concessions from Japan which they neither claimed nor submitted to in their relations with one another."[61] Deeply concerned and disturbed about their racial inferiority, the Japanese were seriously looking for methods to improve it. After visits by some Japanese delegations to Europe and impressed by the mercantile and industrial might of the Europeans, they were getting convinced that "Japanese society as a whole was backward and 'uncivilized'". They got so obsessed by such general feelings of inferiority

[58] Quoted in Jones, note 29, p. 27.

[59] Ibid., p. 47. 16

[60] Quoted in Gong, note 19, p. 25.

[61] Jones, note 29, p. 47.

that it took the form of the admonition, 'You must not be laughed at by foreigners'.[62]

Period of Assimilation

The achievement of equality by the revision of the unequal treaties and the achievement of security became the primary Japanese goals. To achieve these goals, they knew, Japan must first become a "civilized" power. The rallying cry of "Expel the Barbarians" died down because it was no longer useful or proper. The new Meiji Government encouraged the adoption of western ways, their customs and institutions, to assimilate the material and practical features of occidental life which were supposed to be the true foundation of a powerful modern State. For the next two decades, there was almost a craze for western things and western ideas which is sometimes described by some Japanese historians as a "period of intoxication". There was an anxiety among the authorities to show to Western nations that the Japanese people had adopted and assimilated enough of western culture to justify their claims to be treated as member of a civilized modern State. They wanted the Western powers to agree that the Japanese constitution and laws were enlightened and her standards of public and private behaviour were so high that Japan could be considered a worthy member of the international community. The Meiji Government was convinced that the sooner they could display to the western world a recognizable and faithful imitation of western society, the sooner would the unequal treaties be revised. This was the controlling factor in Japanese political life until it was achieved in 1894.[63]

The Japanese were always ready to learn from abroad. Even during the seclusion period there was a strong urge to learn from the West, especially among the so-called Dutch scholars, who were close to the Dutch and had learnt their language. Highranking officials in the very Bakufu, that prohibited travel to foreign lands, strongly desired to see the West with their own eyes and create a navy equal to the Western nations. The first Japanese mission left for the United States as early as 1860. After they returned deeply impressed, the Bakufu sent large and small embassies abroad every year or every other year until its demise in 1868. More than 300 Japanese travelled to foreign lands before the Meiji period. Each of these missions investigated the institutions and civilization of the nations they were sent to and recorded their experiences in books or pamphlets published after their return. The Bakufu missions abroad greatly contributed to the understanding by Meiji

[62] *See* Gong, note 19, p. 173.
[63] *See* Sansom, note 19, pp. 378-385.

Japan of the West by producing popular best-sellers like Fukuzawa's *Conditions in the West.*[64]

Meiji Restoration further strengthened Japan's resolve to learn from the West. On 23 December 1871, the Meiji Government dispatched a great official mission with Ambassador Plenipotentiary Iwakura Tomomi as its leader, and consisting of 48 members, to America and Europe that also took with it 59 students, five of whom were women. While the ostensible objective of the Iwakura mission was to revise the unequal treaties ratified and exchanged in Washington by Tokugawa mission in 1860, the real intention of the mission was to discover conditions in the West and adapt them in Japan to make a new Meiji State. On their return, after an extended stay of 631 days, the Japanese learnt the strong points of each nation. They found, for instance, that England provided a model for industrial and naval development; Prussia, which defeated France in 1871, provided a model for military organization; France was a model for its centralized police system and educational and legal patterns; and America stimulated agricultural development.[65]

Although in the beginning the Japanese were totally dependent on foreign teachers and technicians, it was not long before Japan succeeded in transplanting Western industrial techniques and in training enough talented men to become surprisingly self-sufficient in a relatively short period of 15 to 20 years. Even western clothing became compulsory for government officials in November 1872, and Japan adopted the solar calendar instead of the lunar calendar. Besides formal learning, the foreigners living in Japan provided the Japanese with opportunities to become acquainted with several aspects of western life by observing foreign life styles and daily activities.[66] The Japanese learnt European languages, adopted European manners and clothes, learnt European customs. By 1873, it is interesting to note, watches, gold chains, umbrellas, western hats, jackets, trousers, and shoes were all being used by the elite. Even western literature, philosophies, politics, religion, architecture, painting and music were being studied and emulated.[67]

Adoption of Western Laws and International Law

Japan, like China and some other Asian countries, had been forced to accept unequal, inequitable and humiliating treaties, and forced to relinquish tariff autonomy and concede extraterritoriality, to westerners, in part, because, it

[64] *See* Hiarakawa Sukehiro, "Japan's turn to the West", in Marius B. Jansen, *The Cambridge History of Japan*, vol. 5, *The Nineteenth Century* (Cambridge, 1989), pp. 448-460.

[65] Ibid., pp. 463-465.

[66] *See* ibid., pp. 470-472.

[67] *See* Gong, note 19, pp. 186-187.

was thought, that they were not able to guarantee some basic rights, like life, dignity, property, travel, commerce and religion, to foreigners in their countries and were not even familiar with the obligations of modern international law, including the law of war.[68] To obtain equal status with the West, the early Meiji Government thought it essential to compile legal codes similar to those possessed by the European countries. After a brief flirtation with the Napoleonic Codes,[69] the Meiji Government preferred and adopted the emerging German codes. In 1881 it was decided that the country's first constitution would be modeled on the Prussian Constitution of 1850, a conservative document which could hardly be called democratic. Japan's first constitution was promulgated in 1889 and came into force in November 1890. The constitution, which gave the basic principles of government to Japan for more than half a century, was declared to be a "grant" from the Emperor to his subjects and the army was directly subordinate to the Emperor. A rather unrepresentative parliament existed merely to assist and support the Emperor, and ministers of State were appointed by the Emperor and were responsible to him. Loyalty to the Emperor and filial piety and obedience were proclaimed to be the essence and virtue of the nation. After the adoption of the German-inspired constitution, the German- inspired codes (civil code, commercial code, criminal code, civil and criminal procedure codes) followed as a matter of course. By 1900 Japan had acquired a legal system which looked very German indeed. More relevant and to the point for the Japanese Government, it satisfied the western demands for modernization.[70]

Japan's Introduction to International Law

But even more importantly and more intensely than the national legal system, the Japanese started learning and adopting international law. The foreigners from the West had forced Japan to open up the country using their "tools of civilization", or warships, and announced their requirements based on international law. The first American Consul General in Japan, Townsend Harris, while negotiating the draft Treaty of Amity and Friendship with the commissioners of Shogunate, had started advising the Japanese to follow the rules of international law in their dealings with the western countries and

[68] *See* Gong, note 19, pp. 14-35.

[69] The French legal system was the one which first of all came to the attention of the Japanese when a Tokugawa official traveled to France in 1867 and praised it in his writings. They greeted the French law with enthusiasm and, in 1869, the Meiji Government ordered the translation of all five French law codes, hired an eminent French lawyer to adapt these laws in Japan and to teach Japanese lawyers, but later it was abandoned. *See* Sukehiro, note 64, pp. 473-75.

[70] *See* A.J.G.M. Sanders, "The reception of Western law in Japan", *The Comparative and International Law Journal of Southern Africa*, vol. 28, no. 2 (March 1995), pp. 281-283.

warned them about the grave consequences if they did not accept the tenets of this binding law of nations. He claimed privileges and immunities, such as inviolability of the foreign diplomatic establishments and immunities of officers, recognized under international law. References were constantly made to the concept of the law of nations, not only by Harris but also by other diplomatic missions in their negotiations with the Yedo Government.[71] In trying to understand these demands, the officers of the Tokugawa Government were forced to study international law from some books on international law written by Wheaton and Phillimore which they brought from China. A Chinese translation of Henry Wheaton's *Elements of International Law* (Oxford, 1836) by a Christian Missionary W.A.P. Martin, had been published in 1864 in China on the orders of Prince Kung. The Chinese translation was reprinted in Japan in 1865 and was not only presented to the contemporary last Shogun, Tokugawa Yoshinobu, but was eagerly and enthusiastically read by the authorities and officials of the Tokugawa Government as well as keen intellectuals who held it in high esteem, almost "like holy scriptures".[72] In 1868, a part of Wheaton's book was translated into Japanese. Several other important treatises were translated and published during this period, such as, Theodore D. Woolsey's *Introduction to the Study of International Law* (1864), James Kent's *Commentaries on International law* (1st edition, 1826), and *Le droit International de l'Europe* by J. Bergeon (1873).[73] As early as 1862, the Bakufu had sent eight students abroad. Two of them, Nishi Shu and Tsua Shindo, studied international law under Professor S. Vissering of the University of Leyden. After their return home in 1866, each of them published a book on international law based on Prof. Vissering's lectures.[74] Nishi Amane also started teaching international law in the Kaiseijo. Reversing the old policy, in January 1868, the Emperor declared the opening of Japan to foreign intercourse based on international law and notified the consuls that Japan would "conduct its foreign policy according to the public law of the universe"[75] and started formally receiving them and accepting their credentials.[76]

[71] See for an interesting account of Harris' negotiations with the Japanese Hirohiko Otsuka, "Japan's early encounter with the concept of the 'Law of Nations'", in *Japanese Annual of International Law*, No. 13 (1969), pp. 42-43; Shigeru Kuriyama, "Historical aspects of the progress of international law in Japan", *Japanese Annual of International Law*, vol. 1 (1957), p. 1.

[72] Ibid., p. 46.

[73] *See* Fujio Ito, "One hundred years of International Law Studies in Japan", *Japanese Annual of International Law*, vol. 13 (1969), pp. 20-21.

[74] *See* Otsuka, note 71, p. 44.

[75] *See* Susumu Yamauchi, "Civilization and International Law in Japan during the Meiji Era (1868-1912)", *Hitotsubashi Journal of Law and Politics*, vol. 24 (1996), p. 1-2; also Otsuka, note 71, p. 45.

[76] *See* Otsuka, note 71, pp. 48-49.

International Law Applicable Only to European "Civilized" States or States of European Origin

It is important to note, however, that while Japan was getting keen to learn international law, European powers began to maintain that international law was not the law applicable among all the nations of the world, but applied only amongst Christian States of Europe and America. Thus Thomas E. Holland, Professor of International Law at Oxford, who later had been given the title of Grand Commander of the Rising Sun by Japan,[77] in his book on *Lectures on International Law* (London, 1933), said that international law "grew with the mental growth of the Nations of Europe", all of whom had the Christian religion. Although it was "a purely Christian institution", to avoid the conflict between the Protestants and Catholics, it founded its system on *Jus Naturae*. Therefore, its application was not restricted to nations professing Christian faith, but "its applicability is a question of Civilization than of Creed." He explained that Christian nations and their colonies "have attained a level of civilization perhaps not higher than but at any rate different from that attained by the other races of mankind" and, therefore, "International Law, like many other products of their civilization, is too refined to be applicable, as a whole, very far beyond their limits."[78]

Hall, another authority on international law in his famous *A Treatise on International Law* (1880) declared that the sphere of international law was restricted to "modern civilized states":

> "It is scarcely necessary to point out that as international law is a product of the special civilization of Europe, and forms a highly artificial system of which the principles cannot be supposed to be understood or recognized by countries differently civilized, such states only can be presumed to be subject to it as are inheritors of that civilization."

On the other hand, he said, "states outside European civilization must formally enter into the circle of law-governed countries. They must do something with acquiescence of the latter, or of some of them, which amounts to an acceptance of the law in its entirety beyond all misconstruction."[79]

It is important to note that these were not exceptional views. Most of the European jurists at that time and much later believed in the exclusive family of nations consisting of European States or States of European origin. Wheaton, the outstanding authority for the Japanese, wrote:

[77] He had even been unsuccessfully invited by the Government of Japan to become its legal advisor. *See*Yamauchi, note 75, p. 3.

[78] Thomas Erskine Holland, *Lectures on International Law* (London, 1933), p. 88. Also quoted in Yamauchi, note 75, pp. 4-5.

[79] William Edward Hall, *A Treatise on International Law*, 8th edn. (Oxford, 1924), p. 47.

> "Is there a uniform law of nations? There certainly is not the same one for all the nations and states of the world. The public law, with slight exceptions, has always been, and still is, limited to the civilized and Christian people of Europe or to those of European origin. This distinction between the European law of nations and that of the other races of mankind has long been remarked by the publicists ..."[80]

Wheaton, one of the most popular western authors of international law, whose book had been translated into Chinese in 1864, and into Japanese in 1865, said:

> "There is then, according to these writers, no universal, immutable law of nations, binding upon the whole human race – which all mankind in all ages and countries, ancient and modern, savage and civilized, Christian and pagan, have recognized in theory or in practice, have professed to obey, or have in fact obeyed; – no law of nations similar to the law of right reason of which Cicero speaks...one eternal and immortal law, which can neither be repealed nor derogated from, addressing itself to all nations and all ages, deriving its authority from the common Sovereign of the universe, seeking no other lawgiver and interpreter, carrying home its sanctions to every breast by the inevitable punishment he inflicts on its transgressors."[81]

For Wheaton, the "ordinary *jus gentium*" was only a law that varied from time to time, from religion to religion, and from government to government. The "international law of the civilized nations of Europe and America" was "one thing" and "law of the Mohammedan nations" was "another and a very different thing". So, too, differed the law governing the intercourse between the Eastern nations and the Christians. "The international law of Christendom" had sprung from the "European stock".[82] James Lorimer, Professor of International Law at Edinburgh University, pointed out:

> "As a political phenomenon, humanity in its present condition, divides itself into three zones or spheres – that of civilized humanity, that of barbarous humanity, and that of savage humanity. To these, whether arising from peculiarities of race or from various stages of development in the same race, belong, *of right*, at the hands of civilized nations, three stages of recognition – plenary political recognition, partial political recognition, and natural or mere human recognition ...
>
> The sphere of plenary political extends to all the existing states of Europe, with their colonial dependencies, in so far as these are peopled by persons of European birth or descent; and the states of North and South America ...

[80] Henry Wheaton, *Elements of International Law* (The Literal Reproduction of the Edition of 1866 by Richard Henry Dana, Jr.), (Oxford, 1936), p. 15.

[81] Henry Wheaton, *Elements of International Law with a Sketch of the Science*, 1st edn. (1836), p. 44, quoted in Mark Weston Janis, "American versions of the International Law of Christendom: Kent, Wheaton and the Grotian Tradition", *Netherlands International Law Review*, vol. XXXIX (1992/1), pp. 56-57.

[82] Wheaton, p. 57.

The sphere of partial political recognition extends to Turkey in Europe and in Asia, and to the old historical states of Asia which have not become European dependencies – viz., to Persia and other separate states of central Asia, to China, Siam and Japan.

The sphere of natural, or mere human recognition extends to the residue of mankind; though here we ought, perhaps, to distinguish between the progressive and non-progressive races ...

It is with the first of these spheres alone that the international jurist has directly to deal; ... He is not bound to apply the positive law of nations to savages, or even to barbarians, as such."[83]

Japanese Determination to Westernize

Overawed, as the Japanese were, by the western countries, they did not have the courage to refute these views, nor could they get angry. All they could do was attempt to modernize, or rather 'Westernize' themselves, so that Japan could become a member of the European club of international law, or the 'family of civilized nations', to be able to associate with the European nations on an equal basis. They remembered the Opium War of China, its cause and result, and felt the danger of imperialism and colonization. The only way to maintain her independence seemed to be to imitate Europe in almost every area. They feared that unless they made the nation stronger in military and economic terms, Japan might fall under the aggressive colonization of the Western Powers. They had become well aware that only members of the 'exclusive club' of international law, i.e. European nations, could and would decide on the admission of Japan into that club.[84]

Maintenance of independence of the nation was the greatest concern of the new Meiji Government. They perceived the existing international society as an area where the weak fell prey to the strong. As Iwakura Tomomi, one of the founders and important leader of the Meiji Government, said: "They [the Western Powers] have the heart of tigers and wolves. If we are only frightened and do not resist their violence, our imperial nation will come to be enslaved."[85] Another well-known and influential intellectual leader in Meiji era, Fukuzawa Yukichi, said:

"With respect to a treaty of peace and amity, and with respect to the public law of nations, it should be said that they are all very beautiful in words, but that in the final analysis they are nothing but superficial protocols and names. The reality of

[83] James Lorimer, *The Institutes of the Law of Nations*, vol. 1 (Edinburgh, 1883), pp. 1101-1102.

[84] *See* Yamauchi, note 75, p. 2.

[85] *See Iwakura Ko Jikki or The Record of Duke Iwakura*, quoted in an excellent historical paper by Onuma Yasuki, "'Japanese International Law' in the Prewar Period – Perspectives on the Teaching and Research of International Law in Prewar Japan", in *Japanese Annual of International Law*, no. 29 (1986), pp. 28-29.

> the intercourse among nations is nothing other than a struggle for domination, and an avid appetite for gains. Look at the facts through history, ancient and modern, all over the world. Is it not a common knowledge to everyone that there has been no instance in which a small country, poor and innocent, succeeded in upholding the honour or independence on the strength of treaties and the public law? A hundred volumes of the public law of all nations will not be equal to the power of a single cannon. Numerous copies of treaties of peace and amity will not be equal to the power of a box of gunpowder. Cannons and gunpowder are not the means for upholding the reason that you already have, but a tool for creating a reason where there is none."[86]

If Japan became a member of the family of nations, it was felt, it would be considered as equal because, according to the principles of international law, all States, regardless of their size and power, were accepted as equal. "Now we lack sovereignty in treaties", said Iwakura, referring to extra-territorial, tariff, and other provisions of unequal treaties. But, he said, "the Western Powers took these privileges only by chance, and these are in violation of the principles of law of nations."[87]

Japan's first and foremost diplomatic objective in the beginning of the Meiji era was the revision of the unequal treaties for which international law was supposed to be immensely important. Knowledge and mastery of this law was necessary for negotiating revision of these treaties. But to achieve revision of the treaties, Japan had to demonstrate that it was a "civilized nation." Compliance with the rules of international law would provide evidence thereof. Therefore, to understand and master international law was absolutely important. The Japanese Government not only encouraged translation of major text books from Europe and America, but were eager to employ European and American experts in international law as legal advisors. It even encouraged the establishment of Japanese Association of International Law as early as 1897 when the number of international law experts were extremely limited. The Association started publishing the *Japanese Journal of International Law* as early as 1902. It is important to note that even in the Occidental nations, which were supposed to be the founders of international law and had been practicing it for more than two centuries, academic associations began to be established and journals began to be published around the same time. Thus the International Law Association was established in Europe in 1875 and the American Society of International Law in 1906. The *Revue generale de droit international public* was published for the first time in 1894 and the *American Journal of International Law* in 1907. It just shows the seriousness of the Japanese to learn international law. Studying

[86] Quoted in Hisashi Owada, "Japan, International Law and the International Community", in Nisuke Ando (ed.), *Japan and International Law: Past, Present and Future*, (The Hague, 1999), p. 353; *see also* Onuma Yasuki, note 85, p. 29.

[87] Ibid.

and teaching of international law was carried out as a part of the process of the wholesale westernization of the society.[88] The Meiji Government placed great emphasis on education, especially higher education, to train future leaders of the nation. Imperial University of Tokyo was established in 1877; and the 1870s and 1880s witnessed the mushrooming of several private higher educational institutions specializing in legal education, including public international law.[89]

The Japanese were determined to "Europeanize" themselves with only one purpose, *viz.*, to remove the taint of inequality and join the family of "civilized" States. By 1871, as we have noted earlier, they sent their first major diplomatic mission led by a senior minister in the Meiji Government, Iwakura, not only as a friendship and learning mission, but to explore the possibility of revising the unequal treaties. The Iwakura Embassy traveled to nine major cities in the United States, plus England and Scotland, France, Belgium, the Netherlands, Germany, Russia, Denmark, Sweden, Italy, Austria, and Switzerland. Only the Spanish Civil War prevented it from going to Spain and Portugal. They returned with a clear message: catching up with the West would require dedication and sacrifice but it could be done.[90] The Foreign Minister of Japan, Inouye, declared it clearly in 1887:

> "The only independent countries left in the east are Japan and China. All countries in the West have schemes for engulfing the east by force and we must devise plans for defense against them. To do this we must set up a new 'civilized State' here ... We need to build up a European civilization here on a par with that of European civilized States."[91]

Japan Learns Imperialist Ways

The Japanese were adamant. Not only did they copy the European laws and regulations, adopted European social customs and even dress, learnt European languages, accepted without any question international law made by and only for the European countries, strengthened its army (following Germany) and navy (following the British model), basically on European lines, but they also started following "European" policies of expansion in their relations with the other "uncivilized" peoples of East Asia and its own neighbours. In 1875, only seven years after the Meiji Restoration, Japan began her career of imperialist adventures and annexed Kuriles. Two years later the Bonin Islands were acquired. In 1879, the Ryukyu Islands were incorporated into Japan under the name of Okinawa. The Volcano Islands adjoining the Bonin Islands were taken over in 1891. Japan next looked at the only direction it

[88] *See* ibid., pp. 29-31.
[89] *See* ibid., pp. 33-35.
[90] *See* Gong, note 19, pp. 177-180.
[91] Quoted in Gong, note 19, p. 190.

could go, dictated by geography and history, namely, the Asiatic mainland where the European powers had already begun to divide China, the decadent empire in the nineteenth century. Her eyes first of all fell on China's tributary, Korea.[92] Beginning in the 1880s, there was an increasingly aggressive Japanese involvement in Korea to undermine both the Chinese influence on the peninsula and the authority of the stubbornly traditional Korean Government. In 1875, it even dispatched three gunboats to Korean waters. When one of them was fired on, it retaliated by bombarding the coastal batteries. Later, it sent an embassy headed by a Japanese high official, accompanied by three warships, and like the Perry expedition, forced Korea to conclude a treaty in January 1876 which was similar to the treaties that Japan had been forced to negotiate during the 1850s. The Korean Treaty stipulated that the kingdom was "an independent nation", thereby putting an end to its tributary relationship with the Chinese empire. It also provided for opening of three ports for Japanese trade as well as Japanese consular jurisdiction in Korea.[93] The parallel with the Perry mission is obvious. There is no doubt Japan had learnt its lessons well which it was going to continue to practice.

It is interesting and important to note that it was in the 1880s that the Europeans stepped up their tempo of imperialist domination. In 1881, France established protectorate over Tunis; in 1882, Britain occupied Egypt; in 1883 Germany began its colonial activities in Southwest Africa; in 1884-85, France and Britain extended their respective jurisdictions in Indochina and Burma; in 1885, Africa was divided by the European States among themselves at the Berlin conference; and in 1889, Germany, Britain and the United States divided up the Samoan kingdom into three segments for their tripartite condominium. By the mid-1890s, most of the Middle East, Africa, Asia and the Pacific had been colonized by the Western Powers. China, Japan and Korea were only a few non-colonized States.[94]

During the next two decades, as Japan gathered more military and naval strength sufficient to confront China which until then had Korea in its sphere as a tributary State. Japan got more and more involved in the internal political power struggle in Korea, trying to undermine Chinese influence and the authority of the Korean Government. When the collision finally came in 1894, precipitated in part by Korea's efforts to honour China's ritual demands, Japanese armies quickly drove the Chinese out of Korea, crossed the Yalu River, and occupied the strategic Liaotung peninsula. By February 1895,

[92] The Korean peninsula was regarded by the Japanese "as a dagger pointed at Japan's heart, a source of constant irritation and menace to Japan's security", Hidemichi Akagi, "Japans's Foreign Relations, 1542-1936", quoted in M. A. Aziz, *Japan's Colonialism and Indonesia* (The Hague, 1955), p. 5.

[93] *See* Akira Iriye, "Japan's drive to great-power status", in *The Cambridge History of Japan*, vol. 5, *Nineteenth Century* (Cambridgc, 1989), chapter 12, pp. 745-746.

[94] *See* ibid., p. 747.

they had seized Weihaiwei on the Shantung peninsula. Although the outright annexation of Korea was neither planned nor necessary and would have risked the active opposition of Russia, Japan did expect acquisition of some new territory to enhance its imperial prestige.[95] By the terms of the Sino-Japanese peace treaty concluded at Shimonoseki in April 1895, China was to recognize that Korea was an independent State, cede the Liaotung peninsula and Taiwan to Japan, pay Japan an indemnity of 200 million taels (about 300 million yen) in seven years, open up four treaty ports, grant Japan most-favoured-nation status as well as the right to navigate the Yangtze River, and give the Japanese the right to engage in manufacturing in China. The war and the resulting peace not only gave Japan an equal status with the Western Powers in China, but established its reputation as a great power, and earned it the respect that they had coveted for so long from Europeans and Americans. It also gave Japan as a bonus the indemnity payment to enable it to continue with its industrialization programme.[96]

It is important to note that as Japan strengthened itself militarily and started behaving with China and Korea, just like the Western Powers, in an imperialistic manner, it began to be recognized as a member of the family of "civilized" States. On 16 July 1894, a few days before it went into war with China, it achieved its goal of concluding with Britain a new treaty providing for the abolition of extraterritoriality in five years in return for the opening up of the country for "mixed residence", which did not contain any provision for the appointment of foreign judges in cases involving foreigners. The acceptance of this treaty after thirty years of intensive efforts symbolized the growing status of Japan as a modern State in the eyes of the Western countries.[97]

Japan was quick to exploit the law to its own advantage. Realizing that international legal protection extended only to the "civilized" States, Japan derided the "barbaric" Chinese during the Sino-Japanese war. It is interesting to note that the Japanese intellectual and even public opinion was all in favour of the use of force in pursuit and furtherance of "civilization" because wars formed "one important element of civilization". The foreign minister of Japan wrote in his memoirs:

> "... Japan represents Western civilization and China keeps Asian traditionalism ...We despise China as an extremely conservative State, obstinate and ignorant. China looked down on Japan as a small island of fickle and frivolous nature imitating superficially European civilization ...Therefore, it was obvious that one

[95] *See* Mark R. Peattie, "The Japanese Colonial Empire, 1895-1945" in Peter Duus, *The Cambridge History of Japan*, vol. 6, *The Twentieth Century* (Cambridge, 1989), pp. 224-225.

[96] Akira Iriye, note 93, pp. 766-767.

[97] *See* ibid. p. 756.

day a conflict would appear and its cause would be the collision between the new Western civilization and the old Asian civilization".[98]

Fukuzawa Yukichi, an influential Japanese intellectual and author, writing about the Chinese-Japanese war, called it "a war between civilization and barbarism". China was opposing Japan from stimulating Korea to reform herself toward civilization, and Japan must therefore fight the war to decide the future of civilization. He said:

> "... Japanese who recognized themselves as the most progressive people of the East must be ready to fight not only for their country but also civilization in the world. Japan should attack and defeat China definitely. It is necessary for the Japanese to fight against China until she surrenders herself to civilization."[99]

Another writer, Uchimura Kanzou, expressing similar logic among Japanese intellectuals, affirmed the Korean war as "a righteous war", for Japan intervened in Korea on its behalf because its independence was in jeopardy, and Japan had its "sacred right of neighbourhood". Moreover, "this war was a conflict between a smaller nation representing a newer civilization and a larger nation representing an older civilization, just as Greece versus Persia, the England of Queen Elizabeth versus the Spain of Philip II. It was a historical necessity." Japan, Uchimura felt, stood by "the upward progress of the human race". Japan had its historical mission, he said, and "the Korean War is to decide whether Progress shall be the Law of the East, as it has long been in the West, or whether Retrogression fostered once by the Persian Empire ... and now by the Manchurian Empire of China, shall possess Orient for ever. Japan's victory shall mean free government, free religion, and free commerce for 6,000,000,000 souls in Asia". This was indeed a "holy war".[100]

The Chino-Japanese War and International Law

The Japanese leaders were convinced of the sacred mission of the progressive civilization and, therefore, even the way of waging war itself had to be civilized. The Meiji State, in order to prove that it had become a "civilized nation" and was capable of becoming a member of the family of nations, tried to observe the "civilized" international law. The Chino-Japanese war, which, they said, was "a war between civilization and barbarism", appeared to them to be the first test to show their progress for becoming a member of the family of nations.

Japan formally declared war against China on 1 August 1894, and said that it would conduct the war "consistently with the law of nations".[101] Japan

[98] Quoted in Yamauchi, note 75, p. 11.

[99] *See* Fukuzawa Yukichi, quoted in Yamauchi, note 75, pp. 6-8.

[100] Uchimura Kanzou, quoted in Yamauchi, note 75, p. 8.

[101] *See* Sakuye Takahashi, *Cases on International Law during the Chino-Japanese*

did not want to give the European powers a pretext to intervene in the war but wanted them to follow the rules of neutrality, although neither China nor Japan had so far been recognized by them as members of the family of "civilized" nations. Already ominous opinions were being expressed in Europe. As an article in the *Saturday Review* of 11 August 1894, said:

> "There was no legal war ... The Code of International Law does not apply to barbarians, who have nothing of civilization beyond a chatter of words and supply of deadly weapons."[102]

To avoid any interference by the Western countries, Japan had already concluded a treaty with England, on the eve of its war with China, on 16 July 1894, providing for the cessation of extraterritorial privileges after five years, as we have noted earlier. It gave Japan some status in the exclusive club of international law. The declaration of war by Japan and its promise to carry on the war consistently with the law of nations, as mentioned earlier, was also aimed at dissuading the Western countries from intervening in the war.[103]

Besides using the declaration of war with China as a propaganda tool, to show the Western countries that it was carefully following international law rules, Japan went a step further and sent distinguished international lawyers with the Japanese army and navy as legal advisers who were expected to legally deal with cases on the frontlines during the conduct of war. Ariga Nagao, Professor of the Imperial Military Staff College, went to the battle fields with Governor-General Ohyama; and Takahashi Sakaye, Professor of the Imperial Naval Staff College, was appointed legal adviser to the Imperial Navy and he joined the flagship Matsu-shima and advised Admiral Ito who commanded the Japanese fleet. Both professors carefully kept notes and described the process and cases during the war in their respective books in French and English which they were encouraged to publish after the war. Ariga published *La Guerre Sino- Japanaise au point de vue du Droit International* in Paris in 1896. Takahashi went to Cambridge University and prepared a book under the general guidance of the wellknown Professor John Westlake. He published his book, *Cases on International Law during Chino-Japanese War*, at Cambridge in 1899, and requested Professor Westlake to write an Introduction and Professor T. E. Holland, Professor of International Law at Oxford University, to contribute a Preface to his book. These were like testimonials by the two distinguished British international lawyers to

---

War (Cambridge, 1899), p. 2; Takahashi later wrote another book in Japanese, *The Precedent Practices of the War-Time International Law* (1904), and came to be regarded as "the founder of international law studies in Japan". *See* Fujio Ito, note 73, p. 25.

[102] *See* quoted in Yamauchi, note 75, p. 10.

[103] Ibid., p. 10.

certify that Japan had been faithfully following rules of international law in the Chino-Japanese war and their opinions that Japan was ready to join the family of civilized States. It may also be noted that Professor Westlake looked after Takahashi when he was at Cambridge and "carefully and repeatedly" perused the first draft of his book *Cases*, and gave him "the most accurate and valuable advice both on legal and on literary points", besides writing introduction to his work.[104]

In his Introductory Chapter, Takahashi prudently tried to describe how the Japanese were keen on observing international law during the war. He pointed out that Japan had introduced "European civilization" "with eagerness" 30 years before and had become signatory to the 1856 Declaration of Paris and the 1864 Geneva Convention. Japan had displayed its law-abiding spirit in waging war against China and "it was the earnest intention of the Japanese Emperor to do nothing inconsistent with international law." The Emperor had issued an ordinance for protecting the Chinese people in Japan immediately after the declaration of war. Contrasting the civilized behaviour of Japan with barbarous China, he said:

> "China is signatory neither of the Geneva Convention nor of the Declaration of Paris. She was very barbarous in her methods of carrying on hostilities. She declared that Japanese vessels should be broken up, and even offered a large reward for the head of a Japanese general. She also detained neutral merchant vessels by means of privateers, killed prisoners, and sometimes hacked them to pieces. More than this, she killed not only combatants, but also non-combatants who remained in China after the outbreak of war ...
>
> But Japan refrained from revenge, for it was her intention, in spite of the nature of her opponent, to set an example of generosity by carrying on hostilities in an enlightened fashion."

He went on in the same vein and said that Japan "had the wounded prisoners as well nursed as her own men. She treated all prisoners with the utmost generosity. She governed the people of the occupied districts well, and set at liberty many thousand combatants, who surrendered in Weihaiwei." He pertinently added:

> "It must be confessed that this generosity is chiefly owed to European Civilization, which was introduced thirty years ago, but in general it may be said that if the graft was from Europe, the stock was an ancient one, deep rooted in Japan from the earliest times."[105]

It must be pointed out that, besides praising the Western civilization, Japan actually followed their practices. Right at the beginning of the war, the Japanese Government promulgated the Prize Court Law on 20 August 1894. The Prize Court was established at Sasebo and Higher Court in Tokyo.

[104] Takahashi, note 101, p. viii.
[105] Ibid., p. 3-4.

The German Prize Act (1864) and English Prize Act (1864) were the models for this law. On 7 September 1894, the Prize Law of Japan was also issued based on the work of Professor Holland, the decision of the Institute of International Law (1882), and Instructions for the French Navy. The Japanese Prize law was even more modern, progressive and civilized. While the law of Europe had a private element of gains of war, under which the prize courts generally ordered "a sale of the vessel or goods on condemnation" which sum was "divided among the captors". Under the Japanese law, however, no prize was given to the captors who were deemed to seize property at sea for the sake of their country and not for their own sake.[106]

Certificates or Recommendations from Eminent International Lawyers

All this praise and sychophancy of the Western civilization and countries and their representatives had the desirable effect. In his Introduction, Westlake raised the question as to how far international law, recognized between the States of Christendom, applied "between them and Mahometan or other Oriental States". He answered it by saying that "European States are obliged by their self-respect to observe in their dealings with Oriental States, without regard to reciprocity, all the rules which may be described as prior to treaties, or at least profess to do so; and they require that Oriental states shall observe them towards them, often inflicting severe punishment for any failure in this regard." But institutions, such as extradition and consular jurisdiction, which depended on treaties, was very different and consequently the international law which prevailed between the European States and Oriental States was "very different". But significantly he added:

> "Japan presents a rare and interesting example of the passage of a State from the Oriental to the European class. By virtue of treaties already concluded with the leading Christian states of Europe and America she will shortly be freed from the institution of consular jurisdiction, and in her recent war with China she displayed both the disposition and in the main the ability to observe Western rules concerning war and neutrality."[107]

Professor Holland also certified, in his Preface, that "the war was conducted on the part of the Japanese with an anxious desire that forces should conform to the highest standards of loyalty and humanity". To secure this object Professor Ariga had been attached to the troops on land, and Mr. Takahashi was sent to advise the fleet. "Under his guidance", said Holland, "great pains were taken to observe in all questions of naval capture the best traditions of European Prize Courts."[108]

[106] Ibid., p. 12.
[107] Ibid., pp. xv-xvi.
[108] Ibid., p. vi.

Earlier, commenting on "the great war in the Extreme East", Holland had said that States outside the orbit of the European civilization had to show their qualifications which must be established. Although Europe was accustomed to regarding these Eastern Powers which had signed treaties "as belonging to the charmed circle, though, perhaps, as admitted to it only on probation", that had to be proved. He said:

> "Such might seem to be the position of Japan; but such could hardly be said to be the position of China; for China is far behind Japan in readiness to assimilate the ethical ideas of the West, or to enter into the network of treaties ... Antecedently to the war, therefore, we should have said that Japan was admitted on probation, while China was only a candidate for admission to the 'Family of Nations'."

As regards the conduct of warfare, Holland considered Japan loyal and China indifferent to international law. He affirmed that "China has not accepted the customs, nor has she bound herself by express conventions, which prevail among civilized nations ... [On the contrary,] the conduct of the operation of war by the Japanese seems to have been in accordance with the best European practice ..."[109] He further elaborated:

> "Japan, apart from the lamentable outburst of savagery at Port Arthur, has conformed to the laws of war, both in her treatment of the enemy and in her relations to neutrals, in a manner worthy of the most civilized nations of western Europe; China, on the other hand, has given no indication of her acceptance of the usages of civilized warfare"[110]

Following these certificates by two eminent jurists, other international lawyers followed suit and appropriate editions of Wheaton, Phillimore, Hall, Oppenheim, and others, all recognized Japan's inclination and ability to follow Western international practices concerning war and neutrality.[111] A number of comments and reviews of Takahashi's book on Chino-Japanese war also appeared in academic magazines and newspapers which were also published by Takahashi as appendages to his book once more.[112]

Japan was on its way to becoming a member of the "civilized" family of nations. By the Aoki-Kimberley Treaty concluded between Japan and Britain on 16 July 1894, Britain was the first power to relinquish extraterritoriality in Japan as of 1899[113] when the new Japanese legal codes became fully operational. The other powers followed suit in signing similar treaties. The US Senate approved a new treaty in February 1895; Germany agreed in April, Russia in June of the same year; and France in August 1896. Under the provision that unilateral revision of tariff restrictions could occur in 12

[109] T. E. Holland, *Studies in International Law* (Oxford, 1898), pp. 113-115.

[110] Ibid., pp. 128-29.

[111] *See* Gong, note 19, pp. 185-186.

[112] *See* Fujio Ito, note 73, p. 23.

[113] *See* note 97 above and text relating thereto.

years, Japan gave notice to treaty powers in July 1910 of its intent to renegotiate its tariffs. On 21 February 1911, the United States agreed to a new treaty; Britain followed in April; and most of the other powers in July of that year. Japan thus achieved its goals of revising the "unequal treaties", ended extraterritoriality and regained tariff control.[114]

But did Japan become an *equal* member of the "family of nations"? After signing the Japanese-British Treaty in 1894, by which Britain agreed to renounce extraterritoriality, Aoki, the Japanese representative, said that Japan "can disregard the insults we have suffered over the last thirty years and at one go enter the 'fellowship of nations'." From now on, he advised, "we must try to make our government and people act in accordance with the 'law of nations' and thereby cause civilization to flourish increasingly in our land."[115] But the euphoria over the revised treaties was soon challenged.

Japan Forced to Retreat

Although the Chinese had no choice but to accept after their ignominious defeat, albeit reluctantly and after prolonged negotiations, Japan's harsh demands at Shimonoseki in 1895, alarmed three Western powers, Russia, France and Germany, at the quick tempo of Japanese expansionism in China which they found to be against their own vital interests in China and they decided to intervene. Determined to preserve as much of China as possible for their own exploitation, they decided to intervene and presented their "friendly counsel" that Japan retrocede the just-obtained Liaotung peninsula to China. They collectively threatened military action if Japan did not accept their "advice". Japan had no choice but felt betrayed that their efforts to become a "civilized" equal had been for nought. The warning of some of their people of cunning and deceit of "foxes from the same hole" had proven true.[116] They were forced to conclude that, in the end, only force mattered in international relations. Indeed, as one Japanese historian has pointed out, in order to understand the Japanese nationalism in the twentieth century it is important to comprehend the bitterness and sense of humiliation that swept the country in the wake of the Triple intervention.[117] The "psychological effect of the Triple Intervention", we are told,

> "lasted for decades, and may not have disappeared entirely even today. Western nations had been feared usually, and disliked very often. But on the whole they had been respected by Japan. Now they were distrusted, despised even, as hypocrites."[118]

[114] *See* Gong, note 19, p. 195.

[115] *See* quoted in ibid., p. 196.

[116] Ibid., pp. 197-198.

[117] Storry, *Japan and Decline of the West in Asia*, p. 29, quoted in Gong, note 19, pp. 196-97.

[118] Storry, *A History of Modern Japan*, p. 127, quoted in Gong, ibid.

When these powers started claiming ports in China in the same territory where they had prevented Japan from occupying, i.e. Weihaiwei, Port Arthur, and Kiaochow, "their blatant hypocrisy rubbed salt into old Japanese wounds."[119] Japan realized the truth of Chancellor Otto Von Bismarck's comments to the Iwakura Mission, during their visit to Germany as early as 1871, when Japan was determined to learn, adopt and follow European international law rules without any question to become a member of the "civilized states". The Iron Man of Germany had warned the Japanese:

> "In today's world, it is said that every country interacts with other states on the basis of friendship, harmony, and courtesy (*reigi*). However, this is merely a superficial lip service, behind which lies actual practice, that is, insults to which the strong subject the weak, and scorn in which the big hold the small. When I was a child, my Prussia was poor and weak. [I perceived that] the so-called law of all nations argued for the profit of great powers. If the law of nations contained in it an advantage for them, the powerful would apply the law of nations to the letter, but when it lacked attraction, the law of nations was jettisoned, and military might employed, regardless of the tactics."[120]

There was also trouble in the other territorial acquisition, Taiwan. Although no Western Power questioned its transfer to Japan, the Chinese and the native Taiwanese population strongly objected to its incorporation in the Japanese empire and resisted the Japanese occupation army, numbering 60,000 troops. The Japanese strongly suppressed the uprising but at a tremendous cost of 4,600 casualties and other financial expenses to establish a system of administration for law and order. The main objective of Japanese policy in Taiwan or Formosa was to develop the island so as to serve the economic needs of Japan.[121]

Nor was Korea's independence from China going to end the problems on the peninsula. Independence for Korea meant, in Japanese perception, replacing Chinese with Japanese influence. Japan took steps to "reform" the Korean Government and military administration introducing Japanese measures which had been undertaken by Meiji Japan. These measures provoked Korean resistance which led to anti-Japanese agitation and Koreans turned to Russia for help. Russian influence increased further, much to the dismay and frustration of the Japanese. But the latter were not prepared to leave Korea soon but were determined to push ahead with their imperialism.[122]

Imperialism at that time coincided with rapid industrialization which was deemed to be essential to become a modern State and achieve great-power status. Industrial production, primarily cotton and silk textiles, but also iron and steel, grew rapidly in Japan after the Sino-Japanese war, more than

[119] Gong, note 19, p. 197.

[120] *See* quoted in Hisashi Owada, note 86, pp. 354-355.

[121] *See* Akira Iriye, note 93, p. 769; Aziz, note 92, pp. 7-9.

[122] *See* ibid., pp. 769-770.

doubling between 1895 and 1900. So also, the shipbuilding industry was given impetus by naval construction, the government subsidizing shipyards to construct merchant ships to be used in the expanding opportunities of Korea and China. Japanese growing stature led to signing of the Anglo-Japanese alliance in 1902 which was a recognition of Japan's status as a major power.

Japan Joins the Imperialist Powers

This encouraged Japan even further to behave like the other "civilized" Western States in following imperialistic policies. It tended to rely more and more on force than on law. In 1900-1901, Japan joined the Western Powers in the international expedition to China to suppress the Boxer Uprising and participated in the subsequent conference with the Ch'ing authorities to restore order. In this anti-foreign uprising in China, Japan played the role of a protector of western interests in China, dispatching as many as ten thousand soldiers, about the same number as troops sent by all the Western Powers combined.[123] Japan was rewarded by being invited to a peace conference, and for the first time Japan attended an international conference as a full-fledged member. After 1901 Japan became one of the "Boxer protocol powers" with a right to station troops in the Peking-Tientsin region. Its newly won status made Japan an active member of the power group and politics in China with Britain willing to give Japan a role as its principal partner in Asia. But Russia tried to counter the trend by entrenching itself in Manchuria. The Japanese welcomed the British Alliance, referred to earlier, as a confirmation of their status in the world, but Japanese leaders favoured a Russian alliance to settle the dispute over Korea. Russian influence had been growing in Korea after 1895, and Russia had seized the Liaotung peninsula in China in 1898. Japan wanted recognition of its special interests in Korea by all the interested powers. It was prepared to reach some understanding with Russia so that the latter would recognize Japan's special interests in Korea, in return for Japanese acquiescence to Russian interests in Manchuria. But protracted negotiations between the two countries were not successful. The Japanese were convinced that their position in Korea would be vulnerable as long as Russian influence remained predominant in southern Manchuria.[124]

[123] Ibid., pp. 773-774.
[124] Ibid., pp. 774-775.

Russo-Japanese War

More and more Japanese – political parties, publicists, and other intellectuals – were getting convinced that the struggle between the two powers in Korea (Japan and Russia) would not end unless one of them retreated. Since the Japanese could not even think of retreating in Korea, they had to be prepared to use force to reduce Russian power.[125] "Patriotism, militarism, and imperialism" were deemed to be essential conditions for the existence of the nation as a modern power and the Japanese were prepared to take the risk of waging a war against a big and mighty European power even if it involved taking a big risk and borrowing a huge amount in London and New York to wage the war. But it did challenge and declared a war against Russia. It is important to note that the Russo-Japanese war was essentially an imperialistic war, fought between two powers over issues outside their national boundaries, at the expense of Korea and China who had no say in the matter.[126]

But still, as in the Chino-Japanese war, the Japanese Government wanted to show that it was faithfully observing rules of international law in conducting the war to maintain its reputation as a "civilized" State. It again dispatched Dr. Nagao Ariga in the army as the chief legal advisor of the General Headquarters in Manchuria, and appointed Sakue Takahashi as advisor in Foreign Ministry to deal with international legal problem concerning naval battles. Later both of them wrote books about their experiences and practices in actual battles.[127]

The brilliant victory of the Land of the Rising Sun over the Muscovite giant in the 1904-1905 war enabled Japan to achieve the status of a world power. Its gains were indeed significant. At the peace conference in Portsmouth, New Hampshire, by the socalled Treaty of Portsmouth, concluded on 5 September 1905, Japan acquired Southern Sakhalin as well as Russia's leaseholds to Port Arthur and Liaotung Peninsula, which it had to return to China in the face of the Triple intervention after the Sino- Japanese war of 1894-1895. Russian railway and coal mining rights in south Manchuria and important fishing rights in certain territorial waters of Siberia on the Pacific were also ceded to Japan. China was obliged to accept the treaty arrangements that had applied to Manchuria and consented to transferring to Japan the

[125] Seven professors from the prestigious Tokyo Imperial University asserted in a memorial they submitted to the Prime Minister Katsura Taro in June 1903 that " a fundamental settlement" of the Manchurian problem was needed if Japan were to secure its position in Korea. *See* Akira Iriye, note 93, p. 775.

[126] Ibid., pp. 775-777.

[127] Dr. Ariga wrote *La Guerre Russo-Japanaise us point de vue continental et la droit international in 1908* with a preface by Professor Paul Fauchille, which he later translated into Japanese in 1911. Likewise, Takahashi wrote *International Law applied to the Russo-Japanese War with the Decisions of the Japanese Prize Court in* 1908. *See* Fujio Ito, note 73, pp. 23-24.

Russian lease on Kwantung Province – the Liaotung peninsula – now called Kwantung Leased Territory. Russia furthermore acknowledged Japan's paramount political, military and economic interests in Korea and undertook not to obstruct measures Japan might deem necessary to take there in order to protect its interests. With the last obstacle having been removed, Japan took the unilateral step in Korea to turn it into a protectorate and later, in 1910, annexed it and made it a colony to be ruled as an integral part of the Japanese empire. As a distinguished Japanese statesman, Viscount Ishii, explained later:

> "... Japan attempted to maintain an independent Korea free from the aggressions of Tsarist Russia. But Korea was neither Belgium nor the Netherlands; she was effete, impotent, and supine. She had none of the moral stamina essential to an independent nation. These are harsh words, but I give expression only to the common verdict of critical observers, both Oriental and Occidental ... when we found [our] endeavours [to preserve the independence of Korea] unappreciated, futile, and fruitless, we were forced to the only remaining alternative of establishing a protectorate over Korea. This, to us, was the only practicable means of attaining our own security."[128]

Not a single outside State protested against the Japanese action in Korea or peace settlement. Japan had, by late 1905, emerged indisputably as a major power.[129] Having shown its mettle in its wars against China and a white European power, Russia, and defeated them, there was no more doubt about Japan's entry into the family of "civilized" nations.

The chief criterion or standard of "civilization", the Japanese came to understand well, was power. The connection was too apparent to escape the notice of a Japanese diplomat who said: "We show ourselves at least your equals in scientific butchery, and at once we are admitted to the council tables as civilized men."[130] As a victorious power, the Japanese took "vindictive pleasure" in treating the Russians in their diplomatic correspondence concerning the 1905 Treaty of Portsmouth in the same terms as the Russians had earlier used dictating the Triple Intervention to them.[131]

As the first non-Western nation to emerge as a great power, Japan played a significant role in bringing about a new international order. On the one hand, having successfully resisted western political encroachments and negotiated its way out of the unequal treaty system imposed on it in 1850s, Japan served as a model and inspiration to anticolonial movements in all

[128] Viscount Kikujiro Ishii, "The Permanent Bases of Japanese Foreign Policy", *Foreign Affairs*,Vol. II, No. 2 (January 1933), p. 225.

[129] *See* Akira Irye, note 93, p. 777; Aziz, note 92, p. 6; Mark R. Peattie, " The Japanese Colonial Empire 1895-1945", Chapter 5 in Peter Duus (ed.), note 95, pp. 226-229.

[130] *See* quoted in B.V.A. Roling, *International Law in an Expanded World* (Amsterdam, 1960), p. 27.

[131] *See* Gong, note 19, p. 197.

parts of Asia, as far as India. The Japanese victory over Russia in 1905 made it clear to other non-western peoples that the Europeans were neither omnipotent nor invincible. Several anti-colonial nationalists in Indochina like Phon Boi Chau, and China's nationalists like Ch'i-Ch'ao and Sun Yat-sen, sought refuge or support in Tokyo. It even gave rise to a Pan-Asian feeling that Japan, as the first successful non-European modernized nation, should help uplift its less fortunate neighbours in Asia.

Neither a European nor a Christian nation, Japan became the first non-European country to gain full international status and recognition as a "civilized" State by fulfilling the as yet undefined standard and conditions of "civilization". But within a few months of the Japanese victory over Russia, Oppenheim specified three conditions for a country to be recognized as a member of the Family of Nations:

> "A State to be admitted must, first, be a civilized state which is in constant intercourse with members of the Family of Nations;
>
> Such a State must expressly or tacitly consent to be bound for its future international conduct by the rules of international law; and
>
> Those States which have hitherto formed the Family of Nations must expressly or tacitly consent to the reception of the new member."[132]

Explicitly stated for the first time, these criteria were also reiterated by Wheaton in the sixth edition of his famous *Elements of International Law* in 1929. Stating that "the gradual extension of relations among States has enlarged the field within which international law is applicable", Wheaton said that "the extension necessarily involves three factors":

> "The State to which international law is to be extended must have a form of civilization which renders it able to apply the rules of that law, and it must be in communication with the States already enjoying it;
>
> It must further be prepared to accept the rules of that law as binding upon it; and
>
> The other States must agree to accept the new member of the Family of Nations."[133]

Earlier, discussing "the international status of non-Christian nations", Wheaton questioned China's international status which, he opined, was "semi-civilized". China had also not adopted the rules of war prescribed by the rules of civilized States. In sharp contrast to China, Wheaton praised Japan which had adhered to international conventions, including the 1866 Geneva Convention and The Hague Convention. In the 1895 war, Japan had "striven scrupulously to comply with the highest civilized standards", and had revised its civil and criminal codes so that, as of 1899, "all persons of whatever

[132] L. Oppenheim, *International Law* (London, 1905), pp. 32, also quoted in Gong, note 19, p. 30.

[133] Wheaton, *Elements of International Law*, 6th cdn. (1929), p. 30. *See also* Gong, note 19.

nationality within the confines of Japan have been subject to the Japanese tribunals". The 1902 alliance with Great Britain was a final sign of Japan's qualifications to enter international society. Even before the Russo-Japanese war, said Wheaton, it was "impossible to dispute her right to rank among the powers who are, without reservation, subject to international law."[134]

Japanese Exploitation of its Colonies, Taiwan and Korea

For nearly half a century Japan exploited Taiwan as an imperial power. The main objective of the Japanese policy was to develop the island so as to serve the economic needs of Japan and enhance its national power. It largely succeeded in achieving its purpose and Formosa not only became self-supporting, but supplied foodstuffs and raw materials, besides providing Japan market for industrial products. Although Taiwan was not congenial to Japanese emigrants, its strategic geographical location led Japan to turn the island into a great military base for southward drive against the possessions of the Western Powers. Later, in 1942, Formosa was designated as an integral part of Japan.[135]

Strategically situated and rich in natural resources, Korea was an important cornerstone of the Japanese imperial structure. Recognizing an advantage in employing international law in Korea, Japan modelled the "unequal treaty" it imposed on Korea after the "unequal treaties" the West had imposed on Japan and which it had bitterly denounced. On 26 February 1876, a treaty of amity, friendship, commerce and navigation was signed. Besides providing for the exchange of diplomatic emissaries, it opened three ports to Japanese ships and granted extraterritorial rights to Japanese citizens in Korea.[136]

Like a typical European colonial model, colonial economies were developed by Japan to serve as docile producers of raw materials for the metropolitan power and as a market for its manufactures. For more than three decades, Korea was a source of foodstuffs and raw materials, an outlet for manufactured goods, and a base for further continental expansion. Korea was of prime importance to Japan for its rich mineral wealth – coal, iron ore, gold and alunite, copper, graphite, lead, lithium, mercury, mica, nickel, tungsten – and several other important minerals not found in Japan. The production of all these minerals increased considerably under Japanese control. Korea was also "developed as a rice bowl for Japan". But the tremendous economic development was hardly beneficial for the Koreans. Exploitation was the keynote and virtually every development was undertaken

[134] Wheaton, *Elements of Intenational Law*, 4th edn. (London, 1904), pp. 22-23. *See also* Gong, note 19, pp. 27-29.

[135] *See* Aziz, note 92, pp. 7-12.

[136] Gong, note 19, p. 183.

by the Japanese with the objective of maximizing the benefits which would accrue either directly or indirectly to Japan.

Koreans could hardly accept such treatment and their subjection by the Japanese with equanimity, and the colonial power had to govern the peninsula by military force and martial law suppressing all political organization.[137] Besides attempting to suppress nationalism, Japan adopted the policy of Japanization of the Korean people. They tried to "obliterate all vestiges of Korean culture and national individuality".[138] The teaching of Korean history and literature was suppressed. Textbooks and publications of all kinds were issued in the Japanese language. The Japanese were equally interested in eliminating Western influence. Education, which had earlier been in the hands of Americans, Canadians, Englishmen and Frenchmen, was taken out of their hands and Christians were compelled to compromise themselves by doing homage before Japanese shrines.[139]

In short, learning the art of domination and colonization as well from the Western "civilized" States,[140] Japan surpassed them all in suppressing its unfortunate neighbours which came under its sway.[141] The Japanese Government and publicists sought to justify these actions on the basis of international law. Professor Onuma explained this bitter truth. "For Japan", said Onuma, "the process of learning international law was, at the same time, the process of becoming a colonial power. Really, there is truth and irony in the statement that Japan was an honor student in learning modern Western civilization."[142]

Japan, it is important to note, had accepted European international law not because it was committed to the values and philosophy underlying this law, but because it was too weak to challenge the Western powers. But the Japanese did realize soon enough the truth about the abuse of international law by the strong nations. Once Japan became a Great Power and found

[137] Koreans were effectively deprived of freedom of assembly, association, press and speech. It was said by a Japanese journalist in Korea that "so completely were the people's liberties restricted that the entire peninsula could be said to have militarized". *See* quoted in Peattie, note 95, p. 231.

[138] Aziz, note 92, p. 16.

[139] Ibid., pp. 13-21.

[140] Japanese colonial policy was said to be "European in origin and orientation, and its adoption by Japanese administrators and publicists had much to do with the fact that Japan entered its colonial tasks at the zenith of European colonialism. Its characteristics thus stemmed from the assumptions and predilections common to the 'New Imperialism' of the late nineteenth-century Europe and derived largely from European colonial empires whose territories were geographically dispersed and racially diverse." Peattie, note 173, p. 238.

[141] *See* for a general description of Japan's colonial policy Peattie, note 73, pp. 244-270.

[142] Onuma, note 85, p. 41.

Western international law limiting its ambitions, it did not hesitate to use force to change it and violated international law with impunity.[143]

Having been admitted into the "family of civilized nations", Japan soon fell foul of it. The influence of traditional militarism proved stronger than any emerging democratic movement in Japan. For a while political parties developed and there were even cabinets supported by a political party. Universal male suffrage was introduced. But with the expanding empire, as Japan experienced economic problems and the country increasingly needed ways to expand its exports and secure its imports of raw materials, the military came to the fore. Before long Japan "graduated" to a warring nation.

Japan's Rising Expectations

Having tasted the fruits of power, Japan was not prepared to give up its imperialistic policies. The First World War gave it an opportunity to expand even further and strengthen its hold over China. With the outbreak of hostilities in Europe in 1914, Japan was quick to recognize the slight risk and considerable gain in joining the Allies as a belligerent. It was not only an opportunity to destroy the German influence in Eastern Asia in retaliation of Germany's part in the three-power intervention after the Sino-Japanese war of 1894-1895, which Japan had not forgotten, but also to make the empire secure on the continent. The immediate objective of Japan was to take over Germany's colonial territories in Asia and the Pacific: Tsingtao on the Shantung peninsula and the German possessions in Micronesia – the Marshall, the Carolines, and Marianas – which were isolated and weakly defended. Without much problems Tsingtao fell after a resolute but futile resistance by its German defenders, but isolated island territories were seized without resistance by Japanese naval units. The allied powers wanted Japan to dispatch troops to Europe, but the Japanese Government limited its military operations to sending convoy-escort destroyers to the Mediterranean and stalking German raiders in the Pacific and the Indian oceans. Its main might was concentrated on expanding its sphere of influence in the Pacific.[144] The speed and aggressiveness of the Japanese forces in East Asia and the Pacific aroused the suspicion and hostility of Britain, Australia, New Zealand and the United States. But before the end of the war Japan entered into secret agreements with most of the allied powers confirming its appropriation of these territories which enabled it to press its claims in the Paris Peace negotiations.[145]

Although the Japanese gains after the Russo-Japanese war were significant, military successes and patriotic fervor had raised expectations of the Japanese

[143] *See* ibid.

[144] *See* Ikuhiko Hata, "Continental Expansion 1905-1941", Chapter 6 in Peter Duus, note 95, p 280.

public even more and they were dissatisfied with the fruits of victory obtained at the Portsmouth peace conference and blamed this on the United States which had mediated between the two combatants. Moreover, while Japan gained recognition as a formidable power, its sense of isolation and insecurity were enhanced. The United States, which had expanded into Asia and the Pacific during the 1890s along with the Japanese, now posed a challenge because of its naval expansion, its opposition to Japanese exclusive rights and interests in Manchuria, and, above all, its hostility toward Japanese immigrants. The immigration crisis arose as a result of the influx of Japanese into California after the turn of the century and particularly after the Russo-Japanese war. While the Japanese perceived it as the sign of an expanding nation and a bridge between two countries, the Americans rejected such expansionism and were against the Japanese immigration on racial grounds. Britain, Japan's presumed ally, supported the United States.

Japan became a great power but never earned the respect of the Western countries. Some critics had always warned Japan not to follow the westerners blindly because they would never accept it as equal. At the time of the Russo-Japanese war, a Japanese poet lamented:

Win the war,
And Japan will be denounced as yellow peril,
Lose it,
And she will be branded a barbaric land.[146]

In the meantime, by 1908-1909, the Korean, Chinese, and other Asians were growing increasingly resentful of the Japanese imperialism which they viewed as no less evil than the Western imperialism.[147]

Twenty-one Demands on China

On 18 January 1915, six months after the beginning of the World War, the Japanese Government presented to China the infamous Twenty-one Demands as a draft treaty, divided into five groups, which were to be accepted by China. There is no doubt, as the Chinese President said, that Japan wanted "to take advantage of this war to get control of China."[148] The demands included provisions for the Japanese takeover of German interests in Shantung, for an extension of the leasehold of the Liaotung (Kwantung) peninsula, for an extension of commercial rights in Manchuria, for joint Sino-Japanese control over the Han-yeh-p'ing mines in central China, and for a limitation of China's right to cede control of coastal areas to third powers. The fifth group of demands was really designed to turn China into a

[145] *See* Peattie, note 95, pp. 227-228.
[146] *See* quoted in Gong, note 19, p. 174.

protectorate, a second Korea, by requiring the Chinese Government to use Japanese advisers in its military, police, and financial administrations; purchase from Japan a fixed amount of munitions of war – 50 per cent or more; and the establishment of Chino-Japanese jointly worked arsenals.[149] While presenting the Demands, Japan emphasized the importance of keeping the whole affair secret, in order, according to T. Takeuchi, "not to arouse the suspicion abroad that advantage was being taken of the helpless situation in China and of the world war."[150] It is also important to note, as George Keeton pointed out: "Significantly, the paper upon which the Demands were recorded was water-marked with dreadnoughts and machine guns."[151] Faced with an ultimatum, China had no choice but to accept most of the demands which were incorporated in treaties and notes on 25 May 1915. But Japan had to back off from the radical group five demands when the US Secretary of State, William Jennings Bryan, sent a strong note indicating that the United States could "not recognize" them. The United States held fast to the principles of its "Open Door" policy and consistently expressed its disapproval of Japanese actions that violated Chinese sovereignty. Similar policy of non-recognition was expressed by Secretary of State Stimson in 1931 and Hull in 1941.[152]

As the war progressed, the situation became even more favourable for Japan to extend its control over the continent. The United States entered the war in 1917, and the Russian Revolution erupted the same year. The Japanese were anxious to gain as much ground as possible. In the summer of 1918, a few months before the German surrender, the Japanese Government sent a force of 70,000 to Siberia as part of the joint allied intervention in the Russian Revolution. Even after the other allied powers had pulled out of Siberia, Japanese forces stayed on. Japan also concluded a selfdefense treaty with China under the pretext of preventing the spread of revolutionary forces from Russia to the Far East. By the time the war ended in November 1918, Japanese armed forces controlled a large part of Siberia, the hinterland of the Sinkiang Province of China, and the German-held territories in Micronesia. Even after the withdrawal of the American troops in January 1920, Japan continued to occupy the Maritime Provinces and Northern Sakhalin. The imperialist expansion was simultaneously marked by an increase in economic power. The war had provided Japan with a virtual monopoly of foreign trade with China, the Netherlands Indies, Australia and even India. Japanese

[147] *See* Akira Iriye, note 93, pp. 777-779.

[148] Quoted in Aziz, note 92, p. 23.

[149] *See* Hata, note 144, p. 280.

[150] T. Takeuchi, *War and Diplomacy in the Japanese Empire*, (New York, 1935), p. 189, quoted in Aziz, note 92, p. 24.

[151] George W. Keeton, *China, the Far East and the Future* (London, 1949), p. 147, quoted in Aziz, note 92, pp. 24-25.

factories experienced an unprecedented growth, and, along with the war industries, made Japan a creditor nation with a lot of surplus capital seeking investment abroad.[153]

At the Paris Peace Conference in 1919, Japan largely succeeded in safeguarding her newly-acquired status in East Asia on the basis of secret agreements of February and March 1917 by which England, France, Italy, and Russia had promised to support Japanese claims. In November 1917, on a visit to the United States, Special Japanese Ambassador to the United States, Viscount Ishii Kikujiro, concluded a joint statement with Secretary of State Robert Lansing by which, while recognizing the territorial integrity of China and equal opportunity for commerce and industry, the agreement acknowledged that Japan had special interests in China. It was stated in the agreement:

> "The Governments of the United States and Japan recognize that territorial propinquity creates special relations between States, and, consequently, the Government of the United States recognizes that Japan has special interests in China, particularly in the part to which her possessions are contiguous."

While Secretary Lansing understood that the expression referred particularly to the commercial and industrial advantage which Japan enjoyed in China due to its geographical position, and it had no political significance, Viscount Ishii insisted that these interests of Japan "were principally political."[154] Ishii interpreted the agreement to mean that the United States recognized Japan's exclusive sphere of influence in all of China. In fact the Emperor of Japan honoured Ishii with a gracious message for his "diplomatic victory".[155]

The Japanese Monroe Doctrine

It is important to note that not only did Japan exercise wide and extensive rights in China, but it claimed other powers to recognize and respect its special position in Asia, particularly in China, on the basis of what it called the "Japanese Monroe Doctrine". As the Japanese delegation told the Assembly of the League of Nations, "Japan is responsible for maintenance of peace and order in the Far East".[156] Referring to Article XXI of the League Covenant, which recognized the validity of Monroe Doctrine as a regional understanding, the Japanese Minister of Foreign Affairs, Count Uchida, said:

[152] *See* Hata, note 144, pp. 280-281.

[153] *See* Aziz, note 92, p. 25.

[154] *See* George H. Blakeslee, "The Japanese Monroe Doctrine", *Foreign Affairs*, vol. II, no. 4, (July 1933), pp. 673-674.

[155] *See* Hata, note 144, p. 281; Aziz, note 92, p. 25.

"The League of Nations Covenant very wisely provides that regional understandings shall be respected. In this sense, our government believes that any plan for erecting an edifice of peace in the Far East should be based upon the recognition that the constructive force of Japan is the mainstay of tranquility in this part of the world."[157]

Viscount Ishii told the Americans in Washington D.C. in 1917:

"From our point of view, Japan possesses interests superior to other powers in China as a whole, especially in the contiguous regions, much as the position of your country in the Western Hemisphere, especially in Mexico and Central American countries."[158]

Japan supported this elastic doctrine on the basis of general principles, like self-defense or security; Pan-Asia; special rights and interests; leadership and guardianship; and the right to live or economic necessity. Referring to the need for security, Ishii explained:

"Japan is an island nation. But her distance from the continent of Asia is so small that she cannot be indifferent to what happens in Korea, Manchuria, China and Siberia, any more than England can keep aloof from developments in the Low Countries across the Channel and along the North Sea. Particularly in Korea and Manchuria, we have consistently followed a policy dictated by the sole motive of establishing our own security. We have looked upon their frontiers as our own frontiers ... so Japan attempted to maintain an independent Korea free from aggressions of Tsarist Russia."[159]

On the basis of self-defense, Japan was also opposed to any territorial aggression in China by any foreign State. She fought two wars to drive Russia from Southern Manchuria and Germany from Shantung. In 1915 she obtained a declaration from China, as part of its "twenty-one demands", that "hereafter no port, bay or island along the coast of China will be ceded or leased to any foreign country." As Viscount Ishii pointed out:

"Generally speaking, our policy in China has been based upon the belief that the establishment of an *imperium in imperio* upon her soil by any powerful third nation or group of nations is not only derogatory to her integrity but is also incompatible with our own security. In this we have been actuated by the same principle incorporated in the Monroe doctrine. The wisdom of this policy, especially at a time when China seemed to be harassed by endless internal disorders and constant international difficulties, cannot be questioned. We believed that the break-up of China would bring the formidable powers of the West to our very portals. We thought that, for this reason if for no other, the preservation of China's integrity was essential to our own safety."[160]

[156] Quoted in Blakeslee, note 157, p. 671.
[157] Quoted, ibid.
[158] Quoted, ibid.
[159] Ishii, note 128, pp. 224-225.

No less important for Japan was the economic need of Japan to occupy China. As Viscount Ishii further explained:

> "I shall not invoke statistics and marshal figures to prove how vital Manchuria is to us economically ... It is enough to say that the increase of our population, the congestion of our country, and our lack of raw materials, are such that Manchuria, with its virgin soil and its immense natural resources, has come to be looked upon as our vital protection. Given unobstructed access to those resources, we may still hope to solve our embarrassing population problem. We do not necessarily mean to promote mass emigration to Manchuria; rather, we shall foster our industries by utilizing the raw materials which we can obtain there. Just as England solved her population problem by industrializing herself, so does Japan hope to solve her similar problem. Such was the object of the Sino-Japanese treaty of 1915, though it had strategic significance also."[161]

Having become an imperialist power, Japan was beginning to use imperialist logic and language, howsoever incongruous and impractical they might be. Calling for a policy of "Pan-Asia", or "Asia for the Asiatics", and claiming a "special position" in China and Korea, Japan wanted all European and American influence eliminated from Eastern Asia so that the entire region could be organized under Japanese political control. At one time it even received the support of some Asian leaders, as we have noted earlier. But it was not long before they realized the real motives of Japan.

In fact Japan wanted extensive and exceptional privileges and rights in China and the Japanese generally believed that Japan was entitled to a position of leadership in the Far East which other nations were under an obligation to respect. They interpreted this right of leadership to imply that other powers should take no independent action in China without previous consultation with Japan. They went even further and claimed the "right to live" or the right to economic expansion. They regarded the resources of the region as necessary for the economic life of their country. The "right to live" doctrine demanded and claimed "the right to share in the development and use of the natural resources of China, particularly in Manchuria, whether China gives its consent or not".[162] Such a claim was based, in the words of a Japanese scholar, Matsuoka, upon the "legitimate rights of a nation which is compelled to find an outlet somewhere."[163] Interpreting the Open Door policy, a former Prime Minister of Japan, T. Hara, said:

> "By 'open door' I do not mean a complete throwing down of national boundary stones. What I have in mind is the removal of the economic insecurity of some peoples by extending to them the opportunity for free access to the world's resources, eliminating other artificial barriers, and adjusting as much as possible the inequality arising from the earlier discrimination of nature and history."[164]

[160] Ibid., p. 227.
[161] Ibid., p. 228.
[162] Blakeslee, note 157, p. 675.
[163] Ibid., pp. 675-676.

The Minister of War, General Sadao Araki, an influential leader in the Japanese Government, said that, since "mankind has the right to live upon the earth," no country with abundant resource had a right to deny these to another country which is overcrowded and is insufficiently endowed by nature.[165]

The Western powers were not prepared to accept the Japanese Monroe Doctrine or its contentions. In fact it was pointed out that it was President Theodore Roosevelt who suggested to Viscount Kaneko in 1905 that Japan should devise a Monroe Doctrine for Asia. His intention was the protection of the Orient from European encroachments. Later, Secretary Bryan and Secretary Lansing recognized Japan's special interests in China, especially in the contiguous areas. But the American assumption was that the doctrine would not be used for aggressive purposes. Several other powers, Russia, Great Britain, and the United States, had quite close and important relations with China and they were not prepared to accept Japan as "the guardian of China."[166]

Japan Forced to Roll Back

Although Japan had become a predominant power by the close of the First World War, a colossus of East Asia, the rapid expansion of the Japanese power caused a serious alarm to the Western Powers, particularly the United States, whose interests seemed to be at stake. The Japanese were despised by the Asians ruthlessly ruled by them. And its position neither won adulation nor the admiration of the Western Powers, but indeed their antagonism and strong disapprobation. Japan was forced to renounce her forward policy on the Asian mainland in the face of strong and combined opposition of the new international order formed under the leadership of the victorious powers, especially Great Britain and the United States. At the Washington Conference of 1921-1922, designed mainly to apply brakes to the Japanese policies which she had followed since the Twenty-one Demands of 1915, Japan was made to become party to several Washington treaties – the Four-Power Treaty of 13 December 1921, the Five-Power and Nine-Power Treaties of 6 February 1922[167] – which had the effect of erecting a legal barrier to the expansion of Japanese imperialism. By the Four-Power treaty the Anglo-Japanese alliance was abandoned and was replaced by the Anglo-American bloc, thus devising a new balance of power in the Far East. Japan was

[164] Ibid., p. 676.

[165] Ibid.

[166] *See* ibid., pp. 680-681.

[167] The Four-Power Treaty was concluded between Great Britain, United States, France and Japan; the Five-Power Treaty between Great Britain, United States, Japan, France, and Italy; the Nine-Power Treaty between Great Britain, United States, Japan, France, Italy, China, Belgium, the Netherlands and Portugal. *See* Aziz, note 92, p. 26.

forced to withdraw its troops from Siberia by the Five- Power Treaty, and the naval strength of Japan was reduced to 60% of the Anglo-American figures in capital ships and naval armaments. Japan had to return to China the Kiaochow territory, ceded to her by the Treaty of Versailles, and to withdraw completely the fifth and most objectionable group of the Twenty-one Demands. The Nine Power Pact liquidated all existing treaties between China and the powers and replaced them with the Open Door principles espoused by the United States. Japan had to subscribe to the Open Door doctrine and accept Chinese territorial and administrative integrity. Pressure was also exerted on Japan to withdraw its military forces from the Maritime Provinces and Northern Sakhalin, which were finally restored to the Soviet Union in 1925.[168]

Japan Humiliated and Depressed

The Japanese felt humiliated. Some of them were depressed. As Mochizuki Kotaro, a prominent journalist, complained: "Our empire has lost everything and gained nothing, and only the expense of building warships is spared."[169] Konoe Fumimaro, who later became Prime Minister, felt that Japan "would be left forever a backward country" under the Versailles settlement.[170] But others were satisfied that at least Japan's established special interests, especially in Manchuria and Mongolia, regarded by the Japanese as vital, had not been touched. However, Japan was subdued and for the next few years Japan observed a policy of, as A.J. Toynbee said, "commercial expansion and political goodneighbourliness".[171] But in the field of foreign relations, Japan's position was becoming unfavourable. The United States Restriction of Immigration Act of 1924, which was imitated by several of the British Dominions, came "as an overt political humiliation". The decision of the British Government in 1925 to establish a first class naval base at Singapore was a further blow to Japanese aspirations. Even more serious were the rise of strong Chinese nationalism of the whole of China with the help of the Soviet Union, and the gradual consolidation of the Russian power in the Far East.[172]

The Tanaka Memorial

The Japanese reacted strongly against these humiliations and were getting tired of the conciliatory policy of their government. In April 1927, General Baron Tanaka, a former war minister and militarist came to power with his

[168] *See* ibid., pp. 26-27; Hata, note 144, pp. 282-283.
[169] *See* quoted in Hata, note 144, p. 283.
[170] Ibid.
[171] Quoted in Aziz, note 92, p. 27.
[172] *See* ibid., pp. 27-28.

strong policy towards China. In an important conference with his key officials in June-July 1927, they formulated a new policy towards China called the Tanaka Memorial which was presented to the Emperor on 25 July 1927. Echoing similar views of several other Japanese patriots and statesmen, the Memorial declared that –

> "For the sake of self-protection as well as for the protection of others, Japan cannot remove the difficulties in Eastern Asia unless she adopts a policy of Blood and Iron. But in carrying out this policy we have to face the United States which has been turned against us by China's policy of fighting poison with poison. In the future if we want to control China, we must first crush the United States just as in the past we had to fight in the Russo-Japanese War. But in order to conquer China we must first conquer Manchuria and Mongolia. In order to conquer the world, we must first conquer China. If we succeed in conquering China the rest of the Asiatic countries and the South Sea countries will fear us and surrender to us. Then the world will realize that Eastern Asia is ours and will not dare to violate our rights."

"Having China's entire resources at our disposal", the Memorial went to say, "we shall proceed to conquer India, the Archipelago, Asia Minor, Central Asia, and even Europe."[173] Whether it was Japan's dream of world empire, or mere day dreaming by Premier Tanaka, Japan wanted to push ahead.

Policy in Manchuria

During the Russo-Japanese War, Japan had spent some two billion yen and had shed the blood of nearly 100,000 soldiers. Its material rewards were the Kwantung Leased Territory, including Darien and Port Arthur, and interests in southern Manchuria centering on the South Manchuria Railway Company. After the Chinese Revolution of 1911, Manchuria, the homeland of Ch'ing rulers, slipped out of the reach of central authorities in China. It then came under the control of Chang Tso-lin who enjoyed the backing of the Japanese army, and then his son, Chang Hsueh-Liang. Although the area was Chinese in name, Chinese sovereignty did not extend there.[174]

For those Japanese who could not satisfy their ambitions at home, Manchuria was a new frontier where they could fulfill their dreams and make a fortune. When Japanese- American relations deteriorated as a result of the immigration problem in California, the Japanese Government adopted a policy of concentrating Japanese immigration in Manchuria and Korea. The number of Japanese increased in Manchuria from 68,000 in 1909 to 219,000 in 1930. In 1928, the Japanese army conspired to take over Manchuria by assassinating Chang Tso-lin who had become too strong and difficult to deal with. Although Chang was killed, the plot failed because the Japanese

[173] *See* quoted in ibid., p. 29.

[174] *See* Hata, note 144, pp. 290-295.

Emperor refused to support the Kwantung army. Chang's son, Chang Hsueh-Liang, who took over, began to put more pressure on the Japanese settlers in Manchuria and the Chinese began to construct railway lines parallel to the South Manchuria railway line. Fearing that Japan might be thrown out of Manchuria, the Japanese Kwantung Army is said to have provoked what is known as the "Manchuria incident", and resorted to force to achieve its long-held ambition of bringing the region under Japanese control. On the night of 18 September 1931, an explosive charge was set off on South Manchuria Railway tracks at Liutiaokou, in the suburb of Mukden, with an intention to stir up local confusion by derailing the Dairen Express. Although the train reached Mukden safely in spite of the explosion, the "Manchurian incident" was set in motion. The Japanese Kwantung Army took over Mukden without any bloodshed and advanced outside the railway zone, where Japan had treaty rights, with an intention to occupy all of Manchuria. The defeated soldiers of Chang Hsueh-Liang, after his expulsion, resorted to guerrilla-like attacks across southwestern Manchuria, but Japan was determined. In March 1932, having completed the occupation of whole of Manchuria, the Japanese proceeded to establish a puppet State, Manchukuo, with Henry P'u Yi, ex-Emperor of China, as the Chief Executive, but fully controlled and operated by the Kwantung Army, which had been responsible for the conquest of Manchuria. Foreign powers were informed of the creation of an "independent" and "sovereign" State and invited to extend recognition to it. Japan formally recognized Manchukuo as an independent State. While the new State agreed to respect all the Japanese rights and interests acquired under Sino-Japanese treaties within its territory, Japan was further given the right to station whatever forces it deemed necessary in Manchukuo. The new State severed all ties with China which in future was to be treated as a foreign State for commercial and tariff matters.[175]

The central Government of China appealed to the League of Nations to recover Manchuria through pressure by the great powers. In the United States, Secretary of State Henry Stimson proclaimed the "non-recognition doctrine" and refused to accept the Japanese occupation of Manchuria. But the United States could not take any effective measures being preoccupied with terrible economic depression. Great Britain was also in economic difficulty. The Soviet Government was recovering after a long period of internal strife between Stalin and Trotsky, and wanted to avoid any international disputes. Soviet Russia did not protest the Japanese advance into northern Manchuria, and in 1935 sold the Soviet-owned Chinese Eastern Railway to Japan and withdrew to the Amur River line.[176]

[175] *See* for details about the establishment of the so-called State of Manchukuo and its relations with Japan, Aziz, note 92, pp. 30-45; Hata, note 144, pp. 296-298.

[176] *See* Hata, note 144, pp. 295-297.

The League of Nations' Lytton Commission, which visited the scene in the spring of 1932, fully fathomed the situation inside Manchuria. Expecting the Commission's report to be unfavourable, the Japanese army tried to stir public opinion by promoting a movement to recognize Manchuria's independence. In March 1933, having been defeated by a vote of 42 to 1 in the League Assembly on the acceptance of Lytton Commission's report, Japan withdrew from the League of Nations "deliberately choosing a path of isolation". It adopted a policy of defiance towards the Western Powers for the preservation and expansion of its own colonial and imperialist policy.[177] All references to colonies were eliminated and instead a distinction was made between the "inner territory" (i.e. Japan) and "outer territories" or the overseas possessions, the latter being merely extensions of a single Japanese nation. The European colonial model was not only discarded but declared decadent and evil. Japan was to lead all Asian races (by force, if necessary) in a national war of liberation to drive Western colonialism out of Asia. At the same time the Japanese started showing traces of racism. While referring to Asian racial harmony and co-prosperity, the Japanese Government increasingly spoke of Japan's dominant position within the Greater East Asian Co-Prosperity Sphere and their army officers spoke openly of themselves as "master peoples".[178] Despite all the criticism of the Western States, and attempts to contrast Western colonialism, Japanese colonialism was hardly any different from its Western counterpart. In their colonies, the Japanese lived in luxury, more or less isolated in separate quarters, away from the indigenous majority,[179] and exploited the colonies for the benefit of the mother country.

Japan Moves Deeper into China

Emboldened by the utter failure of the League of Nations as well as the Western Powers to impede the Japanese advance, Russia's apparent indifference in the Far East, ineffectiveness of the United States' policy of "non-recognition of Manchukuo", and above all, the menacing rise of Hitler in Europe, diverting the Western Powers from their interests in East Asia, all led Japan to re-assert her position as the predominant power in Eastern Asia. In 1934, it reiterated the Japanese "Monroe Doctrine for Eastern Asia." On 22 January 1934, Foreign Minister Hiroto, in an address to the Japanese Diet, emphasized Japan's special responsibility and "mission" for the preservation of peace in Eastern Asia. He said, "we should not for a moment forget that Japan, serving as the only corner-stone for the edifice of the peace of Eastern Asia, bears the entire burden of responsibility" and expressed

[177] *See* ibid., pp. 297-298.
[178] *See* Peattie, note 95, pp. 243-244.
[179] *See* ibid., pp. 263-266.

the hope that "eventually this position will be rightly understood by the other powers."[180] Hiroto's views were made even more explicit by Foreign Office spokesman, Eiji Amau, on 17 April 1934. Referring to Japan's "special responsibility in East Asia", he said that the Japanese

> "consider it only natural that to keep peace and order in East Asia we must even act alone on our own responsibility, and it is our duty to perform it. At the same time there is no other country but which is in a position to share with Japan the responsibility for the maintenance of peace in East Asia."

"We oppose," he continued,

> "any attempt on the part of China to avail herself the influence of any other country in order to resist Japan; we also oppose any action taken by China calculated to play [off] one power against another. Any joint operations undertaken by foreign powers even in the name of technical or financial assistance ... are bound to acquire political significance ... Japan therefore must object to such undertakings as a matter of principle ... Supplying China with war aeroplanes, building aerodromes in China, and detailing military instructors or military advisers to China or contracting a loan to provide funds for political uses would obviously tend to alienate friendly relations between Japan, China and other countries and tend to disturb peace and order in Eastern Asia. Japan will oppose such projects."[181]

Japan was clearly intending to extend her domination over the whole of China. In December 1934, Japan issued notification abrogating the Naval Treaty of 1922 making itself free to resume naval building. In January 1936, demanding a parity with the United States and England in naval armament, it withdrew from the general agreement arrived at the London Conference on Naval Disarmament in 1922. The Japanese started dreaming of expanding even beyond China and some of them propagated the superiority of the Japanese race over the white race.[182]

In the meantime, the Japanese Kwantung Army, whose appetite had been whetted further by the success in Manchuria, began to advance into North China, Inner Mongolia and eventually mainland China in the latter part of 1935. As in Manchuria, they relied on subversion, threat of force, and the establishment of puppet governments. The rationale for their policy and actions was to check the emergence of a strong and unified China. After seizing Manchuria's resources, they proceeded toward the main part of China in search of new gains. "Japan-Manchukuo economic bloc" was broadened into "Japan-Manchukuo-China economic bloc". Japanese forces invaded all parts of the Chinese mainland and were soon talking about "Greater East Asia Co-Prosperity Sphere". The targets for further Japanese conquest were

[180] *See* quoted in Aziz, note 92, p. 51.

[181] Quoted in Aziz, ibid. pp. 51-52; *see also* C. J. Chacko, "The Japanese Monroe Doctrine", *Indian Year Book of International Affairs*, 1953, pp. 114-115.

[182] Aziz, note 92, pp. 52-56.

to be extended from East Asia to Southeast Asia and the western Pacific.[183] In 1936, it was decided by the Japanese Government that –

1. Japan must correct the aggressive policies of the great powers and realize the spirit of the Imperial Way (*Kodo*) by a consistent policy of overseas expansion;
2. Japan should complete her national defense and armament to secure the position of the Empire as the stabilizing factor in East Asia;
3. Japan should try to eradicate the Russian menace on the North to realize the steady development of Manchuria and the defense of both Japan and Manchuria. Japan should even be prepared against Great Britain and the United States attempting at the same time close cooperation between Japan, China and Manchuria.[184]

In furtherance of its so-called Co-Prosperity Sphere, Japan adopted a ruthless policy of local plunder. Land was seized for the settlement of Japanese immigrants in Manchuria. On the Chinese mainland business and enterprises were confiscated. Japanese forces fighting in China, and later in the Pacific, lived off the land. The army purchased daily necessities with excessive issues of unbacked military scrip that inevitably led to local inflation. No wonder the Japanese army alienated the local inhabitants of the occupied territories who called the Imperial army an "army of locusts."[185]

Determined as Japan was to occupy China, it used the incident at the Marco Polo Bridge on the outskirts of Peiping on 7 July 1937 as a pretext to start an all-out war against China. The truth about the incident, the question as to who fired the first shot at the Japanese troops engaged in nightly manoeuvres there, remained a mystery. But as the Nanking Government took a confrontational stance and sent a central army to move the day after the Marco Polo Bridge incident, the Japanese army struck hard. Peking fell within a day and the Japanese forces began to move south toward the Yangtze River and later Shanghai. In their desperation, the Chinese decreed a general mobilization on 15 August and the two countries plunged into a full-scale war which lasted for eight years.[186] Although in the beginning the Japanese had quick gains and it took over important towns, its expectations for a quick victory remained unfulfilled. The overextended Japanese lines were constantly exposed to guerrilla counterattacks launched both by Kuomintang regime and the Communist armies, and the hostilities dragged on to a long war of attrition.[187]

Stuck in a long military struggle, Japan blamed the Western Powers for prolongation of the China war by insisting that Chinese military resistance

[183] *See* Hata, note 144, pp. 300-302.
[184] *See* Aziz, note 92, p. 54.
[185] Hata, note 144, p. 302.
[186] *See* Hata, note 144, pp. 302-305.
[187] Hata, ibid., pp. 306-307.

was kept alive by military and psychological assistance from the United States, Britain, the Soviet Union and France. Unable to resolve the conflict with China by negotiations between the principals, Japan sought to find a solution by arranging a military alliance with Germany and Italy to confront Great Britain and the United States. On 27 September 1940, Japan formally signed the Triple Alliance by which Japan undertook to recognize and respect "the leadership of Germany and Italy in the establishment of a new order in Europe" (Art. I) and both Germany and Italy, in return, promised to "recognize and respect the leadership of Japan in the establishment of a new order in Greater East Asia" (Art. II). The three powers agreed "to cooperate in their efforts on aforesaid lines" and "undertook to assist one another with all political, economic and military means if one of three Contracting Powers is attacked by a power at present not involved in the European war or in the Chinese-Japanese conflict" (Art. III). Obviously referring to the United States without naming it, it was explained by the Japanese Foreign Minister, Matsuoka, that both Germany and Japan wanted to prevent the US entry into the war. It was further agreed that the Alliance "affects in no way the political status existing at present between each of the three Contracting Parties and Soviet Russia" (Art. V). It was thought desirable and possible to bring the Soviet Union into the Tripartite Pact thus establishing a continental alliance between the three powers and Soviet Russia.[188]

Japan was determined to move ahead with its plans for an East Asia Co-Prosperity Sphere. By 1940, the original goals of northern advance – the conquest of China south of the Great Wall by way of Korea and Manchuria – had already been achieved. Further northern advance would have meant moving into Siberia, that is, going to war with the Soviet Union which Japan did not want at this stage. The southern advance meant using the Hainan Island as a springboard to solidify the Japanese position in northern Indochina, then heading into southeast Asia, a treasure house of natural resources, centering on the Dutch East Indies. With the outbreak of war in Europe in 1939, two of the major colonial powers in southeast Asia, *viz*. France and the Netherlands, had been overrun by the Germans and a third, Great Britain, seemed on the verge of collapse. Japan did not want to miss this "golden opportunity". By the summer of 1940 it got the first chance to move into the northern part of Indochina. A second chance came with the outbreak of war between Germany and the Soviet Union in the summer of 1941, and it occupied southern Indochina.

The United States and Great Britain, already unhappy with the Japanese aggressive policy, retaliated by announcing an embargo on petroleum and froze Japanese assets.[189] Reacting further to the increasingly intransigent and uncompromising attitude of the Japanese Government in its negotiations

[188] *See* Aziz, note 92, pp. 65-66.
[189] Ibid., pp. 77-78.

with the United States about withdrawal of Japanese troops from Indochina, on 26 November 1941, Secretary of State Cordell Hull submitted to the Japanese envoys a strictly confidential and uncommitted "outline of proposed basis for agreement", called the Hull note, which the Japanese called the Hull ultimatum. As a basis for an American-Japanese agreement, it suggested a complete withdrawal of Japanese military, naval, air, and police forces from China and Indochina; a mutual surrender of extraterritorial rights in China; and recognition of only the Nationalist Government of China. This was totally unacceptable to Japan and the Japanese Ambassador conveyed this clearly to the US Secretary of State.[190] Japan was not old and meek Japan, which was overawed by the United States and Great Britain and wanted to follow their advice. It was no longer afraid of the United States and Great Britain and was prepared to wage war against them for the protection of its interests. As the Japanese Prime Minister, Tojo, said in desperation:

> "How can we let the United States continue to do as it pleases, even though there is some uneasiness? Two years from now [1943] we will have no petroleum for military use; ships will stop moving; when I think about the strengthening of American defenses in southwestern Pacific, the expansion of the U.S. fleet, the unfinished China Incident, and so on, I see no end of difficulties. We can talk about suffering and austerity but can our people endure such a life for long? ... I fear that we would become a third-class nation after two or three years if we merely sat tight."

He added that "there is some merit in making it clear that Britain and the United States represent a powerful threat to Japan's self-preservation".[191]

Imperial Proclamation of War

By the end of November Japan believed that war was unavoidable against the Anglo- Saxon States. While the United States was still seeking Japan's withdrawal from Indochina on 6 December 1941, Japanese air and naval forces launched a big attack on Pearl Harbor in Honolulu on 8 December turning it into "blazing chaos", inflicting a tremendous loss to American life and property.[192] Gone were the old days of scrupulously following international law rules concerning the declaration of war. Unlike the Sino-Japanese and Russo-Japanese wars, when the declarations of war clearly referred to those wars being conducted strictly in compliance with the rules

[190] *See* Alvin D. Coox, " The Pacific War", Chapter 7 in Peter Duus, note 95, pp. 338-339.

[191] Quoted in ibid., p. 136.

[192] Besides loss of nearly half of the 231 US Army and 89 naval aircraft in Oahu, eight battleships damaged or sunk, several destroyers and other ships crippled, American casualties numbered 4,575. *See* Coox, note 190, pp. 342-343.

of international law, the Imperial Proclamation of War issued on 8 December 1941, with which Japan initiated the "Greater Asian War", made no such reference to the laws of war or the need and intention of the Japanese to abide by the rules of international law. In fact, along with Nazi Germany and Fascist Italy, Japan openly challenged the existing international order by force. It showed a contemptuous attitude toward international law rules. The Japanese Government, which zealously gave instructions in international law to members of the army and navy in earlier wars against China and Russia, was no longer interested in its rules in the 1930s and 1940s.[193]

Simultaneously, on 8 December 1941, under Japanese threat, Thailand allowed immediate Japanese occupation of strategic points in its territory. With their Thai flank secured, the Japanese invaded Malaya and landed on the same day on the eastern side of the Malay Peninsula. Two days later, as the naval air force based at Saigon destroyed the core of the British fleet off Malaya, most of Malaya came under Japanese control. Soon thereafter Japanese ground forces drove swiftly toward Singapore and by 15 February 1942 the entire city had been conquered.

By 16 December 1941, a Japanese expeditionary force landed in British Borneo. The official British surrender took place on 19 January 1942. In early January 1942 Japanese forces landed in oil-rich Dutch Borneo and in a short time the Japanese acquired British and Dutch Borneo, as well as Ambon and Celebes, with rich resources and important bases enabling them to screen their sea and air lanes to Singapore.[194]

In December 1941, the Japanese air force destroyed much of the American strength in Philippines islands and Manila was in Japanese hands by 2 January 1942. Even Hongkong, the important conduit into China, had fallen to the seemingly irresistible Japanese in December 1941. By February 1942, the Japanese advanced to Bali, Lombok, and Timor, and ultimately landed in Java by 1 March. Large reserves of fuel were captured essentially intact. With the conquest of the Indies, the end of the European and American empires seemed at hand and Japan's valued Greater East Asia Co-Prosperity Sphere had almost become a reality.[195] Japan was still on its expansion course. On 7 March 1942, the Japanese army went on to defeat the Anglo-India forces in Burma and the Burmese capital, Rangoon, was occupied the next day. In a fierce battle on 13 May they crushed a large number, 20,000 of British and Indian troops. The relative ease of the early Japanese operations and victories led to over-confidence and optimism amongst the Japanese.[196]

[193] *See* scathing criticism of the attitude of the Japanese Government during the 1930s and 1940s by eminent Japanese scholar of international law, Onuma Yasuki note 85.

[194] Ibid., pp. 345-346.

[195] Ibid., pp. 347-348.

[196] Ibid., pp. 348-349.

By the beginning of 1943, the Pacific war started taking a sharp turn and the Japanese started losing. America's enormous economic and industrial resources began to have an overpowering impact on the fight. By 1944, the Japanese were losing on almost all fronts. As defeat followed defeat, Japanese stars waned rapidly, leading to disillusionment bordering on despair. In July 1944, the over-confident, and known as a human dynamo, Prime Minister Tojo could not cope with the pressure and resigned. Almost three and a half years after the outbreak of the Pacific war, in April 1945, none of the Japanese enemies, the United States, Britain, and China, were remotely near capitulation. On the other hand, one of its allies, Italy had surrendered, and Germany was all but defeated. The Third Reich fell in May 1945.

Since Japan still decided in April 1945 to continue the hostilities, it had to face relentless air attacks by American bombers on the home islands. Japanese cities, congested and flammable, were devastated by incendiary raids. Conventional bombing in Japan is said to have killed as many people as did the two atomic bombs which hit Hiroshima and Nagasaki on 6 and 9 August 1945. By the summer of 1945, allied pressure on Japan, from air and sea, grew so severe that it amounted to near-strangulation of the economy. Worse still, on August 9, the Soviet Union declared war on Japan and the Red Army invaded Manchuria.

As Japan was arguing about the conditions for its surrender, the second atomic bomb, often called "the unnecessary bomb", dropped on Nagasaki on 9 August killing or injuring approximately 80,000 to 100,000 people. On 10 August, the Emperor decided to surrender. Disarmament of the loyal armed forces and indictment of its citizens as war criminals were indeed painful to contemplate. But Japan had to bear the unbearable. On 2 September 1945, Japanese Foreign Minister signed the surrender papers on behalf of the Emperor on American battleship Missouri in Tokyo Bay. Japan had to pay an enormous price, in human and material terms, for its part in the Pacific war. By the end of the Pacific war, Japan was isolated and on the brink of starvation.[197]

Japan Occupied

On 14 August 1945, Japan accepted the Potsdam Declaration initially agreed upon by three allied powers, the United States, the United Kingdom and China, and later joined by the USSR, defining terms for Japanese surrender. It is interesting to note that no such terms of surrender were defined in the case of Germany, although both cases are usually understood as unconditional surrender without distinction. The instrument of surrender was in the nature of a preliminary peace treaty, expected to be concluded in the near future,

[197] Ibid., pp. 370-377.

and an armistice agreement. In an unprecedented and unique document, both in substance and procedure, the Instrument of Surrender laid down the conditions for disposition of Japan after its defeat. It declared that:

> "There must be eliminated for all time the authority and influence of those who have deceived and misled the people of Japan into embarking on world conquest, for we insist that a new order of peace, security and justice will be impossible until irresponsible militarism is driven from the world."

And that:

> "We do not intend that the Japanese shall be enslaved as a race or destroyed as a nation, but stern justice shall be meted out to all war criminals, including those who have visited cruelties upon our prisoners. The Japanese Government shall remove all obstacles to the revival and strengthening of democratic tendencies among the Japanese people. Freedom of speech, or religion, and of thought, as well as respect for the fundamental human rights shall be established ...
>
> The occupying forces of the Allies shall be withdrawn from Japan as soon as these objectives have been accomplished and there has been established in accordance with the freely expressed will of the Japanese people a peacefully inclined and responsible government."[198]

It is also important to note that, in the case of Germany, it was occupied jointly and administered directly by each of the allied powers. The administration of occupied Japan was, however, in accordance with the Potsdam Declaration, under the sole authority of the Commander-in-Chief (later, the Supreme Commander for the powers) and was exercised indirectly because in occupied Japan, the Japanese Government remained in existence though it was not really free. Thus, the occupation of Japan was not only operative on a large scale, but its whole purpose was to undermine the political, social and economic structures of the occupied territory. It may also be noted that throughout the period of occupation, the Supreme Commander of Allied Powers (SCAP) was appointed by the US military forces and, therefore, the administration of occupied Japan was exercised in fact according to the policy decisions of the United States.[199] In the initial stage of occupation, during 1945 and 1946, the United States issued important ordinances laying down the fundamentals of occupation policy in accordance with the Instrument of Surrender. Thus, in 1946, the US Government prepared an initial post-surrender policy for the guidance of General MacArthur who had been appointed the SCAP, which stated:

[198] *See* Charles L. Kades, "Introduction: Representative Government in Japan", *Political Reorientation of Japan, September 1945 to September 1948*, Report of the Government Section Supreme Commander of the Allied Powers (1949), p. 89.

[199] *See* Yasuo Ishimoto and Kazuya Hirobe, "Development of Post-war Japanese Studies in Public International Law, Part I: 1945-1964", *Japanese Annual of International Law*, vol. 30 (1987), pp. 93-95.

> "The ultimate objective of the United Nations with respect to Japan is to foster conditions which will give the greatest possible assurance that Japan will not again become a menace to the peace and security of the world and will permit her eventual admission as a responsible and peaceful member of the family of nations. Certain measures considered to be essential for the achievement of this objective have been set forth in the Potsdam Declaration. These measures, among other things, include the carrying out of the Cairo Declaration and the limiting of Japanese sovereignty to the four main islands and such minor islands as the Allied Powers determine; the abolition of militarism and ultra-nationalism in all their forms; the disarmament and demilitarization of Japan, with continuing control over Japan's capacity to make war; the strengthening of democratic tendencies and processes in governmental, economic and social institutions; and the encouragement and support of liberal political tendencies in Japan. The United States desires that the Japanese Government conform as closely as may be to principles of democratic self-government; but it is not the responsibility of the occupation forces to impose on Japan any form of government not supported by the freely expressed will of the people."[200]

Under the occupation regime, the Japanese Government was ordered in October 1945 to suspend its diplomatic activities. Japan had no choice. It closed down all the diplomatic and consular relations it had maintained as an independent nation.[201]

The Tokyo War Crimes Tribunal

The Potsdam Declaration, in Article 10, required prosecution and punishment of Japanese war criminals responsible for conducting an illegal war of aggression and for the violation of numerous rules of war. After the end of World War II, two tribunals, unprecedented in the history of international law, were instituted at Nuremberg and Tokyo. The Tokyo trial, in which major Japanese war criminals were prosecuted, lasted for some two and a half years from May 1946 to 12 November 1948. All of the 25 Japanese prosecuted were declared guilty of committing crimes against peace, and/or conventional war crimes, or crimes against humanity, and punished for their crimes. In spite of serious criticisms of the Nuremberg and Tokyo trials as nothing more than "victor's justice", because they applied *ex post facto* law by recognizing individuals as subjects of international law, introduced new categories of war crimes which had not been recognized in traditional international law and which were technically unwarranted under the formal principles of justice and due process of law, there were only muted comments in Japan. The Japanese were skeptical about the trial. The failure of the allied powers to apply the law to their own conduct – such as atomic bombings of Hiroshima and Nagasaki, the Soviet Union's violation of the Japan-Soviet

[200] Quoted in Kades, note 198, p. 89.

[201] *See* Ishimoto and Hirobe, note 199, p. 96.

Neutrality Pact, and some other postwar events – further undermined the legitimacy of the Trial. But they knew "might is right" and could not do a thing about it. But most of the Japanese intellectuals also knew and were convinced that Japan could not be resurrected without taking responsibility for her resort to "aggressive wars (1931-1945)"; cruelties committed during those wars; and "colonial rule over Korea and Taiwan". Failure to take responsibility for their misdeeds, according to some Japanese intellectuals, had "dulled the moral sensitivities of the Japanese and prompted them to view foreign relations only in economic and political terms."[202] Freed from the wartime suppression of thought and speech and academic freedom, it is pointed out, Japanese intellectuals could for the first time see undistorted the realities of Japanese long wars of aggression against its neighbours and began to inquire into the realities of war crimes committed during those wars, and the cause of the "Greater Asian War" in which they had believed and which had been belied. It is not, therefore, surprising that, with a few exceptions, most of the scholars of international law in Japan approved the punishment meted to war criminals by the Tokyo tribunal.[203]

A New "Peace Constitution" for Japan

After the Meiji Restoration in 1868, as we have seen above, in their desperate attempt to modernize themselves the Japanese promulgated, in 1889, a constitution which was based on Prussian model. Although Japan appeared under the new dispensation to be a constitutional monarchy in the European style, with a representative national legislative assembly, codified laws, what appeared to be a constitutional bill of rights, a centralized system of national and local administration based upon law, it was in reality controlled by a feudal aristocracy and military controlling strictly the life of every community and citizen. Japan had quickly learnt in the nineteenth century that it was not the great or superior civilization of the Western Powers that lay behind their dominance, but their military force and military power. Japan was thereafter determined to make itself militarily strong and a powerful nation. The Japanese leaders worked systematically to unite a feudally divided people into a nation of subjects passionately loyal to the Emperor (*Tennno*) and his increasingly dominant position in a militarist State. Under this constitution, which remained effective till the end of the Second World War, Japan was governed by an Emperor claiming absolute power by divine right as a direct descendant of Sun Goddess. The Emperor *was* the State and was "sacred

[202] Yasuaki Onuma, "Japanese War Guilt, the 'Peace Constitution', and Japan's Role in Global Peace and Security", in Machael K. Young and Yuji Iwasawa (eds.), *Trilateral Perspectives on International Legal Issues: Relevance of Domestic Law and Policy* (1996), p. 525; *see also* Ishimoto and Hirobe, note 199, pp. 96-97.

[203] *See* Ishimoto and Hirobe, note 199, p. 97.

and inviolable", "combining in himself the rights of sovereignty". The slightest criticism of this theory of the Emperor was regarded as sacrilege and a challenge of his authority. Fundamental civil and political rights did not exist. Modern means of mass education and indoctrination – as well as legal, police, and administrative controls – were used over many decades to create an authoritarian, militarist and nationalist government, whose actions were legitimized by legal and quasi-mystical reference to the State sovereignty of a benevolent superhuman Emperor. Virtual annihilation in the service of the Emperor was the ideal.[204] By the 1930s Japan had turned into a modern totalitarian police State.

After the defeat of Japan, the allied powers, in order to make as sure as humanly possible that Japan was never able to wage a war again, wanted to abolish, as the Potsdam Declaration said, "militarism and ultra-nationalism in all its forms in Japan", disarm and demilitarize Japan with a continuing control over its capacity to wage war, and strengthen "democratic tendencies and processes in governmental, economic and social institutions" in Japan. Although they declared that they did not intend to impose on Japan a form of government not supported by the freely expressed will of the people, they "desired" that Japan should have a government based on principles of democratic self-government. After the surrender, Japan had been occupied by the victorious allied powers. But they had no intention to annex or destroy the country. The existing government was left in power to operate under, and subject to, the control of the occupant. It was, therefore, for the Japanese Government to accomplish political and economic reforms to ensure a peaceful Japan once the military forces had withdrawn.[205]

The terms of the Instrument of Surrender signed on 2 September 1945, pursuant to the Potsdam Declaration of 26 July 1945, included the renunciation of Japanese interests overseas and destruction of Japan's power to wage war. In implementing these terms, Japanese territories were occupied by the armed forces of the allied powers, most of which were from the United States. Paragraph 12 of the Potsdam Declaration said:

> "The occupying forces of the Allies shall be withdrawn from Japan as soon as these objectives have been accomplished and there has been established in accordance with the freely expressed will of the Japanese people a peacefully inclined and responsible government."

To give Japan a new government, which the allied powers thought appropriate, a new constitution of Japan was drafted in February 1946, by the staff of the occupation authority under the direction of the US Army General and SCAP, Douglas MacArthur. Contrary to the initial attempts to

[204] *See* Lawrence W. Beer, "Peace in theory and practice under Article 9 of Japan's Constitution", *Marquette Law Review*, vol. 81 (Fall 1998) pp. 816-818; Kades, note 198, pp. xiii-xiv.

[205] *See* Kade, note 198, pp. 82-90.

portray the outcome as the result of a lengthy process of consultation between Japanese leaders and General MacArthur and his colleagues,[206] the 1946 Constitution, which contains an elaborate bill of right in the form of Chapter II on "Rights and Duties of the People", was essentially a foreign imposition reflecting minimal local output. It was said to have been "initially drafted within seven days in February 1946 by a handful of American officials (in the Government Section of the headquarters of the Supreme Commander for Allied Powers), who had no particularly relevant legal or political expertise, and drew very heavily upon the US Constitution."[207] MacArthur subsequently approved it and secretly discussed it with a few government officials before it was presented to the Diet. Extensive debates were held in the Diet but it made little change in the draft which was promulgated by the Emperor's mandate on 3 November 1946, and it became effective on 3 May 1947. It has been rightly pointed out that the 1946 Constitution presents a classic case of foreign transplant breaking entirely from the past. Popular sovereignty was asserted; equality of rights for women were recognized; US-style separation of church and State was mandated; respect for a full range of individual civil and political rights were provided; and a comprehensive American-style system of judicial review was enshrined. In such circumstances, one could expect a dismal failure in its acceptance. Yet, the overwhelming opinion of all commentators is that the Japanese constitution has been a success story. It has never been amended. Even when consideration was given to a far-reaching review of the Constitution in the 1950s and 1960s, the main imported principles, including the bill of rights and judicial review, were supported by the majority of the eminent members of the relevant Commission.[208] Nor has it been possible to revise other important provisions relating to armed forces, as we shall see below. What has become gradually institutionalized is one of the world's most stable and peaceful and democratic States with a constitution as its most widely trusted and respected national institution. Out of some 180 single-document national constitutions of the world, Japan's is one of about 20 ratified before 1950.[209]

The most conspicuous and unique feature of the Japanese Peace

[206] MacArthur suggested at the time that the Constitution had been drafted by the Japanese, over a period of five months, involving "painstaking investigation and frequent conference between the Japanese Government and his headquarters". *See* "Political Reorientation of Japan", note 189, p. 657; *see also* Koseki Shoichi, *The Birth of Japan's Postwar Constitution*, (ed. and transl. by Ray A. Moore), Oxford, (1997), pp. xii, 4ff.

[207] Philip Alston, "Transplanting Foreign Norms: Human Rights and other International Legal Norms in Japan", *European Journal of International Law*, Vol. 10 (1999), pp. 628-629.

[208] "Japan's Commission on the Constitution: The Final Report", quoted in Alston, note 207, p. 630.

[209] Some 130 constitutions were ratified since 1970. *See* Lawrence W. Beer,

Constitution was, as desired by the allied powers, renunciation of war by Japan and its peace provisions. The idea of a pacifist Japan was, we are told, first expressed by Prime Minister Kijuro Shidehara to General Douglas MacArthur. The General enthusiastically accepted the idea and asked his staff to draft a clause in the draft Constitution. As finally adopted by the Japanese Diet, the Preamble of the Constitution proclaimed:

> "We, the Japanese people, [are] resolved that never again shall we be visited with the horrors of war through the action of the government ... [We] ... desire peace for all time and ... an honoured place in an international society striving for the preservation of peace ... free from fear and want."

Article 9 then clearly laid down:

> "1. Aspiring sincerely to an international peace based on justice and order, the Japanese people forever renounce war as a sovereign right of the nation and the threat of use of force as a means of settling international disputes.
> 2. In order to accomplish the aim of the preceding paragraph, land, sea and air forces, as well as other war potential, will never be maintained. The right of belligerency of the State will not be recognized."

Echoing the language of 1928 Kellogg-Briand Pact relating to renunciation of war, and Article 2, paragraph 4, of the Charter of the United Nations, for the first time in modern history, an independent country renounced through its constitution its sovereign right to wage war and use force in the settlement of its international disputes, and even stipulated that it would never maintain armed forces as well as other war potential. Accepted of course under compulsion at that time, Japan has proved true to its words. During more than half a century, it has not used force, it has not fired a single shot against any one, and has adopted a policy of pacifism, which is itself an original and distinct contribution to the theory and practice of international relations.

It is important to mention that to the people and government of Japan, the most important matter after its surrender was how to negotiate an early peace treaty. During the debate on the Constitution in the Diet, Prime Minister Shigeru Yoshida said:

> "The renunciation of war clause in the Constitution might imply no use of the right of self-defence, on condition of access to United Nations membership. I am not concerned with that. What is urgent for us is the recovery of sovereignty and independence as early as possible. This is the question that our government has been most concerned about. We are endeavouring to have the earliest chance of concluding a peace treaty with the Allied nations. On your question concerning the renunciation of war and the right of self-defence what I just said was the right answer."[210]

"Peace in theory and practice under Article 9 of Japan's Constitution", *Marquette Law Review*, vol. 82 (1998), p. 818.

[210] Quoted in Wakamizu Tsutsui, "Conceptions of Japan's Security affecting

The Japanese knew and were certain that acceptance of the Peace Constitution was "the prerequisite to peace with the allied nations."[211] But the negotiation for a peace treaty did not start even after the adoption of the Constitution. While peace with the Axis powers except Germany and Japan had been completed by 1947, peace with the latter two nations got entangled in the growing split within the allied nations. When the Japanese were getting restive about the conclusion of peace treaty, the Korean war broke out on 25 June 1950. The Peace Treaty between Japan and the allied powers was eventually concluded on 8 September 1951, at San Francisco, but only with the Western Powers. The Soviet Union and the People's Republic of China did not participate in the conclusion of this treaty. Under these circumstances, the Peace Treaty could not entail the withdrawal of the US forces from the Japanese territory. To resolve the inconsistency of continued stationing of US forces and making peace with Japan, the Treaty of Mutual Cooperation and Security between Japan and the United States was concluded which came into effect simultaneously with the Peace Treaty. Although, in the words of General MacArthur, more than 95 per cent of the Japanese people were opposed to American bases in Japan, the Japan-US Security Treaty permitted, under Article 6, the stationing of the US forces in Japan to contribute to the security of Japan and to maintain peace and security in the Far East.[212] On 4 April 1952, after the two treaties, the Peace Treaty and the Japan-US Security Treaty, were ratified and became effective, Japan regained its independence seven years after its defeat in the Pacific War, although some of its territories continued to be occupied by the United States (Okinawa and Ogaswara were administered by the United States under the Peace Treaty) and the Soviet Union (which occupied Northern Territories islands off Hokkaido).[213]

In order to resume its normal diplomatic relations, Japan concluded peace treaties with the three Indochina States in January 1952. A peace treaty with the Chinese Nationalist Government was concluded on 28 April 1952, and with India in June 1952. But it was not easy to conclude peace with the Soviet Union which continued in a state of war with Japan. In 1954, negotiations for the conclusion of such a treaty failed because of territorial disputes between Japan and the Soviet Union, and the latter refused to return the so-called Northern Islands of Japan. After tremendous efforts and a lot of controversies about territorial matters and fisheries, a Japan-USSR Joint Declaration was concluded on 19 October 1956, terminating the war between the two countries leading to the restoration of diplomatic relations

---

cooperation with the United Nations", *Victoria University of Wellington Law Review*, vol. 27, no. 1 (April 1997), pp. 3-4.

[211] Tsutsui, note 210, p. 4.

[212] *See* ibid., pp. 4-5.

[213] Ishimoto and Hirobe, note 199, pp. 102-103.

between them.[214] Although Japan had applied for membership of the United Nations on 17 June 1952, it was admitted to the UN only on 18 December 1956, after the conclusion of Japan-USSR Joint Declaration.[215]

Pacifism in Japan

Japan's "Peace Constitution" was a product of war and the national tragedy, ignominious defeat and terrible devastation and destruction, shock of the vast and unbelievable havoc caused by the two atom bombs, helplessness and self criticism, and also perhaps tacit admission of war guilt. Hitoshi Ashida, Chairman of the House of Representatives Special Committee on the Draft Revision of the Imperial Constitution, reported to the Plenary Meeting in the House on 24 July 1946:

> "Our new constitution, which completely removes the possibility of armament and renounces all war, may perhaps be a pioneer in the world. No one would deny that, as a result of atomic bombs produced by modern science, a future war occurring between major powers would produce immeasurable calamity to the human race. It goes without saying that we are ready to propose renunciation of war not only because we have fully realized the abominableness of war from the damage of past wars but also because we hold an ideal of sparing the world from civilizational destruction by any such ... future war."[216]

The "Peace Constitution" has contributed to the reconstruction of postwar Japan as a pacifist nation. In sharp contrast with other major powers, such as the United States, Soviet Russia, UK, France, China, and India, Japan has never resorted to military measures after the Second World War, not even for self-defense, to rescue nationals abroad, by invitation of other governments, or for any other reason. Its constitution has also prevented Japan from "becoming merchant of death". Despite its vast industrial and technological capabilities to produce lethal weaponry, including perhaps nuclear weapons, and to make profit by exporting them, Japan has refrained from producing or exporting weapons and armaments. Further, as Professor Onuma points out, the "Peace Constitution" "has functioned as a substitute for open acknowledgement of guilt and responsibility for its aggressive wars". After the end of the Pacific War, almost everybody was suspicious of Japanese militarism. Japanese leaders were aware that Japan could not prosper, nor even rejoin international society as a respected member, unless it could convince the world that there would never be a resurgence of Japanese

[214] Ibid., pp. 110-113.

[215] Ibid., p. 114.

[216] *See* quoted in Yoshiro Matsui, "United Nations activities for peace and the Constitution of Japan", in Machael K. Young and Yuji Iwasawa (ed.), *Trilateral Perspectives on International Legal Issues: Relevance of Domestic Law and Policy*, (1996), p. 496.

militarism. The acceptance and preservation of Article 9 was like "sending a tacit message to the world: 'we did wrong. We shall never do it again'."[217] When the draft articles of the new Constitution were discussed in the Diet, most members of the Diet, including the cabinet, understood Article 9 as prohibiting even the use of force for self-defense.[218] Postwar Japan concentrated on economic development minimizing its military forces, apparently reflecting a strong condemnation of the prewar policy of seeking military hegemony in Asia. It restricted its military budget to around one per cent of its gross national product, maintaining only defense weapons and limiting other military institutions and activities. But determined and disciplined as the Japanese were, they excelled even in peace. With tremendous initial help from the United States, which also opened a vast market for Japan, the Japanese developed their economy so much that it has become one of the strongest economic powers in the world. With two per cent of the world population, Japan today produces more than 15 per cent of the world GNP. There is a striking similarity here with Germany which has reached new heights of economic prosperity while following the path of peace, protected again by the United States since World War II.

Right of Self-defense under the Japanese Constitution

As originally understood by the Japanese founding fathers of the Constitution in the Japanese Diet, including the government, as we have mentioned earlier, Article 9 did not permit even the use of force for self-defense. But this was really too lofty an ideal to be upheld in postwar international society and raised practical questions of Japan's postwar security policy. The UN collective security system, upon which a nation could or should rely in case of an attack, was bound to be faulty and unreliable because of East-West confrontations. The United States, eager to disarm Japan when the Japanese Constitution was drafted, soon wanted an armed and strong Japan, with its military bases, to co-operate with the United States to effectively contain Soviet military forces. As Professor Onuma explains, Japanese opinion was sharply divided on the issue. One section, critical of the American "imperialism", wanted and urged Japan to strictly follow a policy of non-armament and neutrality. Others, suspicious of communist regimes, insisted that Japan should rely on the United States. Due to a variety of reasons, the latter succeeded and Japan concluded a security pact with the United States and created a Self-defense Force. The United States strongly demanded that Japan should have more effective military forces to face their common potential enemy.[219]

[217] *See* Onuma, note 202, p. 530.
[218] Ibid., p. 529.
[219] Ibid., p. 530.

To implement the new policy of Self-defense Forces, a new interpretation was sought to be given to Article 9. Paragraph 1 of this crucial Article provides, "[a] aspiring sincerely to an international peace based on justice and order, the Japanese people forever renounce war as a sovereign right of the nation and the threat or use of force as a means of settling international disputes". It was pointed out by Japanese international lawyers, as Yasuki Onuma explained, that the use of force "as a means of settling international disputes" meant "*aggressive war* according to the normal terminology of international law, and, therefore, this paragraph, as such, does not renounce the use of force in selfdefense or participation in military enforcement measures of the United Nations."[220]

But this interpretation of Article 9, paragraph 1, is not supported at all by paragraph 2 which clearly states: "... in order to attain the aim of the preceding paragraph, land, sea, and air forces, as well as other war potential, will never be maintained. The right of belligerency of the State will not be recognized." In order to avoid this contradiction, the proponents of this interpretation, Yoshiro Matsui points out that the constitution merely relied "on an understanding that 'the aim of the preceding paragraph' denotes the renunciation of *aggressive war only*". Even though "this interpretation seems to be incompatible with the natural and ordinary meaning of the terms of paragraph 2", it is important to note that it came to be widely supported by constitutional and international lawyers in Japan.[221]

The Japanese Government also slowly and gradually changed its position. After hesitating for a few years, it adopted the interpretation that maintenance of minimal forces for self-defense is permitted under Article 9. Successive governments under the Liberal Democratic Party (LDP) concluded and maintained that the Japan-US Security Treaty and the strengthened Self-Defense Forces (SDF) are permissible by interpreting the Constitution as not prohibiting the right of individual self-defense – in contrast to the right of collective self-defense, which is said to be prohibited by the Constitution. It was, therefore, concluded that the maintenance of military power within the limits of self-defense is permitted. Even after the LDP lost power and was replaced by a coalition of various parties in August 1993, this interpretation was not changed. The Japanese people have also generally accepted this interpretation and the policy to gradually increase Japan's military capabilities.

Although the Supreme Court of Japan has consistently avoided judging constitutionality of the SDF or the Japan-US Security Treaty, in the *Sunakawa* case, the Tokyo District Court decided in 1959 that to permit the US forces to station in Japan under the Japan-US Security Treaty of 1952,

[220] *See* Yoshiro Matsui, note 216, p. 499, quoting the opinion of Yashaki Onuma. Emphasis added.

[221] Ibid., pp. 499-500.

[222] *See* quoted ibid., p. 596 fn.

"cannot but come under maintaining land, sea, and air forces, as well as other war potential, prohibited Article 9, para 2, the first sentence of the Constitution of Japan, and therefore, the conclusion is inescapable that the existence of US forces stationed in Japan is impermissible under the Constitution".[222]

Again in the *Naganuma* case of 1973, the Sapporo District Court, affirming legal interest of the applicants based on the right to live in peace derived from the Preamble of the Constitution, decided that the SDF is clearly "... an armed force, and therefore, the land, sea, and air SDF's must be said to amount to 'forces', the maintenance of which is prohibited under Article 9, para 2, of the Constitution."[223] But both of these cases were reversed by the Sapporo High Court and the Supreme Court on technical grounds.[224] The Supreme Court has held that under Article 9, Japan retains the natural right of self-defense, that the Japan-United States Security Treaty is not on its face unconstitutional, and that, although generally the Court must take into account the political nature of such issues, the Court retains the right to determine whether a law or other government action is clearly and obviously in violation of the Article.[225] In the *Sunakawa* case, interpreting Article 9, the Supreme Court declared: "This Article renounces the so-called war and prohibits the maintenance of the so-called war potential but certainly there is nothing in it which would deny the right of self-defense inherent in our nation as a sovereign power". It added: "Pacifism advocated in our Constitution was never intended to mean defenseless or non-resistance." The Court further argued that if the Japanese people did not maintain the so-called war potential as provided in Article 9, paragraph 2, they could supplement the shortcomings in their national defense. The Constitution, it said, "does not at all prohibit our country from seeking a guarantee from another country in order to maintain the peace and security of the country". In fact, it went on to say, "We are free to choose whatever method or means deemed appropriate to accomplish our objectives in the light of actual international situation." But the Court refused to answer whether Japan could maintain a war potential even for self-defense and explicitly said it would not rule on that point.[226]

It is sometimes said that Article 9 has contributed to restricting the size of the increase of the Japanese military forces by focusing public opinion and strong movements in support of the Constitution. The Constitution of Japan has no provision for the declaration of war or on command and control of

[223] *See* quoted ibid.

[224] *See* Beer, note 204, p. 821.

[225] *See* discussion on the basis of several Japanese cases, Beer, note 204, p. 821.

[226] *See* for an extensive discussion of the *Sunakawa* case, Kisaburo Yokota, "Renunciation of War in the new Japanese Constitution as interpreted by the Supreme Court in the *Sunakawa* case", *Japanese Annual of International Law*, vol. 4 (1960), pp. 16-31.

the armed forces. Japanese military expenditure has been relatively low (about one per cent) compared to its GNP, and Japan has maintained three principles on non-nuclear weapons, namely, not to have, not to produce, and not to introduce nuclear weapons.

But despite all these limitations, there is little doubt that Japan's SDF has already become a formidable force. With an annual expenditure of some 16,465 million dollars (in 1993 alone), Japan ranks sixth in the world. The SDF has more than 237,000 personnel, 1200 tanks, 164 warships, and 1,096 war planes, all of them with sophisticated equipment considering Japan's tremendous technological development. This large military build up by Japan, it has been correctly said, "has brought the contradiction between reality and constitutional requirements to a breaking point." The restrictions imposed by the Constitution, Professor Matsui points out, "have increasingly become obstacles for Japan to be considered a normal State, a State which protects its growing overseas rights and interests by its own military power."[227] Referring to the increasing strength of the SDF forces, an eminent Japanese Professor of International Law, Yasuaki Onuma, comments:

> "... [T]his attitude may be justifiable from a political perspective, but it is difficult to defend from a normative perspective. It contributed, in a sense, to the development of a double standard in Japanese society; on the one hand, Article 9 exists as a supreme ideal; on the other hand, it has been construed as allowing the existence of effective armed forces. The tension surfaced in controversies over the Gulf War and Japan's participation in U.N. peacekeeping operations."[228]

The Japanese Government's interpretation that the Constitution permits SDF forces, it is clear, amounts to *de facto* revision of the Constitution. The right wing of the LDP and Democratic Socialist Party in Japan have demanded revision of the Constitution to authorize expressly the maintenance of self-defense forces. But these arguments for express revision never gained much support from politicians, lawyers or the public. The JSP, which had been the most influential defender of the Constitution and the most consistent objector to the constitutionality of the SDF and of the Japan-US Security Treaty, changed its stance upon coming to power in coalition with in LDP in June 1994. The Prime Minister and Chairman of the JSP, Tomiichi Murayama, said in the House of Representatives on 20 July 1994, that "I understand that the SDF, which is the necessary minimum armed organization for self-defense, is recognized as constitutional".[229] But this interpretation and policy change was strongly criticized by Japanese constitutional lawyers. In a statement issued on 12 August 1994, they said that:

> "the SDF is one of the strongest armed forces in the world, organized and composed

[227] Matsui, note 216, p. 497.

[228] Onuma, note 202, p. 531.

[229] *See* quoted in Matsui, note 207, p. 498.

> in order to use force. Without doubt, this SDF is a war potential which is prohibited to maintain under Article 9, paragraph 2, of the Constitution. A large majority of constitutional lawyers of Japan, in view of the world trends and upon a strict interpretation, have consistently argued that the SDF is unconstitutional. This academic viewpoint must not be treated lightly by the political power. If those who are in power do not respect and defend the Constitution, the basis of constitutional politics would be lost."[230]

It is important to note that the North Korean test firing of the Taepodong-1 missile in August 1998, which violated the Japanese airspace before landing in the Pacific Ocean, profoundly shocked Japanese policy makers. In March 1999, two of North Korea's spy ships, disguised as fishing boats, entered Japanese waters. In an unprecedented move, the Japanese Government authorized ships from the SDF to intercept and fire warning shot at the intruders. But the vessels fled before they could be captured. In August 1999 there were reports of tests of longer-range missiles by North Korea. These threats from North Korea led to both houses of the Diet passing the US-Japan Defense Cooperation Guidelines clarifying the types of non-combatant roles Japan could play in certain situations occurring in areas around Japan. In August 1999, Tokyo and Washington signed a Memorandum of Understanding that spelled out the technologies to be jointly developed, including some components of the system on which Japan would take the lead and provide USD 170 to 260 million for research costs. Tokyo also announced its intention to develop an indigenous surveillance satellite. The Diet also established special panels in both houses to specifically review Article 9 of the Constitution and hold open public discussions from early 2000 onwards.[231]

It is also important to note that after decades of rejecting patriotism as an illegitimate sentiment, the Japanese Diet approved, in August 2000, the national anthem, a song dedicated to the Emperor called *Kimigayo*, and the national flag *Hinomaru*, with its red circle on a white background, as the official symbols of the State. While both of these symbols had long been held in their *de facto* roles of national emblems, the act of legally and formally recognizing them as such had been adamantly opposed by several sections of the Japanese society because of their associations with memories of wartime imperialism and the Emperor system.[232]

[230] Quoted ibid.

[231] *See* Robert M. Uriu, "Japan in 1999: Ending the century on an uncertain note", *Asian Survey*, vol. 40, no. 1 (Jan-Feb. 2000), pp. 147-149; *see also* Michael J. Green and Katsuhisa Furukawa, "New ambitions, old obstacles: Japan and search for an arms control strategy", *Arms Control Today* (July-August 2000), p. 17.

[232] *See* Uriu, note 231, p. 147; Green and Furkawa, note 222, p. 17.

The Constitution of Japan and the UN Collective Security System

Under Article 2 of the UN Charter, all Members of the United Nations are bound to "fulfil in good faith the obligations assumed by them in accordance with the present Charter" (paragraph 2), and must give the UN "every assistance in any action it takes in accordance with the present Charter" and must "refrain from giving assistance to any State against which the United Nations is taking preventive or enforcement action." (paragraph 5). But the drafters of the Japanese Constitution intended Article 9 to prohibit military forces even for the purpose of assisting in enforcement measures under the UN. During the discussion on the Constitution in House of Lords at that time, Kijuro Shidehara, then Minister of State, said on 13 September 1946, that:

> "we sympathize with most of the objects and purposes of the United Nations, therefore, we will cooperate with it. But, as we have Article 9 of the Constitution, we must formulate a reservation on its application. If we are asked to cooperate with a sanction against some State in contravention of our neutrality, we cannot do it at all."[233]

The Japanese application for membership of the United Nations on 16 June 1952, was accompanied with a declaration by the Minister of Foreign Affairs, Katsuo Okazaki, asserting that "the Government of Japan hereby accepts the obligations contained in the Charter of the United Nations, and undertakes to honour them, *by all means at its disposal ...*" Although it was not a formal reservation as such, it is understood by the Japanese scholars as clearly indicating "the intention of Japan at that time that Japan could not cooperate with the United Nations by means not at its disposal, i.e, with armed force."[234]

This interpretation of Article 9, which had long been shared by successive governments, came under attack by the internationalist arguments during the Gulf crisis. When Iraq invaded Kuwait and the US and other coalition powers took UN-supported enforcement action, there arose a strong opinion, supported by mass media institutions, that not only was non-military support to the coalition forces authorized by the UN Security Council, but there was a real need to participate in, or at least cooperate with, the coalition forces. Faced with an increasing demand to participate in UN operations in the Gulf crisis, the Japanese Government introduced a bill in the Diet in October 1990 to enable the SDF to cooperate not only with the UN, but also to participate in the coalition forces in the Gulf. However, it met with such a severe criticism in the Diet and outside that the bill had to be withdrawn without a vote. Although a majority of Japanese had accepted the existence of the SDF, they were extremely reluctant to assign it a positive role and use

[233] Quoted in Matsui, note 216, p. 500.
[234] Ibid., p. 500.

it for such purposes. Although Japan made a massive contribution of USD 13 billion to support the coalition forces, it did not send any forces during the Gulf war. It was only after the war that the Japanese Government decided to send marine mine-sweepers to the Persian Gulf on the request of the United States.[235]

A little more internationalist approach to peace and security was adopted by Japan to bring about peace in Cambodia, where civil wars had been going on since the 1970s. Japan played an important role in persuading the conflicting parties to accept the peace agreements and in October 1991, the Agreement on a Comprehensive Political Settlement of the Cambodia Conflict and other related agreements were concluded. As the UN decided to establish the UN Temporary Authority in Cambodia (UNTAC) to implement these agreements, Japan was naturally expected to participate in the peacekeeping operation. After heated debates in the National Diet, and in academic and legal circles, the Law Concerning Cooperation for UN Peace-Keeping Operations (PKO) and other operations was enacted on 15 June 1992. This law authorizes the government to engage the SDF and other personnel in (1) UN peacekeeping operations, and (2) humanitarian relief operations based on resolutions and requests by the UN or its specialized agencies, like the UN High Commission for Refugees. A separate law had to be enacted for its implementation, and participation of SDF in such activities as monitoring the observance of cease-fire arrangements, patrolling in a buffer zone, and participation in other peacekeeping activities that might involve the use of force. The participation of SDF was limited to such non-military activities as election monitoring, police administration, provision for medical services, and logistical support for other military forces participating in UN peacekeeping operations. Thereafter, Japan sent three electoral monitors to Angola to participate in the Angola Verification Mission in 1992, about 680 personnel, including a 600-member SDF ground unit to Cambodia also in 1992, and a 48-member SDF transport unit to Mozambique to participate in the UN operation in 1993.[236] Japan also sent a small Observer Mission in El Salvador, and a small SDF unit for Humanitarian International Operations in Rwanda.[237]

Summary

Separated by a stretch of a little over 100 miles of rough water from the mainland of Asia, Japan developed in comparative seclusion but was still largely influenced by the Chinese culture and civilization throughout its

[235] *See* Akiho Shibata, "Japanese Peacekeeping Legislation and recent developments in UN Operations", *Yale Journal of International Law*, vol. 19 (1994), p. 308.

[236] *See* ibid., p. 308; *see also* Onuma, note 202, pp. 532-533.

[237] Matsui, note 216, pp. 505-506.

history. While preserving their native quality, Japan owes a lot to the Chinese and never had any qualms about learning from outside. Japan had continuous relations with its neighbours and even with the Portuguese, Spaniards, Dutch and the English from the sixteenth century onwards. However, fearing the evil designs of Christian missionaries, they adopted a policy of almost total seclusion from the outside world for more than 200 years, except the Dutch and the Chinese who were permitted to continue their restricted trade in Nagasaki.

This seclusion policy was rudely shaken by the arrival of the American Commodore Perry in 1853 with his squadron of four "black ships", who wanted to have limited trade relations with the Japanese to replenish the stocks of coal and provisions for the American ships on their journey to and from the Chinese ports, and protection for the shipwrecked American sailors who might be in distress. The local Tokugawa ruler, or Shogun, had no choice but to accept the American demands. The Bakufu Government of Japan could not face the "black ships of the barbarians" when Commodore Perry reappeared with six ships in February 1854, and even against the advice of the Emperor who wanted the barbarians to be thrown out, concluded a treaty of peace, amity and commerce in March 1854. Once Japan signed this treaty, it opened its doors to foreign penetration and it had to conclude several unequal treaties with numerous European countries opening its ports for trade, providing for appointment of diplomatic agents and consuls for the exercise of extraterritorial rights in criminal and civil matters, and fixing custom tariffs at very low rates.

Aggrieved and angry, the Japanese spent the next few decades trying to get rid of these unequal treaties. The Bakufu Government, the once powerful local Japanese authority which concluded these treaties, and its head, the Shogun, lost their face and power and, after a brief civil war, the Emperor's authority was restored and the country submitted to his rule. The Japanese understood well that the only way to revise these humiliating treaties was to join the family of the so-called *civilized States*, which could be done only if they *civilized* themselves and *Europeanized* or *westernized* themselves to join them at the same level. The new Meiji Government encouraged the adoption of western ways. The Japanese, always eager to learn from abroad, adopted the western life with a vengeance. They sent their missions and students to various European countries and the United States, learnt European languages, adopted European manners and clothes, framed new legal codes based on European laws and promulgated a new constitution.

Even more important and vigorously, the Japanese started learning and sought to adopt rules of European international law in the hope that they would be accepted as an equal member of the civilized international community. But while the Japanese were enthusiastically and energetically learning international law, the European powers began to maintain and assert that international law applied only amongst Christian States of Europe or

States of European origin. The Japanese were not prepared to give up their efforts to achieve their goal. They continued their vigorous efforts to learn international law, established a Japanese Association of International Law (in 1897), and started their own *Journal of International Law* (in 1902) as the European countries were beginning to do.

Even more than that, they strengthened their armed forces on European lines and started following "European" policies of intervention and expansion in their relations with their neighbours in East Asia. It aggressively intervened in Korea to undermine the authority of China, and in 1876, forced Korea to conclude a treaty similar to the treaties which Japan had been forced to sign with the Western countries. In 1894, it attacked China to wipe out her influence in Korea and not only drove China out of Korea, but occupied parts of China after defeating it in 1895. Japan claimed a large indemnity from China, besides occupying Taiwan and other parts of China, and joined the Western Powers in exploiting China. All these aggressive policies of Japan had the desired effect on the western powers and Japan was beginning to be recognized as a "civilized" State worthy to be admitted in the European family of nations. After 1894, "unequal treaties" began to be revised, abolishing extraterritoriality in Japan.

Although Japan was forced to retreat from some parts of China by three Western Powers, Russia, France and Germany, after the so-called Triple Intervention in 1895, because Japan was beginning to tread on their toes and infringe their rights to exploit China, it was not long before Japan was back on track. In 1900-1901, it joined the Western Powers to suppress the Boxer Uprising in China and became a member of the power group to exploit China. In 1904-1905, it challenged and declared a war against a big white European power, Russia, to wipe out the Russian influence in Korea. Once it defeated Russia, there was no more doubt about Japan's entry into the family of "civilized" nations. It is interesting to note that not only did Japan scrupulously observe the laws of European warfare in Chino-Japanese and Russo-Japanese wars, but to maintain its reputation as a "civilized" State, published in European universities numerous decisions taken during the wars by the Japanese army and naval forces with the help and guidance of two eminent Japanese Professors of International Law who had been appointed advisors to those forces. These publications led to recommendations by eminent British professors, professional journals, and pressure to accept Japan as a worthy member of the family of civilized nations. Japan also took a firm hold over China by occupying all the areas, and acquiring concession rights earlier held by Russia, to further exploit China. It also turned Korea into a protectorate.

As the first non-western nation to emerge as a great power, Japan was looked upon as a model and inspired anti-colonial movements in Asian countries, as far as India. The Japanese victory also proved that the Europeans were not invincible. It gave rise to Pan-Asian feelings and a hope that Japan, as the first successful non-European nation, would help its Asian neighbours achieve their independence.

But that was not to be. Having enjoyed the fruits of power as an imperialist power, which had also helped it to become a member of the family of "civilized" States, Japan was not prepared to give up its imperialistic policies. The First World War gave it an opportunity to expand its hold over China even further. Taking cognizance of the fact that Britain, France, and other European countries were preoccupied with war, and to take benefit of the predicament of Germany, whose role in the three-power intervention after the Sino-Japanese war of 1894-1895 it had not forgotten, Japan declared war against Germany to side with the allied powers. Without much problem or fight, Japan took over Germany's colonial territories in Asia and the Pacific. This whetted Japan's lust even more. Six months after the beginning of the war, it presented to China its Twenty-one Demands to tighten its control over China, which the latter had no choice but to accept. Although Japan retracted from some of these demands under strong pressure from the United States, the war gave it an opportunity even to expand into Siberia as part of the joint allied intervention in the Russian Revolution.

Japan sought to keep all these areas, especially in China, at the Paris Peace Conference (in 1919) and later, under the pretext of the so-called Japanese Monroe Doctrine and its special rights and interests in China, and the need for its security. It also raised its own imperialist slogans, such as "Pan-Asia" or "Asia for the Asiatics", to claim its "special position" in China and Korea, and a position of leadership in the Far East. Although Japan got large chunks of Chinese territory at the Paris Peace Conference, it was forced to give up some of these areas and accept a balance of naval power with the Western Powers, especially the United Sates and Great Britain, in the Washington Conference 1921-1922, and the treaties concluded there, much to the discomfort and annoyance of Japan.

Though Japan had emerged as the colossus of the Far East, it had caused serious alarm in the Western capitals, and it was disliked and even despised by the Asians it ruthlessly ruled. While it was recognized as a big power and a permanent member of the Council of the League of Nations, it could not persuade the European powers and the United States to include the principle of equality of States or individuals in the Covenant of the League of Nations. Over and above that, the United States passed a law prohibiting immigration of the Japanese to the United States. Japan had agreed to stop on its own emigration of Japanese to the United States, but such a law discriminating against the Japanese was humiliating. However, the United States was not prepared to change its policy.

Japan was not satisfied with the situation. It wanted more space to exploit economically and to settle some of its growing population, as the European colonial powers had done. It sought to do this by establishing a new Chinese State of Manchukuo, completely under the control and supervision of Japan.

The Western Powers were very much against the creation of a new State in Manchuria under Japanese influence. The League of Nations appointed a commission which visited China and gave a report against Japan. In defiance of the international opinion, Japan decided to leave the League of Nations and continue its adventures in China.

After leaving the League of Nations and defying the Western Powers, Japan was prepared to confront them with its new plans and dreams of Greater East Asian Co-Prosperity Sphere under the domination of Japan and free from European colonialism. "Asia for Asians", declared Japan. In fact some Japanese had wild dreams under what is known as the Tanaka Plan of occupying not only China, but all other south-east Asian States, like Indonesia, Malaysia, Philippines, Singapore, Thailand, and even Burma and India. They even dreamt of defeating Europe and, ultimately, the United States.

Determined to occupy the whole of China, Japan used the so-called Marco Polo Bridge incident in July 1937 to start a full-fledged war against China and later blamed the United States, Britain, France, and the Soviet Union for helping China and prolonging the war. On 27 September 1940, it formally signed the Triple Alliance with Germany and Italy recognizing each others' spheres of leadership. Convinced that the United States was the main hurdle in its plans for expansion, having already given it the "ultimatum" to withdraw from China and Indo-China, and that the US, along with Great Britain, represented the most serious threat to Japan's preservation, Japan attacked the United States at Pearl Harbor in Honolulu on 8 December 1942. Joining the Axis powers, it went to war against the United States and Great Britain, without bothering to make a formal declaration.

Simultaneously, it occupied Thailand, invaded Malaya, took over Singapore and the British and Dutch Borneos within a few days and attacked the Philippines, destroying much of American strength there. Hongkong, Bali, Lombok, Timor, Java, all fell in Japanese hands even before 1 March 1942, and Japanese forces marched towards Burma and India.

These early Japanese victories were welcomed by the Asian countries which were struggling for their independence. These developments weakened the European colonialism and helped a lot in the ultimate collapse of the Western colonialism and the emergence of Asian States as independent countries. With the conquest of the Indies by the end of 1942, the end of European and American empires seemed imminent. Although Japan over-extended itself and could not maintain its winning spree against the sustained allied efforts and the tremendous power of the United States, the Japanese early and phenomenal success helped Asians to regain their confidence and independence.

By the beginning of 1943, the Pacific war took a sharp turn. Japan suffered a lot for its foolhardiness and was the first victim of two atomic bombs in August 1945, which brought untold sufferings on Japan at a time when it was already on the verge of collapse. It could not continue the war after this devastation, and had no choice but to surrender. But after the war, China emerged as one of the five Great Powers and a founding member of the United Nations. India became independent. Indonesia, which had been occupied by Japan during the war, was reoccupied by the allied powers. But, in the new wave of independence, and under pressure from newly independent States like India, Pakistan, Thailand, the Philippines and others, it could not be permitted to be re-colonized by the Netherlands and emerged as an independent State. Japan suffered an ignominious and terrible defeat, but helped, even if unintentionally, Asians gain their independence and become members of the "civilized" family of nations.

Having suffered a devastating defeat, Japan was a different State altogether after the war. Horrified by its miserable fate, after three million of its citizens had been killed and its economy almost totally shattered bringing near-starvation conditions, Japan realized that it was on the wrong path. Occupied by the allied forces, headed by the Supreme Commander of Allied Powers, General MacArthur, Japan was constrained to adopt a new "Peace Constitution". Under the new constitution, adopted after a lot of discussion in the Japanese Diet but with no apparent change, Japan renounced "war as a sovereign right" of the nation and declared that in future it would never employ "the threat or use of force as means for settling international disputes." It went further and declared in Article 9 that to achieve these aims, "land, sea and air forces, as well as other war potential, will never be maintained. The right of belligerency of the State will not be recognized."

Japan has so far proved true to its words. Though no longer under any pressure, it has not amended its constitution even after a far-reaching review by its Commission on the Constitution, and thorough studies by its numerous constitutional lawyers. In fact it has proved to be the most trusted and respected national institution. The "Peace Constitution" has contributed to postwar Japan becoming a pacifist nation. It has never used force to protect its interests. However, Japan did set up a Self-defense Force (SDF) that the Japanese scholars, and later the government, felt was permitted under Article 9 of the Constitution. Although the Supreme Court of Japan has consistently avoided judging the constitutionality of SDF, it is generally felt by the Japanese that the maintenance of military power within the limits of self-defense is permitted, a view which has come to be endorsed and supported by the Supreme Court in the *Sunakawa* case. It is another matter that Japan's SDF has already become a formidable force. Although Japanese military expenditure has been about one per cent of its GNP, with annual budget of more than USD 16,465 million (in 1993 alone), Japan ranks sixth in the world. This large military build up of Japan has led, according to some Japanese scholars, to contradiction between reality and constitutional requirements. But the need and demand for the revision of the Constitution to clearly permit Japanese self-defense forces has never gained much support.

So deep-rooted is the new wave of pacifism in Japan that a strong debate has been going on amongst Japanese scholars and statesmen whether under its constitution Japan can and should participate in the United Nations' ever-expanding peace-enforcement and peace-keeping activities. Despite all the pressure from its friends and allies, like the United States, Japan has been extremely reluctant to send its Self-defense Forces abroad on UN missions. Thus, although Japan made a massive contribution of USD 13 billion to support the coalition forces in the Gulf crisis, it could not participate in the UN operations and send its SDF to the Gulf because of strong opposition in the Japanese Diet. It was only in 1992, that after a heated debate, a Law Concerning Cooperation in Peacekeeping and other Operations (Peacekeeping Law) was enacted in the Japanese Diet to permit Self-defense Forces to go abroad on limited UN missions. Thereafter, Japan sent some limited forces to participate in UN missions in Angola, Cambodia, Mozambique, El Salvador and Rwanda in 1992-1993.

In the early 1950s, Japan had entered into a security pact with the United States. Thereafter, protected under the US umbrella, and tremendous initial help by the United States, which also opened its vast market to them, the Japanese adopted the path of peace and concentrated on economic reconstruction of their devastated economy. It has excelled in its economic development so much that it has emerged as the second largest economy in the world. Having achieved tremendous success in peace, Japan is, and should be, now prepared to go even further and help other developing Asian and African countries, struggling to achieve economic development in a world dominated by the developed Western countries, most of whom have achieved far greater standards of development. However, the general perception so far, mostly in Japan itself, is that, despite its past history and background, having achieved tremendous economic progress, Japan is extremely "westernized", a member of the rich men's exclusive group, and following similar economic policies. Indeed, there is said to be hardly any difference "between the approach of Japan in international law and that of the West".[238]

There is no question Japan can play a leading role in the development of a new international law of co-operation which is not individualistic and not merely a law of coordination only amongst independent sovereign States. In the utterly interdependent international society in the new small world, we need a new law of cooperation and help. Japan can play a leading role in this development. It has the resources, it has the technology, it has the expertise, it has a new prestige, and most importantly, it has the will and inclination to help and develop a new atmosphere of co-operation. Japan,

[238] *See* Professor John H. Jackson, "Western View of Japanese International Law Practice for the Maintenance of International Economic Order", in R. P. Anand, "Japan and International Law in Historical Perspective", in Nisuke Ando, note 86, p. 395.

along with some other States, must get its due place in the United Nations as a permanent member of the expanded UN Security Council for the world body to become truly representative of the newly-emerging international society, and in order to become effective. But it must also shed its hesitation to play its real and new role as a leader in the international community for the development of a new law of co-operation. Instead of dwelling on its past deeds it can learn from its own history and lead in helping its neighbours in their development more actively. It has been pointed out by a few Japanese scholars that "since the middle of the nineteenth century, the Japanese had concentrated on catching up with the West and paid little attention to the lives and fates of the non-western peoples in general."[239] The time has come for Japan to make a change and meet new challenges.

[239] Yasuki Onuma, note 202, p. 528.

The Status of Tibet in International Law

Colonization of Free Tibet

Situated between the Himalaya and the wastes of Central Asia, high above the clouds, mysterious, awe-inspiring, forbidding, the unworldly world of Tibet has a fascination hard to resist. Few have, however, dared to go beyond the precipitous barrier of the Himalaya that guards its seclusion, and fewer still have been permitted to do so. Tibet always was, and remains, a poor country made up of large, barren, and tree-less plateaus and secluded valleys. Covering a vast area of about 500,000 square miles, it is bounded on the north by the Chinese Province of Sinkiang; on the south by Nepal, Bhutan, and Sikkim, along with 800 miles of mountainous Indian territory; on the west by the Ladakh area of Kashmir; and on the east by China. In spite of its obvious strategic importance, its recent occupation by Communist China has more or less been ignored. The colonization of free Tibet in the present age of decolonization, and the woes and cries of the three million freedom-loving Tibetans, have failed to elicit any conrete action on the part of the Free World. Under the very nose of the great champions of freedom, a free country has lost its identity, and without so much as a vigorous protest from the ever-vociferous advocates of human rights, its people have had to suffer the most inhuman treatment.

Tibet Through the Ages

In order to understand and appreciate the plight of Tibet today, we must look into the history of this unfortunate country, especially during the last few centuries. Of its history prior to the seventh century after Christ little is known, but there is no need to go into that remote past in order to assess its international status in our age. Divided for a while into numerous petty kingdoms and tribal states, Tibet was united for the first time by the great Songtsen Gampo, who ruled Tibet from A.D. 620 to A.D. 650.[1] At the head of a powerful army, he is said to have conquered Upper Burma and Western China and forced the Chinese to sign a humiliating treaty which stipulated, among other things, the marriage of a Chinese princess to him. During the

[1] All dates in this article are A.D.

reign of Thisong Detsen (about 740), China used to pay a yearly tribute of 50,000 yards of Chinese brocade to Tibet. During the second half of the eighth century and the first half of the ninth, the Tibetans continued their encroachments upon Chinese territory and acquired large parts of it. It is said that they once captured even the Chinese capital. It was only after 850, with the decline of Tibet owing to internal rivalries, that the Chinese were able to push the Tibetans back.[2]

In 1252, Kublai Khan, the Mongol Emperor of China, overran Eastern Tibet, but, instead of bringing the conquered country under Chinese rule, was spiritually "conquered" by the Tibetan scholars. He embraced Lamaism, and conferred the sovereignty of Tibet on the high priest of the Sakya sect. From then on, throughout the time of the Yuan (1277-1367) and Ming dynasties (1368-1634) in China, Tibet functioned as an independent state.[3] In the second half of the seventeenth century, Tibet was blessed with a remarkable Dalai Lama, Lobsang Gyatso, known as the Great Fifth, who united the whole of Tibet and was invited to Peking by the then Manchu Emperor of China and treated as an independent sovereign.[4]

After the death of this Dalai Lama, however, Tibet became involved in internal dissensions and mutual bickerings. His successor was murdered by the Chinese in 1706, and there was trouble in Tibet following the installation of Dalai Lama VII. Taking advantage of the turbulent situation in Tibet, China dispatched a military expedition in 1720 which conquered Tibet and reached Lhasa. This led to the stationing in Lhasa in 1728 (for the first time) of two Chinese Residents designated *Ambans*, each with a thousand troops. The reality of political power in Tibet now devolved on these *Ambans*. During the rest of the eighteenth and most of the nineteenth century, Tibet was virtually a vassal of the Celestial Empire, which, through its *Ambans* in Lhasa, supervised the nomination of every new Dalai Lama. Tibet was without any strong leadership. It is interesting to note that all Dalai Lamas, from the sixth to the twelfth, were discreetly and systematically poisoned before they reached their majority at the age of eighteen.[5]

[2] H. E. Richardson, *Tibet and Its History* (London, 1962), pp. 28 ff; Tsepon, W. D. Shakabpa, *Tibet: A Political History* (New Haven, Conn., 1967), pp. 23 ff.; and Frank Moraes, *The Revolt in Tibet* (New York, N. Y., 1960), pp. 32-36.

[3] See M. E. Willoughby, "The Relation of Tibet to China", *Journal of the Royal Central Asian Society* (London), vol 11 (1924), p. 189; Shakabpa, n. 2, pp. 64 ff.; Ram Gopal, *India-China-Tibet Triangle* (Lucknow, 1964), pp. 2 ff.; and Moraes, n. 2, p. 37.

[4] W. W. Rockhill, *The Dalai Lamas of Lhasa and Their Relations with the Manchu Emperors of China, 1644-1908* (Leyden, 1910), p. 3; Shakabpa, n. 2, pp. 113 ff.; and Ram Gopal, n. 3, p. 4.

[5] Amaury de Riencourt, "Tibetan History", in Raja Hutheesing, ed., *Tibet Fights for Freedom: The Story of the March 1959 Uprising as Recorded in Documents, Despatches, Eye-Witness Accounts and World-wide Reactions* (Bombay, 1960), p. 4.

About the middle of the nineteenth century China's power declined, and China's weak Government was hardly able to maintain its imperial hold over Tibet. Tibet started asserting its authority, and the Chinese Ambans were reduced to the position of envoys. In 1854, Tibet was invaded by the Gorkhas of Nepal and defeated without any Chinese in the foreground or background. But in the Treaty of 1856 between Tibet and Nepal, both parties declared: "We further agree that both States pay respect as always before the Emperor of China and that the two States are to treat each other like brothers."[6]

Tibet Asserts its Authority

The influence of China continued to dwindle, and it was not long before Tibet began openly repudiating China's authority. Thus, in 1878, it did not permit a Russian explorer to enter Tibet though he had obtained a passport from the Government of China to visit Lhasa.[7] In 1886, it refused to recognize the Anglo-Chinese Treaty of 1876, under which the Government of China had agreed to make arrangements for a British mission of exploration to visit Tibet, and the mission was thereupon abandoned.[8] Tibet also erected a stone fortress across the trade road in an area which the British regarded as lying well within the limits of Sikkim, which was then under British control. A protest to China, and China's remonstrances with Tibet, having proved entirely fruitless, the Tibetans were driven out of Sikkim only by a British military force.[9] There was now no doubt that China had lost all control over Tibet.

But despite this dwindling authority of China in Tibet, Britain signed a treaty with China in 1890 delimiting the boundary between Sikkim and Tibet as if the latter had then been a part of China.[10] In 1893, another Anglo-Chinese convention was signed purporting to open Tibetan territory to British trade. But it was all wasted labour.[11] China was in no position to honour the commitments it had made on paper. In 1895, on being questioned about its consistent disregard of the provisions of the Anglo-Chinese Convention of 1893, the Government of Tibet flatly told a British Commissioner that since

[6] See C. V. Aitchison, *A Collection of Treaties, Engagements, and Sanads Relating to India and Neighbouring Countries* (Calcutta, 1929), edn., 5, vol. 14, pp. 15 and 49-50; and Ram Gopal, n. 3, p. 9.

[7] Ram Gopal, n. 3, p. 9.

[8] See International Commission of Jurists, *The Question of Tibet and the Rule of Law* (Geneva, 1959), p. 77.

[9] Ibid.

[10] The British classified the Sino-Tibetan relations as involving Chinese "sovereignty" over Tibet. See Alfred P. Rubin, "The Position of Tibet in International Law", *China Quarterly* (London), July-September 1968, p. 112.

[11] Richardson, n. 2, p. 77.

Tibet was not a party to the Convention, it could not recognize it.[12] It also removed the boundary pillars erected by the British and Chinese authorities. In 1899, Britain made another vain attempt to negotiate with Tibet through the Chinese *Ambans*. Indeed, the Government of Tibet felt so irritated with the British for dealing directly with China in matters concerning Tibetan territory that it even refused to parley with the British and rebuffed the approaches made by them during 1899-1901 for direct negotiations.[13] At least three letters addressed by the British Viceroy in India, Lord Curzon, to the Dalai Lama were returned unopened. The message accompanying the unopened letters said: "We cannot deal with it; we have no dealings with foreigners."[14] By all their gestures and actions, the Tibetans thus tried to assert their independence.

Earlier, in 1894 when Dalai Lama XIII reached the age of eighteen, the national parties in Lhasa had set him on the throne over the loud protests of the Chinese *Ambans*.[15] Powerful and intelligent, the Dalai Lama took advantage of the decline in Manchu authority and embarked on a policy of preserving Tibet's *de facto* independence by clever diplomacy. Faced with British hostility and suspicion, and finding that China was too weak to afford any protection, he turned to Russia in the hope of securing an ally against both China and Britain. Russia, like Britain, was busy those days extending its influence in Central Asia, especially in Mongolia, Manchuria, and Sinkiang. Tibet's cultural and religious influence over Mongolia and other parts of Central Asia and its strategic position bordering India, Nepal, China, and several other, smaller states naturally increased its importance for Russia. In the opening years of the twentieth century, a Russian citizen, Agvan Dorjiev, a lama hailing from Buryat Mongolia, arrived in Tibet. His activities aroused acute British suspicion. Being a lama, Agvan Dorjiev received warm welcome in Lhasa and was said to have had enormous influence over the Dalai Lama. The British, not being able to find out the exact nature of the mission this Russian "agent" had undertaken, entertained the apprehension that the Russians were planning to assume control over Tibet and then threaten their Indian Empire. There was also a rumour that some Russian arms had been imported into Lhasa. The British apprehension became stronger when some Tibetan lamas paid a visit to Russia in August 1901. The British Ambassador in St. Petersburg was instructed to warn the Russian Foreign Office that "His Majesty's Government could not regard with indifference any proceedings that might have a tendency to alter or disturb the existing status of Tibet". The Russian reply that the visit of the lamas had no political or diplomatic object or character failed to satisfy

[12] Aitchison, n. 6, p. 17.

[13] Ibid.

[14] Quoted in Sir Charles Bell, *Portrait of the Dalai Lama* (London, 1946), p. 61.

[15] Riencourt, n. 5, p. 4.

Britain.[16] Britain "believed that Russia was making a secret treaty to help China against those who were pressing her from different directions" and that "Russia was to receive Tibet in return for her service".[17] It felt that its "vastly greater interests in Tibet clashed all along the line with the Muscovite".[18]

Yonghusband Expedition

Rebuffed by the Tibetans and apprehensive of Russian intentions, Britain decided to straighten out its relations with Tibet.[19] Correctly analysing the situation, Lord Curzon said in his letter to the Secretary of State for India: "Chinese suzerainty over Tibet is a constitutional fiction—a political affectation which has only been maintained because of its convenience to both parties." He maintained that the Dalai Lama was the "*de facto* as well as *de jure* sovereign of the country".[20] But as the Dalai Lama refused to negotiate and China had no control over him, Lord Curzon ordered a military expedition to Tibet. The Tibetan defence was no match for the British force which, under the command of Colonel Francis Younghusband, reached Lhasa on 3 August 1904. The Dalai Lama, fearing that he might be arrested, fled to Mongolia. A treaty was signed between the victorious British commander and the Government of Tibet (without the Dalai Lama) on 7 September 1904, under which the Government of Tibet undertook "to respect the Anglo-Chinese Convention of 1890 and to recognize the frontier between Sikkim and Tibet, as defined in Article I of the said Convention, and to erect boundary pillars accordingly". Certain trade rights were granted to Britain. The treaty further laid down, *inter alia*:

(a) No portion of Tibetan territory shall be ceded, sold, leased, mortgaged, or otherwise given for occupation, to any foreign Power;
(b) No such Power shall be permitted to intervene in Tibetan affairs;
(c) No representatives or Agents of any foreign Power shall be admitted to Tibet;
(d) No concessions for railways, road, telegraphs, mining, or other rights, shall be granted to any foreign Power, or the subject of any foreign Power. In the event of consent to such concessions being granted, similar or equivalent concession shall be granted to the British Government;
(e) No Tibetan revenues, whether in kind or in cash, shall be pledged or assigned to any foreign Power, or the subject of any foreign Power.

[16] See Ram Gopal, n. 3, pp. 10-11; and Richardson, n. 2, p. 4.
[17] Bell, n. 14, p. 62; and Richardson, n. 2, p. 4.
[18] See Perceval Landon, *Opening of Tibet* (New York, N.Y., 1905), p. 21.
[19] See Sir Eric Teichman, *Affairs of China* (London, 1938), p. 222.
[20] See quoted in Ram Gopal, n. 3, p. 12.

The Government of Tibet was held responsible for the conditions which had "compelled" Britain to send the expedition, and so was required to pay an indemnity of Rs 7,500,000 (subsequently reduced to a third of this sum). Britain was allowed to be in occupation of the Chumbi Valley until the indemnity had been paid and until its trade marts had effectively functioned for three years.

It is significant to note that neither the Government of China nor its representative in Lhasa uttered a word of protest against the British invasion or the signing of this Convention in the name of the Government of Tibet. It is also interesting that the Chinese *Amban* gave much assistance to the British commander all through the negotiations.[21] There is little doubt that even the last vestige of Chinese control had vanished. Indeed, China was never even mentioned in this instrument, which was later solemnly ratified by Britain on 11 November 1904.

It is submitted that the conclusion of this bilateral treaty was an implied recognition of Tibet as an independent state by Britain. As Ti-Chiang Chen points out: "It is generally agreed that the conclusion of bilateral treaties constitutes recognition."[22] There are in fact several cases of such implied recognition. It is well known that the Republican Government of Turkey was recognized by the United States by the signing of the treaties of 6 August 1923. Similarly, the Soviet Union was accorded recognition by several states through bilateral conventions.[23] It is true that every bilateral arrangements with a new entity, especially if it relates to temporary or local arrangements, does not amount to recognition. But the conclusion of a general trade agreement and a treaty "regulating more or less permanently matters of a general and political nature gives rise to the presumption" of recognition. This presumption is further strengthened by its solemn ratification.[24] Even Sir Hersch Lauterpacht, who was opposed to implied recognition, nevertheless admitted that the conclusion of a general bilateral treaty amounted to recognition.[25] The general character of the 1904 Treaty leaves little doubt about its implication.

Although this Treaty did not define "foreign Power", the general tenor of the Treaty, and Clauses (b), (c), and (d) of Article IX, clearly conveyed the

[21] Sir Francis Younghusband, *India and Tibet* (London, 1910), pp. 421-2; and Richardson, n. 2, p. 93.

[22] Ti-Chiang Chen, *The International Law of Recognition: With Special Reference to Practice in Great Britain and the United States*, L. C. Green, ed. (London, 1951), p. 192.

[23] Ibid.

[24] Ibid., p. 196.

[25] Sir Hersch Lauterpacht, *Recognition in International Law* (Cambridge, 1947), pp. 375 ff. and pp. 405-6.

impression that China was regarded as a foreign Power in Tibet.[26] It is important, however, to remember that the main concern of Britain was to exclude Russia, rather than China, from Tibet since China was then too weak to pose a threat to the British interests in India. Having secured its position in Tibet, and with a view to winning Chinese friendship and confidence, Britain entered into an agreement with China on 27 April 1906, by which it again recognized Chinese overlordship of Tibet. Although it confirmed the Anglo-Tibetan Convention of 1904, the Anglo-Chinese Agreement of 1906 laid down that Article IX (d) of the 1904 Convention denying trade concessions to any foreign Power did not apply to China. Britain further engaged not to annex Tibetan territory or to intervene in the administration of Tibet; and China undertook "not to permit any other foreign state or interfere with the territory or internal administration of Tibet". China also agreed to pay the entire indemnity imposed on Tibet by the 1904 Convention in three instalments, and indeed paid the last instalment about January 1908.[27]

As Sir Charles Bell rightly points out, "the old mistake of concluding a treaty with China about Tibet without consulting the Tibetan Government was repeated".[28] And this gave the Government of Tibet a ground for complaint. However, Britain was engaged in the imperialist game of safeguarding its own interests in India and China rather than the legitimate rights of helpless Tibet. Having thus disarmed China so far as its own rights in Tibet were concerned, Britain turned towards Russia and signed an agreement with it on 31 August 1907. This Agreement defined the spheres of influence of Russia and Britain in Persia, Afghanistan, and Tibet. It also recognized explicitly, and for the first time in history, the so-called "suzerainty" of China over Tibet. The Governments of Russia and Britain engaged not to enter into negotiations with Tibet except through the Government of China as an intermediary;[29] agreed neither to seek nor to obtain, whether for themselves or for their subjects, any concessions or other rights in Tibet; and promised to respect the territorial integrity of Tibet and to abstain from all interference in its internal administration. However, the Government of Russia recognized that "Great Britain, by reason of her geographical position, has a special interest in the maintenance of the status quo in the external relations of Tibet".[30]

[26] International Commission of Jurists, *Tibet and the Chinese People's Republic: Final Report of the International Commission of Jurists by Its Legal Inquiry Committee on Tibet* (Delhi, 1966), pp. 145-6. For the contrary view, see Rubin, n. 10, p. 114.

[27] See Ram Gopal, n. 3, p. 14.

[28] Sir Charles Bell, *Tibet: Past and Present* (Oxford, 1924), p. 88.

[29] It is interesting to note that the Russians also agreed in this Agreement not to deal with Afghanistan except through Britain.

[30] For the full text, see Bell, n. 28, pp. 289 ff.

Whatever might be the meaning and import of the term "suzerainty" in this Treaty, it is important to remember that neither Tibet nor China was a party to it and could not, therefore, be held to be bound by its provisions. In any case, Britain strengthened its own position in Tibet through the Anglo-Chinese and Anglo-Russian Conventions of 1906 and 1907, though these Conventions also helped in the revival of Chinese authority in Lhasa. In 1908, another agreement was signed between Britain, China and Tibet. This Agreement, entitled "Tibet Trade Regulations", granted further trade rights and concessions to Britain—Tibet participating only as a Chinese subordinate. Tibet felt further humiliated as a result, and drifted more and more into the Chinese fold, as the British were to realize later.

Dragon Moves Forward

China was not slow to take advantage of the changed circumstances. During the last decade of the Manchu dynasty, China embarked upon a surprisingly energetic policy towards Central Asia in an attempt to revive its previous imperialist position there. Confident that the British interest in Tibet was restricted to trade matters, it organized a military expedition led by Chao Erh-feng to Tibet. The absence of the Dalai Lama from Tibet and the payment by China of the Younghusband indemnity had strengthened its hands.[31] Moreover, Britain had surrendered its right to intervene by accepting Chinese suzerainty over Tibet and could do nothing to stop the Chinese menace.

As we have mentioned already, before the Younghusband expedition reached Lhasa, the Dalai Lama had fled to Mongolia, where he had a number of followers and immense respect and influence. The Government of China thereupon issued a proclamation in Tibet deposing the Dalai Lama. However, "the Tibetans bespattered [it] with manure, continuing to refer, as far as possible, all important matters to him for his orders".[32] The Dalai Lama's hope was that Russia would help him. The signing of the Anglo-Russian Convention of 1907, therefore, came as a great shock for him. Helpless and forlorn, he was looking for something to lean upon, when he received an invitation to visit Peking to meet the Chinese Emperor. He accepted the invitation and reached Peking in September 1908. Explaining the reasons for his Peking visit later, the Dalai Lama said: "I went because the Great Fifth Dalai Lama and the Manchu Emperor had made an agreement to help each other."[33] Whatever might have been the intention and motive of the Chinese Emperor in inviting the Dalai Lama,[34] there was, according to the

[31] Ibid., p. 93. See also *The Question of Tibet and the Rule of Law*, n. 8, p. 83; and Richardson, n. 2, p. 96.

[32] Bell, n. 14, p. 63.

[33] Quoted, ibid., p. 77.

[34] See Willoughby, n. 3, p. 194.

latter, "no subordination in such a relationship; it is the duty of the layman [the Emperor] to help the priest [the Dalai Lama] in all worldly necessities".[35]

But while the Tibetan God-King was in China, the Chinese troops were pushing towards Lhasa, ruthlessly destroying Tibetan monasteries, killing innocent priests, and tearing up their sacred books and images on the way. Owing to the long absence of the Dalai Lama, the Government of Tibet was disorganized; there was no effective opposition. In December 1909, the Dalai Lama arrived in Lhasa after five years' exile. Within two months the blow fell. Chao Erh-feng with two thousand soldiers arrived within striking distance of Lhasa, and it was not long before an advance guard of the Chinese mounted troops burst into the city. The Dalai Lama had to fly again for his life, this time to his erstwhile foes, the British in India, where he received asylum.

The Government of China again issued a proclamation deposing the Dalai Lama, as it had done earlier in the wake of the Younghusband expedition.[36] But, as Bell says, "the Tibetans paid no attention to this beyond bespattering it with mud".[37] However, the Government of China informed the British Government that "they had no intention of altering the administration of Tibet, still less of converting it into a province of China", which, they admitted, "would be a contravention of treaties".[38] It was not long before both these promises were broken, and a Chinese *Amban*, with over three thousand Chinese soldiers under his command in Lhasa and Central Tibet, took all power into his hands, reducing the Tibetan Government to insignificance. Although the British administrative officers in India strongly felt that "for the security of her northern frontier, India needs a Tibet that is as independent and strong as possible",[39] the British Government had tied its own hands by the Treaties of 1906, 1907, and 1908 and "had deprived itself of the means of enforcing its rights in Tibet and of making Tibet a bulwark for the Indian frontier".[40] It, therefore, decided to remain neutral in the struggle between China and Tibet and abandon Tibet to the tender mercies of China. Encouraged by the neutrality of the British Government, China claimed, about the end of 1910, that it had not merely *suzerainty* but also *sovereignty* over Tibet. It also claimed Nepal and Bhutan as its feudatories.[41]

But Chinese authority did not survive long. Towards the end of 1911, there was a revolution in China. The Manchu Emperor was deposed, and every vestige of Manchu rule swept away. The Chinese troops in Tibet mutinied and killed their own officers, including the Commander, Chao Erh-

[35] Bell, n. 14, p. 77.

[36] Willoughby, n. 3, p. 195.

[37] Bell, n. 14, p. 97.

[38] Idem, n. 28, p. 112.

[39] Idem, n. 14, p. 98.

[40] Idem, n. 28, p. 113; and Richardson, n. 2, p. 101.

[41] Bell, n. 28, p. 114.

feng. The Tibetans besieged the *Amban* and the few troops he had, and they were all unceremoniously expelled from Tibet. By June 1912, the Chinese had lost all power in Central Tibet, and the Dalai Lama returned home after an exile of two years. By August 1912, both Western Tibet and Central Tibet came under his sway, and an agreement was reached by which all Chinese in Tibet gave up their arms and left for China via India.[42]

Independent Tibet

Tibet now left no one in doubt that it meant to preserve its independence. A few months after the Dalai Lama's arrival in Lhasa, Yuan Shih-kai, the President of the Chinese Republic, telegraphed to him, apologizing for the excesses of the Chinese troops, and restoring the Dalai Lama to his former rank. The Dalai Lama replied that he was not asking the Chinese Government for any rank, and that he intended to exercise both temporal and ecclesiastical rule in Tibet. He thus made his declaration of Tibetan independence, indeed if such a formal declaration was necessary.[43]

Thus began a period of complete independence for Tibet. Tibet held that its political connexion had been with the Manchu Emperors. This connexion having snapped, it had nothing more to do with China.[44] Numerous independent observers admit, and no one denies, that China at this time exercised no authority in Tibet. Having told the Chinese President that he would rule over Tibet himself, the Dalai Lama proceeded to establish his rule firmly. He forbade Chinese soldiers and Chinese officials to enter a large part of Tibet which was under his control. "That portion of Tibet", says Bell, "became a completely independent kingdom, and remained independent during the last twenty years of his life."[45] As Hugh Richardson, who represented first the British and later Independent India in Lhasa, points out: "When the Manchu dynasty collapsed in 1911, Tibet completely severed that link, and, until the Communist invasion in 1950, enjoyed full *de facto* independence from Chinese control".[46]

Riencourt also asserts: "And from 1911 to 1950, Tibet ruled itself in all respects as an independent nation."[47] Purshottam Trikamdas in his report on Tibet submitted to the International Commission of Jurists testified: "From 1912 to 1950 Tibet was virtually an independent country. No Chinese writ ran in Tibet; there was no Chinese law, no Chinese newspaper, no Chinese

[42] Aitchison n. 6, p. 20; and Willoughby, n. 3, p. 194.

[43] Bell, n. 14, p. 135; and Richardson, n. 2, p. 105. But cf. Rubin, n. 10, p. 122; and idem, "A Matter of Fact", *American Journal of International Law* (Washington, D. C.), vol. 59 (1965), pp. 586 ff.

[44] Bell, n. 28, p. 213.

[45] Idem, n. 14, p. 391. Dalai Lama XIII died in December 1933.

[46] Hugh E. Richardson, *Red Star over Tibet* (Delhi, 1959), p. 8.

[47] Riencourt, n. 5, p. 5.

soldiers and even no representative of the Chinese government."[48]

Even the British Government, which started the fallacy of Chinese suzerainty in Tibet in 1907, admitted in an official memorandum to the Chinese Government in 1943: "Since the Chinese Revolution of 1911, when Chinese forces were withdrawn from Tibet, Tibet has enjoyed de facto independence. She has ever since regarded herself as in practice completely autonomous and has opposed Chinese attempts to reassert control."[49]

Chinese Suzerainty?

In order to understand and appreciate the international status of Tibet, it is important to evaluate the so-called Chinese suzerainty over Tibet. Because of the juristic imprecision of the term *suzerainty*, it is generally admitted that each case of suzerain-vassal relationship has to be examined on its merits. As Professor John Bassett Moore declares: "The extent of the authority or subordination comprehended by this term [suzerainty] is not determined by general rules, but by the facts of the particular case."[50] It is well known, however, that "suzerainty was originally an institution of feudal law and was used to describe the particular relationship between the feudal lord and his vassal".[51] As Alexandrowicz-Alexander explains: "The latter owed its allegiance to the suzerain ruler, he had to pay him tribute, give him his military support and was entitled to his protection."[52] With the disappearance of feudalism, this kind of suzerainty, which was determined by the constitutional law of the suzerain state, disappeared completely. Suzerainty during the nineteenth and twentieth centuries is a kind of international guardianship. The vassal state of this period is deprived of external sovereignty, but it retains internal sovereignty, which the suzerain state is under a duty to respect. However, stripped of external sovereignty, the vassal state has no position of its own in the family of nations. It is merely a part of the suzerain state which represents it entirely in its relations with other states. "In principle all treaties concluded by the suzerain state are *ipso facto* binding on the vassal; the latter is automatically party to a war in which the suzerain is engaged, and the suzerain state is externally responsible for all

[48] See quoted in Hutheesing, n. 5, p. 15.

[49] See Memorandum of 5 August 1943, Under Secretary of State for Foreign Affairs, Mayhew, to the Chinese Government. Quoted in Marjorie M. Whiteman, *Digest of International Law* (Washington, D.C., 1963), vol. 1, p. 464. See also Willoughby, n. 3, p. 198.

[50] John Bassett Moore, *A Digest of International Law* (Washington, D. C., 1906), vol. 1, p. 27. See also Charles Henry Alexandrowicz-Alexander, "The Legal Position of Tibet", *American Journal of International Law*, vol. 48 (1954), pp. 265 ff; and C. C. Hyde, *International Law* (Boston, Mass., 1957), edn. 2, vol. 1, pp. 48 ff.

[51] Alexandrowicz-Alexander, n. 50, p. 265.

[52] Ibid., pp. 265-6.

actions of the vassal."[53] This position of the vassal state, with minor variations, is generally accepted by international lawyers.[54] It must be mentioned, however, that not infrequently suzerainty, though still based on a historical relationship, becomes just nominal by the increasing participation of a vassal state in international relations as a prelude to its final independence.[55]

Looking at the Sino-Tibetan relations in historical perspective, it is abundantly clear that till the end of the seventeenth century, the relations between the two nations were based on equality and mutual independence. Dalai Lama V visited Peking in 1652 as an independent monarch. Of those old days, Bell writes:

> In the old days Tibet and China waged war with each other on fairly equal terms. Once at least China seized the Tibetan capital: once at least Tibet captured the capital of China. During the seventh and eighth centuries of the Christian era, neither China nor India escaped invasion by the Tibetans, though their lack of organization and culture, combined with their inability to live in hot climates, prevented the latter from holding their gains.[56]

It was only in the second decade of the eighteenth century that the early Manchu Emperors of China were able to establish a considerable measure of control over Tibet. China gave military aid to Tibet to resist the Gorkha invasion of 1791, and thus strengthened its position in Tibet. As a temporal ruler the Dalai Lama became subject to the authority of the Manchu Emperors. He recognized their overlordship in the political, military, and financial fields, and paid them tribute every three years. "This suzerainty", Professor Alexandrowicz-Alexander rightly emphasizes, "was obviously one of Chinese feudal law."[57] To preserve their authority in Tibet, the Manchu Emperors maintained their permanent representatives (*Ambans*) in Lhasa, who exercised all rights of external sovereignty, and even interfered in the internal affairs of Tibet. During all this period, almost till the end of the nineteenth century, Tibet was entirely outside the family of nations. But so was China before the middle of the nineteenth century: it emerged as a fully sovereign state only after the First World War.[58]

It must be said that Tibet's link with Manchu China could not be described strictly in Western terms. As Richardson points out: "Tibet was a sort of Papal state under the protection of the Chinese Emperor, whose supremacy

[53] Ibid., p. 266.

[54] See W. E. Hall, *International Law* (Oxford, 1917), p. 29; Hyde, n. 50, pp. 48 ff; and L. Oppenheim, *International Law*, Hersch Lauterpacht, ed. (London, 1955), edn. 8, vol. 1, pp. 190-1.

[55] For instances of the participation by vassal states in international relations before their Independence, see Oppenheim, ibid.

[56] Bell, n. 28, p. 208.

[57] Alexandrowicz-Alexander, n. 50, p. 267.

[58] Ibid., p. 268.

was acknowledged and with whom there was an indefinable mystico-political bond."[59] According to the Tibetans, the Dalai Lama was the spiritual guide and the Manchu Emperor his lay supporter. "It is the duty of the layman to help his priest in all ways possible, but the priest does not on that account become the layman's servant."[60] Whatever help China might have rendered to Tibet, the Tibetans explain, it was rendered in that capacity and did not in any sense put Tibet under China. There was never any treaty, they point out, by which Tibet recognized that China was its overlord.[61] If Tibet had been under China, they argue, the latter would have defended its dependency whenever foreign nations attacked it. They point out that the war against Kashmir in 1841, the war against Nepal in 1855, the wars against Britain in 1888 and 1904, and the ancient wars between Tibet and Bhutan were all fought and settled by the Tibetans themselves. They assert that even if Tibet had at any time been subordinate to China, the latter had, by failing to give Tibet assistance on so many occasions in defending itself, failed to keep its part of the bargain and could not expect Tibet to continue to regard itself as a vassal of China.[62]

In any case, the fact is that with the gradual decline of the Chinese power in Tibet, China's so-called suzerainty became increasingly nominal. By 1904, the British signed a bilateral agreement with Tibet, thus according an implied recognition to the latter as an independent nation. China was, of course, not happy with this situation. It wanted to keep Tibet under its control, not only for its own sake but also because of the growing influence of the Dalai Lama as a spiritual authority over the Buddhist communities outside Tibet—in Mongolia, Nepal, Bhutan, Sikkim, and India. In order to make China happy and friendly the British later thought it expedient to recognize China's authority over Tibet; this was a "convenient arrangement" for them not only because they would then have only one authority to deal with, but also because they would be able to exploit successfully "the vast potentialities of trade with China".[63] They also hoped to prevent Russia from spreading its influence in Tibet and posing a danger to their interests in India.[64] Chinese suzerainty was, therefore, sought to be revived by the Anglo-Chinese Conventions of 1906 and 1908 and the Anglo-Russian Treaty of 1907.[65] It was—as even the British imperialist agent, Charles Bell, later admitted—

[59] Richardson, n. 46, p. 8. Also idem, n. 2, p. 103. vol. 10, no. 4.

[60] See Bell, n. 14, p. 356; and David Howarth, ed., *My Land and My People: The Autobiography of His Holiness the Dalai Lama* (Bombay, 1962), pp. 65-66.

[61] Bell, n. 14.

[62] Ibid.

[63] See Alexandrowicz-Alexander, n. 50, p. 268.

[64] See Bell, n. 14, pp. 352-3.

[65] For the contrary view, see Tieh-Tseng Li, "The Position of Tibet", *American Journal of International Law*, vol. 50 (1965), p. 395.

nothing short of "an outrage that they [the British] should sell Tibet in order to increase their own commercial profits in China".[66]

But even the British support for China's suzerainty over Tibet did not succeed in reviving it. In 1911, there was a revolution in China which ended Manchu rule in China and established a republic. And with the end of Manchu rule, the personal allegiance of the Dalai Lama to the Manchu Emperor, as the Tibetans understood it, also came to an end. The last of the sentimental and religious bonds that Tibet had with China was snapped. The exchange of presents with the Government of China was discontinued. All Chinese representatives and garrisons stationed in Tibet were expelled from the country. Tibet declared its complete independence, and "thereafter depended entirely on its isolation, on its faith in the wisdom of Buddha, and occasionally on the support of the British in India for its protection".[67] Says Alexandrowicz-Alexander: "It is difficult to consider Tibet now otherwise than in her initial stage of independence."[68] The International Commission of Jurists in its preliminary report correctly declared: ". . . the events of 1911-12 mark the re-emergence of Tibet as a fully sovereign state, independent in fact and in law of Chinese control."[69]

Simla Conference

China, however, gave up neither its hope nor its intention of bringing Tibet back to its control. As soon as things settled down after a period of turmoil following the Revolution of 1911, the President of the Republic of China, Yuan Shih-kai, proclaimed, on 12 April 1912, that Tibet would thenceforth be treated as a Province of China.[70] He also dispatched troops to Tibet to restore the Chinese position there. The Tibetans stood their ground and repulsed the Chinese attack with whatever force they were able to muster. Although the British recognized China's suzerainty over Tibet, they disapproved of the Chinese move, which, they felt, threatened the peace of their Indian Empire. In a Memorandum addressed to China on 17 August 1912, they said that they did not recognize China's sovereignty over Tibet, and declared that China was no more than a suzerain. They conceded China's right to station a representative in Lhasa, but said that they would not agree to the stationing of an unlimited number of troops in Tibet. They took exception to China's interference in Tibet during the past three years, and warned that unless China behaved in a manner consistent with the British

[66] Bell, n. 14, p. 353.

[67] See the text of the cablegram sent by the Tibetan Kashag to the United Nations on 11 November 1950 in *Tibet in the United Nations 1950-1961* (Issued by the Bureau of His Holiness the Dalai Lama) (New Delhi, 1965), p. 2.

[68] Alexandrowicz-Alexander, n. 50, p. 270.

[69] *The Question of Tibet and the Rule of Law*, n. 8.

[70] Tieh-Tseng Li, n. 65, p. 397.

position, they would not recognize the new Chinese Republic and would forbid the entry of the Chinese into Tibet via India.[71] They also demanded a written agreement on the foregoing lines. China at first refused to comply, and fighting continued between Tibet and China. Later on, recognizing the strength of the Tibetan position, China agreed to a tripartite conference between China, Britain, and Tibet to settle the status of Tibet. Invitations for this conference had already been issued by the British in May 1913. It is significant to note that China agreed not only to the conference being held at Simla in India, a neutral country friendly to both the other parties, but also to the presence of a Tibetan Plenipotentiary *on an equal footing* with the Plenipotentiaries of China and Britain. According to Bell: "It was clear that. unless a Tibetan Representative attended, Tibet, as in the past, would refuse to recognize any resulting Agreement, and that, if the negotiations were conducted in Peking, the Tibetan Representative would be overawed."[72]

Plenipotentiaries of the three Powers met at Simla in October 1913. After several months of protracted negotiations, an agreement was reached and a convention initialled by the three Plenipotentiaries on 27 Aril 1914. Under the terms of this Agreement Tibet was to be divided into two parts, Outer Tibet and Inner Tibet. the former was the part nearer India, including Lhasa; the latter was the more remote part nearer China. Chinese suzerainty over the whole of Tibet was to be recognized in return for the Chinese undertaking not to convert Tibet into a Chinese Province. Outer Tibet was to be recognized as fully autonomous, and no Chinese interference was to be permitted. The Government of Tibet was to retain the administration of Inner Tibet as well, but the Chinese were to be allowed to maintain their own communities and to protect them by their own officials. The Chinese representative was to be re-established in Lhasa with a military escort limited to three hundred men. The British trade agents were also to be allowed to stay in Tibet with a limited escort.[73]

This was quite a gain for China, but as it was not satisfied with the boundaries between Outer Tibet and Inner Tibet as laid down in the Treaty, China repudiated the action of its Plenipotentiary and refused to sign the Convention.[74] In the changed situation, the Plenipotentiaries of Great Britain and Tibet signed the Convention on 3 July 1914, with an express declaration that "so long as the Government of China withholds signature to the aforesaid Convention, she will be debarred from the enjoyment of all privileges accruing therefrom".[75]

[71] *Tibet and the Chinese People's Republic*, n. 26, pp. 139 and 318; and Bell, n. 28, p. 149.

[72] Bell, n. 28, p. 150; and Richardson, n. 2, pp. 107 ff.

[73] See Bell, n. 28, pp. 154-5.

[74] Ibid., p. 157.

[75] See quoted in *Tibet and the Chinese People's Republic*, n. 26, p. 140.

It is thus clear that while Britain, in order to secure peace on its Indian frontier, persuaded Tibet to agree to Chinese suzerainty,[76] China, by refusing to accept the Convention, missed the chance thus afforded to it to get its suzerainty acknowledged internationally. D. K. Sen, therefore, correctly points out that "the Convention in no way prejudiced the position of complete independence which Tibet had attained after the outbreak of the Chinese revolution".[77] Professor Alexandrowicz-Alexander also asserts: "China did not become a party to the agreement from which she withdrew and could not therefore claim rights of suzerainty on its basis."[78] The International Commission of Jurists concludes its report:

> The Chinese refusal to sign the Convention meant quite simply that Great Britain and Tibet agreed to withhold the recognition of suzerainty, and with it the understanding that Tibet was part of Chinese territory. *Vis-a-vis* Tibet, China was thus faced with a reversion to the status quo, namely the proclamation of Tibet's independence in 1912 by the thirteenth Dalai Lama, with the expulsion of the Chinese from Tibet in the same year.[79]

Indeed Tibet's claim of independence was considerably strengthened by the Simla Conference, for Tibet participated in this Conference on an equal footing with China and Britain, and by the Simla Convention, which it concluded with Britain as an independent and sovereign state.[80] Tibet's claim was further strengthened by another agreement that it concluded with Britain in respect of trade regulations for Outer Tibet in consequence of the cancellation by the Simla Convention of the trade regulations which had been established under the Anglo-Chinese Conventions of 1893 and 1908 and which the Tibetans were no longer prepared to accept on the ground that they were not a party to them.[81] In fact, after 1914, until the end of British rule in India in 1947, the British always dealt directly and exclusively with the Government of Tibet in respect of their mutual interests.[82] British diplomacy, however, kept up the myth of Chinese suzerainty. In 1921, for instance, the British informed the Chinese officially that they recognized the status of Tibet "as an autonomous state under the suzerainty of China".[83]

[76] It is interesting to note that seven years after the Simla Conference, the Dalai Lama wanted to know from the British representative in Tibet the real reason for the proposed division of his country into two parts. See Bell, n. 14, p. 206.

[77] Quoted in *Tibet and the Chinese People's Republic*, n. 26, p. 141.

[78] Alexandrowicz-Alexander, n. 50, p. 276; and Richardson, n. 2, pp. 114-16.

[79] *Tibet and the Chinese People's Republic*, n. 26, pp. 140-1. For an opposite view challenging the validity of the Simla Convention, see Tieh-Tseng Li, n. 65, pp. 400-1.

[80] For the contrary view, see Rubin, n. 10, p. 127; and idem, n. 43, pp. 587-8.

[81] See Bell, n. 14, p. 206.

[82] *Tibet and the Chinese People's Republic*, n. 26, p. 142.

[83] See Rubin, n. 10, p. 130.

Again, in response to an inquiry by the Government of China on the status of Tibet, the British Under Secretary of State for Foreign Affairs said on 5 August 1943:

> They [the British] have always been prepared to recognize Chinese suzerainty over Tibet but only on the understanding that Tibet is regarded as autonomous. Neither the British Government nor the Government of India have any territorial ambitions in Tibet but they are interested in the maintenance of friendly relations with, and the preservation of peaceful conditions in, an area which is coterminous with the North-East frontiers of India. They would welcome any amicable arrangements which the Chinese Government might be disposed to make with Tibet whereby the latter recognized Chinese suzerainty in return for an agreed frontier and an undertaking to recognize Tibetan autonomy and they would gladly offer any help desired by both parties to this end.[84]

It is probable that the Britain expected to use Chinese "suzerainty" as a vague threat to frighten Lhasa into being solicitous of British interests in Tibet. According to Rubin:

> With a weak Tibet potentially under British influence, and China given an empty classification of "suzerain" no longer linked to any particular powers, although with the implication of Tibetan external affairs remaining in Chinese hands, both the political objective of an impotent neighbour to the north of India, and the commercial objective of unobstructed trade, could be expected to be fulfilled. The British apparently felt that no question of principle was involved.[85]

In considering British policy, further, we must take due note of the continued Russian presence and influence in the Tibetan-Mongolian area. On 21 October 1912, Russia signed an agreement with Mongolia, converting a large part of what had for long centuries been Chinese territory into a virtual protectorate.[86] On 5 November 1913, it signed another agreement with China and recognized Outer Mongolia as being under Chinese suzerainty.[87] It thus seems to have been convenient both for Britain and for Russia to support the empty legal title of China in their efforts to establish their influence in this area.[88]

There is little doubt, however, that the so-called Chinese suzerainty over Tibet was after 1912 nothing more than a ghost elusive to grasp. International lawyers may well disregard this meaningless term in the context of Tibet, for it has no factual basis whatsoever. As Professor Alexadrowicz-Alexander rightly asserts, in case of "discrepancy between *de facto* arrangements and

[84] See Whiteman, n. 49, p. 465.
[85] Rubin, n. 10, p. 120.
[86] See Bell, n. 28, Appendix 12, p. 298.
[87] Ibid., Appendix 14, p. 305.
[88] See Alexandrowicz-Alexander, n. 50, p. 272.

legal title, the first, which, after all, matter most, call for legal reformulation by international lawyers".[89]

Tibet had become independent, and it continued to behave and conduct its relations with other states on that basis. In January 1913 it entered into a treaty with Mongolia. The two countries by this Treaty recognized each other's sovereignty and independence of China.[90] In 1926 the representatives of the Government of Tibet met the representatives of the British Government and of the Princely Indian State of Tehri to discuss the boundary between Tehri and Tibet.[91] It is also generally admitted that Tibet was never a party to any military conflict during the two world wars or in the inter-war period, although China was continually engaged during all this time as a belligerent.[92]

China's Futile Attempts to Regain Control

All this does not, however, mean that China gave up for good its aspirations in Tibet. Fighting between Chinese and Tibetan forces continued after the Simla Conference, despite temporary cease-fires and occasional negotiations. In 1917, the Tibetans inflicted a crushing defeat on the Chinese forces. By the end of 1918, the Government of Tibet was in control of territory beyond the traditional Sino-Tibetan border.[93] In 1919, the victorious Tibetans rebuffed Chinese overtures for negotiations. In January 1920, a Chinese Mission arrived in Lhasa, with the reluctant permission of the Government of Tibet, but failed to reach any agreement.[94] The Chinese are said to have been subjected to indignities during their short stay of four-and-a-half months in Lhasa.[95]

In 1928, the Kuomintang Government in China sent a Mission to Lhasa to invite Tibet to join the Chinese Republic,[96] but failed to convince Tibet of the advantages of acceding. Nevertheless, in 1931, the Government of China declared Tibet to be a part of China.[97] But such a unilateral declaration,

[89] Ibid. See also idem, "Comment on the 'Legal' Position of Tibet", *Indian Year Book of International Affairs* (Madras), 1956, pp. 172 ff.

[90] For a text of the Treaty, see Bell, n. 28, Appendix 13, p. 304. Doubts have been expressed not only about the authority of the one who negotiated on behalf of Tibet, Agvan Dorjiev, who was a Russian Buryat, to enter into such a treaty but also about the existence of the Treaty itself. Ibid., pp. 151 and 228-30; and Rubin, n. 10, p. 123. However, in 1960 the present Dalai Lama asserted that this Treaty was entered into under the authority of his predecessor. See Howarth, n. 60, p. 240.

[91] Howarth, ibid., p. 240; and Rubin, n. 10, p. 130.

[92] Alexandrowicz-Alexander, n. 50, p. 272.

[93] *The Question of Tibet and the Rule of Law*, n. 8, p. 87.

[94] Ibid.

[95] Bell, n. 14, p. 231.

[96] See *Tibet and the Chinese People's Republic*, n. 26, p. 145.

[97] Ibid.

unsupported by facts, had obviously no legal significance.[98] When the Chinese Government once again attempted to exercise control in a part of Tibet in 1931-32, it was strongly resisted, and the Chinese forces were obliged to withdraw.[99]

In December 1933, Dalai Lama XIII died in Lhasa. A Mission was sent by China in 1934 "to convey condolences and restore official relations" with Tibet. This Mission managed to stay on in Tibet and established its permanent headquarters in Lhasa. But there is no evidence that the Mission had any official status or effective part in the Government of Tibet.[100] In fact, soon after, Britain also sent a representative to Lhasa, and in 1936 it established a permanent Mission there. Nepal followed suit, and even the Maharaja of Bhutan sent his agent. Thus Tibet was in direct communication with most of its immediate neighbours during this period.[101]

The Chinese representatives in Tibet usually preferred to travel to Tibet through India, and not overland directly from China. It is important to note that the British authorities always granted or refused transit visas to them according to the wishes of the Government of Tibet.[102] It is also important to note that the permission of the Government of China was never sought by the nationals of Britain or the nationals of any other European state visiting Tibet between 1920 and 1950, while there are numerous documented instances when the permission of the Government of Tibet was felt to be essential.[103] All this shows that in practice the Government of Tibet was master of its own external affairs and did not need to make any reference to China.

China's Pretensions

In 1938, the fourteenth incarnation of the Dalai Lama was "discovered" in the Chinese Province of Chinghai. According to the Chinese claim, Wu Chunghsin, the Chinese envoy, presided over his installation in 1940.[104] Howsoever, insignificant this fact might be to prove Chinese authority in Tibet, there is little doubt that the story is a fabrication as the testimony of several writers, including some eye witnesses, clearly proves.[105]

[98] Alexandrowicz-Alexander, n. 50, p. 273.

[99] Ibid. Also see *The Question of Tibet and the Rule of Law*, n. 8, p. 88.

[100] Rubin, n. 10, p. 131.

[101] Ibid., p. 132.

[102] *Tibet and the Chinese People's Republic*, n. 26, p. 147.

[103] Rubin, n. 10, p. 133.

[104] See Tieh-Tseng Li, *Tibet: Today and Yesterday* (New York, N. Y., 1960), pp. 178-84; idem, n. 65, p. 397; and *Concerning the Question of Tibet* (Peking, 1959), p. 195.

[105] Bell, n. 14, pp. 399-400; Sir Basil John Gould, *Jewel in the Lotus: Recollections of an Indian Political Observer* (London, 1957), p. 234; Richardson, quoted in *Tibet and the Chinese People's Republic*, n. 26, p. 146; Howarth, n. 60, pp. 33 ff.; and Richardson, n. 2, p. 154.

During the Second World War, the question of Tibet's independence arose when supply lines for transporting war material from India to China via Tibet were being considered by Britain, the United States, and China. Owing to its fear of Chinese penetration and its reluctance to get involved in the war against Japan, Tibet refused permission to establish a supply route across its territory.[106] It is important to note that Tibet did not regard the fact of the whole of China being at war as significant to its status and that it actually prevented a Chinese attempt to send a survey party into Tibet.[107] On 7 August 1942, the Head of the Far Eastern Department of the British Foreign Office wrote to the Counsellor of the American Embassy in London:

> In point of fact the Tibetans not only claim to be but actually are an independent people, and they have in recent years fought successfully to maintain their freedom against Chinese attempts at domination. Their distinct racial, political, religious and linguistic characteristics would seem to entitle them, therefore, to benefits of...the memorandum. . . .[108]

In a letter dated 15 February 1943 to President Franklin Delano Roosevelt of the United States on the subject of the Allies being allowed to establish a supply route, the Tibetan Regent wrote that Tibet "*has been free and independent from her earliest history*".[109]

This assertion, however, did not pass unchallenged, for China reasserted its claim that Tibet was a part of China.[110] The Government of Britain, while reiterating its view that Tibet was under the suzerainty of China, stressed that it was under no obligation to continue to recognize Chinese suzerainty "unless she [China] in turn agrees to Tibetan autonomy". It declared:

> If the Chinese Government contemplate, the withdrawal of Tibetan autonomy, His Majesty's Government and the Government of India must ask themselves whether in the changed circumstances of today it would be right for them to continue to recognize *even a theoretical subservience for a people who desire to be free and have, in fact, maintained their freedom for more than thirty years*.[111]

Although convinced of Tibet's autonomy, it added: "Great Britain's alliance with China makes it difficult [for it] to give effective material support to Tibet."[112]

[106] US Department of State, *Foreign Relation of the United States: Diplomatic Papers: 1942: China* (Washington, D. C., 1956), p. 626.

[107] Richardson, n. 2, p. 159.

[108] *China, 1942*, n. 106, p. 145. Quoted in *The Question of Tibet and the Rule of Law*, n. 8, p. 89.

[109] US Department of State, *Foreign Relations of the United States: Diplomatic Papers: 1943: China* (Washington, D.C., 1957), p. 622. Emphasis added.

[110] Ibid., pp. 626-7, 634, and 642.

[111] Ibid., p. 636. Emphasis added.

[112] Ibid., p. 635.

In an effort not to offend Chinese susceptibilities, which were said to be important in connexion with the war effort, the Government of the United States successfully avoided taking any positive stand on the matter.[113] It said that no "useful purpose would be served by opening at this time a detailed discussion of the status of Tibet".[114] It was, however, not unaware of the Chinese weakness and recognized the *de facto* existence of the Government of Tibet and its neutrality.[115]

It was not without a lot of British pressure that the Government of Tibet ultimately agreed to the transportation through its territory of non-military supplies for China on the condition that "(1) no military supplies of any sort be thus transported; and (2) no foreign supervision of shipments while in Tibet would be permitted".[116] It specifically refused to allow Chinese officials into the country and declined to have direct dealings with the Government of China without British participation.[117]

There were reports in 1943 that China was getting ready to occupy Tibet. The Chinese anxiety to occupy Tibet was perhaps due to a feeling that the British and American acquiescence in the refusal by the Government of Tibet to open a supply line through its territory except on its own terms amounted to implied recognition of Tibet's independence.[118] However, the invasion, if ever actually contemplated by China, was never launched.[119]

Tibet came out of the Second World War unscathed. But while the Yalta Agreement between the Allied Powers recognized the independence of Outer Mongolia under pressure from Joseph V. Stalin, Tibet's status was left undefined. Tibet failed to get such a formal recognition of its independence in spite of its being independent for all practical purposes because it did not have the patronage of a Great Power like the Soviet Union to press its claim on its behalf. However, Tibetan independence was an accomplished fact. In order to assuage Tibetan feelings, Chiang Kai-shek made a statement on 25 August 1945 that "if and when" the Tibetans reached the stage of complete independence in political and economic matters, China would adopt the same attitude with regard to it as it did about Outer Mongolia, and would support the "independence" of Tibet.[120]

But despite the continued resistance of the Government of Tibet and its repeated rebuffs to China's attempts to assert its authority in Lhasa, China continued to view Tibet as a part of itself. It misconstrued every move on the part of the Government of Tibet as lending support to this view. Thus, it

[113] Ibid., pp. 629 and 630.
[114] Ibid., p. 630; and *The Question of Tibet and the Rule of Law*, n. 8, pp. 90-91.
[115] See Richardson, n. 2, p. 164.
[116] See *China*, 1943, n. 109, pp. 629-30.
[117] Richardson, n. 2, p. 161.
[118] Ibid., pp. 161-2; and *China*, 1943, n. 109, pp. 632 ff.
[119] Richardson, n. 2, p. 162; and Rubin, n. 10, p. 134.
[120] Tieh-Tseng Li, n. 65, pp. 397-8.

treated the goodwill mission sent by the Government of Tibet after the war in 1946 as Tibet's delegation to the Chinese Constituent Assembly which drafted the Republican Constitution in 1946. It claimed that the Tibetans also participated in the Chinese National Assembly in 1948. Similarly, it described the congratulatory message sent by the Government of Tibet to Chiang Kai-shek on his assumption of office as President of the Chinese Republic as a message of loyalty and submission. These Chinese tactics were not dissimilar to the diplomatic technique of the Chinese Emperors of old, who treated all communications received by them from the Pope and other European sovereigns as evidence of their vassalage and submission.[121] They are good examples of what has been described as "the infinite Chinese capacity for misrepresentation". There is no evidence that the Tibetan delegation had any other business or authority but to offer greetings to the Government of China on its victory in the war. The members of the delegation attended the session of the Chinese National Assembly in 1946 and 1948 merely as "observers". They did not recognize or sign the new Constitution of China.[122]

In any case, in the Chinese Constitution of 1 January 1947, Tibet was declared a self-governing Province of the Republic of China. This, however, could not, and did not, change of factual position or the legal status of Tibet, which continued to play its limited but independent role in international affairs. In March 1947, a few months before the Independence of India, Tibet sent a delegation to represent it as an independent country in the Asian Relations Conference held in New Delhi, where, along with the national flags of the other independent countries participating in the Conference, the national flag of Tibet was flown.[123] In 1948, a Tibetan delegation, led by the Finance Minister, visited Britain, France, India, Italy, and the United States, with travel documents issued by the Government of Tibet and accepted by the host countries as sufficient.[124] The protest of China in the matter were just ignored.[125] In July 1949, on the eve of the collapse of the Nationalist Government of China, the Government of Tibet expelled all Chinese representatives in its country in an effort to make clear that China had no rights over Tibet, and a public declaration was made of Tibet's neutrality in the Chinese Civil war.[126]

[121] See *The International Position of Tibet* (New Delhi, 1959), p. 29; and D. K. Sen, "China, Tibet and India", *India Quarterly* (New Delhi), vol. 7 (1951), p. 113.

[122] See *The Question of Tibet and the Rule of Law*, n. 8, p. 93; *Tibet and the Chinese People's Republic*, n. 26, p. 148; and Rubin, n. 10, p. 135.

[123] Purshottam Trikamdas in *Tibet in the United Nations, 1950-1961*, n. 67, p. viii; Richardson, n. 2, p. 168; and Rubin, n. 10, p. 135 (n.).

[124] See Richardson, n. 2, p. 177.

[125] See *The Question of Tibet and the Rule of Law*, n. 8, p. 93; *Tibet and the Chinese People's Republic*, n. 26, p. 157; and Peter Calvocoressi, *Survey of International Affairs 1949-50* (London, 1953), p. 369.

[126] *Tibet and the Chinese People's Republic*, n. 26, p. 160.

Independence of Tibet in 1950

Tibet's feeling at this time was undoubtedly one of independence. It was reported late in 1949 that the Dalai Lama, having rid his capital of the Chinese Nationalist Mission, proposed to strengthen his position as an independent ruler by appointing his own Ambassadors in Britain, China, India, Nepal, and the United States. The Chinese Communists, however, who had in the meantime captured power in China, established a provisional Government of Tibet in Chinghai and issued a notification that the Dalai Lama had no right to dispatch independent Missions abroad and that the reception of any such Mission by a country would be an act hostile to China.[127]

As we have seen, throughout the period between 1912, when Tibet declared itself independent, and 1950, when Communist China invaded the hermit country, China only asserted its claim but never exerted its authority in Tibet. The Chinese pretensions, however, could not change the facts or their legal effect. Although Britain did not formally recognize Tibet as a state, it dealt with Tibet after 1912 as with an independent state. One really wonders if *de facto* independence asserted progressively, and more and more openly, over a period of nearly forty years, and asserted, especially during the last decade, in such a way as to defy completely a status of subordination, is not sufficient to establish a right of independence under international law. According to a well-established doctrine of international law, lack of recognition cannot be used as an argument against the factual existence of a state and its rights of independence and territorial integrity.[128] It is generally admitted that states do exist irrespective of recognition. There is a strong school of thought which believes that recognition is merely declaratory, and not constitutive, of statehood. Once an entity has got the necessary ingredients of statehood, it has an "international legal personality" which may or may not be recognized immediately by other states for political reasons.[129] No one can seriously deny or doubt the existence of a more or less defined territory of Tibet from 1912 to 1950 and a more or less stable population in the habit of obedience to the Government of Lhasa, which exercised during this period all the powers of a sovereign authority in internal as well as external matters without any subordination to any other authority or Power. It is strongly believed that a state, if it exists in fact, must exist in law.[130] To say that a state may exist in fact but not in law would be a contradiction in terms and would create an intolerable legal vacuum within the borders of

[127] See Calvocoressi, n. 125, pp. 369-70.

[128] Cf. Ti-Chiang Chen, n. 22, p. 33; and Lauterpacht, n. 25, pp. 38 ff.

[129] Ti-Chiang Chen, n. 22, pp. 30 ff.

[130] See L. Oppenheim, *International Law* (London, 1937), edn. 5, vol. 1, p. 120; idem, n. 54, pp. 125 ff; Hans J. Kelsen, "Recognition in International Law: Theoretical Observation", *American Journal of International Law*, vol. 35 (1941), p. 605.

that state,[131] as Ti-Chiang Chen has persuasively shown. Sir Hersch Lauterpacht goes to the extent of maintaining that there is a duty to recognize a state if "it fulfils the conditions of statehood as required by international law".[132] Hall also says that "no state has a right to withhold recognition when it has been earned".[133] But whether recognition is a matter of duty or policy,[134] it certainly does not create the personality of a state.[135] Nor, it is submitted, can non-recognition of a full-grown state amount to a negation of its personality in the eyes of international law.

Tibet had certainly become a full-fledged state by 1950. The absence of explicit recognition by third states cannot be used as an argument against its existence. There was no explicit recognition by third states because there was no opportunity for recognition, thanks to Tibet's policy of conscious isolation, a policy that was encouraged by Britain.[136] The British view remained characteristically ambiguous. Owing to various politico-economic reasons, it continued to recognize Tibetan "autonomy" under an undefined Chinese "suzerainty". Britain's relations with Tibet showed, however, that Tibet's "autonomy" included a large measure of freedom which ultimately became identical with "independence" and made the term "suzerainty" more or less meaningless in its context.[137] As late as November 1950, the Government of Britain declared: "We have over a long period recognized Chinese suzerainty over Tibet, but only on the understanding that Tibet is regarded as autonomous. For many years this Chinese suzerainty has been no more than nominal, and indeed, since 1911, Tibet had enjoyed *de facto* independence."[138]

In order to avoid hurting the feelings of China, a war-time ally, the United States also refrained from according recognition to Tibet. And yet both Powers—Britain and the United States—treated Tibet as an independent state. So did India, as we have already seen, after its Independence in 1947. In these circumstances, it is impossible to escape the conclusion that Tibet had emerged as an independent state by 1950, and the Government of Tibet

[131] Ti-Chiang Chen, n. 22, pp. 30 ff.

[132] Lauterpacht, n. 25, p. 6.

[133] W. E. Hall, *A Treatise on International Law*, A.P. Higgins, ed. (London, 1924), p. 127.

[134] John Fischer Williams, "Some Thoughts on Recognition in International Law", *Harvard Law Review* (Cambridge, Mass.), vol. 47 (1933-34), pp. 776 ff.; Charles de Visscher, *Theory and Reality in Public International Law*, P. E. Corbett, trans. (Princeton, N. J., 1957), pp. 228 ff.; and Ti-Chiang Chen, n. 22, pp. 52 and 62.

[135] Ti-Chiang Chen, n. 22, pp. 53-54, 77-78, and 133 ff.

[136] See Rubin, n. 10, pp. 127-8.

[137] See *China*, 1942, n. 108, p. 145; and *China*, 1943, n. 109, p. 636.

[138] Statement by the Under Secretary of State for Foreign Affairs in an oral answer to a question in Parliament on 6 November 1950. Quoted in Rubin, n. 10. p. 137.

had every right to claim that "Tibet was a sovereign and independent country at that time".[139]

The Dragon Strikes

The independent status of Tibet, however, did not deter Communist China from making the oft-repeated Chinese claim of Tibet being a part of China.[140] On 1 January 1950, China announced that one of the "basic tasks" of the People's Liberation Army would be the "liberation" of Tibet.[141] The Chinese claim of suzerainty was certainly unjustified and untenous claim to independent Tibet. Just because a country had once occupied another country or had exercised domination over it during some period of its history, it cannot be said to have a permanent claim to the country it had subjugated. If that were the case, London could still claim the United States to be a part of Britain, and the whole of Asia, Africa, and the Americas would become part of a colossal European empire. Apart from the logical untenability of such an argument, international law does not banish revolt or revolution as a means of achieving independence. And, as we have seen, Tibet had emerged as an independent state by 1950. But apparently logic or law did not mean much for China.

The Government of Tibet, while reaffirming its independence in 1950, was under no illusions as to its ability to withstand a military attack by China. It did, however, expect India to continue the British policy of safeguarding its autonomy.[142] In a desperate attempt to retain its independence, it sought an understanding with the new Chinese Government. In February 1950, it sent a Mission to talk things over with the Chinese Communists in the neutral territory of Hong Kong. But since the British Government refused to grant visas to the Tibetans, the venue of the talks was shifted to New Delhi. The Tibetan delegation arrived on 5 September to meet the Chinese Ambassador, and as the talks made little headway, it was suggested that the discussions should be continued in Peking. While arrangements were being made for the second round of talks, a Chinese army began to move into

[139] See Shakabpa, n. 2, p. 301. According to Tieh-Tseng Li, owing to the absence of political consciousness among the Tibetans to form an independent and sovereign state, "the utmost that scholars can do is to classify Tibet as among the entities of doubtful or unusual legal status". Tieh-Tseng Li, n. 65, p. 403. He thus admits that Tibet was not a part of China. But it was not a no-man's land either. It was an independent nation. See also Lauterpacht classfying Tibet as a half-sovereign state normally under the protection or suzerainty of China. Oppenheim, n. 54, p. 258.

[140] On 2 September 1949, the Chinese Communists made a statement to that effect. See Calvocoressi, n. 125, p. 368.

[141] See *Tibet and the Chinese People's Republic*, n. 26, p. 160.

[142] Ibid.

Tibet suddenly on 7 October 1950, without any warning.[143] On 24 October, China announced that the "Chinese liberation forces" had been ordered "to advance into Tibet to liberate three million Tibetans from imperialist aggression".[144]

To the Government of India, which had all along been counselling that the Sino-Tibetan dispute should be settled peacefully, this development was a great shock. It had made it clear earlier, in a Note delivered to the Government of China on 26 October 1950, that it would not interfere in the dispute except diplomatically even if China invaded Tibet.[145] It could thus only express its "deep regret that the Chinese Government should have decided to seek a solution to the problem of their relations with Tibet by force". In reply, the Government of China declared: "Tibet is an integral part of China and the problem of Tibet is entirely a domestic problem of China. The Chinese People's Liberation Army must enter Tibet, liberate the Tibetan people, and defend the frontiers of China." There was also a suggestion that the Government of India had acted under some foreign influence hostile to China.[146]

In another Note on 31 October 1950, the Government of India strongly repudiated the Chinese charges, and suggested that a settlement of the Tibetan problem might be possible on the basis of Tibetan autonomy under Chinese suzerainty. It stated that "Tibetan autonomy is a fact", and described military operations against Tibet as unprovoked and unjustifiable. It also specified the existing rights of India in that country—an agent in Lhasa, trade agencies at Gyantse and Yatung, maintenance of post and telegraph offices on a trade route up to Gyantse, and a small military escort for the protection of the trade route—which, it averred, did not prejudice Chinese suzerainty over Tibet. The Government of China was in no mood to argue. In reply, it reaffirmed its position with an additional charge that India was trying to prevent it from exercising its sovereignty over Tibet.[147]

The writing on the wall was ominously clear, for the Chinese forces had already marched quite deep into Tibetan territory, and in quick succession several places of strategic importance had fallen. On 19 October 1950, Chamdo, in Eastern Tibet, was taken, and the Tibetan army decisively defeated.[148]

In a desperate appeal to the United Nations on 11 November 1950, the Government of Tibet begged "the nations of the world to intercede in our

[143] Ibid., pp. 160-1; Calvocoressi, n. 125, p. 370; and *The Question of Tibet and the Rule of Law*. n. 8, p. 93.

[144] *The Question of Tibet and the Rule of Law*, n. 8, p. 94.

[145] See Calvocoressi, n. 125, p. 371.

[146] See quoted in Ram Gopal, n. 3, pp. 32-33; and Richardson, n. 2, p. 184.

[147] See Richardson, n. 2, p. 184.

[148] See *Tibet and the Chinese People's Republic*, n. 26, p. 161.

behalf and restrain Chinese aggression". It pointed out that the Chinese claim that Tibet was a part of China conflicted radically with the facts and with Tibetan feelings. It expressed the view that if China wanted to press its claim over Tibetan opposition, there were other, civilized methods available, methods not involving the use of force or coercion. "The armed invasion of Tibet for the incorporation of Tibet in Communist China through sheer physical force", it declared, was "a clear case of aggression". As long as the people of Tibet were compelled by force to become a part of China against their will and consent, it continued, "the present invasion of Tibet will be the grossest instance of the violation of the weak by the strong". It assured the United Nations that "Tibet will not go down without a fight, though there is little hope that a nation dedicated to peace will be able to resist the brutal effort of men trained to war, but *we understand that the United Nations has decided to stop aggression wherever it takes place*".[149]

The United Nations had certainly so decided. Attack by China was a clear violation of the sacred principles of international law prohibiting the use of force in international relations and enshrined in Articles 1(1), 2(3), 2(4), 2(6), of the UN Charter. It is widely recognized that the Charter obliges not merely the Members of the United Nations but also non-Members to settle their disputes by peaceful means, and to abstain in their relations with other states from the threat or use of force.[150] In any case, the United Nations must ensure, in the words of Article 2(6), that "states which are not Members of the United Nations act in accordance with these principles so far as may be necessary for the maintenance of international peace and security". It must also be mentioned that even an unrecognized state is not devoid of an "international legal personality" and is entitled to certain minimum rights. It is certainly entitled to its territorial integrity and political independence, which cannot be violated with impunity.[151] Communist China, although not a Member of the United Nations, had no right to use force even against formally unrecognized but independent Tibet.

The United Nations Abdicates its Duty

A small country from a far-off continent, EI Salvador, alone found the courage to move that the unprovoked aggression by Communist China should be condemned. Reminding the United Nations of its primary responsibility to maintain international peace and security, the delegate of EI Salvador

[149] See *Tibet in the United Nations*, 1950-1961, n. 67, pp. 1 ff. Emphasis added.

[150] See Hans Kelsen, *The Law of the United Nations* (New York, N.Y., 1950), pp. 106 ff.; and L. M. Goodrich and Edvard Hambro, *Charter of the United Nations* (London, 1949), pp. 108 ff.

[151] See Ti-Chiang Chen, n. 22, p. 33; and H. W. Briggs, *The Law of Nations: Cases, Documents and Notes* (New York, N.Y., 1952), pp. 114-15.

said: "It is true that Tibet is not a Member of the United Nations, but it is also a clear fact that the responsibilities of this organization are not limited to the maintenance of international peace among Members, but, on the contrary, that they extended to the whole world."[152]

The case came up for discussion before the General Committee of the General Assembly on a proposal by El Salvador that the Tibetan appeal should be put on the agenda of the General Assembly. The delegate of that country appealed to the Members of the United Nations not to dismiss the Tibetan case unheard.[153] The British delegate pleaded ignorance of the exact course of events and declared that the legal position of Tibet was yet uncertain. He, however, expressed the bland hope that the dispute would be settled amicably, and proposed that the matter should be deferred.[154] The representative of India, the country most closely affected, supported the British proposal. He pointed out that the Chinese forces had ceased to advance after the fall of Chamdo, a town some 480 kilometers from Lhasa. "The Indian Government was certain that the Tibetan question could still be settled by peaceful means, and that such a settlement could safeguard the autonomy which Tibet had enjoyed for several decades while maintaining its historical association with China." He, therefore, thought that the best way to obtain this objective was to postpone the issue.[155] The Soviet and the Chinese Nationalist delegates opposed discussion on the ground that Tibet was an integral part of China.[156] The United States agreed to an adjournment solely because even the Government of India entertained the hope that the question could be peacefully and honourably settled.[157] The debate was, accordingly, adjourned *sine die.*

The Tibetans found it hard to believe that they could receive such treatment from the civilized world. They sent an agonized telegram to the United Nations on 8 December 1950. Concerned and dismayed at the indifferent treatment of "the peace appeal of the weak and peace-loving people . . . beleaguered by their powerful neighbours", they asked for a UN fact-finding commission to carry out investigation in Tibet.[158] They received no answer. The United Nations had abdicated its duty.

China Consolidates its Power

To some extent, of course, Tibet is to be blamed for this indifferent attitude of the world body. It still remained, by and large, "a mysterious *terra*

[152] *Tibet in the United Nations, 1950-1961*, n. 67, p. 5.
[153] Ibid., p. 10.
[154] Ibid., p. 11.
[155] Ibid.
[156] Ibid., p. 12.
[157] Ibid., p. 14.
[158] Ibid., pp. 15-16.

incognita", and "no foreign government had much knowledge of or material commitment in the area". The Tibetans had made no serious effort till then "to beak out of their traditional isolationism and join the family of nations" although they had had "ample opportunity to do so" in the past fifty years.[159]

Being assured that the United Nations would take no action, China did not take long to consolidate its position. By the end of November 1950, the Chinese forces had strongly established themselves in Eastern Tibet and had also gained a foothold in the western part of the country. On 21 November 1950 the Dalai Lama, who had assumed full powers at the unusually early age of sixteen, left Lhasa and, along with some important officials of his Government, reached the Chumbi Valley near the Indian border. His idea was to negotiate with the invaders only at arm's length, if at all there were to be negotiations or, alternatively, to seek refuge in India. For four months thereafter, the Tibetan mountain passes being frozen in the winter cold and impassable, and the Chinese choosing not to move out of their camps at lower altitudes, there were exchanges of messages between the Chinese and the Tibetans. Eventually, in April 1951, a Tibetan delegation went to Peking to "negotiate", and concluded an agreement with China on 23 May 1951. Tibet is said to have committed its *harakiri* by this Agreement "for the peaceful liberation of Tibet", popularly known as the Seventeen-Point Agreement. The Agreement declared that "the Tibetan nationality is one of the nationalities with a long history within the boundaries of China" and that the Tibetans had agreed to "return to the big family of the Motherland—the People's Republic of China". It guaranteed the continuance of the existing political system in Tibet, including "the established status, functions and powers" of the Dalai Lama and the Panchen Lama, and conceded internal autonomy to Tibet in matters of custom and religion. It, however, made the Tibetan army a part of the national defence forces of China, and declared that the external relations of Tibet would be handled exclusively by the Peking Government.[160]

At the request of the newly appointed Chinese Commissioner in Tibet, who met him in the Chumbi Valley, and in response to the appeals of his own high lamas, the Dalai Lama returned to Lhasa on 17 August 1951. On 9 September, three thousand picked Chinese Communist troops arrived in Lhasa. They were followed soon after by another twenty thousand soldiers, who were stationed at key points throughout Tibet. Under the shadow of the bayonets, on 24 October 1951, the Dalai Lama ratified the Seventeen-Point Agreement, by which, as he said later, "we were expected to hand ourselves and our country over to China and cease to exist as a nation". But there was

[159] See George Ginsburgs, "Peking-Lhasa-New Delhi", *Political Science Quarterly* (New York, N.Y.), vol. 75 (1960), p. 339.

[160] See the text of the Agreement in *The Question of Tibet and the Rule of Law*, n. 8, pp. 139 ff.

no alternative. As the disillusioned Tibetan leader put it: "We were helpless. Without friends, there was nothing we could do but acquiesce, submit to the Chinese dictates in spite of our strong opposition and swallow our resentment. We could only hope that the Chinese would keep their side of this forced, one-sided bargain."[161]

About eight years later, however, the Dalai Lama and his Government attacked this Agreement on the grounds of forgery and coercion. After his flight to India in 1959, the Dalai Lama declared: "The agreement which followed the invasion of Tibet was also thrust upon its people and Government by the threat of arms. It was never accepted by them of their own free will. The consent of the Government was secured under duress and at the point of the bayonet." Elaborating his charges further, he said:

> My representatives were compelled to sign the agreement under the threat of further military operations against Tibet by the invading armies of China leading to utter ravage and ruin of the country. Even the Tibetan seal which was affixed to the agreement was not the seal of my representatives but a seal copied and fabricated by the Chinese authorities in Peking and kept in their possession ever since.[162]

It may be argued that whatever the truth in regard to the alleged use of force against the representatives of Tibet in Peking or in regard to the fabrication of the Tibetan seal affixed to the Agreement, the Dalai Lama conferred legitimacy on the Agreement by ratifying it through the exercise of his deliberate will. There is little doubt, however, that the Agreement was signed under coercion and under a threat of further use of force against Tibet. This is just not allowed under the general norms of international law and is in violation of the principles of the UN Charter. Coercion is generally regarded as vitiating the validity of international agreements.[163] As the International Law Commission declared in 1966: "The invalidity of treaty procured by the illegal threat or use of force is a principle which is *lex lata* in the international law of today."[164] Article 49 of the Commission's Draft

[161] Howarth, n. 60, p. 82.

[162] Statement by the Dalai Lama on 29 June 1959. For the text, see *The Question of Tibet and the Rule of Law*, n. 8, p. 196. See also Howarth, n. 60, p. 80; and Shakabpa, n. 2, p. 304.

[163] Under traditional doctrine prior to the Covenant of the League of Nations, when unrestricted right of war was permitted, the validity of a treaty was not affected by the fact that it had been brought about by the threat or use of force. See "Report of the International Law Commission on the Work of Its Eighteenth Session", American Journal of International Law, vol. 61 (1967), p. 407. Cf. Julius Stone, "The International Law Commission and Imposed Treaties of Peace", *Virginia Journal of International Law* (Charlottesville, Va), vol. 8 (1968), pp. 356 ff.

[164] "Report of the International Law Commission on the Work of Its Eighteenth Session", n. 163. See also *The Question of Tibet and the Rule of Law*, n. 8, pp. 96-97.

Articles on the Law of Treaties, therefore, laid down: "A treaty is void if its conclusion has been procured by the threat or use of force in violation of the principles of the Charter of the United Nations." If that is the case, the Seventeen-Point Agreement is void *ab initio* and cannot be said to affect the international status of Tibet.[165]

India Capitulates

With Independence India inherited the rights established by the British in Tibet and the policy pursued by them in regard to Tibet. As we have already seen, the British had their own selfish motives for recognizing China's suzerainty over Tibet. It is important, however, to remember that they always insisted on Tibet's autonomy, for they knew that a strong and free Tibet "would furnish a northern frontier for India of unparalleled strength".[166] They wanted to maintain it as a buffer between India and the Russian Empire.[167] As Charles Bell puts it:

> We want Tibet as a buffer to India on the North. Now there are buffers and buffers; and some of them are of very little use. But Tibet is ideal in this respect. With the large desolate area of the Northern Plains controlled by the Lhasa Government, Central and Southern Tibet governed by the same authority, and the Himalayan border states guided by, or in close alliance with, the British-Indian Government, Tibet forms a barrier equal, or superior, to anything that the world can show elsewhere.[168]

The British knew that "if China reoccupied Tibet, their troops stationed in Lhasa, and even further south, might well form a focus of Bolshevist intrigue against India".[169] Out of these conflicting desires to appease China on the one hand, and keep India's northern border secure on the other, was born the "suzerainty-cum-autonomy" formula which India inherited.

On 6 December 1950, the Prime Minister of India, Jawaharlal Nehru, said in the Indian Parliament: "We were anxious that Tibet should maintain the autonomy it has had for the last forty years. We did not challenge or deny the suzerainty of China over Tibet." On 7 December, he repeated: "Please note that I used the word suzerainty, not sovereignty. There is a slight difference, though not much." But he stressed: "Since Tibet is not the

[165] The US Government declared on 29 April 1953 that it "neither recognizes nor condones the so-called 'agreement' of May 1951, under which the Chinese Communists deprived the Tibetan people of the *de facto* political autonomy which they long enjoyed". See Whiteman, n. 49, p. 464.

[166] Bell, n. 28, p. 190; and Rubin, n. 10., p. 144.

[167] See Teichman n. 19, p. 223.

[168] Bell, n. 28, p. 246.

[169] Ibid., p. 191; and Bell, n. 14, p. 342.

same as China, it should ultimately be the wishes of the people of Tibet that should prevail and not any legal or constitutional arguments."[170]

But when the matter came before the United Nations, India took, as we have seen, an equivocal stand and refused to condemn China for violating Tibet's autonomy. Nehru was perhaps taken in by Communist China's assurance of its intention to reach a peaceful settlement with Tibet. He was, further, extremely anxious to forge a friendship with the new, united, and powerful China that had emerged and did not want to displease it for the sake of forlorn Tibet. It was in pursuance of the latter objective that Nehru agreed, by the Sino-Indian Agreement on Tibet of 29 April 1954, to terminate all the privileges that India had inherited in Tibet from the British. Trade missions were no longer maintained as of right, but only on the basis of strict reciprocity: the Chinese secured the right to open trade agencies in New Delhi, Calcutta, and Kalimpong, and allowed the Indians in return to maintain similar agencies at Gyantse, Yatung, and Gartok. Indian garrisons stationed in the trading posts ever since 1904 were withdrawn. All installations—post-and-telegraph installation and public telephones—heretofore owned and occupied by the Government of India were sold and transferred to the Chinese authorities "at a reasonable price".[171] India later decided, "as a gesture of goodwill", to waive even the compensation due to it for those installations.[172]

More significant than the surrender of privileges is the fact that India signed the Trade Agreement with China in Peking, no longer with Tibet in Lhasa, thus recognizing China's sovereignty over Tibet by implication. The Chinese claim to sovereignty over Tibet was further reinforced by frequent references in the preamble and even in the text, to "the Tibet Region of China", thereby making it clear that the Government of India accepted the Chinese position that Tibet formed an integral part of China. Nehru left no one in doubt as to what he had done. Defending his action in Parliament, he said on 15 May 1954:

> So far as Tibet is concerned, it is a recognition of the existing situation there. ...Some criticism has been made that this is a recognition of Chinese sovereignty over Tibet. Apart from that fact, I am not aware of any time during the last few hundred years when *Chinese sovereignty, or if you like suzerainty*, was challenged by any outside country and all during this period whether China was weak or strong and whatever the Government of China was, China always maintained this claim to the sovereignty over Tibet. It is true that occasionally when China was

[170] Quoted in Ram Gopal, n. 3, p. 53.

[171] For the text of this Agreement and the Notes exchanged on the same day, see Richardson, n. 2, pp. 278 ff. This Agreement expired on 2 July 1962. Because of the strain that developed in Sino-Indian relations, it was not renewed. Following the expiry of the Agreement the Indian trade agencies in Tibet and the Chinese trade agencies in India were closed. See Shakabpa, n. 2, p. 309.

[172] Moraes, n. 2, p. 125.

weak, this sovereignty was not exercised in any large measure. When China was strong, it was exercised. Always there was a large measure of autonomy of Tibet, so that there was no great change in the theoretical approach to the problem from the Chinese side.[173]

This was not an objective assessment of history. Nehru looked at the problem of Tibet only from the Chinese side without taking into consideration the fundamental change that had come in its status during the past forty years. No Government of India had ever taken this change into consideration. Although the experience of Tibet in 1950 showed Chinese expansionism and imperialism, Nehru accepted without question Chinese assurances of good faith and good conduct. The preamble to the Sino-Indian Agreement enunciated for the first time the now famous five principles of peaceful co-existence, known in India as the *Panchasheela*. Nehru thought in his simplicity that China would abide by those principles.

India had to pay dearly for this mistake. By a decision, dictated more by expediency and less by prudence, India agreed to regard the Indo-Tibetan border as the Sino-Indian border, which China did not take long to question. Frank Moraes rightly remarks:

No reasonable person or government expected India to go to war with China over Tibet in 1950. . . . But by refraining from recognizing Tibet as a sovereign, independent state between 1947 and 1949, at a time when neither the Chinese Communists nor the Nationalists could have effectively intervened, India lost the opportunity of bringing Tibet into the forum of independent nations and simultaneously of ensuring the existence of a buffer state between herself and China.[174]

Nehru failed to appreciate the usefulness of an independent Tibet as a buffer. While he condemned the British policy in Tibet as "imperialist"[175] and willingly surrendered the privileges that India had inherited in Tibet, he supported, strangely enough, the Chinese claim of suzerainty over Tibet, which was no less "imperialist" since Tibet had never willingly submitted to Chinese authority.[176] Indeed, he even went further and accepted Chinese sovereignty over Tibet. This was an endorsement, by an apostle of freedom, of the subjugation and enslavement of a free country and free people in this age of freedom and self-determination. At the same time, all unwittingly, he magnified the problem of India's security which he had sought to solve by this endorsement.

Nepal followed India's example. On 20 September 1956, it signed the

[173] See quoted in Ram Gopal, n. 3, p. 54. Emphasis added.

[174] Moraes, n. 2, p. 118.

[175] See also for such a view, K. M. Panikkar, *Asia and Western Dominance* (London, 1953), pp. 161-2.

[176] See Moraes, n. 2, pp. 127-8.

Sino-Nepalese Agreement on Trade and Intercourse between the Tibet Region of China and Nepal, and recognized Chinese sovereignty over Tibet.

Tibet Rebels

Having annexed Tibet by invoking an outworn, imperialist formula, without any serious opposition or even a protest from the Free World, China felt free to slow down the implementation of its plan to destroy Tibet's personality completely. It needed time to build roads and strengthen its military establishments. But as soon as it had sufficiently entrenched itself, it began to tighten the screws. Contrary to the provisions of the Sino-Tibetan Agreement, it took steps to undermine the Dalai Lama's position. It sought to erode the authority of the Dalai Lama, both secular and ecclesiastical, and that of the Kashag (the Tibetan Cabinet), especially after 1956. In the name of introducing reforms, it interfered in everything, in matters of religion as well as administration. This led to periodic flare-ups of violence and sporadic armed uprisings throughout 1956, 1957, and 1958, which were all suppressed with a firm hand. About the end of 1958, the resistance to Chinese rule became strong enough to take the form of a regular uprising. On the night of 17 March 1959, the Dalai Lama, in disguise, escaped and fled towards India. He reached India on 30 March, and was immediately granted political asylum.[177]

On 11 March 1959, the Kashag proclaimed in Lhasa the independence of Tibet.[178] During their flight to India, the Dalai Lama and his party learnt that the Chinese had dissolved the Tibetan Government. They, therefore, formed on 29 March 1959 a Government in exile.[179] On 20 June 1959, the Dalai Lama publicly repudiated the Seventeen Point Agreement. He declared: "The Sino-Tibetan agreement imposed by the Chinese in accordance with their own desires has been violated by the Chinese themselves, thus giving rise to a contradiction. Therefore, we cannot abide by this agreement."[180]

Commenting on this statement, the International Commission of Jurists declared:

> The classic doctrine on denunciation of treaties is that if one side violates its obligations under a treaty, the injured party "may by its own unilateral act terminate a treaty as between itself and a state which it regards as having violated such treaty. ..."[181] It is essential...that the treaty be actually repudiated, for, unless this is done, the treaty remains in force, i.e. it is voidable only.[182]

[177] See generally Richardson, n. 2, pp. 199 ff. and 206 ff; and Shakabpa, n. 2, pp. 316 ff.

[178] See *Tibet and the Chinese People's Republic*, n. 26, pp. 15

[179] See Shakabpa, n. 2, pp. 319-20.

[180] See *The Question of Tibet and the Rule of Law*, n. 8, p. 202.

[181] See Green Haywood Hackworth, *Digest of International Law* (Washington, D.C., 1932-34), vol. 5, p. 346.

[182] *The Question of Tibet and the Rule of Law*, n. 8, p. 99.

The Commission concluded: "Tibet discharged herself of the obligations under the Agreement, the principal one being the surrender of her independence."[183]

We have argued, however, that the 1951 Agreement being void *ab initio*, Tibet never lost its independent status. In any case, even if the Agreement was valid, in the words of the International Commission, "Tibet lost her sovereignty but regained, possibly on the ground of duress and for violation by China".[184]

It is unfortunate, however, that despite China's increasingly intransigent and aggressive behaviour and Tibet's continued suffering, India refused to give even moral support to Tibet. This was apparently because India did not want to displease China. Thus, when on 20 June 1959 the Dalai Lama made a simple statement to the effect that wherever he was, accompanied by his Government "the Tibetan people recognize us as the Government of Tibet",[185] the Government of India issued a rejoinder that the Government of India did not recognize any separate Government of Tibet and that there was no question of a Government of Tibet functioning under the Dalai Lama in India.[186]

The Dalai Lama, finding the prospect for his country becoming "immeasurably darker and gloomier", again thought of an appeal to the United Nations "for the verdict of the peace-loving and conscientious nations of the world" and for their "support to our cause of freedom and justice".[187] The Government of India, feeling that such an appeal would be embarrassing in its relations with China, sought to discourage the Dalai Lama from taking his case to the United Nations and warned him that such a move would serve absolutely no purpose and that it would make the plight of his people even worse.[188]

Tibet in the United Nations

The Dalai Lama, however, felt that he could not escape his duty to his own people. In a message to the UN Secretary-General on 9 September 1959, he pointed out that "the area of aggression has been substantially extended" since the matter was discussed and adjourned in the United Nations in 1950, "with the result that practically the whole of Tibet is under the occupation of the Chinese forces", and urged that "in view of the inhuman treatment and

[183] *Tibet and the Chinese People's Republic*, n. 26, p. 165.

[184] *The Question of Tibet and the Rule of Law*, n. 8, p. 99.

[185] Ibid., p. 202.

[186] Statement by a spokesman of the Indian Ministry of External Affairs on 30 June 1959. Quoted in Ram Gopal, n. 3, p. 57.

[187] Statement by the Dalai Lama on 30 August 1959. Quoted, ibid., p. 57.

[188] Statement by Nehru in the Lok Sabha on 4 September 1959. Quoted ibid., pp. 57-59. See also Howarth, n. 60, p. 206; and Shakabpa, n. 2, p. 321.

crimes against humanity and religion to which the people of Tibet are being subjected", the United Nations should intervene at once. He emphasized "that Tibet was a sovereign state at the time when her territorial integrity was violated by the Chinese armies in 1950". He enumerated numerous acts of persecution and genocide being committed against the Tibetan people and appealed to the United Nations to do something, so that "this wanton and ruthless murder of my people should be immediately brought to an end".[189]

When, however, the matter was discussed in the General Committee of the General Assembly on the initiative of Malaya and Ireland on 9 October 1959, and again in the General Assembly on 12 October, 13 October, 20 October, and 21 October 1959, Tibet received only lukewarm support from the Members. While numerous delegates condemned China for its suppression of the Tibetan people and for the violation of human rights, few supported Tibet's status as an independent state.[190] The General Assembly adopted on 21 October 1959—by 45 votes to 9, with 26 abstentions—a mildly worded resolution calling "for respect of the fundamental human rights of the Tibetan people and for their distinctive, cultural and religious life". Without supporting Tibet's status as an independent state, it merely said that the General Assembly was "mindful...of the distinctive cultural and religious heritage of the people of Tibet and of the autonomy which they have traditionally enjoyed".[191] India took more or less an indifferent attitude, and neither supported nor rejected the resolution: it abstained.[192]

Though repeatedly rebuffed, the Dalai Lama appealed to the United Nations in 1960 for the third time. In a letter to the Secretary-General of the United Nations on 29 September 1960, the Dalai Lama reasserted the independent status of Tibet on the basis of certain historical facts which he enumerated, and once again made an appeal "in the hope that the United Nations will take measures to get China to vacate its aggression".[193] The question of Tibet had earlier been raised by Thailand and Malaya for further consideration by the General Assembly on 19 August 1960,[194] but pressure of work prevented this from being considered during the fifteenth session.[195] In the sixteenth session of the General Assembly in 1961, the question of Tibet

[189] See *Tibet in the United Nations, 1950-1961*, n. 67, pp. 17-19.

[190] See speeches by the delegates of Belgium, Cuba, El Salvador, Ireland, and New Zealand. Ibid., pp. 88 ff.

[191] For the text of the resolution, ibid., p. 230.

[192] See the speech of V.K. Krishna Menon, the Indian representative, ibid., pp. 199 ff.

[193] For the text of the letter, ibid., pp. 233-8.

[194] Ibid., p. 231.

[195] See a short discussion in connexion with the inclusion of the item in the agenda of the fifteenth session, ibid., pp. 238 ff.

was again debated.[196] On 20 December 1961, the Assembly adopted another harmless resolution—by 56 votes to 10, with 29 abstentions—by which it expressed grave concern "at the continuation of events in Tibet including the violation of fundamental rights of the Tibetan people".[197]

The plight of the Tibetans and the continued and increasing suppression of their rights again attracted the attention of the General Assembly in the twentieth session.[198] The world body passed yet another resolution on 18 December 1965—by 43 votes to 26, with 22 abstentions—by which it "deplored the continued violation of the fundamental rights and freedoms of the people of Tibet" and declared its conviction that the violation of such rights increased international tension and embittered relations between peoples.[199]

India Modifies its Stand

There was a noticeable shift in India's stand when in 1965 it supported in the United Nations a resolution condemning the Chinese atrocities in Tibet. Speaking in the Indian Parliament on 14 July 1967, India's Minister for External Affairs, M. C. Chagla, expressed deep sympathy for the sufferings of the people of Tibet. But he reminded the House that there was an "important distinction between the political status of Tibet and the people of Tibet". "However much we might regret [it]", he said, "we have admitted a certain political status of Tibet. We have accepted, admitted and recognized the fact that China has sovereignty over Tibet."[200]

He said that he was sorry that history could not be rewritten and that India was just in no position to help Tibet.

Conclusion

This brief survey of the long and rather complicated history of Tibet leaves us in no doubt that racially, culturally, geographically, and politically the Tibetans are a separate nation. They are a homogeneous people, and "though they are akin to the Chinese, the relationship is no closer than that between

[196] Ibid., pp. 253 ff.

[197] For the text of the resolution, ibid., p 311.

[198] *Official Records of the General Assembly of the United Nations* (GAOR), session 20, plen. mtgs, mtg 1394, 14 December 1965; mtg 1401, 17 December 1965; and mtg 1403, 18 December 1965. Earlier, in a letter to the Secretary-General on 23 September 1965, the Dalai Lama had drawn the attention of the United Nations to the alarming and most distressing news from Tibet. See GAOR, session, 20, Agenda Item 99, Annexes.

[199] GA Resolution 2079 (XX).

[200] India, Lok Sabha, *Debates*, col. 12009, 14 July 1967.

Frenchmen and Italians".[201] As a distinct and ancient nation, they enjoyed for many centuries a relationship of mutual respect with China. After 1720, some kind of Chinese control was established in Tibet which continued almost till the middle of the nineteenth century. Even after that, as China started loosening its hold over Tibet, there were times when the latter sought, but did not always receive, the protection of the Chinese Emperors from foreign invaders. Whatever the political implications of this relationship, there is little doubt that on the fall of the Manchu Empire in China in 1911, Tibet severed all its connexions with China and declared its independence. After that, it continued to act as a fully independent state, attended at least two international conferences (in 1913-14 at Simla, and in 1947 in New Delhi) as a sovereign state, signed international agreements, sent trade delegations to various countries, and resisted Chinese pressure, all through by force and otherwise in assertion of its independent status. Although not expressly recognized, it had been tacitly accepted by Britain and India, and also by some other countries which received its trade delegations, as a state which was independent of China. In any case, since recognition does not confer personality upon a state, the non-recognition of Tibet cannot amount to a negation of its international personality. The invasion of Tibet by China in 1950 was, therefore, a clear case of aggression prohibited under the UN Charter. The Sino-Tibetan Agreement of 1951, which was forced on Tibet with a view to perpetuating an act which was a flagrant violation of the sacred principles of the Charter, cannot be accepted as valid and does not affect the independent status of Tibet. Tibet's legal position is not affected by a situation dictated by mere physical compulsion. Even the absence of one or more criteria of statehood, like people or territory, over relatively long periods have not been regarded in recent times as depriving such states of legal personality in international law.[202]

It is unfortunate, however, that even after the lapse of forty years, the ghost of Chinese suzerainty should continue to haunt Tibet. It is hard to believe that, along with Britain, even independent India and the United States[203] have chosen to bless this imperialist concept of China being Tibet's suzerain and overlord. When Tibet fell, India did nothing apart from lodging a mild protest against Chinese high-handedness, and it contented itself by appealing to China to act peacefully. Indeed, it did something worse, something totally incomprehensible and unprecedented, by accepting China's sovereignty over Tibet in 1954. No Indian or even British Government had

[201] Bell, n 28, p. 217; and idem, n. 14, p. 352.

[202] See Briggs, n. 151, pp. 66 and 73 ff. Cf. Tieh-Tseng Li's using the arguments in favour of China after the 1911 Revolution in China and declaration of independence by Tibet. Tieh-Tseng Li, n. 65, p. 397.

[203] For the British, Indian, and American official positions in 1959, see Whiteman, n. 49. pp. 463-8.

ever recognized Chinese sovereignty over Tibet. It had in fact never existed. It is, of course, true that India could not go to war with China over Tibet. But it could certainly have raised its voice against the gross injustice of the Chinese action. As Jayaprakash Narayan has pointed out: "It is true that we could not have prevented the Chinese from annexing Tibet. But we could have saved ourselves from being party to a wrong."[204]

Though the hard reality to Tibet's present occupation and suppression by China cannot be denied, it is submitted that Tibet is not dead. At least not legally.

[204] *Report of the All India Tibet Convention* (Calcutta, 1959), p. 12.

Enhancing the Acceptability of Compulsory Procedures of International Dispute Settlement

Law and Peace

If peace without law is unthinkable, peace under law is much to be strived for and desired. In the humanity's long struggle for peace, one of the oldest, most important and appropriate, approaches to peace has been the peaceful settlement of disputes on the basis of law. In all civilized societies, disputes between individuals are settled in courts under the rule of law. But the law of jungle still prevails as the ultimate mechanism to settle disputes between nations. If we want to avoid the bloodbath of continuous warfare we see all around in our international society, we should be prepared to resolve our disputes through impartial third-party settlement, if direct negotiations between parties fail. That is the only civilized way to settle disputes. Supremacy of law within nations insures freedom of individuals. Supremacy of law in the community of nations, it is hoped, will free mankind from the dread of endemic violence and destruction we see and hear everyday all over the world.

International Law Deficient: "Pyramid without a Base"

But as regards institutions and procedures for adjustment of disputes, international law has been woefully deficient—a jungle law imperfectly ameliorated by a fragmentary and hesitant progress in the direction of a legal order. The precariousness of the present situation can be visualized from the fact that whereas it is difficult to establish arbitration courts—which in any case remain *ad hoc* and impermanent—and the Permanent Court of Arbitration has been little used, we have an International Court of Justice, which is sitting "precariously at the peak of a pyramid which has no enduring base. To say that the institutions of which the pyramid consists are primitive and incomplete is to speak mildly."[1] Although, as we shall see, the jurisdiction of the World Court has been progressively extended and it has gained tremendous and well-deserved prestige and confidence by its excellent and conscientious work, it is unable to realize fully "the potentialities of its

[1] See, Edwin Dewitt Dickinson, *Law and Peace* (Philadelphia, 1951), p. 113.

greatness", it is pointed out, because of the insecure foundations upon which its enterprise must rest.[2] It needs, it has been suggested, a more enduring base if it is to fulfil the hopes which it has engendered. For, as Edwin Dickinson put it,

> " ... building peace requires effort from top to bottom. Reflecting some aspects of the task, one is tempted to say from bottom to top. Clearly the overall objective must be something better coordinated and more nearly complete. Work on the foundations may be more arduous and less dramatic, but ultimately such work must be done and done well if confidence is to be cultivated and the good order extended.[3]

Proliferation of New International Tribunals

Although it has been done rather haphazardly and "without any overall plan", there has been a proliferation of several new international tribunals during the last 50 years. Besides, several *ad hoc* arbitration tribunals which have been set up, and the so-called "commercial arbitrations" held under established rules such as UNCITRAL or the ICC or ICSID, or under municipal arbitration law, quite a number of other international judicial or quasi-judicial institutions have been established, such as Iran-United States claims Tribunal, and new mechanism under the auspices of the WTO.

There are too many such institutions to be enumerated. At the regional level, Europe has its European Court of Justice in Luxembourg; its Commission and the Court of Human Rights at Strasbourg; and a European mechanism for conciliation and arbitration set up within the framework of the CSCE.

Several administrative tribunals have been established to deal with disputes arising between international organizations and their staff: the ILO Administrative Tribunal; the UN Administrative Tribunal; the World Bank Administrative Tribunal; and so on.

The horror of war in Yugoslavia and Rwanda have led the UN Security Council to create two International Tribunals for crimes committed in the former Yugoslavia and in Rwanda. A new permanent International Criminal Court is now proposed to be established.[4]

Even more interesting for us today is the International Tribunal for the Law of Sea which has been established under the Montego Bay Convention concluded in 1982 as part of a comprehensive system for the settlement of disputes laid down in the Convention. The Convention came into force in

[2] Dickinson, *ibid.*, p. 121.

[3] Dickinson, *ibid.*, pp. 121-22.

[4] See, Gilbert Guillaume, "The Future of International Judicial Institutions", *International and Comparative Law Quarterly* (I.C.L.Q), vol. 4 (October 1955), pp. 848-49.

November 1994. Although there is a considerable overlapping in the jurisdictions of the Hamburg Tribunal and the International Court of Justice, the Law of the Sea Tribunal can deal with some important classes of disputes[5] that probably could not go before the Hague Court.

No Structured Relationship, or System Between Different Kinds of Courts

But despite all this proliferation of Courts, there is no "structured relationship" or "hierarchy or system" between them. As Judge R.Y. Jennings, President of International Court of Justice, pointed out, "they have just appeared as need or desire or ambitions promoted yet another one".[6] As a result :

> "In this particular respect, contemporary international law is just a disordered medley. Suffice it to say that it is very difficult to try to make any sort of pattern, much less a structured relationship, of this mass of tribunals, whether important or petty. It is sometimes difficult to find out what is going on, much less to study it."[7]

This lack of "structured relationship" among different kinds of courts in international system, where diverse organs exercising parts of judicial system are not related to each other is, it is sometimes pointed out, a rather disturbing trend which may lead to conflicts of "jurisdiction or contradiction in decisions increasing the indetermination rather than the determination of law".[8] Some well-meaning scholars and judges are concerned about 'the dangers that international law as a whole will become fragmented and unmanageable."[9]

[5] Disputes like the prompt release of vessels and crews under Art. 292 of the L.O.S. Convention and in the matter of provisional measures under Art. 290, paragraph 5, and disputes concerning the international seabed area as provided in Part XI of the Convention. See Judge P. Chandrasekhara Rao, "The ITLOS And its Guidelines", *Indian Journal of International Law* (IJIL), vol. 38, nos. 3 and 4, pp. 371-72.

[6] R.Y. Jennings, "The Judiciary, International and National, and the Development of International Law", *ICLQ*, vol. 45 (January 1996), p. 5.

[7] Jennings, *ibid.*, p. 5.

[8] George M. Abi-Saab, quoted in R.Y. Jennings, "The Role of the International Court of Justice", *British Yearbook of International Law*, vol. 68 (1997), p. 61. But cf. Shabtai Rosenne who points out that "there is no evidence to support the view that multiplicity of international judicial institutions for the settlement of disputes seriously impairs the unity of jurisprudence (a difficult proposition at the best of times). The Convention requires ITLOS to perform tasks that are beyond the capacity of the International Court under its present Statute. If only for that reason the cautious observer will hesitate before crying redundant." Shabtai Rosenne, "Establishing the ITLOS", *American Journal of International Law* (AJIL), vol. 89 (1995), p. 814; see also Alexander Yankov, "ITLOS: Its place within the dispute settlement system of UN Law of the Sea Convention, IJIL, vol. 37 (1997), p. 304.

[9] Jennings, *ibid.*, p. 60.

Jurisdiction of International Courts

Besides the problems relating to creation or establishment of different structures of peace and their relationship with each other, the most important issues relate to the jurisdiction of these courts. It is all too well-known that no state is under an obligation to submit its disputes to any third party settlement without its own consent. As the International Court of Justice has made it clear beyond any doubt that the jurisdiction of an international court "depends on the will of the parties" and that the jurisdiction exists in so far as the states have accepted it.[10]

Leaving aside *ad hoc* arbitration and other specialized international criminal tribunals on which jurisdiction is conferred by special agreements relating to their establishment, it may be mentioned that when the Permanent Court of International Justice was established in 1920 and again when its Statute was revised and the new International Court of Justice was formed in 1945, general compulsory jurisdiction could not be conferred on the Court. The obligatory jurisdiction of the Court could be accepted either under treaties, bilateral or multilateral, or by unilateral declarations under the optional clause (Art. 36(2)) of its Statute. The optional clause constituted an invitation to States to take courage and undertake this commitment even if only for a trial period and even if only for a limited range of disputes. But the unilateral form of these declarations and complete freedom assumed by States left them free to exclude wide matters from coming before the Court. This also made State practice under the optional clause dependent on international confidence in the Court. After 1920, as confidence in the Court grew, many States accepted its jurisdiction. At certain time as many as 41 States out of 48 States parties to the Statute had accepted its jurisdiction under the optional clause. In 1939, 36 States had made much declarations.[11]

Permanent Court of Justice largely a "European Court":

Although the Permanent Court of International Justice had proved its worth and was the subject of general and well-merited praise at the San Francisco Conference for its decisions and advisory opinions—between 1922 and 1940 the Court pronounced 29 judgements and gave 27 advisory opinions—general compulsory jurisdiction could not be conferred on the new Court which replaced it.[12] The Permanent Court truly represented the international

[10] See, R.P. Anand, quoting numerous cases in the World Court, *International Courts and Contemporary Conflicts* (Bombay, 1974), pp. 194 ff.

[11] See R.P. Anand, *Compulsory Jurisdiction of the International Court of Justice* (Bombay, 1961), pp. 36-37.

[12] See for an interesting comparison between jurisdiction conferred on the PCIJ and the ICJ, Philippe *Couvreur*, in A.S. Muller, D. Raic and J.M. Thuranszky (ed.), *International Court of Justice: Its Future Role After Fifty Years* (The Hague, 1997), pp. 96-97.

community of its time. It was largely a "European Court" with a majority of European judges (with the notable exception of post-revolutionary Russia) in addition to judges from the USA, some Latin American Republics, as well as from China and Japan. The Court also reflected in its pronouncements, it is said, "the legal outlook of the Eurocentric community, which was strongly imbued with nineteenth century positivism."[13]

International Court of Justice

The situation had entirely changed when the Court started functioning in its new reincarnation as a part of the UN Organization under its new name, the International Court of Justice. Since it started functioning in the late 1940s, there was a general deterioration in the international situation. The division of the world into two main groups and the advent of the cold war led to a general weakening of the position of law in international relations. Not only was there a totally negative attitude of the Soviet Union and its allies towards the Court, but there was a general "decline of the optional clause" in the later part of the 1940s and 1950s.[14] Several Western and other countries, led by the United States, accepted the optional clause jurisdiction with such wide and far-reaching reservations that it amounted to negation of the Court's jurisdiction.[15]

The same trend has continued to this day. Although 23 countries which had accepted the jurisdiction of the Permanent Court were deemed to have accepted the jurisdiction of the ICJ under Article 36(5) of its Statute in 1945, not many more countries have come forward to accept the jurisdiction of the new Court. In fact 17 countries which had accepted the jurisdiction of the PCIJ under its optional clause, let their declarations lapse or terminated them. In 1998, out of 187 members of the international judicial community, including 185 members of the United Nations and 2 non-members (Switzerland and Nauru) only 60 States, or less than one-third, had accepted the jurisdiction of the Court under Article 36(2) of its Statute. Since 1951, 12 other declarations under the optional clause have either expired, been withdrawn or been terminated without being subsequently replaced. These declarations were made by Bolivia, Brazil, China, El Salvador, France, Guatemala, Iran, Israel, South Africa, Thailand, Turkey and the USA.[16]

Not only do most of these declarations which are still valid contain far-reaching reservations, but nearly 50 per cent of them may be terminated by a

[13] George M. Abi-Saab, "The International Court of Justice as a World Court", in Vaughan Lowe and Malgosia Fitzmaurice (ed.), *Fifty Years of the International Court of Justice: Essays in honour of Sir Robert Jennings* (Cambridge, 1996), p. 4.

[14] See C.H.M. Waldock, "The Decline of the Optional Clause", *British Yearbook of International Law*, vol. 32 (1955-56), p. 244.

[15] See Anand, n. 11, pp. 53 ff.

[16] See *Yearbook of the ICJ, 1997-98*, p. 83.

simple notice which may take effect immediately or in some cases after a specified time.

It is interesting to note that President Mikhail Gorbachev of the former Soviet Union called the permanent members of the Security Council to set an example by submitting to the ICJ. This aroused great interest and the Five held a number of meetings at legal advisers level with a view to drawing up a list of subjects which could be submitted to the Court in the event of a dispute. But no agreement could be reached.[17]

Compulsory jurisdiction of the Court may also be accepted through compromissory clauses in international treaties. But we find the same hesitation in accepting the Court's jurisdiction among most of the countries.

Jurisdiction of the Law of the Sea Tribunal

There is a similar lack of enthusiasm in accepting the jurisdiction of the only other permanent court which has been recently created, viz., International Tribunal for the Law of the Sea which should have a great potential in the settlement of disputes relating to the law of the sea. Since not all countries were equally enthusiastic about this new Tribunal, the 1982 Law of the Sea Convention identifies in Part XV other means of settling disputes and leaves it to States to choose between the Tribunal, the ICJ, and various forms of arbitration. At present out of 112 States which have ratified or acceded to the LOS Convention, 17 have made a choice of procedure under Section 2 of Part XV. The rest are deemed to have accepted arbitration as the method of settlement of disputes. Of the 17 States, 9 have chosen the Tribunal. They are Argentina, Austria, Cape Verde, Finland, Germany, Greece, Oman, Tanzania and Uruguay.[18]

Further, States are not obliged to submit to the Tribunal their disputes which they consider of vital national concern. Thus, practically all disputes arising out of the exercise of sovereign rights or jurisdiction by a State in the exclusive economic zone concerning marine scientific research and fisheries are excluded from the compulsory procedures. Moreover, a State may declare in writing that it does not accept any compulsory procedure with regard to, *inter-alia*, disputes concerning boundary delimitation, military activities and law enforcement activities in regard to marine scientific research and fisheries in the EEZ, as well as disputes in respect of which the Security Council is exercising its functions under the Charter.[19]

[17] See President of the ICJ Judge Bedjaoui, in his address to the General Assembly on 11 October, 1995.

[18] See Gudmundur Eiriksson, "The Role of ITLOS in the Peaceful Settlement of International Disputes", *Indian Journal of International Law* (IJIL), vol. 37, no. 3 (Special Issue on ITLOS) (1997), p. 350.

[19] See Law of the Sea Convention, Part XV, Sections 2 and 3; see also Guillaume, n. 4, p. 855; Shigeru Oda, "Dispute Settlement Prospects in the Law of the Sea",

International Court of Justice in Crisis from the very Beginning

From the very beginning the International Court of Justice was portrayed as in crisis as a result of the lack or loss of confidence by one or the other part of the international community. None of the big powers put much faith in the Court and avoided it as far as possible. If United States included self-judging Connally reservation relating to domestic jurisdiction in its declaration under the optional clause which reduced the acceptance to a mere nullity, the United Kingdom revised its declaration four times within a few years, each time changing its reservations to suit its convniences.[20] France withdrew its declaration after the *Nuclear Test* cases in 1974.

After 1960, with the acceleration of decolonization process, as numerous Asian and African countries became independent, "the 'crisis of the Court' was perceived and analysed in terms of the distrust manifested by newly independent States towards the Court."[21] Several explanations were sought to be given for this supposed distrust on the part of the Asian-African States in the judicial process and their preference for the diplomatic procedures. Besides their cultural differences and national traditions, lengthy and onerous character of the judicial procedure, under-representation of the Asian-African States on the bench, and the dissatisfaction of the new States with large parts of classical international law which legitimized their subjugation and generally favoured the interests of the erstwhile colonial powers, were given as the reasons for the hostile attitude of the new States towards international adjudication.[22]

The strongest blow to the confidence in the Court, especially amongst the Asian-African States, came in 1966 when the Court, by the casting vote of the President[23] (Sir Percy Spender), after nearly six years of proceedings costing millions of dollars, more than a dozen volumes of written proceedings, almost 300 hours of oral testimony, and more than 100 Court sessions, decided—or refused to decide—the *South-West Africa* cases by declining to go into their merits on the basis of a matter of "antecedent character" which was not even argued by either of the parties. This most controversial decision—or lack of decision—frustrated and enraged politically conscious

International and Comparative Law Quarterly(ICLQ), vol. 41 (October 1995), p. 863.

[20] Anand, n. 11, p. 39.

[21] Abi-Saab, n. 13, p. 5.

[22] See R.P. Anand, "Attitude of the 'new' Asian-African countries towards the International Court of Justice", in his *Studies in International Adjudication* (New Delhi, 1969), pp. 53 ff; Abi-Saab, n. 13, p. 5.

[23] The Court being equally divided 7 votes to 7. See *South-West Africa* Cases (Second Phase), *ICJ Reports*, 1966, p. 6.

Africans, undermined the confidence of newly independent countries in the Court and its capacity to do justice and thrust the Court into an acute crisis.[24] The African States, in particular, adopted "the cynical view that the ICJ was a white man's Court, dispensing white man's justice."[25] It also evoked an extended and critical debate on the role of the Court in the General Assembly, leading to readjustment in the composition of the Court to make it more representative of the various parts of the international community.

There was a steep decline in the work of the Court. So steep was the decline that for some time—from June 21, 1971 to August 30, 1971—there was not a single case pending before the Court.[26] For the next nearly three years after 1971 it had little to do and "it was the subject of some humour about there being few cases and many judges."[27]

Self-Assessment and Change on the Part of Court

One of the most important consequences of this crisis was a new self-assessment, a new self-awareness and change of attitude on the part of the Court itself. While earlier the Court was reserved in its relations with the UN, after this crisis the Court missed no opportunity to emphasize that it was part of the United Nations and its principal judicial organ, and put forward the law and principles of the Charter.[28] The Court also revised its rules of procedure in 1972 and 1978 to make itself more efficient.[29]

In 1971 the Court gave its advisory opinion in the *Namibia* case[30] declaring illegal the continued occupation of Namibia by the Republic of South Africa following the termination of its mandate. The Court's stock further rose in the eyes of African countries when in 1975 it gave its advisory opinion in the *Western Sahara* case.[31] In this case the Court had occasion to discuss further the principles of decolonization and self-determination and made an important pronouncement on the concept of occupation as a means of acquiring title to territory in Africa.

[24] See R.P. Anand, "International Status of South-West Africa", n. 22, p.119.

[25] Andronico O. Adede, "Judicial Settlement in Perspective", in A.S. Muller, D. Raic and J.M. Thuranszky (ed.),: *The International Court of Justice: Its Future Role after Fifty Years* (The Hague, 1997), p. 51.

[26] See R.P. Anand, "Role of International Adjudication", in Leo Gross, *The Future of the International Court of Justice* (Dobbs Ferry, N.Y. 1976), p. 2.

[27] See Judge Mohamed Shalabuddeen, "The World Court at the Turn of the Century", in Muller, Raic and Thuranszky, n. 25, p. 20.

[28] See Abi-Saab, n. 13, p. 6.

[29] See Guillaume, n. 4, p. 851.

[30] *ICJ Reports*, 1971, p. 16.

[31] *ICJ Reports*, 1975, p. 12.

International Court Regains Confidence

The Court was beginning to regain its confidence, especially the trust of the African countries. The confidence in the ICJ reached its high water mark after its final judgement on the merits on 27 June 1986 in the *Nicaragua* case. Nicaragua appeared before the Court on the basis of its own and US declarations under the optional clause and charged that the United States was "using military force against Nicaragua and intervening in Nicaragua's internal affairs in violation of Nicaragua's sovereignty, territorial integrity and political independence and of the most fundamental and universally accepted principles of international law." The Court unanimously rejected US objections and boldly held that it had jurisdiction to entertain the case on merits.[32] Over the strongest objections of the United States, which withdrew from the case and cancelled its optional clause jurisdiction, the Court gave a decision on merits holding the United States responsible for its actions, as charged by Nicaragua.[33]

This was indeed a bold decision and the Court was well aware of the political risk it was taking in deciding the dispute against the only Super Power and leader of Western group of States even if it was "upholding the basic principles of contemporary international law and the Charter in the way it did in its judgement, and which it could not help doing as a court of law."[34]

This led to what was supposed to be a new crisis. Earlier it was said that the Third World had no confidence in the Court. But with this judgement, some people "started to contend that it is now the Western world that no longer has confidence in the Court, where it risks systematically being put into the minority."[35] France had already withdrawn its jurisdiction under the optional clause in 1974 after the *Nuclear Test* cases. United Kingdom was the only permanent member of the Security Council which had accepted optional clause jurisdiction which itself was full of gaps and reservations. The Court had, therefore, decided the Nicaragua case at a very high cost, it was feared.[36]

Increase in Court's work

But these fears proved to be short-lived and unnecessary panic. The Court had indeed given proof of its impartiality, objectivity and independence.

[32] *ICJ Reports*, 1984, pp. 415-19.

[33] *ICJ Reports*, 1986, p. 14.

[34] Abi-Saab, n. 13, p. 6.

[35] Abi-Saab, n. 13, p. 6.

[36] See R .P. Anand, "The World Court on Trial", in R.S. Pathak and R.P. Dhokalia, *International Law in Transition: Essays in Memory of Judge Nagendra Singh* (New Delhi, 1992), pp. 253ff.

Even if, therefore, it would suffer in the volume of its work in the short run, it was bound to increase its credibility.

Furthermore, with the collapse of communism, international tension between Eastern and Western bloc decreased and cold war between them subsided. This new period was ushered in by a momentous event, the collapse of Berlin Wall on one memorable day in 1989. "Other walls", as Judge Bedjaoui told the General Assembly in his address on 11 October 1995, "erected in the minds of world's leaders and which previously constituted so many impediments to the Court's work" then began to fall.[37]

Charles de Visscher said, "general and prolonged political tensions are one of the gravest obstacles to regular recourse to international justice".[38] Although tension is not altogether gone, it is much less prominent and much less debilitating.

All these factors have led to tremendous increase in the Court's work. In fact the Court was never so busy and has never had so many cases simultaneously in its docket. There are at present 24 cases pending before the Court, many of them brought by the much-maligned Third World, who, it used to be said, did not trust the Court. Even those who were sceptical yesterday are beginning to see the Court's potentiality. As President Mitterand of France some ten years after France had withdrawn its declaration under the optional clause said in 1984 in an address in the Great Hall of the Court:

> "[T]here can be no civil peace without judges, no peace in our international society without judges who are chosen at that level and represent the powerful moral and legal force of the Hall where all the peoples of the world gather."[40]

President Mikhail Gorbachev of the Soviet Union in an article on "The Realities and the Guarantees of a Secure World", published in Pravda on 17 September 1987, said:

> "One should not forget the capacities of the International Court either. The General Assembly and the Security Council could approach it more often for consultative conclusions on international disputes. Its mandatory jurisdiction should be recognized by all on mutually agreed upon conditions. The permanent members of the Security Council, taking into account special responsibility, are to take the first step in that direction."[41]

[37] See Address by President Bedjaoui to the General Assembly on 11 October, 1995.

[38] Charles de Visscher, *Theory and Reality in Public International Law* (1968), p. 369.

[39] See Judge Gilbert Guillaume, President of ICJ, Address to the General Assembly, February 2000.

[40] Quoted in Shahabuddeen, n. 27, p. 24.

[41] See quoted in Adede, n. 25, p. 62.

The Court is now overloaded with judicial work. Judge R.Y. Jennings, President of the Court, said to the General Assembly in his 1991 address:

> "Glancing at this list of cases, we can say one thing with assurance: this is indeed now a World Court, exhibiting in its daily work that quality of universality which is also a feature of the General Assembly. I think there is every reason to believe that this new buoyancy of the Hague Court, which has been developing now for some time, is set to continue. A reason for that belief is that there is perhaps now a greater understanding among Governments of the role that an international Court can and should play in their relations with one another."[42]

It may also be mentioned that a Legal Aid Fund was established by the Secretary General of the United Nations in 1989 to help the poor countries pursue their cases before the Court. This is an excellent move and can help some countries seek justice at the international level which many a time is beyond their reach.[43]

Chambers of the Court

The International Court of Justice has also adapted itself to the new situation under its new rules revised in 1978. The Court offers access by States in a case to chambers of the Court consisting of a group of judges less than the whole Court. While "the number of judges to constitute such a chamber" is determined by the Court with the approval of the parties (Article 26(2)), under Art. 17(2) of its revised rules, "when the parties have agreed, the President shall ascertain their views regarding composition of the chamber, and shall report to the Court accordingly." According to Article 27 of the Statute, a judgement by a chamber "shall be considered as rendered by the Court."

The chambers of the Court, it has been pointed out, offer "an attractive half-way house between international arbitration and adjudication", because it gives the States a more attractive "forum by permitting them a voice in the choice of judges."[44] Proceedings before a chamber would be much less expensive than the establishment and funding of an arbitral tribunal.[45]

But despite the attractiveness of the chamber procedure for its "speed and informality", as well as the opportunity it provides the litigating parties to

[42] *ICJ Yearbook*, 1991-92, p. 207. See also Judge Shahabuddeen, n. 27, p. 22ff; K. Highet, "The Peace Palace Heats up: The World Court in Business Again", *AJIL*, vol. 85 (1991), p. 646.

[43] See Judge Shahabuddeen, n. 27, p. 23.

[44] E. Jinenez de Archega, "The Amendments to the Rules of Procedure of the ICJ", *AJIL* vol. 67 (1973), p. 2.

[45] See Stephen H. Schwebel, "Reflections on the Role of the ICJ", *Washington Law Review*, vol. 61 (1986), p. 1061.

choose certain members,[46] the system of chambers has been strongly criticized on several grounds. Firstly, it is pointed out, it reduces "the ICJ to another Permanent Court of Arbitration, a mere list of judges or arbitrators from whom the parties pick and choose those they want to sit in their case." It diminishes the "institutional character of the Court and the stability and continuity of its composition." Moreover, as happened in the first chamber constituted in the *Gulf of Maine* case where "the parties insisted on having a chamber composed exclusively of Western judges," this would endanger "the universal character of the Court".[47] Luckily, this pitfall was avoided in the other three cases referred to chambers so far.[48]

Fears have also been expressed that the chamber system may fractionalize the Court disrupting the universal development of international law.[49]

Apart from these theoretical objections, Judge R.Y. Jennings has referred to some practical difficulties for the Court and the waste of resources that chamber procedure leads to. As he pointed out:

> "The members of the Chamber are also at the same time members of the full Court. If, therefore, a chamber has one of these major cases on hand, the members of the Court who are also members of the chamber can do little else until the case is disposed of. In other words, whilst the chamber is working full time over its case, the rest of the Court in effect have to mark time until the chamber case is over.[50]

At this time when the full Court has a long list of important cases pending, he said, it "would seem intolerable that those cases should be held up by a chamber case involving perhaps only three of the members of the Court, but involving also just as much work for the Registrar and staff as a full Court case."[51]

It is important to note, however, that in spite of the very full docket of the Court, none of the cases before it at present have been referred to a chamber and in fact none has been since 1987.

Encouraging Trend

As we have seen, there has been a lot of judicial activity during the last few years. Several new international tribunals have been created and we are sitting in the new building of the newest permanent court which has been

[46] See Jennings, n. 8, p. 38.

[47] Abi-Saab, n. 13, p. 9. See also Jennings, n. 8, p. 38.

[48] *Frontier Dispute* (Burkina Fago vs. Mali), *ICJ Reports*, 1985, p. 6. *Elettronica Sicula* (United States vs. Italy), *ICJ Reports*, 1987, p. 3. *Land, Island and Maritime Frontier Dispute* (El Salvador Vs. Honduras), *ICJ Reports*, 1987, p. 3.

[49] See Anand, n. 36, p. 264.

[50] Jennings, n. 8, pp. 38-39.

[51] Jennings, *ibid.*

established for the settlement of disputes under the Law of Sea Convention. Although extensive compulsory jurisdiction has not been conferred on this Tribunal for the Law of the Sea, nor for that matter even on the International Court of Justice, the case load in the latter Court shows increasing interest of States in the judicial settlement of international disputes. There have of course been swings before in the work-load of the International Court and certainly variations will occur in the future. But an awareness seems to be increasing of the need to recourse to judicial settlement as a useful procedure for resolving disputes in a civilized way, in much the same way as individuals do within a domestic system. States seem to be appreciating more and more the dictum of the PCIJ that, "judicial settlement of international disputes, with a view to which the Court has been established, is simply an alternative to the direct and friendly settlement of such disputes between the parties."[52]

Limitations of the Judicial Process

It must be realized, however, that the judicial process has its own limitations. Law is not a panacea to solve all the problems of the international society. As the Court itself said in the *Northern Cameroon*'s case that even if it finds that it has jurisdiction,

> "the Court is not compelled in every case to exercise that jurisdiction. There are inherent limitations on the exercise of the judicial function which the Court, as a court of justice, can never ignore. There may thus be an incompatibility between the desires of an applicant, or, indeed, of both parties to a case on the one hand, and on the other hand the duty of the Court to maintain its judicial character. The Court itself, and not the parties, must be the guardian of the Court's judicial integrity."[53]

It must be confessed that judicial procedure cannot, on the plane of mere fact, be a substitute for war. The judicial approach is limited by the fact that, given the fundamental nature of major disputes that arise in international relations and the clashes of political and economic interests, a judgement does not constitute a settlement. There is no doubt that the much-disputed line between legal and political questions is purely a subjective phenomenon of the minds and wills of the disputants. But the fact still remains that many issues will be as far from settlement after a judge has said all that a judge can properly say as they were before any such pronouncement. It must be admitted that by the very nature of international life, not all disputes can or will be submitted to the international courts. The problem is not that the courts cannot decide the disputes because of their inherent "political" nature. But the problem is that the States won't be prepared to submit disputes or to

[52] *Free Zones* case, Order PCIJ, Series A, No. 22 (1929), p. 13. See also Shahabuddeen, n. 27, p. 23.

[53] *I.C.J. Reports*, 1963, p. 29.

accept judicial decision in cases which involve their vital interests.[54] Professor David Forsythe correctly stated:

> "The ICJ remains marginal in international relations because of the 'up-stream' concern by States that their 'vital' interests not be entrusted to independent judges who will decide disputes with reference to legal rules. Even when the Court finds that the States have given their consent to ICJ jurisdiction, if the resulting judgement is bothersome enough, States from Albania to Iran, from Libya to the US will display defiance rather than compliance. That most States have complied with ICJ and PCIJ judgements means primarily that States gave their consent for World Court adjudication previously because the dispute was not seen as 'vital'.[55]

The assertion that if general compulsory jurisdiction could be established, the problem of war and illegal force would be solved, said Judge R.Y. Jennings, rests—

> "upon an egregiously mistaken assumption that wars and other resorts to force are about what international lawyers would recognize as legal 'disputes' which would answer to the adversarial procedure of a court of justice. Some uses of force, or resort to war have indeed had legal disputes at the core of the matter—notably disputes about boundaries or entitlement to territory, both land and sea—but many again have not. Neither of the World Wars have even remotely lent themselves to so simplistic an analysis."[56]

So long as the world remains as unorganized as at present, and the security and welfare of each State are left in fact to depend upon itself alone, the world history can not be turned into a Court procedure. Similarly, when States demand a change in the law, which they challenge as obsolete, a decision according to law can hardly help in solving the dispute. Indeed, the authoritative declaration of legal rights and wrongs may even impede settlement by encouraging the rigidity of one side in the controversy which might have been settled by a political compromise.[57] To again quote Judge R.Y. Jennings, who said about grave disputes which are neither simply legal nor simply political:

> "[A] Court, in deciding the legal question in legal terms, might be prejudicing or indeed frustrating decisions of which it may not itself be in a position even to understand, other than perhaps marginally. The Court has no expertise or even experience in the political, military and strategic criteria that a political body would expect to apply to this kind of political decision."[58]

[54] See J.L. Brierly, "Vital Interests and the Law", *BYIL*, vol. 21(1944), p. 51. See also Louis B. Sohn, "The Jurisdiction of the ICJ", *AJIL*, vol. 38 (1944), p. 694ff.

[55] David P. Forsythe, "The International Court of Justice at Fifty", in Muller, Raic, Thuranszky, n. 12, p. 397.

[56] Jennings, n. 8, p. 53.

[57] See Anand, n. 10, pp. 231 ff.

[58] R.Y. Jennings, n. 8, p. 31.

He added that sometimes it is better not to settle at all but to *manage* the dispute and referred to "the successful treaty regime for Antarctica which wholly depends upon an agreement *not* to settle the underlying disputes."[59]

It has been correctly pointed out that generally "States have mutual, vested interests in settling (or managing, or just continuing) disputes out of Court. It is because of States' perception of what is in their national interest, i.e. freedom of maneuver as compared to submission to a workable and effective rule of law—that the ICJ has averaged only about three cases per year over the last 50 years."[60]

Wider Compulsory Jurisdiction Helpful

But though compulsory adjudication in comparatively ordinary, non-political, so-called "run of the mill" cases is not an effective substitute for war, that does not mean that it is not in itself a powerful constituent element of peace. While admitting that adjudication must be supplemented by approaches of a different order and that other more informal political methods of pacific settlement of international disputes must be provided, it is essential to increase the jurisdiction of the courts. Even by solving minor day to day disputes, they can help create a law habit among States and create an atmosphere of peace. By deciding these ordinary economic, business or even boundary disputes without much fanfare, they can render a most useful service, as courts do in the traditional field, because by far the greatest number of disputes relate to these matters which, if peacefully settled, can encourage smooth intercourse between States in the present inter-dependent world. It has been well said by an experienced judge:

> "After all, it is the habit of living under the law, and with habitual and normal recourse to the agencies of the law, that will make violence and aggression in defiance of the law more difficult. What we need is not just a crisis law but a law for normal existence."[61]

Basically the principal function of law "is to provide clear principles and rules for the routine ordering of a society by the rule of law".[62]

Conclusion

Institutions and procedures for the settlement of disputes under law are at once the hope and despair of all those who reflect seriously upon relations among nations. One of the basic functions of a civilized legal order is a

[59] Jennings, *ibid., footnote*. Emphasis in original. See for a detailed discussion of this dichotomy of legal and political disputes, Anand, n. 10, pp. 230-241.

[60] See Forsythe, n. 55, p. 401.

[61] Jennings, n. 8, p. 54.

[62] Jennings, *ibid.*

system of courts with jurisdiction to decide every dispute that might arise. In the international society, besides *ad hoc* arbitration courts, we have a number of courts established during the last 50 years but without any regular plan or structured relationship. We have the International Court of Justice which is truly a World Court without any regional restriction as to subject matter in its contentious jurisdiction. But it is restricted as to parties of cases which come before it. Under Article 34(1) of its Statute, "only States may be parties in cases before the Court." Although individuals can and do enjoy "rights" directly under modern international law, the Hague Court is increasingly cut off from a growing and very important part of international law system. Neither multilateral corporations, nor NGOs, nor even the United Nations itself can appear before the Court as applicants or respondents. This is an anachronism created in 1922 which has not been rectified. There is a dilemma. According to a former President of the World Court, if Article 34(1) of that Statute is modified, it "would probably produce a flow of cases with which the Court, with its present staff, organization, resources, could not possibly cope."[63]

Another possible remedy is of course the creation of other kinds of international tribunals and courts which has been done with a lot of enthusiasm. Although the proliferation of new, specialized and permanent courts, like the Law of the Sea Tribunal, are welcome, they all have limited jurisdiction, limited sometimes by region, sometimes by subject matter, sometimes by both. But because of their rather haphazard and unplanned growth, there is a serious danger that international law may "become fragmented as each tribunal ... will tend to produce a specific variety of international law.[64]

In a developed system of courts, as we find in most States, there are legally defined relationships between courts, whether legally defined subordination or legally recognized independence. There is usually one court at the top of the hierarchy. It is suggested that "the ICJ, being the principal judicial organ of the United Nations, and moreover having a general jurisdiction over all questions of international law, would seem apt to fill this role."[65] But we will have to solve the problems of Article 34(1) of the Statute, and its relationship with the specialized tribunals.

Although far-reaching jurisdiction has not been conferred on the International Court, nor is it likely to solve important economic or political problems involving vital interests of States, it is still by far the most successful organ of the United Nations. It is too much to expect States to accept unqualified compulsory jurisdiction immediately. The maxim "calculate the limits of the possible" should be kept in mind. The busier the Court gets, the

[63] Jennings, *ibid.*, pp. 38-39.
[64] See Abi-Saab, quoted by Jennings, *ibid.*, p. 61.
[65] Jennings, *ibid.*, p. 63.

better it is for the world society because it can help promote a more peaceful and less lawless world. It can certainly help reduce tension between States by sorting out intricate facts and clarifying complicated law in numerous disputes that arise between them. Let us remember that each day of peace is a time for the extension of law and every extension of law a reinforcement of peace.

The World Court on Trial

International Court established with Great Hopes

In spite of its glorious record and the respect which was attached to the name of the Permanent Court of International Justice (PCIJ) in 1945,[1] when a new international organization was formulated at the San Francisco conference, the Court was re-established under a new name, the International Court of Justice (ICJ), for political rather than juristic considerations.[2] But in its "reincarnation", the loose connection of the old World Court with the League of Nations was replaced by the integration of the new Court into the United Nations as its "principal judicial organ" and the Statute of the Court was made part of the United Nations Charter (Art. 92). Thus all members of the United Nations became *ipso facto* Parties to the Statute of the Court (Art. 93). But though it was a new Court with a new name which came into existence in 1945, the chain of continuity was not broken, and the new Court stepped into the shoes of the old Court, with the same organization and virtually the same Statute.[3] With a satisfactory record, of PCIJ and its international composition having a body of highly competent and great jurists of the world as its judges, there is little wonder that the ICJ was inaugurated with high hopes and great expectations. As P.H. Spaak, first President of the General Assembly, said at the inaugural sitting of the International Court of Justice on April 18, 1946:

> I would not venture to assert that the International Court of Justice is the most important organ of the United Nations...but I am convinced that it is of quite exceptional importance...I am deeply convinced that peace will not be established until countries have recognized the truth that there can be no civilized world nor any lasting peace, if there be not complete and absolute respect for international jurisdiction and its judgments.[4]

Although compulsory jurisdiction could not be conferred on the new Court as well because of the hesitation and strong opposition of several sovereignty-enamoured big powers, especially the Soviet Union and the

[1] See Report of the UN Committee of Jurists which said that the Court "had functioned to the satisfaction of the litigants". *UNCIO DOC.* vol. 14, p. 822.

[2] See R. P. Anand, *International Courts and Contemporary Conflicts*, (Bombay, 1972), p. 64.

[3] Report of Subcommittee IV/1/A, *UNCIO DOC.* vol. 13, p. 384.

[4] *Year Book of the International Court of Justice* (1946-47), p. 31.

United States, it was hoped that as the Court started functioning and helped in solving some controversial and difficult issues, it would engender in course of time more and more confidence in its working and greater faith in its impartiality. It was expected that the jurisdiction of the Court, which could be conferred only by the consent of States, either by *ad hoc* agreements or under treaties, [Art. 36(1)], or by declarations made under the Optional Clause [Art. 36(2)] of the Court's Statute accepting compulsory jurisdiction before hand in future disputes, would come to be widely accepted as had happened in the case of the Permanent Court of International Justice. Thus as many as 42 out of 52 members of the Statue of the Permanent Court (or nearly 73% of the "international judicial community") had accepted its jurisdiction under Article 36(2) of its Statute.[5] Moreover, almost all the then existing States of the world (all save Nepal, Saudi Arabia, Vatican and Yemen) took part in concluding hundreds of treaties which conferred jurisdiction on the Court. During the eighteen years of its existence in the 66 disputes which came before it, the Court gave 32 judgments, 27 advisory opinions, and more than 200 orders. Its decisions, some of which were of major importance, commanded universal respect and its jurisprudence became a new store-house of international law. Paying "tribute to this remarkable achievement" of the Permanent Court, the *Rapporteur* of the First Committee of Commission IV at the San Francisco Conference foresaw:

> a significant role for the new Court in the international relations of the future. The judicial process will have a central place in the United Nations for the settlement of international disputes by peaceful means... It is confidently anticipated that the jurisdiction of the tribunal will be extended as time goes on, and past experience warrants the expectation that its exercise of the jurisdiction will command a general supprot.[6]

Hopes Belied

These hopes were however woefully belied after 1945 in the tension-ridden bipolar world and amidst power and ideological struggle that ensued between the Communist and the non-Communist States. Although 23 countries which had accepted the jurisdiction of the Permanent Court were deemed to have accepted the jurisdiction of the ICJ under Article 36(5) of its Statute in 1945, not many more countries came forward to accept the jurisdiction of the new Court. In fact 17 countries which had accepted the jurisdiction of

[5] See Leo Gross, "Compulsory Jurisdiction under the Optional Clause: History and Practice:, in Lori Fisler Damrosch, *The International Court of Justice at a Cross-roads*, (Dobbs Ferry, N.Y, 1986), p. 21; Shabatai Rosenne, *The Law and Practice of the International Court*, (New York, 1965) vol. I, p. 419.

[6] Report of the Rapporteur of Committee IV/1, *UNCIO DOC*.913, IV/1/74(1), vol. XIII, p. 393.

the PCIJ under its Optional Clause, let their declarations lapse or terminated them. In 1990, out of the 164 members of the "international judicial community" (including 160 members of the UN and 4 non-members), only 51 States (about 30%) had accepted the jurisdiction of the International Court under Article 36(2) of its Statute.[7] These included 16 States from Africa, 9 from Latin America, 3 from Asia and 23 from West European and other States. The then Soviet Union and the former Communist States of East Europe never accepted the jurisdiction of the Court. China withdrew its declaration in 1972 shortly after the People's Republic of China replaced Taiwan as the legal representative of the Chinese people at the United Nations. France terminated its declaration in 1974 after it refused to appear before the Court in *Nuclear Test cases*. Not only have very few countries accepted the jurisdiction of the Court but even these declarations under the Optional Clause have been made with far-reaching reservations which are found in almost 40 out of 51 declarations. These reservations include questionable self-judging Connally-type reservations concerning matters within the domestic jurisdiction of a country as determined by that country, first made by the United States and originally followed by 10 other countries,[8] and other exclusions, no less damaging.[9] Further, many of these declarations (25 of them) may be terminated by a simple notice which may take effect after a specified time or immediately.[10] Although the United Kingdom is the only permanent member of the Security Council, which at present has accepted the compulsory jurisdiction of the International Court under the Optional Clause, the United Kingdom itself terminated its declaration four times and each time added new reservations in order to avoid being arrainged before the Court.[11]

[7] Since 1951, 11 declarations under the Optional Clause had either lapsed or been terminated. These declarations were made by Bolivia, Brazil, China, France, Guatemala, Iran, Israel, South Africa, Thailand, Turkey and the Untied States. See *Year Book of the International Court of Justice,* (1989-90), p. 63.

[8] Five countries have withdrawn Connally-type reservations but it is still found in five declarations (Liberia, Malta, Mexico, Philippines and Sudan) under the Optional Clause. For details and an analysis of these damaging reservation, See Gross, note 5, pp. 22 ff.

[9] Thus the United States declaration included "Vandenbarg" reservation which excluded all "disputes arising under a multilateral treaty unless (1) all parties to the treaty affected by the decision are also parties to the case before the Court or (2) the USA specially agrees to jurisdiction". This reservation has been included by El Salvador, India, Malta, Pakistan and Philippines in their declarations. See *Year Book of the International Court of Justice,* (1989-90), pp. 62 ff.

[10] See J. Patrick Kelly, "The International Court of Justice: Crisis and Reformation", *Yale J. Int'l,* (1987), vol. 12, p. 350.

[11] See C.H.M. Waldock, "Decline of the Optional Clause", 32 *Brit. Year Book Int. L.* (1956), p. 269; See also Kelly, ibid.

Underutilized Court

In almost forty-six years of its existence, the International Court of Justice has been markedly underutilized. Between 1946 when the Court met for the first time and July 1990, a total of 81 cases i.e. 61 contentious cases and 20 advisory opinions were filed with the Court. In these cases, it gave 51 judgments and 21 advisory opinions and made 242 orders.[12] In 11 of the contentious cases, there was no apparent basis for jurisdiction because the other party had not accepted the Court's jurisdiction.[13] In fact only 17 disputes have been filed on the basis of compulsory jurisdiction under its Optional Clause. In 4 of these cases, a party either failed to appear or refused to comply with the Court's judgments.[14] Nine cases have been filed on the basis of special arrangements. In two of these, the losing party refused to comply with the Court's judgments.[15] The remaining seven were boundary disputes which were amicably settled.[16] In 4 cases in which jurisdiction was based on treaties referring disputes to the Court, the defendants refused to appear before the Court.[17]

Thus, it may be found that even those States which have consented in advance to be bound by the jurisdiction of the Court have sought to wriggle themselves out when subsequently cases were brought against them. What was once a trend has almost become the rule. Since 1972 the respondents in 12 out of 13 contentious cases brought before the Court have contested the jurisdiction of the Court and in most of these cases have chosen either not to appear or not to participate at some stage in the proceedings.[18]

[12] *Year Book of the International Court of Justice*, (1989-90), p. 3.

[13] 9 out of 11 cases were filed by the United States or its Allies against the Soviet bloc countries. See *Year Book of the International Court of Justice*, (1984-85), p. 54.

[14] *Trial of Pakistani Prisoners of War (Pak v. India), ICJ Reports,* 1973, p. 347; *Nuclear Tests* cases (*Australia* v. *France* and *New Zealand* v. *France*), *ICJ Reports,* 1973 pp. 99, 145; *Military and Paramilitary Activities in and against Nicaragua* (*Nicaragua* v. *USA*) *Merits, ICJ Reports*, 1986, p. 14, *Hostages case* (*USA* v. *Iran*) *ICJ Reports*, 1984, p. 3.

[15] *Corfu Channel Case, ICJ Reports* 1949, p. 244; and *Asylum* (Second Phase) and *Haya de la Torre Case, ICJ Reports*, 1951, p. 71.

[16] See Kelly, note 10, p. 363.

[17] *Fisheries Jurisdiction* cases (Iceland), *ICJ Reports*, 1972, pp. 12, 30; Aegean Sea Continental Shelf case (Turkey), *ICJ Reports* 1978, p. 4; Hostages case (Iran), *ICJ Reports*, 1980, p. 3; Nicaragua case, (Merits) *ICJ Reports* 1986, p. 14.

[18] These cases included the two *Fisheries Jurisdiction* cases, *ICJ Reports* 1972, pp. 12 & 30; two *Nuclear Test* Cases, *ICJ Reports*, 1973, pp. 99, 135; *Pakistani Prisoners of War*, *ICJ Reports*, 1973, p. 347; *Aegean Sea Continental Shelf* case (*ICJ Reports*, 1978, p. 4), *Hostages* case, *ICJ Reports*, 1980, p. 3; *Nicaragua* case, *ICJ Reports*, 1984, p. 392, *Border and Transborder Armed Actions* (*Nicaragua* v. *Honduras*) *ICJ Reports*, 1987, p. 69; Certain *Phosphates Lands in Nauru* (*Nauru* v. *Australia*) *ICJ Report*; 1989, *Aerial Incident of 3 July 1988* (*Iran* v. *USA*), *ICJ*

The reluctance of States to appear before the Court is further indicated by the fact that despite endless disputes between them not a single case was brought before it in 1952, 1963-66, 1968 and 1969, and for some time in 1971 not a single case was pending before it. The reticence of the States to make use of the Court is also reflected in the reluctance of the General Assembly and the Security Council, as well as other authorized organs of the United Nations and the specialized agencies to use the advisory procedure of the Court for clarification on numerous issues that come before them. Whereas the Council of the League of Nations requested 27 advisory opinions from the PCIJ, the UN Security Council has requested only one and the General Assembly 13 advisory opinions. Seven opinions were requested by specialized agencies (Economic and Social Council, UNESCO, WHO, IMO and the Committee on Applications of Review of Administrative Tribunal Judgments).

World Court: A Noble Institution

It must be stressed, however, that if the World Court was not kept busy it was not because there was supposed to be something seriously wrong with the Court. In spite of all the imperfections and weaknesses of the International Court, it is considered as "one of the noblest institutions we have achieved in modern times, designed to preserve peace on earth".[19] The Court has magnificently fulfilled its task. All the greatest jurists of the world have almost unanimously acclaimed the work of the Court. Judge Philip Jessup expressed the feeling of competent professional opinion when he said that "by and large the judgments of two permanent international courts give these courts a reasonable claim to be included among tribunals of acknowledged impartiality".[20] William Samore hardly exaggerated the position by declaring that "sweeping allegations to the contrary (notwithstanding), the scales of justice at the international level have generally been balanced with as pleasing a degree of impartiality as ever graced on American court house".[21] It is, of course, possible to disagree with some of the decisions here and there, but generally speaking the quality and integrity of the Court's decisions are accepted by commentators as excellent.

Reports, 1989; *Boundary and Maritime dispute* (*Qatar* v. *Bahrain*) *ICJ Reports* 1991.

[19] E. Foda, *The Projected Arab Court of Justice*, (The Hague, 1957), p. 168.

[20] P.C. Jessup, *The Use of International Law*, (Ann Arbor, 1959), p. 20; See also H.W. Briggs, "Confidence, apprehension and International Court of Justice", *Proc. Am. Soc. Int. L.*, (1960), pp. 25-28; Arthur Larson, "The Law Structure of Peace", *Tenn. L. Rev.*, (1960) vol. 27, p. 505.

[21] William Samore, "*National Judges* v. *Impartial Decisions*: A Study of World Court Holdings", *Chi.-Kant L. Rev.*, (1956), vol. 34, p. 194.

Despite all the political colourings of the election process, the present method has succeeded on the whole in the appointment of praiseworthy judges. It is true that nationality has been a prominent factor during election, and a few candidates less qualified (than others available) might have been elected because of political considerations. But it must be said that the vast majority of judges have been eminently qualified.

After the election is over, the Court is given every facility to maintain its independence. Its judges are given reasonably good salaries and a fairly long tenure at their age. It has been located at The Hague so as to permit a measure of detachment from the political atmosphere of the seat of the United Nations. Moreover, the judicial activities of the Court are never the subject of discussion, much less of approval, by any other organ. As an experienced judge of the International Court has said, the Court thus works:

> in an "ivory tower" isolated from all political pressures and national prejudices: a "tower" in which there is neither east nor west; and to which no allegiance is admitted, other than the pledge to perform the judicial duties and exercise the judicial powers honourably, faithfully, impartially and conscientiously.[22]

Court has an Impeccable Record

Although the Court has not been entirely free from criticism of its decisions by the disgruntled defeated States or their spokesmen and is also accused of partiality and political motivations, none of such accusations stands to reason. The allegation that judges vote merely according to the views of their governments, has been proved to be wrong and without any basis again and again. Various studies closely examining the voting records of judges on the Court have shown that national judges do not merely register and sanction the views held by their own governments.[23] As Weiss, after a close look at the Court's record, recently concluded:

> The statistical analysis of the Court's historical voting behaviour does not reveal regional or political voting alignments.

She further found that:

> A review of the voting record of the ICJ does not indicate that the judges of the

[22] John E. Read, "The place for international law and Justice in the years to come", *Report of 48th Conference of the International Law Association held in 1958*, London, (1958), p. 663.

[23] See R. P. Anand, "The International Court of Justice and Impartiality between nations", in R. P. Anand, *Studies in International Adjudication*, (New Delhi, 1969), pp. 73, ff; Peter J. Liacorous, *The International Court of Justice*, (Durham, 1962) Vol. II, p. 527; Samore, note 21, p. 201; G. Terry, "Factional behaviour on the ICJ: An analysis of the first and second Courts (1945-51) and sixth and seventh Courts (1961-67), *N. U. L. Rev.*, (1975) vol. 10, p. 59.

> Court persistently vote in a predetermined way. Rather it lends strong support to the proposition that the Court has generally functioned as an independent and impartial international judicial body.[24]

Each and every judge stands on his own record. Even when the judges support their government's cases, it is not necessarily a manifestation of bias and can at least partly be explained by similarity of outlook and legal tradition. Moreover, they always support their votes by meticulous statements and cogent reasonings. As Judge Jessup pointed out:

> It is one of the cases which show that a dissection of the views of the judges of the Court to prove some kind of national alignment is often not supportable and may be quite misleading.[25]

With its impeccable record, no knowledgeable person has seriously doubted the Court's impartiality or questioned the integrity of its judges or judgments. It has not only helped in the settlement of some controversial issues between States, but has also fulfilled the essential function of clarification and development of international law. Even within the limited sphere of its activity, hedged in by the sacrosanct limits of consent and curbed by the absence of any execution machinery, the International Court has done a remarkable job in building up a case law which is evidence of existing international law of the highest value. It has also been very helpful in guiding the United Nations in its work and in the development of what has been called "constitutional law" of the United Nations.

If, in spite of all the contributions and considerations, States did not want to accept the World Court's jurisdiction, or hesitated to come to the Court, it was generally because of their own fears of losing the case or avoiding the settlement of their disputes in the tension-ridden multipolar international society. Several explanations were sought to be given why States, particularly newly-independent States from Asia and Africa, were reluctant to appear before the Court. While some observers thought that it was against the cultural mores of Asian-African States to settle their disputes according to law or through law courts, others argued that since international law was a product of the Western Christian Civilization it was no longer suitable in a multicultural world and could not be relied upon to settle disputes by a court applying traditional law.[26] Some scholars felt that not only was international

[24] Edith Brown Weiss, "Judicial independence and impartiality: A preliminary enquiry", in Lori Fisler Damrosch (ed), *The International Court of Justice at a Cross-roads*, (Dobbs Ferry, N.Y, 1986), pp. 128, 129, 133.

[25] Quoted in Edward Gordon, "Observations on the independence and impartiality of the members of the ICJ", *Conn. J. Int. L.*, (1987) vol. 2, p. 404.

[26] See views of Scholars like Quincy Wright, F.S.C. Northrop, Adda Bozeman discussed by R. P. Anand, "Attitude of the 'new Asian-African Countries towards the ICJ", in R. P. Anand, *Studies in International Adjudication*, (New Delhi, 1969), pp. 53 ff.

law Eurocentric, but the International Court was dominated by European and American judges and was not trusted by the newly-independent Asian and African countries.[27] It is important to note, however, that most of these so-called reasons or explanations were merely unfounded conjectures because even the European or American countries never showed more enthusiasm for the settlement of disputes through international judicial procedures.

Court, a Prestigious Body

Be that as it may, it is important to note that, even in its non-use or under-utilization and comparative idleness with so little work, looking at its potentiality, the International Court has its own serenity, prestige and indeed majesty. Even if it was seldom used, it has helped the international society in many ways and is considered as the most successful organ of the United Nations. Free from political controversies and bickerings, it can be extremely useful if used. The United Nations General Assembly several times recommended the States to make more use of it.

United States Challenges the World Court

The World Court was recently challenged by the United States, which not only questioned its authority but even its usefulness as it is organized today. It is important to note that the United States not only claims to be a champion of the rule of law in national as well as international society, but the World Court is said to be its own "child".[28] It is claimed by Americans that:

> The World Court is essentially our idea. We argued for it, we laboured for it and finally it worked out, very largely, by the best American brains. It is of American origin. It came into world because of American initiative; it is American in its conception and in its reflection of our strong national belief in courts of justice.[29]

But in spite of all this rhetoric, the attitude of the Government of the United States towards the World Court has been rather cold, if not altogether hostile. It had never adhered to the Statute of the Permanent Court of International Justice. In 1945, the new Court came into existence, and, the United States as a member of the United Nations, became a party to the Statute of the Court. It then accepted the compulsory jurisdiction of the Court under its Optional Clause with questionable self-judging Connally reservation relating to domestic jurisdiction and far-reaching Vanderbilt

[27] See R. P. Anand, ibid, pp. 58-63. It is interesting to note that the position has reversed today because the Western countries are said to have lost confidence in the Court because of the presence of Asian-African judges. See supra.

[28] See James Brown Scott, *The Relation of the United States to the Permanent Court of International Justice*, (New York, 1923).

[29] A.S. Bustamante, *The World Court*, (New York, 1925), Introduction, p. (ix).

reservation concerning the multilateral conventions. This was, as Sir Hersch Lauterpacht said in the *Interhandel* case, "no acceptance at all".[30] The United States "both accepted and rejected the jurisdiction of the World Court". In the "appearance of almost complete submission to the World Court", there was in reality "virtually no submission".[31] And yet, presenting the American declaration to the UN Secretary General, US Ambassador Herschel Johnson said that it demonstrated US commitment "to a great development of the rule of law in international relations through a broad acceptance of the function of the Court in the spirit of the Charter".[32] Despite strong criticism of the US declaration by numerous American scholars, all efforts to withdraw its reservations failed.[33]

The United States also never wanted to appear before the Court as a defendant. Although it sought to bring before the Court East European countries in seven *Aerial Incident cases*,[34] and instituted proceedings against Iran in *US Hostages case*, it willingly agreed to appear before the Court as a defendant in only one case which related to certain *Rights of Nationals of the United States in Morocco* which was decided by the Court in 1952. In the *Interhandel* case, brought by Switzerland against the United States in 1957, the latter invoked Connally reservation though the Court declined to have jurisdiction in the case on the ground that local remedies had not been exhausted by the Swiss Company.[35]

Nicaragua case

The real test of the United States' commitment and adherence to the rule of law came only on 9 April 1984, when Nicaragua appeared before the Court and charged that the United States was "using military force against Nicaragua and intervening in Nicaragua's internal affairs in violation of Nicaragua's sovereignty, territorial integrity and political independence and of the most fundamental and universally accepted principles of international law." The charge further states that the US was supplying money and training to the rebel forces fighting the Sandinista Government in Nicaragua's civil conflict. Nicaragua, therefore, wanted the Court to decide that the United States must

[30] Interhandel case, dissenting opinion by Sir Hersch Lauterpacht, *ICJ Reports*, 1959, pp. 101-102.

[31] Thomas M. Franck, *Judging the World Court.* (New York, 1986), p. 2.

[32] See quoted in Thoms Franck and Jerome M. Lehrman, "Messianism and Chauvinism in America's commitment to Peace through Law", in Damrosch, note 24, p. 17.

[33] See R. P. Anand, "The United States and the World Court", in R. P. Anand, note 23, pp. 1-36.

[34] All these cases were discontinued because the other parties had not accepted the jurisdiction of the Court.

[35] *ICJ Reports*, 1959, p. 6.

cease and desist immediately from all use or threats of force against Nicaragua, whether direct or indirect. Further, the United States was bound to pay reparations to Nicaragua.[36]

The United States, sensing that such a case was imminent, sought to modify its declaration by a letter to the UN Secretary-General just three days before Nicaragua filed its application before the Court, on 6 April 1984, announcing that for the next two years it would not recognize the Court's jurisdiction concerning issues in Central America.[37] The Court later in its judgment on jurisdiction and admissibility of Nicaragua's application, rejected the US withdrawal in the case on the ground that the United States "by its own choice", and "formally and solemnly" had assumed an "inescapable obligation not to change its 1946 Declaration except upon six month's notice.[38]

The United States challenged the jurisdiction of the Court on the grounds, *inter-alia*, that Nicaragua had not validly accepted the jurisdiction of the Court under its Optional Clause, having failed to deposit the ratification of its Protocol of Signature to the Statute of the PCIJ with the Secretary General of the League of Nations, though notification about its due ratification had been sent. But even more importantly, the United States advanced five separate objections to the admissibility of the Nicaraguan Application "as a legal bar to adjudication", or as calling for judicial discretion "in the interest of the integrity of the judicial function". It pleaded (1) that Nicaragua had failed to bring before the Court "indispensable parties"—Honduras, Costa Rica and El Salvador whose participation was necessary for the rights of those parties to be protected and for adjudication of the issues raised in the application; (2) that the dispute and Nicaragua's allegations that US was engaged in unlawful threat or use of force was essentially within the competence of the UN Security council, and not the Court; (3) that the concept of "collective self defence" could not appropriately be subjected to judicial examination; (4) that the judicial function could not adequately deal with situations involving on-going conflicts; and (5) the Nicaragua had failed to exhaust the regional negotiating processes for the resolution of the conflict.

The Court in its judgment on November 26, 1984, not only unanimously rejected the objections to admissibility of Nicaragua's application, but held by 15 votes to 1 that it had jurisdiction to entertain the case on merits.[39]

[36] *Military and Paramilitary activities in and against Nicaragua, ICJ Reports*, 1984, pp. 169, 170.

[37] Letter from Secretary of State George Shultz to the UN Secretary General (April 6, 1984) to modify the 1946 Declaration in Damrosch, note 24, p. 471.

[38] *ICJ Reports*, 1984, pp. 415-19.

[39] By a Vote of 11 Votes to 5, the Court decided that Nicaragua had accepted its jurisdiction under the Optional Clause despite its failure to "formally" deposit its ratification, *ICJ Reports*, 1984, p. 392. For a valuable critique of the case see B.S. Chimni, "The International Court and the maintenance of Peace and Security. The

US withdrawal from the Nicaragua case

The United States felt grievously hurt because the Court had the temerity to reject US objections to its jurisdiction. After giving "deepest and careful consideration" to the judgment and its reasoning, the United States concluded "that the judgment of the Court was clearly and manifestly erroneous as to both fact and law". the Untied States remained:

> firmly of the view...that the Court is without jurisdiction to entertain the dispute, and that the Nicaraguan application of 9 April 1984 is inadmissible. Accordingly....the United States intends not to participate in any further proceedings in connection with the case, and reserves its right in respect of any decision by the Court regarding Nicaragua's claims.[40]

In a background paper explaining further the US decision, the Department of State reiterated:

> The conflict in Central America... is not a narrow legal dispute: it is an inherently political problem that is not appropriate for judicial resolution. The conflict will be solved only by political and diplomatic means not through a judicial tribunal. The International Court of Justice was never intended to resolve issues of collective security and self-defence and is patently unsuited for such a role.[41]

Asserting that it was "one of the foremost supporters of the ICJ", being one of only 44 of the 159 Member States of the UN, and along with the UK the only other permanent member of the Security Council, to accept the Court's compulsory jurisdiction, the United States pointed out that:

> of the 16 judges now claiming to sit in judgment on the United States in this case 11 are from countries that do not accept the Court's compulsory jurisdiction.... Nevertheless, out of its traditional respect for the rule of law, the US has participated fully in the Court's proceedings this far.[42]

But no more. Said the United States:

> The Court's decision is a marked departure from its past, cautious approach to jurisdictional questions. The haste with which the Court proceeded to a judgment on these issues—noted in several of the separate and dissenting opinions—only adds to the impression that the Court is determined to find in favour of Nicaragua in this case.
>
> For these reasons, we are forced to conclude that our continued participation could not be justified.[43]

Nicaragua Decision and the US response" in *Int. & Com. L. Q.*, (1986) vol. 35, pp. 960 ff.

[40] Letter by the Davis R. Robinson, Legal advisor of Deptt. of State, to the Registrar of the Court, *Am. J. Int. L.* (1985) vol. 79, p. 439.

[41] "US Statement concerning US withdrawal from the Nicaragua case, January 18, 1985" in Damrosch, note 24, p. 473. Also *Am. J. Int. L.*, (1985) vol. 79, p. 439.

[42] Ibid.

[43] Ibid., p. 440.

The United States felt that it could not trust the World Court to do justice to its case. Furthermore, to add insult to the injury the United States went on to say:

> In addition, much of the evidence that would establish Nicaragua's aggression against its neighbours is of a highly sensitive intelligence character. We will not risk US national security by presenting sensitive material in public or before a Court that includes two judges from Warsaw Pact nations. The problem only confirms the reality that such issues are not suited for the International Court of Justice.[44]

Throughout the history of the World Court, nobody had ever doubted the personal honesty and character of individual judges.[45] The United States not only challenged the personal integrity of the Soviet and the Polish judges, but expressed doubts about the future of the World Court itself:

> We are profoundly concerned also about the long-term implications for the Court itself. Decision of November 26, 1984, represents an over reaching of the Court's limits, a departure from its tradition of judicial restraint, and a risky venture into treacherous political waters. We have seen in the United Nations, in the last decade or more, how international organizations have become more and more politicized against the interests of the Western democracies. It would be a tragedy if these trends were to infect the ICJ. We hope this will not happen, because a politicized Court would mean an end of the Court as a serious, respected institution. Such a result would do grievous harm to the goal of the rule of law.
>
> ...because of our commitment to the rule of law, we must declare our firm conviction that the course on which the Court may now be embarked could do enormous harm to it as an institution and to the cause of international law.[46]

Earlier, at the 1984 annual meeting of the American Society of International Law, US Ambassador in the UN, Jeane Kirkpatrick, charged that the World Court judges reflected the political biases and proclivities predominant in the political organs of the United Nations.[47] She was later supported by a former legal adviser in the US Department of State, Monroe Leigh. Leigh said that the "selection procedure for judges and the composition of the Court has increased the impression of the Court as a political organization in which many, if not a majority, of the members oppose US interests".

[44] Ibid., p. 440.

[45] But see comments by Judge Schwebel in his dissenting opinion against the President of the Court, Judge T.O. Elias. Judge Elias is reported to have said in a press interview in December 1984, that "if a State withdraws its acceptance of our jurisdiction without notice, that leads to anarchy and disorder". He added: "A State that defies the Court will not get away with it. Although some States try to show that they do not care, they do in reality". *ICJ Reports*, 1986, pp. 314-15; see also Gordon, note 25, pp. 424-25.

[46] Robinson, note 40, p. 441.

[47] Quoted in Franck, note 31, p. 37.

He pointed out that the emergence of 100 new Member States in the UN system had altered both the composition of the Court and the attitudes of judges. In 1946 there were six judges from the Americas and four from Western Europe. Moreover, the judges from China and Egypt reflected West European influence. In contrast, in 1985 there were only three judges from the Americas, the same number as from Communist States. There were thus "a significantly greater number of judges from nations that are at least sympathetic to interests adverse to those of the United States".[48] He added:

> Besides producing a Court with more members from countries less sympathetic to the US view of international law, the increased geographic diversity of the Court has added to the perception of the Court as a political rather than a judicial body...... While geographic diversity may have enhanced the *political* balance of the Court, it has also undermined the perception of the Court as a judicial rather than a political body.[49]

US withdraws Compulsory Jurisdiction

Having lost all hope and confidence in the Court, on October 7, 1985, the United States took the next logical step of withdrawing its declaration accepting compulsory jurisdiction of the Court, howsoever limited it might have been. Explaining the reasons for such withdrawal, the United States said:

> Our experience with compulsory jurisdiction has been deeply disappointing. We have never been able to use our acceptance of compulsory jurisdiction to bring other States before the Court but have ourselves been sued three times. In 1946 we accepted the risks of our submitting to the Court's compulsory jurisdiction because we believed that the respect owed to the Court by other States and the Court's own appreciation of the need to adhere scrupulously to its proper judicial role would prevent the Court's process from being abused for political ends. These assumptions have now been proved wrong. As a result, the President has concluded that continuation of our acceptance of the Court's compulsory jurisdiction would be contrary to our commitment to the principle of the equal application of the law and would endanger our vital national interests.[50]

[48] See Monroe Leigh and Stephen D. Ramsey, "Confidence in the Court: It need not be a 'Hollow Chamber'", in Damrosch, note 24, p. 108; see to the same effect Leigh quoted in Franck, note 31, p. 38; Abraham D. Sofaer, "The United States and the World Court", *Proc. of the 80th Annual Meeting of Am. Soc. Int. L.*, (1986) p. 207.

[49] Leigh and Ramsey, ibid., pp. 108-109. See to the same effect Fred L. Morrison, "Potential Anthony Clark Arend (ed.). *The United States and the Compulsory Jurisdiction of the ICJ*, (Charlottesville, Va. 1985), pp. 29 ff. Michael Reisman "Termination of the US declaration under Art. 36(2) of the ICJ", ibid., pp. 71 ff.; Anthony Clark Arend, "The ICJ, International Law, US Foreign Policy", ibid., pp. 190-96.

[50] See Damrosch, note 24, p. 477; see also Sofaer, note 48, pp. 207-208.

US "Disappearance" from the *Nicaragua* case

Such an extreme step by the United States, of walking out of the Court after the jurisdictional decision was rendered and before the merits phase got under way, was entirely unprecedented. No other State—not even South Africa in the *South-West Africa cases*[51]—had ever walked out after losing on jurisdiction but before arguing on the merits. The United States' non-appearance, aptly described by the President of the American Society of International Law, Keith Highet, as "disappearance"[52] was, as he said:

> in essence a confession and avoidance—a plea of guilty conscience—as to the propriety of US actions in Nicaragua under international law. Why else quit the Court, which only 4 years earlier had been used in the Hostages case by the United States, with such great success, to uphold international law and acceptable standards of international conduct?[53]

Professor Oscar Schachter also said that:

> the technieal argument by the United States understandably left the impression in many quarters that its case was too weak on the merits to withstand judicial scrutiny.[54]

The US stand was strongly criticized by various scholars, most importantly in the United States itself. Keith Highet called it "an unmitigated disaster".[55] Professor Schachter said that "withdrawal not only prevented the United States from presenting its own case fully to the Court, but it raised the more profound and disturbing question of its commitment to abide by the legal principles on the use of force".[56] Even if one disagreed with majority of the judges whether Nicaragua's 1929 declaration was "in force" in 1945 or not, it could not be said that "their reasoning was patently unsound or their conclusions arbitrary". He added:

> To charge that most of the highly respected judges who supported that position were anti-American is absurd. They include judges who were nominated by the United States and nearly all of them received US support when they were elected. Moreover, it is somewhat ironic that the United States emphasized a highly technical point to try to overcome Nicaragua's willingness to accept compulsory

[51] *ICJ Reports*, 1962, p. 312.

[52] Keith Highet, "Between a rock and a hard place—the United States, the International Court and the *Nicaragua case*", *Int. Lawyer*, (1987) vol. 21 no. 4, p. 1085.

[53] Keith Highet, "Litigation implications of the US withdrawal from the Nicaragua case", *Am. J. Int. L.*, (1985) vol. 79, p. 1002.

[54] See remarks by Oscar Schachter in discussion on "The United States and the World Court", Proc. of the 80th Annual Meeting of Am. Soc. Int. L. (1986), p. 212.

[55] Keith Highet, "You can run but you can't hide'—Reflections on the US position in the Nicaragua case", *Virginia J. Int. L.*, (1987) vol. 27, p. 571.

[56] Oscar Schachter, note 54, pp. 210-211.

jurisdiction when the United States had for so many years urged all States to do just that, and criticized the Soviet bloc and Third World States for not accepting jurisdiction under Article 36(2).[57]

About the State Department's contention that it would not risk US national security by presenting sensitive evidence in public or before two judges from Warsaw Pact States, Professor Thomas Franck said that:

> Those who drafted this statement undoubtedly realized that it would be greeted by nearly universal skepticism.... Most observers, even those of pro-American leanings, will reluctantly group this explanation with the too familiar use by national governments of the 'national security' rationale to withhold evidence of their own wrongdoing. In this they may be wrong but their response will be both human and predictable.[58]

Political Impartiality of Judges

Although judges generally avoid making public comments about their judgments, Judge Manfred Lachs of Poland felt so deeply hurt by imputations of partiality on his part[59] that in his separate opinion he sought to dispel any doubt about the impartiality of judges. "A judge", he asserted, "is bound to be impartial, objective, detached, disinterested and unbiased".[60] Stating that "each and every judge stands on his own record", he quoted Judge Jessup to the effect that "a dissection of the views of the judges of the Court to prove some kind of a national alignment is often not supportable and may be quite misleading".[61] Although the goal of a true judge may be attainable to the very few, he said, every judge can and should attempt—

> to uphold the dignity of a profession to which society for centuries has attached profound importance.... it appears unseemly to doubt a judge on account of the place where he was born or the passport he may carry. And this case is probably unique as one in which these are by implication claimed to impair a judge's status, standing, wisdom, discretion and impartiality and to warrant the limitation of the knowledge made available to him for the discharge of his trust.[62]

In his own restrained way, Judge Sir Robert Jennings in his dissenting opinion expressed his "regret that, in a court which by its Statute is elected in such a way as to assure the 'representation of main forms of civilization and of the principal legal systems of the world', the United States in its

[57] Oscar Schachter, ibid.

[58] Thomas Franck, "Icy day at the ICJ", *Am. J. Int. L.*, (1985) vol. 79, p. 379.

[59] The Soviet Judge, Platon Morozon, had resigned from the Court for reasons of ill health and his successor had not been appointed.

[60] *ICJ Reports*, 1986, p. 158.

[61] Ibid., p. 159.

[62] Ibid., p. 160.

statement . . . should have chosen to refer to the national origins of two of the judges who took part in the earlier phases of the case".[63]

In a brief comment in Columbia Journal of International Law in 1987 Judge Manfred Lachs again felt constrained to defend his voting record to prove his impartiality. He pointed out that "judges from Socialist nations (had) voted in ways not evincing a nationalist or Socialist bias". He himself "while differing on specific issues, (had) voted with the majority of his colleagues in eighteen of the nineteen judgments and four of the five advisory opinions in which he (had) participated while in the Court, being in the minority in this case along with the judge from the United States". He added:

> I simply wish to point out that the concordance of a judge's role with his country's interests or viewpoint does not occur more especially in relation to any particular type of political system. I say one should look at the man and his record, and not make lazy assessments in terms of the labels of political regimes.[64]

He, therefore, decried opinions of some scholars finding judges from countries "allied to the United States" as "friendly to our country" and performing "their judicial functions with competence and independence". This opinion was surely contradictory, he said, for "one should not be 'friendly' to any country if one is to perform one's judicial functions 'with competence and independence'. 'Friendliness' is far removed from legal independence, for a true judge may even vote against his own country". It was deplorable, he added, "when hasty and unjust conclusions are drawn on nationality grounds. As often as not, the drawers of such inferences seem prejudiced against allowing foreigners to decide matters of State interest".[65] And yet, there is little doubt that "if an International Court has to exist at all, nations must submit to be judged by persons of other nationalities. For it is an inevitable and in fact useful feature of the international judiciary that each judge comes to the bench with all his cultural, social and intellectual baggage, including his nationality. A bench of stateless individuals would be tongue-tied or sham".[66]

Dr. Edvard Hambro, formerly Registrar of the ICJ and a keen observer of the Court, also said:

> It should be emphasized that a judge may share the point of view of his government. This does not, however, necessarily mean that the judge votes for his government or for the policy pursued by that government.

Noting the importance of Article 9 of the Statute, Hambro said that "a

[63] *ICJ Reports*, 1986, p. 528.

[64] Judge Manfred Lachs, "A few thoughts on the independence of Judges of the ICJ", *Colum. J. Int. L.*, (1987) vol. 25, pp. 596-597.

[65] Ibid., p. 597.

[66] Ibid., p. 594.

judge, although he does not represent a government, does in a way represent a legal tradition". It means that "the whole experience and philosophy of the judges must be brought to bear in the case. One must expect this to give different results according to the background of the individual judge". This is the reason, he pointed out, "why the voting at times looks as if it goes according to nationality; but this does not in any way even remotely imply that the judges receive any kind of intimation, let alone instructions, from their governments as to how they should vote".[67]

It is indeed unfortunate that aspersions have been cast against some judges without any basis whatsoever so much so that some of them have found it necessary to defend themselves as if they are on trial. It has been shown time and again that even in most difficult circumstances the Court has acted with tremendous restraint and dignity. As several detailed studies have proved its judges are not swayed by political considerations. It is difficult to find any political divisions on the Court and its record so far shows that it can competently and objectively dispose of international disputes without being entangled in such political controversies. Deprecating the criticism made against the integrity of the Court and impartiality of its judges before the US Senate Foreign Relations Committee in 1960, Herbert Briggs said at that time what is equally valid today:

> The muddy flow of misrepresentation about the Court and its judges... is demonstrably the product of ignorance, prejudice and fear, not a rational fear of caution based on knowledge or experience, but a morbid fear of foreigners and of the integrity, impartiality and knowledge of the law of foreign judges. At this level the correlation between apprehensive ignorance, on the one hand, and lack of confidence on the other, is almost 100 per cent.[68]

Reluctance of 'Sovereign' States

If the Court has not been given enough work it is not because there is anything wrong with its working or there exists any distrust among most of the States in the competence and impartiality of its judges.[69] It is rather because of lack of confidence in the legality of their own cases and their continued reliance on the outdated and worn-out principle of sovereignty. Or they subscribe to:

[67] See Edvard Hambro, quoted in Gordon, note 25, pp. 406-407.

[68] See H.W. Briggs, "Confidence, apprehension and, the ICJ", Proceedings of the Am. Soc. Int. L. (1960), pp. 31. See also Professor Dugard in discussion on "Untied States and the World Court", *Proc. of the 80th Meeting of Am. Soc. Int. L.* (1986), pp. 217-221;

[69] See Philip C. Jessup. *The Use of International Law*, (Ann Arbor, Mich. 1959), p. 124.

The good old rule,
The simple plan;
that they should take
Who have the power
And they should keep who can.[70]

It is indeed discouraging to see "nations, large and small, still suffering from the cancer of trust in a false god (of sovereignty) which seems to flatter their vanity but is always served at the expense of their well being".[71]

In today's almost wholly inter-dependent world, sovereignty has to be controlled because it embodies the evil spirit of selfishness which knows no restraint and no standard of judgment other than its own. It perpetuates chaos in international relationships and cannot lead to pacification of the world.

We are convinced that, in spite of all the imperfections of the UN System a better world order and universal peace can be guaranteed only by international law in all its ramifications. Of course it cannot be built in a short time or without tremendous efforts. But as a first step we must use and develop the institutions at hand to better advantage. We can and should use the International Court for the settlement of disputes as much as possible. It cannot do miracles. But it is certainly capable of strengthening peace in an infinity of ways.

Court Busier than Ever

It is encouraging to note that in spite of the ungracious refusal by the USA to accept the decision of the International Court in the *Nicaragua* case and its arrogant refusal to abide by the Court's judgment on merits[71a], the Court has not lost its credibility. In fact, during the last two years, besides *El Salvador-Honduras* dispute pending before a Chamber of the Court, ten more disputes have been brought before it,[72] seven of them by the much-

[70] See quoted by Daniel Patrick Moynihan, "International Law and International Order", *Det. Coll. L. Rev.* (1984), vol. 4 p. 878.

[71] J.H. Ralston, *A Quest for International Order* (Washington D.C., 1941) p. 55.

[71a] The Court gave its final judgment on merits on 27 June 1986 in favour of Nicaragua. *ICJ Reports*, 1986, p. 14 The UN Security Council twice addressed the question of enforcement of the *Nicaragua* judgment on July 31 and October 28, 1986, but the United States vetoed the draft resolutions. On Nov. 6, 1986, the General Assembly passed a resolution (by 93 votes to 3, with 47 abstentions) urgently calling for full and immediate compliance with the judgment of the Court. UN Doc. A/41/PV.53, p. 92 (Nov. 6, 1986). This is the first time that a veto has been used to bar application of Art. 94 of the Charter for enforcement of the Court's decision. See Keith Highet, note 48, pp. 1092-1095.

[72] These are (1) *Maritime delimitation in the areas between Greenland and Jan Mayen* (*Denmark* v. *Norway*); (2) *Aerial incident of 3 July 1988* (*Iran* v. *USA*); (3)

maligned Third World, especially Asian-African States, who, it used to be said, did not trust the Court. The International Court was never so busy in its history. Its dockets are full and the cases are diverse. Even Iran, which refused to appear before the Court in the two cases brought before it *Anglo-Iranian Oil Company and US Hostages* has now found it necessary to seek justice through the Court in *Aerial Incident* case involving international responsibility of the United States for the shooting down in 1988 of Iran Air Flight 655 by the USS *Vincennes* in the Persian Gulf during the Iran-Iraq war. It is important to note that the US has decided to appear before the Court albeit to contest its jurisdiction in the first instance.[73]

Chambers of the Court

The International Court of Justice has also adapted itself to new situations and revised its rules in 1972 and 1978 to facilitate access by States to Chambers of the Court to a group of judges less than the whole Court for a particular case. The main change, as a former President of the Court said, was "to accord to the parties a decisive influence in the composition of *ad hoc* Chambers".[74] This was done by introducing into the Rules of the Court in 1978 a provision that where the parties have agreed upon the formation of a Chamber to deal with a particular case, the President of the Court "shall ascertain their views regarding the composition of the Chamber, and shall report to the Court accordingly". According to Article 27 of the Court's Statute, a judgment by a Chamber "shall be considered as rendered by the Court".

It has been rightly pointed out that the Chambers of the Court offer "an attractive half-way house between international arbitration and adjudication". While it would be ideal to submit disputes to the full Court, Chambers may offer some of the States a more attractive "forum by permitting them a voice in the choice of judges". It provides them advantage of arbitration while providing the advantages over an *ad hoc* arbitration of an accepted body of rules of procedure and the facilities of the Court in The Hague. Proceedings

---

Certain Phosphetes Lands in Nauru (*Nauru* v. *Austrlia*); (4) *Arbitral Award of 31 July 1989* (*Guinea Bissau* v. *Senegal*; (5) *Territorial Dispute* (*Libya* v. *Chad*); (6) *East Timor* (*Portugal* v. *Australia*); (7) *Maritime Boundary* (*Guinea Bissau* v. *Senegal*); (8) *Passage through the Great Belt* (*Finland* v. *Denmark*); (9) *Sovereignty over islands. Shoals and Maritime boundary* (*Qatar* v. *Bahrain*); and *Dispute Concerning Crash of Pan Am Flight 103* on December 21, 1988 in Lockerpie (UK) (*Libya* v. *UK*/*Libya* v. *USA*).

[73] See Keith Highet "The Peace Palace Heats Up: The World Court in business again", *Am. J. Int. L.* (Oct. 1991) vol. 86, p. 650.

[74] de Archega, "The amendments to the rules of procedure of the ICJ", *Am. J. Int. L.* (1973), vol. 67, p. 2.

before a Chamber of the Court would be much less expensive than the establishment and funding of an arbitral tribunal.[75]

The first Chamber was constituted by the Court in response to a request by the United States and Canada in the *Gulf of Maine* case.[76] The second case decided by a Chamber of the Court was *Frontier dispute* between Burkina Faso and Mali.[77] The United States and Italy submitted a case, *Elletronica Sicula S.P.A.* to a Chamber.[78] Another Chamber has been dealing with a long case between El Salvador and Honduras relating to *Land, Island Maritime Frontier* dispute.

Some knowledgeable observers have questioned the advisability of the Chamber procedure in which too many of the same judges are being used for Chamber assignments while other judges are left with little to do. This also leads to the detriment of the functioning of the whole Court. According to some scholars the fully consensual Chambers, in which judges are handpicked by the parties, are inconsistent with the Statute.[79]

Fears have also been expressed that the Chamber system may fractionalize the Court disrupting the universal development of international law. However, there does not seem to be any such indication in a few cases decided by the Chambers of the Court.[80] It may be mentioned, however, that at least seven new cases have recently been submitted to the full court, not to Chambers.[81]

Conclusion

If the great hopes and expectations with which the World Court was established and then revived after the Second World War, have not been fulfilled it is not because the Court has failed to perform its assigned task admirably. Undoubtedly, the World Court has proved to be a very useful body which has not only helped States in the settlement of their numerous disputes but in the clarification, elucidation and development of a useful body of international law. In spite of all the weaknesses of the election procedure for the selection of judges, some of the most competent international lawyers have been elected to the bench. Not all the judges have been equally competent, but once elected, practically all of them have done their job in an impartial and objective manner as judges. One may disagree with the Court's

[75] See Stephen M. Schwebel, "Reflections on the role of the ICJ", *Wash. L. Rev.*, (1986) vol. 61, p. 1061.

[76] *ICJ Reports*, 1984, p. 246.

[77] *ICJ Reports*, 1986, p. 554.

[78] *ICJ Reports*, 1991, p. 15.

[79] Judge Shahabuddeen expressed such doubts in his dissenting opinion to the Order of the Court concerning the *Nicaragua Intervention in the EL Salvador-Honduras* case. *ICJ Reports*, 1990, p. 18. (order of Feb. 28).

[80] See Stephen M. Schwebel, note 75, p. 1061.

[81] Keith Highet, note 73, p. 649.

judgments here and there, but one can not dismiss them lightly because of the meticulous reasons and reasonings which the Court and its judges always provide in their judgments. Indeed, if the States do not bring their cases before the Court it is not because of their lack of faith in the Court's integrity and impartiality, but for the reason of their distrust in the soundness of their own cases and weakness of their own reasons.

It must be admitted that the World Court is not a panacea to solve all the problems in the international society. It works in a tension-ridden, multipolar, divided world society and has only a persuasive authority over authoritative sovereign States. It can certainly help reduce tension between States by sorting out intricate facts or clarifying complicated law in numerous disputes that arise between them. The busier the Court is the better it is for the world society because it can help promote a more peaceful and less lawless world. It needs all the constructive support of all knowledgeable persons of such a world. But it is important to emphasize that the World Court is not a "court" if it is only respected by a party when it renders a favourable judgment. Unfavourable and unpopular judgments too should be accepted as faithfully as victories. President Eisenhower of the United States put it simply and well: "It is better to lose a point now and then in an international tribunal, and gain a world in which everyone lives at peace under the rule of law."[82]

[82] See quoted in Franck, note 31, p. 23.

Common Heritage of Mankind: Mutilation of an Ideal

Common Heritage of Mankind: Arvid Pardo's Initiative

Ever since Arvid Pardo, Malta's representative to the United Nations, startled much of the international community with his unique proposal that the UN declare the seabed and ocean floor "underlying the seas beyond the limits of present national jurisdiction" to be the "the common heritage of mankind," and not "subject of national appropriation in any manner whatsoever," the nations of the world have been busy in attempting to build on a largely outdated and outmoded extant oceanic law a regime to govern the ever-increasing uses of the oceans and their resources.[1] By early 1960s, it had come to be known that beyond the continental margin, generally referred to as the deep sea-bed, there lay extensive deposits of valuable manganese nodules. Potentially mineable, these nodules contain at least 25 per cent manganese, 1.25 per cent nickel, 1 per cent copper and 1.22 per cent cobalt, all metals essential for a modern industrial economy.

In a very comprehensive, well-documented and forthright speech before the First Committee of the General Assembly on 1 November 1967, Pardo referred to rapid technological progress made by a few advanced countries which had made it possible to exploit the tremendous resources, far greater than the resources known to exist on dry land, of the sea-bed and the ocean floor. The area, he pointed out, was also of vital and increasing strategic importance and technology permitted its effective exploitation for military and economic purposes. Some countries might be tempted, he apprehended, "to use their technical competence to achieve near-unbreakable world dominance through predominant control over the seabed and the ocean floor." Indeed, the process had already started, he informed the committee, "and will lead to a competitive scramble for sovereign rights over the land underlying the seas and oceans, surpassing in magnitude and in its implication last century's scramble for territory in Asia and Africa".[2] The sequence of a competitive scramble for sovereign rights over the sea-bed, he said, could be "very grave":

[1] See *Note verbale* dated 17 August 1967, from Permanent Mission of Malta to the UN Secretary General. Doc. No. A/6695. *UN GAOR*, 22nd Sess., Agenda item 92, annexes (1967), p. 1.

[2] *UN GAOR*, 22nd Sess., 1st Cmtee, 1515th Mtg, 1 November 1967, p. 12.

> At the very least, a dramatic escalation of the arms race and sharply increasing world tensions, caused also by the intolerable injustice that would reserve the plurality of the world's resources for the exclusive benefit of less than a handful of nations. The strong would get stronger, the rich richer, and among the rich themselves there would arise an increasing and insuperable differentiation between two or three and the remainder. Between the very dominant Powers, suspicions and tensions would reach unprecedented levels. Traditional activities on the high seas would be curtailed, this is a virtually inevitable consequence of the present situation.[3]

He emphasized the need for the creation of an effective international regime for the sea-bed and ocean floor beyond a clearly defined national jurisdiction and acceptance of that area as "common heritage of mankind" to be used and exploited for peaceful purposes for the exclusive benefit of mankind as a whole.[4]

Sea-Bed Committee: A Forum for Developing New Law

The General Assembly responded by not only unanimously declaring the sea-bed and ocean floor beyond the limits of national jurisdiction as "common heritage of mankind" which could not be appropriated by any state, but by establishing an *ad hoc* Sea Bed Committee, which was later made permanent and which became a forum for preliminary negotiations on a new law of the sea. On 18 December 1970, on the recommendation of this Committee, the General Assembly unanimously adopted a Declaration of Principles Governing the Sea-Bed and Ocean Floor, which said, *inter alia*, that the Sea-bed beyond national jurisdiction was not subject to national appropriation or sovereignty but was "the common heritage of mankind," and that it must be "exploited for the benefits of mankind as a whole, and taking into particular consideration the interests and needs of the developing countries."[5] Earlier, in 1969, over the objections of the technologically advanced countries, which wanted to maintain their legal right to exploit the new found precious resources of the sea-bed, the General Assembly declared that the sea-bed must be exploited "under an international regime including appropriate international machinery." Until such a regime was established, it declared a moratorium on all exploitation activities in the sea-bed beyond national jurisdiction.[6]

[3] Arvid Pardo, in UN Doc. A/C, I/PV. 1515, 1 November 1967, pp. 57-60.
[4] Pardo, in UN Doc. A/C, I/PV, 1516, 1 November 1967, p. 6.
[5] UN GA Resolution 2749 (XXV).
[6] UN GA Resolution 2574 D (XXIV).

Legal Value of the Principle

The principle of deep seabed beyond the limits of national jurisdiction being the "common heritage of mankind", iterated and reiterated by the UN General Assembly in numerous resolutions, not only symbolized the interests and aspirations of the developing countries, but had been endorsed by all the developed countries, including the United States. As early as 1966, President Lyndon B. Johnson wanted to "ensure that the deep seas and the ocean bottoms are, and remain, the legacy of all human beings."[7] In 1970, President Richard Nixon, renouncing all sovereign rights to the seabed and its resources and announcing the American policy to help establish an international machinery to administer the licensing of exploration and exploitation of the resources of the seabed, declared:

> The International Seabed Area would be the common heritage of mankind and no State could exercise sovereignty or sovereign rights over this area or its resources.[8]

Presidents Gerald Ford and Jimmy Carter recognized these principles without any question and enthusiastically participated at the UNCLOS-III to develop an international regime to govern seabed mining activities. In spite of all these endorsements, several Western scholars and statesmen called the concept merely a "neologism", which meant different things to different people.[9] It was said to have "no legal content"[10] and was unknown in international law. They objected to its inclusion because it was not clear as to what its "legal implications" would be.[11] Others believed, as Professor Brown said:

> [T]he concept of the common heritage of mankind is not a legal principle but embodies rather agreed moral and political guidelines which the community of States has undertaken as a moral commitment to follow in good faith in the elaboration of legal regime for the area beyond the limits of national jurisdiction.[12]

On the other hand, most developing states supported the concept of

[7] Quoted by Jon Van Dyke and Christopher Yuen, "Common Heritage' Vs. 'Freedom of the High Seas', Which Governs the Seabed"? *San Diego Law Review*, vol. 19 (1982), pp. 526-27.

[8] "Summary of Provisions of the Draft proposed by the United States for a 'UN Convention on the International Seabed Area' 3 August 1970", *AJIL*, vol. 65 (1971), p. 180.

[9] See Belgian delegate, Debergh, in Seabed Committee, quoted in R.P. Anand, *Legal Regime of the Seabed and the Developing Countries* (New Delhi, 1972), p. 206.

[10] See Canadian delegate Alan Beesley, quoted ibid.

[11] See French, Japanese and Soviet delegates, quoted ibid.

[12] E.D. Brown, "The 1973 Conference on the Law of the Sea: The Consequences of Failure to Agree", Paper presented at the Sixth Annual Conference of the Law of the Sea Institute, University of Rhode Island, on 21 June 1971, *Proceedings*, p. 18.

'common heritage', which, as the Indian representative said, "symbolizes the hopes and needs of the developing countries, which can legitimately expect to share in the benefits to be obtained from the exploitation of the resources. These benefits would help to dissipate the harsh inequalities between the developed and the developing countries."[13]

The Brazilian delegate said that "this key concept should provide the cornerstone for a legal regime for the area and, in particular, for the exploration, use and exploitation of its resources." Referring to the general criticism that it lacked 'legal content' and was not a 'self-explanatory legal concept', he referred to the report of the Legal Sub-committee where it had said that "before their adoption, all legal concepts are devoid of legal content."[14]

The principles on which the new legal regime was to be based, said Ambassador Pardo of Malta,

> could not be sought in traditional doctrines of international law; they must be new, equitable and moral.... The concept that any area was to be administered in common for common good was somewhat alien to existing international law. Nevertheless, its introduction as the basis of international law on the sea-bed and ocean floor was essential, not only for the development of that environment but also for the peaceful development of the world.[15]

The Chairman of the Sea-bed Committee, Amerasinghe of Ceylon, stated:

> There are, we realize, many who are alarmed by what they consider to be the formulation of a novel concept hitherto unknown, but the traditional legal concepts are not, we feel, applicable to this unique area and its resources. If the area and its resources are to be saved from competitive exploitation restricted necessarily to those with financial resources and the technological power to exploit them, it is necessary for us to abandon those traditional concepts and evolve a new concept.

Traditional international law, especially customary law, he said:

> ...has in the past found its origin in the convenience and power of the few. It is the duty of this Organization to see that the resulting inequalities are removed and that in the future, international law is designed to serve the interests of all mankind, especially the economically weaker sections of mankind.[16]

Ballah of Trinidad and Tobago considered the concept a "useful rallying cry, for it symbolized the interests, needs, hopes, desires and objectives of all peoples."[17]

[13] Sen (India) in UN Doc. A/C 1/PV. 1878. 31 October 1969, p. 28.

[14] Saraiva Guerreiro (Brazil) in UN Doc. A/C 1/PV. 1674, 31 October 1969, pp. 7-10.

[15] Pardo (Malta), in UN Doc. A/AC. 135/WG, 1/SR. 3; 6-14, 3 September 1968, p. 52.

[16] UN Doc. A/C, 1/PV. 1673. 31 October 1969, pp. 18-20.

[17] UN Doc. A/C, 138/SC. 1/SR, 12-29, 6 November 1969, p. 47.

Kanchet of Kuwait said that if the concept "has no legal content at present, there is nothing to prevent us from imparting such a content to it." He pointed out that "international law is in gestation, as it were: it is in a constant state of flux; it evolves, since in international relations there arise new and special circumstances for which provision must be made in terms of new rules that would correspond to them." He called this principle "the very backbone of the entire system that should in future govern the exploitation of and exploration of the sea-bed and ocean floor."[18]

In an eloquent and brilliant speech, the veteran Norwegian Ambassador, Edvard Hambro, very strongly supported the concept of 'common heritage of mankind'. Referring to the criticism that it was not an established term in the vocabulary of international law, he said:

> That may be, but the problems with which we are confronted are novel and the solutions we must offer in this area in order to establish international justice and maintain international peace can hardly be found in the bookshelves of international term libraries. We must not be afraid of new concepts or of new terms to explain them. New words are needed for new concepts.

The deep-ocean floor, he insisted, "is not free for all where everybody can do what he wants for various purposes." Basic principles of law govern those areas, "but those principles are so rudimentary in substance and so general in form that they obviously must be further elaborated and supplemented to suit the host of problems which the technical revolution has created and will continue to create in those areas." The term 'common heritage of mankind', he suggested,

> ...points to something valuable, referring to the past as well as to the present and future, emphasizing that those areas and the riches contained therein with their possibilities and problems, have been passed on to the present international community as a heritage of mankind and for common benefit as a whole, not to any individual nation or group of nations.[19]

Mrs. Alva Myrdal of Sweden regretted a tendency on the part of some industrialized countries to avoid expressing conviction in the 'supreme principle' of the 'common heritage of mankind'. We were standing, she said, at "crucial crossroads," and "if different positions were taken on this fundamental principle, it would amount to more of a parting of ways than is generally accounted for" and "would entail differences on practically all the remaining issues, however technical they have appeared in the discussion." On the other hand, if this principle was accepted as a foundation, the Sea-Bed Committee could proceed with formulating "a definite set of international

[18] UN Doc. A/C, 1/PV. 1675, 3 November 1969, p. 51.

[19] UN Doc. A/C, 1/PV, 1676. 4 November 1969. pp. 27-28. See also Venezuela in UN Doc. A/C. 1/PV. 1678. 6 November 1969. pp. 63-65.

legal precepts in order to save the sea-bed area and its resources from competitive exploitation."[20]

Although some states had objected to the phrase 'common heritage of mankind' on the ground that it lacked precision and legal content, none of them was opposed to the essential ideas it expressed. Most of them referred to certain general principles like (a) inappropriability and indivisibility of the sea-bed beyond national jurisdiction; (b) international regulation of the exploration and exploitation activities of this common property; (c) equitable distribution of benefits among all countries irrespective of the geographical location of states; (d) freedom of access, use, and navigation; (e) use of the sea-bed only for peaceful purposes' and (f) international co-operation. All of these ideas were supposed to be subsumed in the generic term 'common heritage of mankind' and were emphasized by most of the countries in different words and with varying emphases. These were also the principles which came to be elaborated upon and accepted in the General Assembly Resolution 2749 (XXV) of 18 December 1970, on 'General Principles'.

International Machinery for Area Beyond National Jurisdiction

Although it became possible, after extensive negotiations and diplomatic bargaining and with express reservations by several delegations, to reach agreement on the 'general principles' "as a compromise, with all its attendant inadequacies—warts and all,"[21]—and this was no mean achievement—,it did not solve the most difficult questions relating to the exploration of the deep sea-bed and exploitation of its resources. It emphasized, however, that the sea-bed area beyond national jurisdiction should be explored and exploited 'for the benefit of mankind as a whole', and that an 'international regime' and 'appropriate machinery' for the exploration and exploitation of the area should be established. At the same time it postponed resolving the difficult problems about the nature of this machinery, its powers, and functions.

There was much dispute and little agreement as to how this area should be exploited for the common benefit of all. Since the industrialized countries of the West had both the resources and the fast-developing technology to exploit the mineral wealth of the sea-bed they did not want to be hampered in their projects in this regard. They wanted and suggested the creation of an International Sea-bed Resources Authority which would license and regulate private companies, with guaranteed non-discriminatory access to the resources for a reasonably long period, without strict limits on production and with

[20] UN Doc. A/C. 1/PV. 1680, 7 November 1969, pp. 12-17. See also Solomon (Trinidad and Tobago), ibid., p. 11 Schram (Iceland) in UN Doc. A/C, 1/PV. 1678. 6 November 1969, p. 42.

[21] Amerasinghe (Ceylon) in UN Doc. A/C, 1/PV. 1772. 25 November 1970, p. 18-20.

royalties to be shared for common purposes. They also wanted the regime and the machinery to be structured in such a manner as to reflect realistically the principal interests of different groups of states and permit the technologically advanced countries to exercise a dominant role. In line with this trend of thought, some technologically advanced countries, like the United States, the United Kingdom, France, the Soviet Union and Poland, submitted drafts and working papers regarding proposals for an international regime, including an international machinery, to the Sea-bed Committee during the 25th and 26th sessions of the General Assembly.[22]

These proposals were, however, totally unacceptable to the developing countries. Unable to exploit the seabed resources themselves, and skeptical about the intentions of the developed countries which might soon begin to exploit the resources with the striding marine technology, the under-developed countries wanted the international seabed area to be held in trust by the proposed Seabed Authority and developed as a common resource. They felt that they could be assured of real participation only if the Authority itself carried out deep seabed mining on behalf of the international community as a whole. A regime based on licences or concessions would not be equitable because it would give advantage to the technologically advanced countries, create a monopoly for them and serve only the interests of individual countries or companies, rather than those of mankind as a whole.[23] They, therefore, pleaded for the creation of a strong international machinery with comprehensive powers, including the power to explore and exploit the deep sea-bed and its resources. In accordance with these idea, during the 1971 session of the Sea-bed Committee, several developing countries submitted proposals for a centralized, democratically structured international regime and an international machinery with comprehensive powers for the exploration and exploitation of the seabed and its resources.[24]

While the international society, almost for the first time in history, came to agree on a large part of international law of the sea, and the Third United Nations Conference, despite its cumbersome and time-consuming rules of procedure, settled most of the issues that looked in the beginning unsolvable, one issue that could not be resolved and which threatened to disintegrate the entire conference many a time, was the mining of deep seabed manganese nodules. Although this activity had not yet started and was likely to have less immediate effect on the basic interests of most states than other activities on which agreement had been reached, it had caught the imagination of the whole mankind because it contained an unimaginable amount of precious

[22] See for details and discussion of these drafts, Anand, note 9, pp. 215-20.

[23] See for this and other views of the developing countries, Anand, ibid., pp. 220-24.

[24] See for a description and discussion of these proposals by Tanzania. 13 countries of Latin America and Malta, Anand. ibid. pp. 224-32.

mineral resources. A handful of companies and multinational consortia in the United States, Japan, Canada, the United Kingdom, West Germany and some other technologically advanced countries were already prospecting for the mineral rich nodules and were developing the technology to recover them from the ocean floor and extract their metals. Some American companies claimed to have invested more than 100 million U.S. dollars in these ventures even before the beginning of the conference.

Numerous proposals had been made in the conference both by the developed and the developing countries for the exploitation of mineral resources of the seabed, which had been a subject of intense discussions and acrimonious debates. After prolonged negotiations and innumerable bargaining sessions, compromise proposals were put forward and revised again and again in informal negotiating texts (SNT, RSNT, ICNT and Draft Convention). A consensus on most aspect of this difficult issue seemed to have been reached in the August 1980 Informal Draft Convention. It was agreed that the exploration and exploitation of the area, declared as "common heritage of mankind", should and would be conducted by or under the authority of an International Seabed Authority to be created for this purpose (Article 153). According to the "Basic conditions of prospecting, exploration and exploitation", contained in 1980 Draft Convention,[25] the Authority (through its functional organ, Enterprise), state parties and private companies might simultaneously explore and exploit the mineral resources after authorization by the Authority under a parallel or dual system. Each state or company (other than Enterprise), seeking permission to exploit deep seabed mineral resources, must submit two mining sites of equal estimated commercial value out of which the Authority would choose one site to be exploited directly by itself or under contract with private entities, leaving the other site to the state or company for exploitation under certain conditions laid down by the Authority, which would include, *inter alia*, transfer of technology to the Authority and the Enterprise "on fair and reasonable terms and conditions", and financial guarantees 'to enable the Enterprise to engage in seabed mining effectively at the same time as the other entities".[26] Agreement was said to have been finally reached on such controversial issues as the powers and functions of various organs of the International Seabed Authority (the Assembly, the Council, the Economic Planning Commission, the Legal and Technical Commission, the Seabed Tribunal and the Enterprise), and the procedures for them to take decisions.[27]

[25] Draft Convention, op.cit., Annex III, pp. 130-51. Similar provisions may be found in Annex I. SNT and RSNT and Annex II of ICNT.

[26] Ibid., Annex III, Article 13, p. 139.

[27] See for details on the compromise "United States" Delegation Report on Resumed Ninth Session of the Third United Nations Conference on the Law of the Sea. July 28-August 29, 1980" (Geneva), pp. iii-v, 16-18, 23.

But as the goal of a final treaty on the law of the sea seemed to be in sight, the newly elected United States administration of President Ronald Reagan put the whole process of negotiations in disarray by its surprise announcement on the eve of the tenth session on 8 March 1981, that the United States would want to review thoroughly the 1980 Draft Treaty before deciding any policy toward it. Some of the leading and influential American mining companies were reported to feel that "too many concessions" had been made by the previous American negotiators, and that "a better deal" could be extracted for U.S. interests from other participants, most of whom possessed neither the financial nor the technological means to engage in deep seabed mining.[28]

The Strong US Objections

Smelling "an ideological rat"[29] in the establishment of the International Seabed Authority which was described as "nothing less than a new socialist international economic order",[30] the United States did not want to get a raw deal. After nearly ten months of policy review, while the whole world waited rather impatiently for Uncle Sam to reassure himself that the Draft Convention was a reasonable compromise document containing wholesome rules for the multifarious uses of the sea, on 29 January 1982, President Reagan announced that the United States would indeed return to the negotiating table and try to achieve an acceptable treaty. He went on to say that "while most provisions of the draft convention are acceptable and consistent with U.S. interests", in the deep seabed mining regime 'we will seek changes'.[31]

The United States objected that the proposed regime for the exploitation of deep seabed resources beyond the limits of national jurisdiction laid down in Part XI of the Draft Convention failed to provide the United States and other industrialized Powers that would be affected by seabed mining "a voice commensurate with those interests", giving undue authority to small countries on the basis of their numbers and voting rules. Moreover, the legal regime, by creating an international sea-bed authority and a machinery for the exploration of deep seabed resources, was based on principles for the organisation of economic activity that would interfere with market forces

[28] See *New York Times*, March 9, 1981, pp. A-1, A-22; Louis Wiznitzer, "U.S., Blocks Law of the Sea Treaty," *Christian Science Monitor*, March 9, 1981, p. 5; John N. Moore, "Sea-law Treaty Could Come Soon," Honolulu Advertiser, June 22, 1981, p. A-6.

[29] Daniel D. Nossiter, "Under-Water Treaty: The fascinating story of how the Law of the Sea was Sunk", *Barron's*, July 26, 1982, p. 10.

[30] See David L. Larson, "The Reagan Administration and the Law of the Sea", *Ocean Development and International Law Journal*, vol. 11 (1982), p. 298.

[31] *Department of State Bulletin* (March 1982), p. 54.

and effectively pre-empt private investment in deep seabed mining. The United States did not like that the Convention's provisions could be amended by a future review conference by a three-fourths majority and even theoretically bind the US without its consent. Moreover, future revenues from seabed mining might be distributed to liberation movements, such as the PLO or SWAPO.

The United States also objected to Part XI because of the requirement that commercial enterprises, as a condition to the awarding of mining rights, must undertake to transfer their mining technology to a competing arm of the Sea-bed Authority, known as the Enterprise, or possibly to the developing countries. It did not like the Enterprise benefiting from discriminatory and competitive advantages over other commercial enterprises through provisions which required funding of its initial operations by state parties through loans and loan guarantees, and a 10-year holiday from paying royalties. They objected as well to the regime's production control arrangements, which would limit the level of the production from the seabed in order to protect land-based producers of the minerals that would be produced from the seabed. The United States complained also about the regime's onerous system of financial payments that must be made by potential miners, in particular a US one million dollar annual fee payable, beginning with the exploration stage when an area was registered by a miner.[32]

On instructions from Washington, the US delegation presented a 68-page book suggesting amendments to more than half of the seabed provisions of Part XI.[33] After nine long, tedious sessions of the Conference and fourteen years of strenuous negotiating efforts, the United States now wanted to renegotiate essential elements of a package that had already commanded widespread support and near consensus. Stunned by the US announcement, the treaty process came to a grinding halt.[34]

Despite all the efforts of the international community, especially the President of the Conference, Tommy Koh of Singapore, to accommodate the American interests and allay US fears,[35] the United States was not satisfied. The gulf was too great. In the end, with all efforts to arrive at a consensus having failed, on 30 April 1982, the United States called for a vote and voted against the Convention along with Israel, Turkey and Venezuela. The

[32] Ibid. See also R.P. Anand "The Convention on Law of the Sea and the United States," *IJIL*, vol. 24 (1984), pp. 171-76.

[33] Statement by Leigh S. Ratiner, Deputy Chairman of the U.S. delegation to the 11th Session of UNCLOS III in "U.S. Foreign Policy and the Law of the Sea", *Hearing before the Committee on Foreign Affairs of the House of Representatives*, 97th Congress, 2nd sess., June 17, Aug. 12, Sept. 16, 1982 (Washington, D.C, 1982), pp. 193-95.

[34] See "United States Delegation Report", quoted in Larson, note 30, p. 54.

[35] See L.S. Ratiner, "The Law of the Sea: A Crossroads for American Foreign Policy", *Foreign Affairs*, vol. 60 (1982), p. 1016; Ratiner, note 33, p. 201.

smaller countries, which opposed the Convention along with the USA, did not share the US views on the treaty but had entirely different reasons of their own for their negative votes.[36] The Soviet group, Thailand, as well as the west European countries abstained but kept their opinions open to sign the Convention.

Although, accepted by a divisive vote (of 130 in favour to 4 against with 17 abstentions, which included the Soviet bloc and a few Western European industrialized countries), everyone realized that it was a monumental achievement in multilateral negotiations".[37] Called "a comprehensive constitution for the oceans", it was said to be "the most significant international agreement since the Charter of the United Nations"[38] providing a legal regime for nearly 70 per cent of the earth's surface. On 10 December 1982, the Convention was opened for signature and immediately 119 delegations signed the Treaty, the largest number ever to sign a treaty on the very first day of its opening for signature. These included 117 nations (15 from developed countries, all of the Eastern block, and 92 developing countries) and delegations from two entities which are not full states (the Cook Islands and the UN Council for Namibia).[39] Although later the Soviet Union and its allies, Japan and even France decided to sign it, the United States, West Germany, UK and Italy continued to oppose the Convention which thus remained a truncated treaty although it had come to be accepted by a vast majority of states. The Convention was kept open for signature till 9 December 1984. It was signed by then by 155 states and four entities (the Cook Islands, Niue, Namibia and the European Economic Community). According to Article 308 of the Convention, it was to come into force one year after its ratification or accession by sixty states. Having received the sixtieth ratification by Guyana on 16 November 1993, the Convention entered into force on 16 November 1994, providing a reasonably clear and codified law of the sea which had been a subject of intense controversy and disputes among states all through history.

[36] Israel voted against the Convention since it gave fuller standing to P.L.O., Turkey wanted to make reservations in regard to provisions, not permitted under the Convention, and Venezuela because of its opposition to provisions on delimitation of marine and submarine areas between states with opposite or adjacent coasts. See *U.N. Chronicle*, vol. 19 (June 1982), pp. 16, 22. See also the Statement by President Reagan on 9 July, 1982, "Law of the Sea and Ocean Policy", *Current Policy*, No. 416, U.S. Deptt. of State, Bureau of Public Affairs (Washington, D.C., 1982), p. 1.

[37] Tommy T.B. Koh (President of the Third UN Conference on the Law of the Sea). Statement at the Opening Meeting of Montego Bay Session in Jamaica on 6 Dec. 1982. UN Doc. No. SEA/MB/1/Rev. 1, 6 Dec. 1982, p. 1.

[38] Edward Seaga, Prime Minister of Jamaica, UN Doc. SEA/MB/2, 6 Dec. 1982, 185th Meeting, p. 1. Hug L. Shearer, Deputy Prime Minister and Foreign Minister of Jamaica, UN Doc. SEA/MB/10 Dec. 1982, p. 2.

[39] See Anand, note 32, 154.

It is important to note that even before 1993, when the Convention was ratified by the sixtieth state, and before it came into force, it had already become effective. Most of the states including the Western industrialized Powers, had adopted most of its provisions in their national legislations. Moreover, the Preparatory Commission (Prepcom), established under the Convention, had been meeting in Jamaica since 1983 to lay down rules, regulations and procedures for the exploitation of the seabed in the common interests of mankind by the International Sea-bed Authority proposed to be established under the Convention and its various commissions. It had also been dealing with the problems of land-based producer states, preparing a draft mining code, and was making arrangements for the establishment of an International Tribunal for the Law of the Sea and framing its rules. Some countries had already applied for permission to explore the resources of the seabed. Four states—France, India, Japan and the Soviet Union applied for registration as pioneer investors in 1983-84. After examination by the Group of Technical Experts, India was registered as a pioneer investor on August 17, 1987 for an area of 52,300 square kilomeres in the Central Indian Ocean. France, Japan and the Soviet Union were also so registered and each of them was allocated a pioneer area of 7,500 square kilometres in the Clarion-Clipperton Fracture Zone in the North Pacific Ocean on 17 December 1987.[40]

The U.S. Accepts Part of the 1982 Convention

As we have noted earlier, the Convention had been accepted as 'a package' and 'an integral whole'.[41] It was for this reason that, as President of the Conference, Tommy Koh, explained—

> ...the Convention does not provide for reservations. It is therefore not possible for States to pick what they like and disregard what they do not like. In international law, as in domestic law, rights and duties go hand in hand. It is, therefore, legally impermissible to claim rights under the Convention without being willing to assume the correlative duties.

He added: "Let no nation put asunder this landmark achievement of the international community."[42]

But having been accepted by a vast majority of states, the Convention, or a large part of it, had become part of customary international law even before its formal ratification and was supposed to be binding on signatories

[40] See R.P. Anand, "UNCLOS: Compromise or Mutation", *World Focus*, No. 177 (New Delhi, September 1994), p. 3.

[41] See Koh, note 37, pp. 3-6.

[42] Ibid., p. 6.

and non-signatories alike.[43] Even the United States, which had refused to accept the final version of the Convention, agreed with this view. It believed that a large part of the law of the sea codified in the Convention relating to coastal state jurisdiction of territorial sea, EEZ., or continental shelf; as well as rules relating to navigation and overflight through territorial sea and straits, had all become part of customary law.[44] As Ambassador Malone said: "The Convention does not make the navigation and overflight provisions parochial to just the Convention [and] they apply to all parties and non-parties."[45] Proclaiming a 200-mile exclusive economic zone, on 10 March 1983, President Reagan also declared that besides deep seabed mining provisions, objected to by the United States, "the Convention also contains provisions with respect to traditional uses of the oceans *which generally confirm existing maritime law* and practice and fairly balance the interests of all States."[46]

But while claiming benefit of these various rules laid down in the Convention as customary law which would serve a wide array of US national interests—the mobility of air and naval forces, commercial navigation, fisheries, environmental protection, scientific research, marine mammals, dispute settlement, and more—President Reagan asserted:

> Deep seabed mining remains a lawful exercise of the freedom of the high seas open to all nations. The United States will continue to allow its firms to explore and, when the market permits, exploit those resources.[47]

Ambassador Malone also said that while the navigational and overflight provisions would apply to parties and non-parties alike, "under Article 137, your deep seabed provisions are parochial to the Convention and only parties could take advantage of those."[48]

Despite the universal acceptance of the principle of "common heritage of mankind" in successive resolutions of the General Assembly and at the Conference, it was said to be no more than a "moral" or "political" principle since its implementation was conditioned by the acceptance of a legal regime in a universally agreed treaty. In the absence of such a treaty, it was no more

[43] See also Hasjim Djalal, Indonesian Ambassador to the UNCLOS-III, in S.A. Clingan (ed.), *Law of the Sea: State Practice in Zones of Special Jurisdiction*, Proceedings of the 13th Annual Conference of the Law of the Sea Institute, 1979 (Honolulu, 1982), pp. 512-13; see discussion on this point, ibid, pp. 516-24.

[44] The Reagan administration's policy was based on this unquestioned assumption "It was taken for granted", see Ratiner, note 35, pp. 1011-12.

[45] U.S. Ambassador Malone, *Hearings*, note 33, p. 102, 105. See also Powell A. Moore, Assistant Secy. of State. ibid, Kronmiller, ibid., p. 294.

[46] "Oceans Policy and the Exclusive Economic Zone", *Current Policy*, No. 4711, U.S. Dept. of State (Washington, D.C., March 10, 1983), p. 3: emphasis added. See also Malone, ibid., p. 2.

[47] President Reagan, ibid.

[48] Malone, *Hearings*, note 33, p. 102.

than an agreement to agree. No matter how well motivated, the common heritage principle was, therefore, said to be "still devoid of any legal content whatsoever."[49]

Interim Seabed Mining Regime

Following the US views, besides the United States, some other developed States as well, Germany, U.K., France and later the Soviet Union and Japan, enacted unilateral legislations to license their nationals to mine the deep seabed mineral resources, establishing interim seabed mining regimes until the Law of the Sea Convention came into force.[50] But although, again following the United States, they all considered seabed mining as a freedom of the high seas, no company or country ever thought that it would provide a secure legal foundation for investment, because it would be violative of the universally recognized principle of the common heritage of mankind. In any case, nobody has so far reached the stage of actually exploiting the seabed minerals. If somebody were to do so, it would create a conflicting situation because according to Article 137(3) of the 1982 Convention, "No State or natural or juridical person shall claim, acquire or exercise rights with respect to the minerals recovered from the area except in accordance with this part. Otherwise, no such claim, acquisition or exercise of such rights shall be recognized."

A licence or permit issued by any state outside the Law of the Sea Convention, once the Convention entered into force for a substantial number of states, would be of questionable legal validity.[51]

Fresh Negotiations Under the Auspices of The UN Secretary-General

The world community was of course deeply upset that some of the biggest maritime Powers, including the only Super Power, had refused to accept the Convention although even they had adopted more than 90 per cent of its rules in their national legislations and practice. In the beginning not many countries came forward to ratify it hoping that the United States and its allies would change their mind. But when they refused to budge, the international community agreed to change the Convention to satisfy the United States, because the Convention was too important to be left in a limbo.

In July 1990, the UN Secretary-General, Javier Perez de Ceullar, took the initiative to convene "informal consultations" aimed at achieving universal participation in the 1982 Convention, which represented many years of

[49] Dennis W. Arrow, "The Customary Norm Process and the Deep Seabed" *Ocean Development and International Law Journal*, vol. 9 (1981), p. 29.

[50] See Anand, note 32, p. 179.

[51] Anand, ibid., pp. 179-183.

negotiations and which had already made a significant contribution to the international legal maritime order. He noted that in the eight years since it was adopted, certain significant political and economic changes had occurred, which had a marked effect on the regims for deep seabed mining contained in the Convention. First, he pointed out, prospects for commercial mining of deep seabed minerals had receded into the next century, against the initial expectations when the Convention had been negotiated. Secondly, there was a discernible shift towards a more market-oriented economy. Thirdly, there had emerged a new spirit of international co-operation in resolving outstanding problems of regional and global concerns. All these factors, said the Secretary-General, should be taken into account in considering the problem relating to seabed mining.[52]

Between 1990 and 1994, a series of "informal consultations", under the aegis of the Secretary-General, were held on outstanding issues relating to deep seabed mining and to meet the US objections to Part XI of the Convention. In 1992, the new Secretary-General, Boutros Boutros-Ghali, continued these so-called "informal consultations" in which some 75 to 90 delegations participated. On August 3, 1993, representatives of several developed and developing states circulated what was called a "boat paper" as a contribution to the process of consultations. After several revisions of the "boat paper" and at the end of the last meeting of the consultations (May 31 to June 3, 1994) there emerged a Draft Agreement Relating to Implementation of Part XI of the UN Convention on Law of the Sea of 1982. On November 16, 1993, as the Convention received its 60th instrument of ratification by Guyana, the imminent entry into force of the Convention on November 16, 1994 added a sense of urgency to these consultations.[53]

The New Agreement

At the resumed 48th Session of the UN General Assembly, convened from July 27 to 29, 1994, a resolution was adopted by 121 votes to none, with seven abstentions, whereby the Draft Implementing Agreement was adopted and opened for signature. According to Article 4 of this agreement, any instrument of ratification or accession to the 1982 Convention, after the adoption of this agreement, "shall also represent consent to be bound by this agreement". Even states which had already ratified the 1982 Convention

[52] See Bernard Oxman, "Law of the Sea Forum: The 1994 Agreement on Implementation of the Seabed Provisions of the Convention on the Law of the Sea", *AJIL*, vol. 88 (1994), p. 687 ff. Louis B. Sohn, "International Law Implications of the 1994 Agreement", *AJIL*. vol. 88 (1994), p. 696.

[53] See U.S. Ambassador David A. Colson, "Current Status of the Convention on the Law of the Sea", *Hearings Before the U.S. Senate Committee on Foreign Relations*, on August 11, 1994, pp. 11-17.

"shall be deemed to have consented to be bound by the agreement" 12 months after its adoption unless they notified otherwise. The Implementing Agreement shall come into force 30 days after 40 states have signed or accepted its provisions and shall be applied provisionally with effect from November 6, 1994 itself. Such provisional application, including provisional membership of states, which have signed but not ratified the 1994 agreement, can continue up to November 16, 1998 with all the rights and obligations of members.[54]

The United States Gets All It Wanted

On substantive issues and objections by the United States against Part XI of the 1982 Convention, the international community bent backwards to make sure that Washington was satisfied and got all it wanted and more. Thus:

1. A US seat is guaranteed on the Council or the executive organ of the proposed International Sea-bed Authority.
2. The United States and a few other industrialised states acting in concert can block decisions in the Council. The Assembly of the proposed Sea-bed Authority cannot act without the Council's recommendations.
3. Future amendments to the regime cannot be adopted over US objections.
4. Provisions compelling the transfer of seabed mining technology were dropped.
5. Provision of the power of the Sea-bed Authority to limit production from the seabed to protect the interests of land-based producers was dropped. In its place restrictions on subsidisation of seabed mining based on GATT were adopted.
6. Seabed mine sites to three US-led multinational consortia on terms no less favourable than those granted to Japanese, French, Russian, Indian or Chinese claimants which have already been registered.
7. The provision for large annual fees that miners were to pay prior to commercial production was dropped.
8. The Enterprise, the engineering arm of the Sea-bed Authority, was restructured, subjecting it to the same requirements as other commercial enterprises; eliminating the requirement that parties to the Convention fund its mining activities or provide it technology; and providing that it operates through joint ventures with commercial enterprises.[55]

But the United States and several other states have still not ratified and accepted the Convention.

[54] See Anand, note 32, p. 6.

[55] Ibid., p. 7. See also Oxman, note 52, pp. 690 ff.

The "Common Heritage" Principle Assailed

Although the area of the deep seabed beyond the limits of national jurisdiction is still called and declared as the common heritage of mankind, the term has lost its original meaning and substance when it symbolised the interests, needs, hopes and aspirations of a large number of poor peoples. The principle has lost its lustre and soul. The deep seabed will not be explored and exploited in future as common property "primarily in the interests of mankind with particular regard to the needs of poor countries," as Arvid Pardo had dreamed and the General Assembly desired in 1967 and expressed as an ideal again and again. The deep seabed will now be exploited on commercial terms, irrespective of the needs and interests of the weaker members of the international community. All this is justified partly on the ground that seabed exploitation of minerals is only a distant dream not to be fulfilled until well into the next century. Moreover, this is an age of free enterprise and the new agreement is said to be in accord with the new trend.

Be that as it may, the international community is still said to be better off with a universally recognized, comprehensive treaty on law of the sea with a new agreed law for the twenty-first century which in itself is no mean achievement.

Navigation through Territorial Sea and Straits—Revisited*

Innocent Passage through Territorial Waters

By the beginning of the nineteenth century it came to be universally accepted amongst the maritime states of Europe that the sea, constituting the great highway for commerce and communications between civilized nations and the remotest regions of the earth, should remain unrestricted during the continuance of peace for the complete enjoyment of every nation. Although a small part of the adjacent sea was deemed to be essential for the security of that coastal state and was accepted as under its dominion, even this part, it was felt, should be held subject to the right of innocent passage by foreign ships.[1] The right of innocent passage was, therefore,

> the result of an attempt to reconcile the freedom of ocean navigation with the theory of territorial waters. While recognising the necessity of granting to littoral States a zone of waters along the coast, the family of nations was unwilling to prejudice the newly gained freedom of the seas.[2]

But although everyone agreed and accepted the concept of the freedom of innocent passage through the territorial sea, the meaning of "innocent passage" was not clear and there was a continuing controversy about the passage of warships. Because the chief, or perhaps the sole, reason for the acceptance of a right of innocent passage was "because of a recognition of the freedom of the sea for the commerce of all States",[3] this right came to be confined to merchant vessels or other governmental vessels, and did not extend to warships. As the Harvard Draft on Territorial Waters declared in its commentary on the eve of the 1930 Hauge Codification Conference:

> There is...no reason for innocent passage of vessels of war. Furthermore, the passage of vessels of war near the shores of foreign States and the presence without prior notice of warships in marginal seas might give rise to misunderstanding even when they are in transit. Such considerations seem to be

* Part of the lectures delivered at the Institute of International Public Law and Relations, Aristotle University, Thessaloniki, Greece, on 23-27 September 1996.

[1] See Paul Morgan Ogilvie, *International Waterways* (New York, 1920), p. 104.

[2] See Philip C. Jessup, *The Law of Territorial Waters and Maritime Jurisdiction* (New York, 1927), p. 120.

[3] Ibid., p. 120.

the basis for the common practice of States in requesting permission for the entrance of their vessels of war into the ports of other States.[4]

Jessup confirmed this state of the law:

As to warships, the sound rule seems to be that they should not enjoy an absolute right to pass through a State's territorial waters. As Mr. Root has said; Warships may not pass without consent into this zone, because they threaten, merchant ships may pass and repass because they do not threaten.[5]

The right of innocent passage, even for merchant ships, did not exist in internal or inland waters, nor when the vessel of another state was "approaching the port of a state through its marginal seas or when she is entering or leaving a port of that state".[6] These rules, forming part of customary law, came to be codified for the first time in 1958 in the Convention on the Territorial Sea and Contiguous Zone.

Guaranteeing ships of all states the right of innocent passage through the territorial sea under Article 14(1), the 1958 convention defined "passage" to mean "navigation through the territorial sea for the purpose of traversing the sea without entering internal waters, or of proceeding to internal waters, or making for the high seas from internal waters" [Article 14(2)]. Article 14(3) explained that "passage includes stopping and anchoring, but only in so far as the same are incidental to ordinary navigation or are rendered necessary by force majeure or by distress".

Defining the innocence of passage, Article 14(4) declared a passage to be "*innocent so long as it is not prejudicial to the peace, good order or security of the coastal state. Such passage shall take place in conformity with these articles and with other rules of international law*" (emphasis added).

There is little doubt that apart from military threats or activities by a passing ship which are clearly prejudicial to the peace, good order and security of a coastal state and which render such a passage non-innocent, the coastal state may also require compliance by foreign vessels with its laws and regulations. The International Law Commission in its report gave several examples of areas in which the coastal state might make regulations: (1) the safety of traffic and the protection of channels and buoys; (2) the protection of water of the coastal state against pollution of any kind caused by ships; (3) the conservation of living resources of the sea; (4) the rights of fishing and hunting and analogous rights belonging to the coastal state; (5) any hydrographic survey; (6) use of the national flag; and (7) customs and health.[7]

[4] See "Harvard Law School Draft on Territorial Waters". AJIL. (Supp.), vol. 23 (1929), p. 245; see also C. Colombos, *The International Law of the Sea* (London, 6th ed., 1967), p. 261.

[5] See Jessup, note 2, p. 120.

[6] See *Harvard Draft*, note 4, p. 295.

[7] See Report of the International Law Commission, *Yearbook of the International Law Commission*, 1956, vol. II, p. 274.

Serious infringement of these rules might have far-reaching consequences for the peace, good order and the security of a coastal state. Although it leaves a wide amount of latitude to a coastal state to declare a passage non-innocent, it would be certainly unreasonable to make "security" the sole criterion of innocent passage. That the 1958 Convention rejects it is also clear from Article 14(5) which lays down:

> Passage of foreign fishing vessels shall not be considered innocent if they do not observe such laws or regulations as the coastal State may make and publish in order to prevent these vessels from fishing in the territorial sea.

While exercising their right of innocent passage, submarines were "required to navigate on the surface and to show their flag" [Article 14(6)]. Though Article 14(6) was less specific, failure of even non-military submarines to navigate on the surface and show their flag would render their passage non-innocent.

Once the coastal state finds that a particular passage by a foreign vessel is not innocent – and it has the right to decide the issue at least in the first instance – under Article 16(1), it "may take the necessary steps in its territorial sea to prevent" such passage. It may also, under Article 16(3), "without discrimination amongst foreign ships, suspend temporarily in specific areas of its territorial sea the innocent passage of foreign ships if such suspension is essential for the protection of its security. Such suspension shall take effect only after having been duly notified". The International Law Commission in its commentary made it clear that a temporary suspension in definite areas was permissible and asserted that it was "of the opinion that the article states the international law in force".[8]

Innocent Passage of Warships

Ever since the doctrine of innocent passage came to be established in the middle of the nineteenth century, the question of the right of passage of warships has remained controversial and coastal states have been reluctant to permit passage without previous authorization or at least notification. State practice was conflicting.[9] The U.S. Agent in the North Atlantic Coast Fisheries Arbitration, Ellihu Root, argued that warships did not have such a right "without consent...because they threaten. Merchants ships may pass because they do not threaten."[10] This statement has often been seized on by governments and jurists to deny the existence of a right of passage for warships.[11] In response to a questionaire addressed to governments by the

[8] Ibid., p. 273.

[9] See D.P.O'Connell, *The International Law of the Sea*, I.A. Shearer [ed]. (oxford, 1984), pp. 274-281.

[10] See Jessup, note 2, p. 120.

[11] O'Connell, note 9, p. 277.

Preparatory Committee of the Hague Codification Conference in 1930 on the right of innocent passage for warships, sixteen governments replied negatively, including the United States, or were of the opinion that previous authorization was required before the right of passage could be exercised. At the Conference in 1930, not all delegations discussed the passage of warships. But the United States, for one, bluntly denied that there was such a right, because innocent passage existed primarily for commerce, and, so far as warships were concerned, it was wholly a question of usage and comity.[12] The United States was not an exception in this regard. The general discussion at the conference:

> revealed almost no support for the equivalent rights of warships and merchant ships to traverse the territorial sea, but rather a tendency to favour the view that in times of a threat to national security passage of warships could be prohibited, and even the view that in normal times previous authorization, or at least previous notification, was required.[13]

The International Law Commission, in its 1956 draft presented to the 1958 UN Conference on the Law of the Sea, suggested that:

> The coastal State may make the passage of warships through the territorial sea subject to previous authorization or notification. Normally it shall grant innocent passage subject to the provisions of Articles 17 and 18.

In its commentary, the Commission said:

> While it is true that a large number of States do not require previous authorization or notification; the Commission can only welcome this attitude which displays a laudable respect for the principle of communications; but this does not mean that a State would not be entitled to require such notification or authorization measure. Since it admits that the passage of warships through the territorial sea of another State can be considered by the State as a threat to its security, and is aware that a number of States do require previous notification or authorization, the Commission is not in a position to dispute the right of States to take such a measure.[14]

If, however, a coastal state had not enacted and published such a restriction, the Commission added, the foreign warships could pass without previous notification or authorization provided they did not enter a port.

The International Law Commission's text, as it was presented to the conference, favoured the policies of the Soviet bloc and was supported by them. However, the United States, which until the Second World War was always opposed to the passage of warships through territorial sea without authorization, had changed its stance. Having emerged as the greatest maritime Power, it was interested in the widest freedom of navigation even for its warships. The United States and its allies in NATO were strongly opposed

[12] Ibid., p. 252.

[13] Ibid., p. 283.

[14] *ILC.*, note 7, p. 277, Emphasis added.

to any limitation on the freedom of the seas, whether in the form of an extension of the territorial sea or a limitation on the passage of warships. Such a limitation, they thought, favoured the Soviet Union which possessed the largest fleet of submarines which could operate undetected for long periods in neutral States' territorial waters without surfacing. Extension of territorial waters coupled with restrictions on free passage of warships. they felt, would have the effect of exposing the mobility of NATO warships and aircraft to crippling jurisdictional restrictions.[15]

But in spite of strong opposition by the United States and other NATO Powers, the ILC's proposed text of draft Article 24 was adopted in the First Committee on 10 April 1958.[16] When the matter came before the Plenary Meeting on 27 April 1958, procedural tactics were employed by the NATO countries to reverse the situation. Italy sought a separate vote on the words "authorization or" in ILC draft Article 24 and the motion was carried, by a vote of 45 to 27 with 6 abstentions, to delete these words.[17] The effect now was to subject innocent passage of warships to procedures of notification only. Denmark, arguing that there was now no question of the need to seek permission of the coastal state, suggested that the Article be redrafted. The Conference was left with the option of either accepting a text requiring only prior notification by the coastal state, or of rejecting the text altogether. Although a majority of states still wanted the coastal state to have at least the right to require notification, several states which wanted the right of "authorization" by the coastal state refused to accept this truncated right mentioned in the draft convention. They, therefore, voted against the article in its emasculated form and it was defeated and eliminated from the Convention.[18] Defeated on the substance of the article, the Soviet Union organized sufficient support to ensure that the truncated article did not obtain the requisite two-thirds majority. It was, therefore, not included.

The bizarre result of this diplomatic struggle at Geneva is that the 1958 Convention contains no provision on the subject of passage of warships through the territorial sea. These provisions are found in a sub-section containing "rules applicable to all ships", including government ships other than warships, as well as, it is claimed, warships. However, Articles 21 and 22 specifically declare that government ships, whether operated for commercial or non-commercial purposes, enjoy the right of innocent passage

[15] See Arthur H. Dean, "Geneva Conference on the Law of the Sea; What Was Accomplished, *AJIL.*, vol. 52 (1958), pp. 610-12, see also O'Connell, note 9, pp. 288-9.

[16] See *UNCLOS Official Records* (1st Committee), vol. 3, UN Doc. A/CONF. 13/ C1/L 37/Con. 212 (1958), See also ibid., p. 131. para 25.

[17] *UNCLOS Official Records*, Plenary Meetings (1958), p. 67, para 28.

[18] Ibid., p. 68, para 46. It failed to receive the two-thirds majority. The vote was 43 to 24.

defined under Articles 15-17. Articles 22(2) also recognizes the usual immunities granted to government ships operated for non-commercial purposes.

It is curious, however, that there is no clear mention about innocent passage for warships. The only provision relating to warships, Article 23, blandly declares:

> If any warship does not comply with the regulations of the coastal States concerning passage through the territorial sea and disregards any request for compliance which is made to it, the coastal State may require the warship to leave the territorial sea.

The provision survived because the Commission had fortuitously made it a separate article rather than a part of the composite article on straits.[19]

The absence of an article on innocent passage of warships is sometimes interpreted by scholars and diplomats to mean that no restrictions are permissible on the passage of warships. This is said to be supported by Article 14 in which "all ships", including warships, it is asserted, are given the right of innocent passage. Furthermore, Article 23 is said to permit the coastal state to regulate the use of the territorial sea by foreign warships, but not to require previous permission for their transit.[20]

On the other hand, it is argued by some countries and publicists that the expression "ships" in Article 14 means merchant ships because the inclusion of warships, in the light of long-standing customary law, would have required express and clear provision; that Article 23 authorizes the coastal state to insist on prior permission as part of its regulatory competence; and that this interpretation is supported by customary law which authorized the coastal state to exclude foreign warships from the territorial sea at will.[21] It is important to note that the Soviet bloc countries, while ratifying the Geneva Convention, made declarations that they considered that the coastal state had a right to establish procedures for the authorization of the passage of foreign warships through its territorial waters.[22]

With this historical record, it is difficult to conclude that warships have an untrammelled right of innocent passage through territorial waters. Because the 1958 Convention is silent on the subject, it must be interpreted in the

[19] O'Connell, note 9, p. 298.

[20] This is not only the position taken by NATO Powers, Australia and New Zealand, but it is supported by several writers like Verzil, Kelsen, Jessup, Pharandand and Fitzmourice, ibid., p. 290, n. 204.

[21] Besides the Soviet Union and its allies, this interpretation was supported by the Philippines, Indonesia and Malaysia. Several Scholars such as Brownlie, Groethem, Slomina, Colombos and Tunkin, also agree with this interpretation, See O'Connell, note 9, p. 291.

[22] Quoted in ibid., p. 291.

light of customary law. The consequence of the rejection of the controversial articles relating to warships by the Geneva Convention was merely to shelve the issue and relegate the question of innocent passage to customary law[23] which did permit coastal states to require notification and authorization before such passage was permitted. Sorensen also points out that "the proceedings of the conference leave no room for doubt" that the majority of delegations did not want warships to have the same rights as other ships.[24] In fact, it may be noted, that a large number of states still require authorization and a majority of them require at least prior notification for transit of warships.[25]

UNCLOS-III and the Passage of Warships

During the Third UN Conference on the Law of the Sea (UNCLOS III), the Soviet Union and its allies quietly dropped their strong objections to innocent passage of warships through territorial waters. The new identity of interests among the major naval Powers led to substantially identical proposals by NATO and Warsaw Pact countries to include warships in the rules relating to innocent passage.[26] This led to the adoption of the concept of equal treatment between warships and merchant, ships in the Informal Single Negotiating Text of 1975 [(Article 29(2)].

The opposition to the right of innocent passage of warships shifted during the Conference from the Soviet bloc to a few Third World countries,[27] which were afraid of both the Super Powers and wanted to protect their coastal areas from becoming involved with their military manoeuvres.

It is significant that the revision of the Single Negotiating Text between

[23] Ibid.

[24] See Max Sorensen, "Law of the Sea", *International Conciliation*, vol. 520 (1958), p. 235.

[25] See O'Connell, note 9, p. 290, n. 205; I. Brownlie, *Principles of Public International Law* (London, 3rd ed., 1979), p. 198. See also Myron Nordquist, Testimony in Hearings before the Subcommittee on Oceanography, Gulf of Mexico and the other Continental Shelf of the Committee on Merchant Marine and Fisheries, House of Representatives on "The Law of the Sea Treaty and Reauthorization of the Deep Seabed Hard Mineral Resources Act", on April 26, 1994, US House of Representatives Serial No. 103-97 (Washington, D.C. 1994), p. 220. See also for numerous restrictions on innocent passage of various types of ships by several countries which the United States felt excessive and protested against in US Department of State, *Limits in the Sea, No. 112; United States Responses to Excessive National Maritime Claims* (March 9, 1992), pp. 51-61.

[26] See U.K., Bulgaria, G.D.R., Poland, U.S.S.R., Malaysia, Morocco, Oman, Yemen and Fiji, *UNCLOS-III Official Records*, 3 v., pp. 183, 192, 196 and 203.

[27] For example: Bangladesh, Somalia, Sri Lanka, Maldives, Sudan, Yugoslavia and Yemen, passed laws requiring prior authorization before transit of warships, see O'Connell, note 9, p. 293.

the 1975 and 1976 sessions of the Conference omitted the reference to warships and thus restored the situation that existed under the 1958 Geneva Convention. The requirement that warships comply with the law and regulations of the coastal state, provided in the 1958 Convention, was included without any change and without any discussion except for a reference to leaving the territorial sea "immediately".[28] It is important to note that a vote on the issue of navigation of warships through territorial waters (which, according to Dr. Myron Nordquist, "The United States expected to lose"), was "avoided at the LOS Convention only because of the outstanding diplomatic skill and extraordinary effort by the President of the Conference."[29] The result is that the legal situation concerning the innocent passage of warships through the territorial sea remains practically the same in the 1982 Convention as it was under the Geneva Convention in 1958.

It may be noted, however, that although the 1982 Convention defines innocent passage in the same terms as the 1958 Convention as a passage that "is not prejudicial to the peace, good order or security of the coastal State" (Article 19(1), unlike the 1958 Convention, it contains a catalogue of actions, applicable to all ships, that render the passage non-innocent. Proposed originally by both NATO and Warsaw Pact blocs in order to minimize fears concerning the innocent passage of warships, the catalogue was included in the Convention even after reference to "warships" had been removed. They are now applicable to "all ships" exercising the right of innocent passage as provided in Part II, Section 3, of the convention. The catalogue of actions contained in Article 19 refers to such actions as "any threat or use of force against the sovereignty, territorial integrity or political independence of a coastal State"; "any exercise or practice with weapons of any kind"; the collection of information prejudicial to the defence or security of the coastal state; acts of propaganda affecting the security of the coastal state, etc. (Article 19(2). The adoption of this catalogue to some extent presumes the right of innocent passage for warships, because the activities generally concern the mode of passage of warships.[30]

Like the 1958 Geneva Convention, the 1982 Convention requires submarines and other underwater vehicles "to navigate on the surface and show their flag" while exercising their right of innocent passage (Article 20).

[28] Article 30, UN Convention on the Law of the Sea (1982).

[29] Nordquist, note 25, p. 220; see also *Limits in the Sea*, No. 112, note 25, pp. 55-56.

[30] See also O'Connell, note 9, p. 292.

Innocent Passage of Warships With or Without Notification and/or Permission

Even if it is assumed that all ships, including warships, have a right of innocent passage through territorial waters, a question still remains whether warships can exercise this right without at least notification, if not specific permission, of the coastal states. It is important to note that at least 43 states (several of them developed states of Europe) have imposed such a condition for notification by warships, and many of them require clear permission, before the warships can exercise their rights of innocent passage through territorial waters.[31] Besides, some states imposed some restrictions on passage of ships carrying nuclear weapons or other dangerous cargo.[32]

In a statement on 24 November 1982, the Soviet Union declared that:

> Foreign warships and underwater vehicles shall enjoy the right of innocent passage through the territorial waters (territorial sea) of the USSR in accordance with the procedure to be established by the Council of Ministers of the USSR.[33]

Then, in 1983, the Soviet government published rules for warship navigation in the Soviet territorial sea. In these rules the Soviet Union provided for the innocent passage of foreign warships only in limited areas of the Soviet territorial sea in the Baltic, the Sea of Okhotsk, and in the Sea of Japan.

Rejecting all these so-called "excessive national maritime claims", the United States said in a policy statement on March 10, 1983, that its policy was to:

> accept and act in accordance with the balance of interests relating to traditional uses of the oceans – such as navigation and overflight. In this respect, the United States will recognize the rights of other States in the waters off their coasts, as reflected in the Convention, so long as the rights and freedoms of the United States and others under international law are recognized by such coastal States.

In addition, the United States added, its policy was to:

> exercise and assert its navigation and overflight rights and freedoms on a world wide basis in a manner that is consistent with the balance of interests reflected in the Convention. The United States will not, however, acquiesce in unilateral acts of other States designed to restrict the rights and freedom of the international community in navigation and overflight and other related high seas uses.[34]

[31] See *Limits in the Sea*, No. 112, note 25, p. 59; see also Hearings before the US Senate Committee on Foreign Relations on "Current Status of the Law of the Sea Convention", 103rd Congress, 2nd Session, on August 11, 1994, pp. 28, 38, 49-51; see also Hearings, note 25, pp. 20.

[32] Admiral William D, Centre Hearings before the Senate Committee on Foreign Relations, ibid., p. 25. D.O.D. Ocean Policy Review, 1993, ibid., pp. 87-88.

[33] Quoted in *Limits in the Sea*, No. 112, note 25, p. 53.

[34] Ibid.

In order to assert its navigation and overflight rights and test other countries' resolve in this connection, the United States started as early as 1979, a "Freedom of Navigation Programme" and sent its warships, submarines and aeroplanes to other countries territorial seas and straits and protested against what the US believed were their excessive claims.[35] In March 1986, two US warships, the *USS Caron* and *USS Yorktown*, exercised the right of innocent passage through the Soviet territorial sea in the Black Sea. The incident created an exchange of protest notes by both sides. The Soviet Union accused the United States of violating Soviet borders. The United States rejected the Soviet claims.

In 1988, the same two US warships were again involved in an incident in the Black Sea. On 12 February 1988, two Soviet vessels "bumped" the two US Navy ships in the Soviet territorial sea. In an unpublished article offered to major newspapers, the United States stated in part,

> Our disagreement with the USSR involves Soviet efforts to limit, indeed virtually to abrogate, the right of innocent passage for warships through the Soviet territorial sea. According to Soviet legislation, foreign warships may exercise innocent passage in only five specified locations out of the thousands of miles of Soviet coastline. The Soviet made no provisions for innocent passage in the Black Sea.[36]

It is significant to note, however, that on the eve of the disintegration of the Soviet Union in 1989, the latter made a volte face in its policy. Under pressure from the United States, the two countries issued a joint statement, called Jackson Hole agreement, adopting a uniform interpretation of the rules governing innocent passage through the territorial sea. It was asserted in the Joint Statement of September 23, 1989, that:

— The LOS Convention contains the relevant rules of international law governing innocent passage of ships in the territorial sea.
— All ships, including warships, regardless of cargo, armament, or means of propulsion, enjoy the right of innocent passage, for which neither notification nor authorization is required.
— The list set out in Article 19(2) is an exhaustive list of activities that would render passage not innocent. A ship not engaging in any of these listed activities is in innocent passage.
— A coastal State that questions whether a ship is in innocent passage must give that ship an opportunity to clarify its intentions, or to correct its conduct.
— Ships exercising the right of innocent passage, must abide by all laws and regulations of the coastal State adopted in conformity with international law, as reflected in Articles 21, 22, 23 and 25 of the LOS Convention.
— If a warship acts in a manner contrary to innocent passage, and does not correct its action upon the coastal State's request, the coastal State may

[35] The United States filed more than 140 such protests including more than 110 since FON Programme began. See, *Limits in the Sea*, No. 112, note 25, p. 1.

[36] Ibid., p. 53.

require it to leave the territorial sea, in accordance with Article 30. In such cases the warship shall do so immediately.

— Without prejudice to the exercise of rights of coastal and flag States, all differences regarding a particular case of innocent passage shall be resolved between the coastal State and the flag state through diplomatic channels or other agreed means.[37]

But while Russia has come under the influence of the United States, not all states are prepared to accept the American viewpoint or give up their right to demand notification or even permission before warships may enter their territorial waters. The United States cannot take upon itself to force all the states to adopt its view without a tremendous cost. It is sometimes questioned in the United States itself if it is all worth it.[38]

Passage Through Straits

Convinced of the need for free navigation without let or hindrance for the development of commerce and communications all over the world, Great Britain and other maritime Powers have been trying, since the beginning of the nineteenth century, to make all international waterways free so that their vessels might sail all seas and affluent waters without suffering burdensome restrictions. Freedom of passage or navigation through straits, or those natural narrow passages that join two parts of the high seas was considered as a necessary concomitant of the freedom of the seas. Geographically defined as a narrow passage or sea channel "connecting two larger bodies of water"[39] the term "strait" is used for waterways ranging in breadth from 800 yards to over 150 miles.[40] A relatively narrow waterway lying between areas of land,

[37] Ibid., pp. 48-49; 84-85.

[38] See *Limits in the Sea* No. 112, note 25, pp. 58-68, 73-76; see also Robert E. Osgood, Ann L. Hollick, Charles S. Pearson, James C. Orr, *Toward a National Ocean Policy: 1976 and Beyond* (Washington, 1975), p. 22; see also Elliot L. Richardson, "Law of the Sea: Navigation and Other Traditional National Security Considerations", *San Diego Law Review*, vol. 19 (1982), pp. 554-5, see also Osgood et al, ibid., p. 45 for US bilateral agreements with Indonesia; R. Darman, "The Law of the Sea: Rethinking U.S. Interests", *Foreign Affairs*, vol. 56 (1967), p. 376.

[39] See D. Stamp (ed.,) *A Glossary of Geographic Terms* (1968), p. 436.

[40] At its narrowest point the Dardanelles Strait is only 800 yards wide. On the other hand, the Hudson Straits are about 155 miles wide. See K.L. Koh, *Straits and International Navigation: Contemporary Issues* (1982), p. 11. Some scholars refer to the difficulty of separating "in principle" gulfs from straits. Thus Hall refers to the Strait of Juan de Fuca (ranging from 10 to 15 miles in width) which he says possesses some of the characteristics of a gulf, W.E. Hall, *A Treatise on International Law* (Oxford, 8th ed. 1924), p. 195, noted in Koh, ibid. See 1958 Geneva Convention on Territorial Sea and Contiguous Zone guaranteed in Article 16(4) passage through Strait of Tiran connecting the Gulf of Aqaba and the Red sea, See Koh, ibid.

a strait may be a channel between continents, a continent and an island, or two islands, connecting two oceans, two adjoining parts of the some ocean, two by-oceans, or an ocean and a by-ocean. The concept covers islands of an archipelago and is sometimes also known as a "sound".[41] Unless these more than two-hundred waterways all over the world—some important and some not so important—are kept open and free, they can act as bottlenecks for navigation and communication between states. Some oceans and even some states are accessible from the rest of the high seas only through these passages. Thus the Mediterranean and Aegean Seas open to the oceans of the world through the Strait of Gibraltar, and the Black Sea is connected with the Mediterranean and other waters through the narrow straits of the Bosporus and Dardanelles. The Baltic Sea flows to the outer ocean through the Danish Straits, and the straits of Malacca join the Pacific and the Indian Oceans. The strategic character of a strait is based on the fact that passage through the strait saves time, cost and distance for commercial and military ships. Some intercontinental straits (Gibraltar, Dardanelles, Kattegat, Bab-cl-mandeb, Hormuz) are strategic because an alternate route does not exist. In some straits, like Malacca and Hormuz, the amount of traffic that transits through them is extremely heavy because of their convenience and unavailability of viable alternate route.[42] Others may not be so critical though still important for international traffic. Without going into the geographical details of these various straits[43] it may be asserted that they are all important as corridors of international maritime traffic and essential for the freedom of the seas.

These natural gateways to the ocean could not be permitted to be closed to ships in peace or war, even if the strait states had to sacrifice part of their territorial sovereignty and independence for this purpose. Under the patronage and active participation of the big maritime Powers—especially Great Britain which as the biggest naval power had become policeman of the vast oceans—even those straits lying within the territorial waters of coastal states were kept open by agreement or otherwise. A number of agreements were

[41] Koh gives a list of 220 such straits from a list by W. Smith, *Strategic Quality of International Straits* (1973) (unpublished M.A. dissertation available at the University of Rhode Island), quoted in Koh, ibid., pp. 24-26. See also Robert W. Smith, "An Analysis of the Strategic Attributes of International Straits: A Geographical Perspective", Maritime Studies Management, vol. 2 1974), pp. 88 ff.

[42] Approximately one-sixth of the world's oil goes through the strait of Malacca, and about 92 per cent of Japan's oil comes from Persian Gulf via this strait. See Smith, ibid., p. 28.

[43] See Smith note 41, pp. 97 ff; R.H. Kennedy, *A Brief Geographical and Hydrographical Study of Straits Which Constitute Routes for International Traffic*, Preparatory Document No. 6, 1958 UN Conference on the Law of the Sea (hereafter UNCLOS), UN Doc. A/CONF, 13/6 (23 Oct. 1957).

concluded to declare freedom of passage through straits in the late nineteenth and early twentieth centuries which are valid even today. Thus the Turkish Straits are regulated by the Montreux Convention of 1934; the Straits of Magellan by the Treaty between Argentina and Chile of 1881 opening the straits to vessels of all nations, the Straits of Gibraltar by the Anglo-French Declaration of 1904 to which Spain adhered by the Franco-Spanish Treaty of 1912; the Danish Straits by notes exchanged between Denmark and Sweden accompanying the Danish-Swedish Declaration of 1932.[44] An instance of this process of opening an international waterway to free use by all nations was the recognition by Japan, after receiving notes from the French, German and Russian ministers, of the Straits of Formosa as a "great sea highway of nations, beyond the exclusive control or appropriation of that country".[45] Not content with natural channels, the maritime powers constructed artificial straits or waterways of Suez and Panama to serve the same purposes in terms of economic geography and navigation, namely, piercing an isthmus to afford easy access between two portions of the high seas.

Despite the importance of straits for navigation and communication between states in the heyday of the freedom of the seas doctrine, however, there was always some hesitation on the part of numerous strait states to accept the unquestioned right of all ships to pass through their waters irrespective of their security and other interests. Most of the strait states claimed territorial sea jurisdiction in straits unless the straits were much wider than double the territorial sea claimed by them. The big maritime states disagreed, contending that if a strait was wider than double the limits of the so-called traditional territorial sea of three miles claimed by them, i.e. broader than six miles, there was supposed to be a high seas corridor in the strait, open to free navigation by the ships of all nations. This, in practice, was never accepted. Indeed, coastal states generally claimed jurisdiction over the entire strait beyond even the limits it normally claimed for its territorial sea. Thus by a Protocol of 10 March 1873, the United States and Great Britain fixed the northwest water boundary between the United States and Canada as a line running midway in the Strait of Jaun de Fuca which ranges between 10 and 15 miles in width.[46] In his exhaustive study on straits in 1947, Bruel said that the situation in which a strip of high sea runs through an entire strait "rather belongs to the literature than to reality.[47] Especially during the war, the strait states' concern was to protect their territories or maintain their neutrality and they could not permit unrestricted

[44] See K.D. Shaw, "Juridical Status of the Malacca Straits in International Law", vol. 14 (1976), pp. 35-6.

[45] Quoted in R.R. Baxter, *The Law of International Waterways* (Cambridge, 1964), p. 8.

[46] Ibid., p. 5.

[47] Erik Bruel, *International Straits* vol. II (London, 1947), p. 41.

navigation through straits and subject themselves to the crossfire of belligerents just because nature had put them on the crossroads of the world's oceans.[48]

The tension between the demands of the international community—especially the maritime Powers—to keep the straits open and free for navigation, on one hand, and demands of the coastal states to protect their security, economic and other interests on the other, continued and became even more pronounced after the Second World War. Despite all the desires and pressure of the maritime Powers to keep the straits free for navigation (and although several conventions or agreements had been concluded about navigation in some important straits) international law was still ambiguous and uncertain about (1) the definition as to what constituted a legal strait;[49] (2) the "use" or "indispensability" of a strait for communications; and (3) whether innocent passage through a strait was an exceptional right or an application of the rule relating to the territorial sea.[50] Further, while it was generally conceded that warships had a right of passage through straits, in time of war as of peace, this was tied to the question of innocent passage of warships through the territorial sea, and might have been the only exceptional feature that legal straits possessed. These ambiguities persisted until the *Corfu Channel* case and although it was generally felt that the coastal state could not legally forbid passage through its international straits, the doctrinal basis of such a right remained a matter of controversy.[51] It was always considered to be merely a specific instance of innocent passage through the territorial sea. This is how it was treated at the Hague Codification Conference in 1930.[52] It is important to note further that the concept of "innocent passage" through territorial waters was not clear, and the limits of these waters remained a subject of intense dispute among states.

Corfu Channel Case and Straits Regime

In this case, two British warships were fired upon by Albanian coastal batteries while the ships were within the Albanian part of the strait of Corfu, which lies between the island of Corfu, a part of Greece, and the coasts of Albania and Greece. Part of the strait is within the territorial waters of Albania and part within that of Greece. The 1946 incident touched off a

[48] Chile declared the Strait of Magellan as part of its territorial sea for the purposes of defending its neutrality, see Baxter, note 45, p. 7.

[49] At the Hague Conference in 1930, the German delegate pointed out that while there was a geographical notion of a strait, "no general definition of the term exists in international law", quoted in Koh, note 40, p. 13.

[50] Ibid.

[51] O'Connell, note 9, pp. 301-305.

[52] Ibid, pp. 303-306.

controversy between the United Kingdom and Albania regarding the claim of innocent passage for the former and the requirement of notification and authorization for passage by foreign warships and merchant vessels of the latter. Because the dispute could not be settled, the United Kingdom decided to test the Albanian attitude by sending warships through the strait. During the attempted passage through the Albanian part of the strait, two British destroyers struck mines and forty-four officers and men lost their lives, forty-two officers and men were injured, and serious damage was caused to the two ships. In November, 1946, the United Kingdom announced its intention to mine-sweep the Albanian part of the strait to collect evidence of mine laying and proceeded to do so without the consent of Albania. On the recommendations of the UN Security Council, the dispute was submitted to the International Court of Justice. Rejecting Albania's contention that the passage by British warships through the strait was a violation of Albanian sovereignty for which the United Kingdom was responsible, the Court said:

> It is, in the opinion of the Court, generally recognized and in accordance with international custom, that States in times of peace have right to send their warships through straits used for international navigation between two parts of the high seas without the previous authorization of a coastal State, provided the passage is innocent. Unless otherwise prescribed in an international convention, there is no right for a coastal State to prohibit such passage through straits in time of peace.[53]

The Court noted that the two riparian states, Greece and Albania, did not maintain normal relations, that Greece considered itself technically at war with Albania, and that Albania considered it necessary to take certain measures of vigilance in the region. "In view of these exceptional circumstances", said the Court, Albania "would have been justified in issuing regulations in respect of the passage of warships through the strait, *but not in prohibiting such passage or in subjecting it* to the requirement of special authorization".[54]

Whether the coastal state can require notification before the passage of a warship is not clear from the judgment. It is clear, however, that the Court rejected the Albanian arguments (a) that the Corfu Channel was the type of strait that would require prior authorization, (b) that it was not an important strait, (c) that it was not a necessary route between open sea areas, and (d) that it was used mainly for local traffic between Corfu and Sarvanda. The Court said:

> It may be asked whether the test is to be found in the volume of traffic passing through the strait or in its greater or lesser importance for international navigation. But in the opinion of the Court, the decisive criterion is rather its geographical situation as connecting two parts of the high seas and the fact of its being used

[53] *Corfu Channel Case* (Great Britain v. Albania), *ICJ, Rep.* 1949, p. 28.
[54] Ibid., p. 29 (emphasis added).

for international navigation. Nor can it be decisive that this strait is not a necessary route between two parts of the high seas, but only an alternative passage between the Aegean and the Adriatic seas. It has nevertheless been a useful route for international maritime traffic.[55]

It is clear from the decision that the coastal authority over passage of warships and other ships is limited to the exclusion of non-innocent passage. The Court interpreted the term "innocent passage" broadly in this case. Even an otherwise provocative passage of a British force consisting of two cruisers and two destroyers, close to the coast of Albania, was held to be innocent because its purpose was to assert a right against previous and anticipated forceful attempts to deny it. It must be stressed, however, that even under such a restrictive interpretation of the coastal state's right to refuse passage, it still has wide discretion and, of course, the authority, at least in the first instance, to decide whether a passage is or is not innocent.

Straits in the 1958 Geneva Convention

In its 1956 draft submitted to the Geneva Conference, the International Law Commission recommended that:

> There must be no suspension of the innocent passage of foreign ships through straits normally used for international navigation between parts of the high seas...

In its commentary, the Commission said that "it would be in conformity with the Court's decision" to insert the word "normally" before the word "used" in this article, "which was suggested" by the *Corfu Channel* decision.[56] In the final provision relating to straits, however, the word "normally" was deleted from the Commissoni's draft on an amendment proposed by the United States. It was said that the *Corfu Channel* decision had not so qualified the word "used".[57] The objective of the proponents of the amendment was to assure passage through straits which were actually used and to avoid friction over the concept of normal use.[58] Article 16(4), as finally adopted, stated:

> There shall be no suspension of innocent passage through straits which are used for international navigation between one part of the high seas and another part of the high seas *or the territorial sea of a foreign State.*

The *italicized* words, called the Aqaba Clause, were added over the strong objections of Indonesia, Saudi Arabia, and other Arab countries because of the Arab-Israeli dispute over access to Israel's territorial waters in the Gulf of Aqaba through the strait of Tiran. It is thus apparent that the 1958 Geneva

[55] Ibid., p. 28.
[56] *Yearbook of the International Law Commission*, vol. 2 (1956), p. 273.
[57] *UNCLOS Official Records*, 3. v., UN Doc. A/CONF. 13/cl/L.39, p. 220.
[58] Ibid., 95, para 66.

Convention not only reaffirmed the broadly conceived conception of straits in the *Corfu Channel* case through which warships and merchant vessels have a right of innocent passage and which cannot be arbitrarily denied by the coastal state, but extended it further and made it more liberal.

But it is important to note that the 1958 Convention, like past practice dealt with the question of straits in the context of innocent passage in the territorial sea,[59] provided for in Section III ("Right of Innocent Passage"), Sub-Section A ("Rules Applicable to All Ships"). Thus although Article 16, paragraph 4, provides for innocent passage through straits, paragraph 3 permits a state "to suspend temporarily in specified areas of its territorial sea the innocent passage of foreign ships if such a suspension is essential for the protection of its security." The assimilation of the regime of straits with that of the territorial sea in the 1958 Convention was a step backward for all those supporting a special regime for straits.[60]

Extension of Territorial Sea and Straits

After the failure of the 1958 and 1960 Conferences to reach an agreement on the limits of the territorial sea, extension by many states of coastal state maritime zone and jurisdiction to 12 nautical miles, threatened to enclose within double the territorial sea limits another 116 straits. The three-mile rule would have left at least theoretically a strip of high seas between them. Freedom of navigation through several strategic straits, such as the Dover Strait, the Strait of Gibraltar, the Bering Straits, Bab-el-Mandep, and the Strait of Hormuz, became even more precarious, because they came under the coastal states' problematic territorial sea jurisdiction and discretion. Moreover, the territorial seas regime required submarines to come up on the surface and show their flag, and there was no right of innocent passage for aircraft through the airspace above the territorial sea. This regime thus left the coastal state with wide discretion to declare any particular passage as non-innocent, the passage of nuclear-powered ships, for instance, or big oil tankers.

It is also important to recall the changed political environment after the UN Conferences on the Law of the Sea. Before the Second World War, most of the strategic and vital straits, especially in Asia and the Middle East, were under the control of the maritime powers interested in keeping them open (and claiming narrow territorial sea of three miles). With the collapse of colonialism, new states emerged which were more concerned about their own security and economic interests and were not enamoured by the "freedom of the seas" doctrine which had for a long time been used and abused to their disadvantage. Indeed, feeling that unlimited freedom of the seas was

[59] See O'Connel, note 9, p. 316.

[60] See Baxter, note 45, pp. 166-167.

against their interests, they wanted to curb it.[61] Some of these newly independent states were strait states now able and willing to control these important waterways to protect their vital interests. The threat of oil spills, dumping on the high seas, and other sources of pollution in a period of growing ecological concern, added still another reason for expanded jurisdictional claims by coastal states. As the trend to extend territorial waters gathered momentum after 1960, most of these straits became part of the territorial seas subject to numerous controls and limitations imposed by the coastal states. In fact, some of these states went further and sought to make certain important straits internal waters subject to their absolute sovereignty. Thus, Indonesia and the Philippines, two newly-independent archipelagic states, sought to employ the method of straight baselines joining the outermost points of the outermost islands of the archipelagoes for delimitation of their extended territorial waters,[62] thereby enclosing some of the most important straits, e.g., Sunda, Lombok, Ombai-Wetar, Macassar, and Malacca. Indonesia enjoys a monopoly over all deep water straits between the Asian mainland and Australia connecting the Pacific and the Indian Oceans. The closure of those straits like Sunda, Lombok, Ombai-Wetar or Macassar would necessitate a diversion of traffic around Australia or through the Panama Canal resulting in time delays, higher consumer prices, and the reduced mobility and flexibility of naval forces.

U.S.—U.S.S.R. Agreement on Keeping Straits Open

This trend was totally unacceptable to the maritime powers. The Soviet Union, which until the 1958 Geneva Convention was opposed to a special regime for straits, quietly changed its position and became interested in keeping the straits as free as possible. Concerned about the increasing prospect of their closure, both the U.S.S.R. and the United States agreed in 1967:

(1) to fix the maximum breadth of the territorial sea at 12 nautical miles; and
(2) to preserve explicitly in international straits traditional freedoms of navigation as had existed in the pre-12 mile territorial sea regime.

They also contemplated calling an international conference on the law of the sea limited to these issues and began soliciting support of various countries through diplomatic means.[63] At the same time, Ambassador Arvid Pardo of

[61] See R.P. Anand, "Tyranny of the Freedom of the Seas Doctrine", *Interntional Studies*, vol. 12, no. 3 (July-September 1973), pp. 79-93.

[62] See R.P. Anand, "Mid-Ocean Archipelagoes in International Law: Theory and Practice", *IJIL*, vol. 19 (1979), pp. 238-42.

[63] See B. Harlow, "UNCLOS III and Conflict Management in Straits", *Ocean Dev. & Int Law J.*, vol. 15 (1985), p. 199.

Malta focused international attention on the great potential value of the deep seabed minerals and suggested that they be declared "the common heritage of mankind", and that an international regime be established for their exploration and exploitation. As a result, a consensus developed for a law of the sea conference, but it was to be comprehensive in nature, and not confined to the navigational issues as contemplated by the United States and the Soviet Union. Nevertheless, for both the Super Powers, navigational freedom through territorial seas and straits was the most important issue to be addressed and resolved at the Conference.[64]

As the Seabed Committee (established by the General Assembly to prepare for the Third UN Conference on the Law of the Sea) started functioning, the maritime powers made clear their intention to keep the straits open. In his 1970 ocean policy statement, President Nixon emphasized the need for a treaty establishing a 12-mile limit for territorial sea and "free transit through international straits".[65] The maritime powers realized, however, that in spite of their strong intention to retain a three-mile limit, they could not force others to roll back their territorial sea. To deal with the situation, the United States introduced a set of Draft Articles on the Breadth of the Territorial Sea, Straits and Fisheries in a Sub-Committee of the Seabed Committee on 3 August 1971. After recognizing the right of the coastal states to extend their territorial sea to 12 miles, Article 2 provided:

> In straits used for international navigation...all ships and aircraft in transit shall enjoy the same freedom of navigation and overflight as they have on the high seas. Coastal States may designate corridors suitable for transit by all ships and aircraft through and over such straits....

The United States representative said in the sub-committee of the Seabed Committee that "in addition to the importance of sea navigation for their international trade, many States depended upon air and sea mobility in order to exercise their inherent right of individual and collective self-defence".[66] He pointed out that "the security of the United States and its allies depended to a very large extent on the freedom of navigation and on the overflight of the high seas. More extensive territorial seas, without the right to free transit of straits, would threaten that security.[67] The United States maintained that the invulnerability of its nuclear missile submarines (SSBNs)—currently the Polaris/Poseidon fleet—and their indispensable role as an adequate second strike force depended on their right to pass through straits submerged and

[64] Ibid., pp. 199-200.

[65] Sub-Committee II of the Committee on the Peaceful Uses of the Sea-bed (hereafter Seabed Committee), *UNGA Official Records*, Session 26, suppl. no. 21A/8421, p. 241, UN Doc.A/A.C.138/S.C.II/L.48.

[66] See Stevenson (U.S.), UN Doc. A/A.C. 138/S.C.II/SR8, pp. 45-47 (3 August 1971).

[67] See Stevenson, UN Doc, A/A.C.138/S.C.II/SR.37, p. 65 (28 July 1972).

unannounced.[68] In the U.S. view, the right of free transit through straits was "an indispensable adjunct to the freedom of navigation and that of overflight on the high seas themselves". Moreover, the regime of innocent passage provided for in the 1958 Convention on the Territorial Sea was "inadequate when applied to international straits" because it was a subjective standard subject to abuse. Some states, he said, had in fact claimed that certain types of passage—by nuclear-powered ships and super oil tankers—should be considered as non-innocent *per se*.[69]

The United States made it clear time and again that it would not accept any extension of the territorial sea from three miles to twelve miles unless the right of free passage through international straits was accepted. It demanded freedom of unobstructed passage for warships, including nuclear submarines, on the surface or submerged without notification and irrespective of mission. Further, it wanted freedom of civilian and military flights through the superjacent airspace. All these rights were claimed not only in those straits that were wider than six miles and were supposed to have, at least theoretically, a corridor of high seas in their midst, but *in all straits irrespective of their breadth or importance.*

The United States was willing to accept and "observe reasonable traffic safety and marine pollution regulations", that is to say, regulations that were "consistent with the basic right of transit". The safety standards to be applied in straits however, should be established by international agreement and should not be unilaterally imposed by the coastal State.[70]

As to the free transit of aircraft, the United States stated that civil aircraft already enjoyed transit rights over national territory of other states, under the Convention on International Civil Aviation and the International Air Service Transit Agreement. But such rights were not available to State aircraft. The United States demanded a right of free transit for all aircraft over straits, but also stated that such aircraft need not be routed over the strait itself but, at the coastal state's discretion, could be directed through "suitable corridors over land areas".

The United States was supported on this issue not only by the Western maritime powers, like the United Kingdom, France, West Germany and others but also by the Soviet Union and Communist bloc countries which also insisted that the limited right of "innocent passage" was not sufficient and "had never been and could never be applied to such straits as those of Gibraltar, Dover, Malacca, Singapore and Bab-el-Mandeb, where freedom of navigation had always been enjoyed."[71] In accordance with these views

[68] Osgood, et al, note 38, p. 45.

[69] Stevenson, note 67, p. 63.

[70] Ibid., p. 25.

[71] See Kolesnik (USSR), UN Doc.A/A.C.138/S.C.H/SR.69, pp. 2-4 (24 July 1973), see also Sapozhnikov (Ukranian SSR), UN Doc. A/A.C. 138/S.C.II/SR.71, p. 23 (8 August 1973).

on 25 July 1972, the Soviet Union proposed "Draft Articles on Straits used for International Navigation.[72]

Although "the coastal State should be given appropriate guarantees of its security and protection against pollution of the waters of its adjacent straits", the Soviet Union, like the United States, was absolutely convinced that "the concept of innocent passage could not be accepted as applying to the principal straits used for international navigation because it was too widely interpreted as a concept giving, so to speak, the last word to the coastal State or States concerned". Refusal to recognize the principle of free passage would mean, according to the Soviet Union, "establishing the domination of only 12 to 15 States adjacent to straits over the passage of vessels of some 130 States of the world".[73] The reversal of the Soviet Policy from its stand in 1958 was, of course, the result of the emergence of the Soviet military capability—naval, fishing and merchant maritime—during the subsequent two decades.[74]

Opposition by Strait States

Skeptical of the true intentions of the maritime Powers and fearful for their own security and sovereignty, the small coastal and strait states strongly objected to the right of "free passage" (instead of "innocent passage") through international straits. Any attempt to set up separate regimes for the territorial sea and for straits, they felt, would "clearly violate the fundamental principle of the sovereignty of the coastal State over its territorial sea". Strait states, they pleaded, could not "be expected to sacrifice any part of their national sovereignty for the exclusive benefit of the military and strategic interests of a few other States."[75]

The 1982 Law of the Sea Convention

Despite all the misgivings and apprehensions of the smaller coastal strait states which they repreated at the Caracas session in 1974, the maritime powers were not prepared to give up their demands. Both the Super Powers and their allies left no one in doubt that "unless unimpeded passage on, over and under straits used for international navigation was conceded to all commercial vessels and warships, including submarines, there was simply no possibility of coming to an agreement on the subject of national jurisdiction and other issues."[76] They were prepared to make concessions on other issues,

[72] UN Doc.A/A.C.138/S.C.II/L.7 (25 July 1972).

[73] See Kolesnik, note 71.

[74] See Mark W. Janis, *Sea Power and the Law of the Sea* (Lexington, 1976), p. 31.

[75] R. Morales (Spain), UN Doc A/AC.138/SR.60, p. 88 (4 April 1973). See also Djalal (Indonesia), ibid., p. 191.

[76] See Supra p. 19.

e.g., the exploitation of deep seabed resources[77] and to accept wide coastal jurisdiction, even the claims of archipelagic States,[78] provided their naval mobility was not affected.

Over the objections of the strait states, an agreement seemed to be emerging at Caracas for the acceptance of unimpeded transit passage through straits. A large number of countries from the "Group of 77" supported this position. The Single Negotiating Text of 1975 reflected this position. The Single Negotiating Text of 1975 reflected this agreement and provided for a non-suspendable "transit passage" through straits which, after several revisions, came to be included in the1982 Convention. As finally adopted, the Convention provided for the guaranteed non-suspendable transit passage through straits and archipelagic waters, subject only to the power of the coastal state to make certain rules related to navigational safety, pollution, and fishing. For the first time, the Convention provides separate regimes for "innocent passage" through territorial sea, laid down in Part II, Section 3 (Article 17 to 32), and "Transit Passage" through International Straits, laid down in Part III, Section 2 (Articles 37 to 44), and Section 3 (Article 45), the latter applicable only to special straits. The right of transit passage applies to "straits which are used for international navigation between one part of the high seas or an exclusive economic zone and another part of the high seas or an exclusive economic zone" [Article 37]. But transit passage does not apply to:

(1) Straits formed by an island of a State bordering the strait and its mainland if there exists seaward of the island a route through the high seas or through an EEZ of similar convenience with respect to navigational and hydrographical characteristics [Article 38(1)].
(2) Straits used for international navigation between one area of the high seas or an EEZ and the territorial sea of a foreign State [Article 45(1)(b)].

For these two categories the right of "innocent passage" is deemed sufficient which however cannot be suspended [Article 45(2)].

Transit passage is defined as:

> the exercise in accordance with the part of the freedom of navigation and overflight solely for the purpose of continuous and expeditions transit of the strait between one part of the high seas or an EEZ and another part of the high seas or an EEZ. However, the requirement of continuous and expeditious transit does not preclude passage through the strait for the purpose of entering, leaving or returning from a

[77] The Nixon administration was prepared for this trade-off. See L. Ratiner, quoted in R.P. Anand, "UNCLOS and the US", *IJIL*, vol. 24 (1984), p. 162.

[78] Most of the objections to the wide archipelagic claims of countries like Indonesia and the Philippines were raised because of the threat to international navigation, see Anand, note 62, p. 250.

State bordering the strait, subject to the conditions of entry to the state [Art. 38(2)].

Article 39 lays down the duties of ships and aircraft while exercising the righ. of transit passage, such as, (1) to proceed without delay through or over the strait; (2) refrain from use of force against the sovereignty, integrity or independence of the bordering States, or in any manner in violation of the principles of international law; (3) refrain from any activities other than those incidental to their normal modes of continuous and expeditious transit unless rendered necessary by *force majeure* or by distress. The ships and aircraft are also expected to comply with the generally accepted international regulations, procedures, and practices for preventing collisions and avoiding pollution; and aircraft must comply with the rules of the air established by ICAO or otherwise [Article 39(2) (3)].

The coastal states have been authorized under Article 41 to designate sealanes and prescribe traffic separation schemes for navigation after receiving the approval of the IMO. They may also adopted rules and regulations regarding navigation, pollution, fishing, and loading and unloading in transit.

Does Transit Passage Include Submerged Passage?

Serious criticism has been made of these provisions and some scholars have questioned whether "transit passage", as defined in Article 38, includes a right of submerged transit for submarines.[79]. It is suggested that because the term "freedom of navigation" in Article 38 is accompanied by so many qualifications and restrictions, and since there is no express mention of submerged passage, this "freedom" was not intended to include submerged passage. Even if the negotiations sought to include such a right, it is argued, it is substantially qualified and hedged by numerous restrictions so that the text does not clearly and unequivocally "guarantee" a right of submerged passage. Knight feels, for example, that the phrase "solely for the purpose of continuous and expeditious transit", qualifies the exercise of "freedom of navigation" so that it cannot be given its traditional meaning when bound by such a limitation.[80]

Second, it is felt that the reference to "normal modes of continuous and expeditious transit" in Article 39(i) (c) does not refer to and does not authorize

[79] Such criticisms were made and doubts raised by II. Gary Knight and Michael Reisman in a memoranda submitted to Senator Barry Goldwater as Chairman of a Senate Committee on the Law of the Sea Negotiation in 1976, quoted extensively in W.T. Burke, "Submerged Passage Through Straits: Interpretations of the Proposed Law of the Sea Treaty" *Washington L. Rev.*, vol. 52 (1977) p. 193. See also Michael Reisman "The Regime of Straits and National Security: An Appraisal of International Law Making", *AJIL*, vol. 74 (1980), p. 48.

[80] Knight, qoted in Burke, note 79, p. 207.

submerged transit and ought to be understood to mean surface transit. According to Reisman, the terms "normal" might or might not mean submerged transit, because the significance of "normal" depends upon "a great many variables in a given instance."[81]

But, in fact, considering the history of the drafting of these provisions and the emphasis that the United States, the Soviet Union and other maritime Powers put on unimpeded passage through straits, including submerged passage for submarines and right of overflight for the aircraft, there can be no doubt that transit passage through straits clearly covers those rights.[82] As John Norton Moore said: "To argue that Article 34(1) prohibits submerged transit in the face of the overwhelming textual evidence to the contrary is logic chopping at its worst".[83] He added "And in the real world of ocean politics, it is nonsense to believe that either the United States or the Soviet Union would accept a law of the sea treaty that did not fully protect freedom of navigation through straits".[84]

Although customary law never permitted a right of overflight over the territorial sea, the UNCLOS text states explicitly that transit passage includes overflight rights, Article 38(1), (9). Article 39 specifies the duties of aircraft in transit, and under Article 44, the State is prohibited from hindering the transit passage of an aircraft.

Archipelagic Passage

Part IV of the Convention establishes a right of "archipelagic sea lanes passage" through the archipelagic waters and adjacent territorial sea seaward of archipelagic baselines. This right, spelled out in Articles 52 to 54, is in all major respects the same as the right of transit passage through straits as defined in Articles 37 to 45. In fact, Article 54 expressly incorporates this right by reference to Articles 39, 40, 42 and 44 of the straits chapter. It is well known that the concept of mid-ocean archipelagoes was accepted only subject to "archipelagic sea lanes passage," including rights of overflight and submerged transit.[85]

[81] Reisman, quoted in Burke, Ibid.

[82] See Ellion L. Richardson, "Law of the Sea and Other Traditional Security Considerations", *San Diego Law Review*, vol. 19 (1982), pp. 564-565, see also John Norton Moore, "The Regime of Straits and the Third UNCLOS", *AJIL*, vol. 74 (1980), p. 89.

[83] Moore, note 82, p. 93.

[84] Ibid., p. 121.

[85] Ibid., p. 111. See also Richardson, note 82, pp. 566-8.

Package Deal

The above analysis shows that although the importance of straits as necessary doorways to make freedom of the seas effective had always been recognized, a separate straits regime has come to be accepted for the first time in history in the 1982 Convention on the Law of the Sea. As Reisman points out, 'transit passage' is a neologism; it lies somewhere between 'freedom of navigation' on one hand, and 'innocent passage' on the other, it is a compromise, a concession or a second-best solution".[86] The 1982 Convention is a classic example of the progressive development of international law, which cannot be divorced from the codification of existing international law.

The Convention was negotiated and accepted as a "package deal". The issues were interconnected. Several delegations made it clear that their willingness to accept one or more of the claims and proposals were dependent upon the acceptance of the other clàims and proposals.[87] The emphasis on the integrity of the "package deal" dominated the debates at various sessions.

Although the Convention was binding as a "package", these novel provisions, including transit passage through straits, at variance with customary law or based on uncertain practice and adopted for the first time, could not be said to give rise to binding customs in a short time without sufficient practice.[88] Nor can non-parties take benefit of certain provisions without accepting the burden of others.

United States Accepts Some Parts of the Convention

This is what the United States sought to do in March 1983. The United States claimed sovereign jurisdiction over a 200-mile EEZ as provided in the UN Convention. In an accompanying statement President Reagan stated:

> The United States is prepared to accept and act in accordance with the balance of interests relating to traditional uses of the ocean—such as navigation and overflight. In this respect, the United States will recognize the rights of other States in the waters off their coasts, as reflected in the Convention, so long as the rights and

[86] See Reisman, note 79, p. 68.

[87] John R. Stevenson and Bernard Oxman, "The Third UNCLOS: The 1974 Caracas Session", *AJIL*, vol. 69 (1975), p. 1 ff.

[88] Reisman observes: "By its nature submerged passage is not the sort of practice that generates customary rights. The notoriety and opportunity for parties thereafter subordinated – requisite components of formation of prescriptive rights – can hardly be fulfilled when the strait state does not or cannot know of the passage or lacks the means of stopping it. And even if such practices were deemed to have generated customary rights in one strait, they could not ipso facto be applied to all straits, nor would they be probative of features of surface or aerial passage". Reisman, n. 79, p. 57; see also Anthony D'Amato, The Concept of Custom in International Law (London, 1971), p. 104 for a detailed discussion of treaty-custom dichotomy.

the freedoms of the United States and others under international law are recognized by such coastal States.

He made it clear that:

> The United States will exercise and assert its navigation and overflight rights and freedoms on a world-wide basis in a manner that is consistent with the balance of interests reflected in the Convention. The United States will not, however, acquiesce in unilateral acts of other States designed to restrict the rights and freedoms of the international community in navigation and overflight and other related high sea uses.[89]

Also in this statement, President Reagan rejected the Convention's deep seabed mining provisions "as contrary to the interests and principles of industrialized nations".[90]

Although 78 countries claimed a territorial sea of 12 miles (and another 26 claimed even wider limits),[91] the White House said that:

> The President has not changed the breadth of the United States' territorial sea. It remains 3 nautical miles. the U.S. will respect only these territorial sea claims of others in excess of 3 nautical miles, to a maximum of 12 nautical miles, which accord to the U.S. its full rights under international law in the territorial sea.
>
> Unimpeded commercial and military navigation and overflight are critical to the national interests of the United States. The United States will continue to act to ensure the retention of the necessary rights and freedoms.[92]

This is precisely what the other countries were not prepared to accept. During the March 1983 session of the Preparatory Commission, the Group of 77 declared "its firm opposition to any action by States which have not signed the Convention to apply selectively, whether unilaterally or jointly, the provisions of the U.N. Convention on the Law of the Sea while continuing to reject the provisions relating to the international seabed area."[93]

On 23 April 1983, the Soviet Union said that:

> The United States...ignores the fact that the Convention is integral and indivisible. It is a thoroughly balanced package of accords on all closely interlinked problems related to the regime of marine expanses, the use of the ocean's living and mineral resources.
>
> Any attempt arbitrarily to pick out some of its provisions, while discarding

[89] See Larson, "Security Issues and the Law of the Sea: A General Framework", *Ocean Dev. & Int'l L.J.*, vol. 15 (1985), pp. 136-7, Appendix B.

[90] Ibid., p. 136.

[91] See *Summary of Territorial Sea and Fishing Claims*, U.S. Dept. of State (1984) in Larson, ibid., . 140.

[92] Larson, note 89, p. 140.

[93] *Soundings*, vol. 18 (1983), p. 4; see also Schreiber (Peru), Seabed Committee (195th mtg.) UN Doc. S.E.A./M.B./25 (6 Dec. 1982); Castaneda (Mexico)., ibid.; Ballati (Trinidad & Tabago), ibid., p. 6; Nandan (Fiji), UN Doc. 3 (7 Dec. 1982).

others, are incompatible with the law and order established by the Conventions on the seas and directed against the legitimate interests of the other States.[94]

Still insisting on the largely rejected 3-mile limit for the territorial sea, along with some of its allies and some small countries unable for geographical reasons to extend it farther,[95] the United States realized that it could not force other states to limit their territorial waters jurisdiction. Any challenge to their sovereignty in these extended waters by a preponderant majority of states would be strongly resisted. Thus, in 1979, there were media reports that the United States had instructed its forces to exercise the freedom of the high seas up to the 3-mile limit of the coasts of other nations. Various governments requested immediate clarification some issuing statement that such a policy was illegal and would violate their sovereignty.[96] The Group of Coastal States at UNCLOS III also declared:

> The Group of Coastal States noted with surprise and concern recent media reports that the Government of the United States had "ordered its Navy and Air Force to undertake a policy of deliberately sending ships and planes into or over the disputed waters of nations that claim a territorial limit of more than three miles."
>
> In the view of the Group of Coastal States such a policy... is highly regrettable and unacceptable being contrary to customary international law, whereby a great majority of States exercise full sovereignty in their territorial seas up to a limit of 12 nautical miles, subject to the right of innocent passage. That policy is also inconsistent with the prevailing understanding at the UNCLOS which has recognized the validity of such a practice.... The Group of Coastal States considers the statement that the regime of the high seas commences beyond three miles as clearly an anachronism.[97]

Statements criticizing the U.S. position were made by Angola, Argentina, Brazil, China, Colombia, Costa Rica, Ecuador, El Salvador, Peru, the Philippines, and Vietnam. The Soviet Union said that the group of coastal states was "justified in its anxiety to which the Soviet delegation was sympathetic".[98] In this environment, Oxman was correct when he said that "it should be a warning to those who, in preference to a treaty, would rely on the major powers to make and enforce the law."[99]

The United States insisted that it would not accept the 12-mile territorial

[94] *Soundings*, ibid., p. 3.

[95] See a list of 26 such states including Bahrain, Belize, Brunci, Chile, Dominica, Qatar, Saint Vincent and the Grenadina, Singapore, Solomon Islands, Tuaolu and UAE, Larson, note 89, p. 141.

[96] See Un Doc. A/Conf. 62/85 (23 August 1979) (declaration by Foreign Minister of Columbia, Ecuador, Chile and Peru), quoted in Oxman, "The Third UNCLOS: The Eighth Session, 1979", *AJIL*, vol. 74 (1980), p. 9.

[97] See Oxman, ibid., p. 10.

[98] Ibid., p. 11.

[99] Ibid.

sea adopted in the 1982 Convention unless its freedom of transit passage recognized in the Convention was also accepted. It is important to note, however, that the transit passage regime for straits came to be accepted in UNCLOS III through hard bargaining and as a concession to the maritime Powers for their agreement to accept wider coastal state jurisdiction in the EEZ and continental shelf, and an international machinery for the exploration and exploitation of deep seabed resources. Since the United States sought to reject its part of the "package", the other states—strait states—argued that they were not bound to accept their part of the bargain. Thus, at the concluding session of UNCLOS III, Arias Schreiber of Peru, spokesman of the Group of 77, ruled out third state rights under the Convention.[100] Iran specifically denied the right of non-parties to transit passage in its declaration of the convention.[101] Spain, Morocco and Oman also were reported to have declared that they recognized "innocent passage" rather than "transit passage" through Gibraltar and Hormuz. Indonesia and Democratic Yemen spoke against third state rights at the final session of UNCLOS III.

Although these arguments are no longer valid since the United States has become party to the Convention in 1994, some of the small strait states still have reservations about the unobstructed right of transit passage through straits lying within their territorial waters. They may not be able to oppose the United States' or other maritime Powers' warships from exercising their right of passage.[102] But they are not prepared to accept this right as part of customary international law or roll back their claims.

[100] UN Doc. A/CONF. 62/PV. 185 (1983).

[101] Ibid., p. 191.

[102] See *Limits in the Sea*, No. 112, note 25, pp. 58-76.

South Asia and the Law of the Sea: Problems and Prospects

South Asia: Geographical Limits

The South Asian region, dominating the northern half of the Indian Ocean and extending from the Persian Gulf to the Straits of Malacca, occupies an important strategic location in an area that has been hotbed of international politics and conflicts for more than two decades. Inhabited by almost one-fifth of the human race in about three percent of the world's land surface, whose magnitude of deprivation is matched only by their desire to have a place in the sun, all of these countries have emerged from colonial domination after the Second World War. Geographically, besides the seven countries of the Indian subcontinent with common land frontiers – Afghanistan, Pakistan, India, Bangladesh, Nepal, Bhutan, and Burma—the region includes Sri Lanka and Maldives Islands with common maritime borders with India.

It may be noted, however, that because of their infrequent interactions with this region and their distinct social and cultural identities, Afghanistan is generally accepted as part of Central Asia and Burma as part of Southeast Asia. It may also be mentioned that for the last nearly twenty years, Afghanistan has been embroiled in a terrible war of attrition and could not, therefore, participate in any peacetime regional activities even if it were accepted as part of the region. On the other hand, Burma, for its own internal reasons, has adopted for the last nearly four decades a policy of self-imposed isolation. It has opted to stay out of all regional organizations. During the last two decades, it has turned down two invitations to join the Association of Southeast Asian Nations (ASEAN), and one proposal to join the South Asian Association of Regional Cooperation (SAARC). It has even declined to continue as part of the British Commonwealth and has left the Non-aligned Movement (NAM).

The seven countries of South Asia, it is significant to note, form the largest geopolitical reality of the Indian Ocean community. Unlike Southwest Asia and Southeast Asia, which are highly fragmented, South Asia is almost a continental whole. It physically dominates the northern part of the Indian Ocean, which serves as a vital link between the West and the East, connecting Europe through the Middle East with Southeast and East Asia. The region is traversed by important sea lanes of international trade and of vital oil supplies from the Gulf. Its island territories of Andaman and Nicobar screen, as it were, the Malacca Straits. The only significant trade routes that escape this domination are those that directly connect Southern Africa and Australia.

Geographically, South Asia is easily identifiable, lying south of the Himalayan range and forming a littoral of the Indian Ocean. Culturally, it is not difficult to find broad uniformities with respect to the political, administrative, legal, and economic structures found in all the seven countries, largely because of their common colonial domination and their historical emergence as independent nation States. These nations and their peoples are bound together by common bonds of historical ties, religious and cultural traditions, linguistic affinities, and common values and social norms.

Special Traits

As a region, South Asia has certain special traits. First of all, it is an Indo-centric region. India is central to it, geographically, culturally, politically, and even economically. While no other South Asian nations share a common border, four of them have land borders with India and two of them—Sri Lanka and the Maldives—maritime borders. The South Asian nations are related to India individually in terms of sociocultural bonds and historical experiences. India's geographical position bestows upon it a strategic strength in relation to the Indian Ocean that no other country can claim. Moreover, India's size gives it political and economic clout. It bestrides the region like a colossus. In terms of area and demographic and economic resources, India is bigger than all the other countries of the region put together.

According to the World Development Report of the World Bank, India's population is three times more than the combined population of the other six regional States and nearly eight times bigger than that of Bangladesh, the second most populous State in the region. India occupies 73 percent of the total region and is four times bigger than Pakistan, the second largest State in South Asia in area.[1] Its GNP is 78 percent of the total in the region and is

[1] Covering an area of 3.28 million square kilometers (sq.km.), India has a population more than a billion. Bangladesh, the second most populous country in South Asia, has an area of 144,020 sq.km. and a population of 100.59 million.

Situated in the Eastern Himalayas and bounded on the east-west and south by India, Bhutan covers an area of 46,600 sq.km. and has a population a little over one million. Pakistan has a total area of 804,000 sq.km. and a population of about 94.93 million.

The Republic of Maldives, 400 miles southwest of Sri Lanka, consists of some 2000 low-lying coral islands (only 220 inhabited) covering an area of 298 sq.km. and a population of .195 million.

Nepal covers an area of 147,400 sq.km. and has an estimated population of 16.14 million.

Sri Lanka, lying south-west of India, has a total area of 65,610 sq.km. and has a population of 16.4 million. See *SAARC Perspective*, vol. 1, no. 3 (1987); *Asia Year Book* (1989).

four times bigger than the combined GNP of Bangladesh and Pakistan. Moreover, India has one hundred percent of the uranium, iron ore, bauxite, copper, gold, lead, silver, zinc, asbestos, and diamonds in South Asia, and more than 80 percent of the coal, crude oil, and salt.[2] India, it is important to note, is at the center and all the other countries are bordering on its periphery. It is said to be the "fulcrum of the area." India's neighours among themselves have very few common attributes and their relations with each other—both economic and political—are very minimal. The crux of their diplomacy is how to gain maximum leverage vis-a-vis India. In other words, India is the axis around which the wheel of South Asia revolves.[3]

This high level of disparity between South Asian countries and asymmetrical relations between them has perhaps been the single most important factor impinging on cooperation in the region and the cause of tension and dissensions amongst them. All the small—and not so small[4]—neighbours of India have had misgivings, misapprehensions, and anxieties about India's intentions and fear of its actions and behaviour.

This mistrust and suspicion has led to high walls which have been built between countries of the region by an interplay of global, regional, and bilateral animosities. It may be noted, however, that because of geographical and historical factors, the intraregional security of South Asian States has been marked by the absence of any bilateral or multilateral issues among the six smaller nations of the group. At the same time, India is a common factor in all major disputes existing within the region. The great divide is between the six and the seventh. But then it must be borne in mind that India is the only country that has common land or sea frontiers with all other members

[2] See Emajuddin Ahamad, *SAARC: Seeds of Harmony* (Dhaka, 1985), pp. 44-45. See table, p. 46. According to another permutation, within South Asia, India is said to account roughly 76 percent of the population; 79 percent GOP; 68 percent of manufacturing exports; 62 percent of the import market; 41 percent of external reserves; 46 percent of the total armed forces; and 72 percent of estimated defense spending. see Iftekharuzzaman, "Bangladesh and SAARC Reflections on the Region and Motivations for Cooperation," in Muzaffar Ahmad and Abul Kalam (eds.) *Bangladesh Foreign Relations: Changes and Directions* (Dhaka, 1989), p. 81 (hereafter cited as BFR). Also some 85 percent of the land under permanent cultivation and 70 percent of the irrigated land of the region is in India. See Abul Kalam, "Bangladesh and India: A Perspective of Cooperative Relationship in a Regional Strategic Environment," in Muzaffar Ahmad and Abul Kalam, *BFR*, p. 96.

[3] See V. Suryanarayan, "Partners in Progress or Uneasy Coexistence? An Indian View," *The Island* (Colombo: July 26, 1985).

[4] Bangladesh and Pakistan are the eighth and ninth most populous countries in the world. Indeed, except for Bhutan and Maldives, the other nations of the region, including Sri Lanks, and Nepal, by international standards, come within the top 30 percent of the nations of the world. See M.D. Dharamdasani (ed.) *Contemporary South Asia* (Varanasi, 1985), p. 20.

of the group. Since the five countries have common borders only with India and not with each other, the entire security problem tends to be blown up out of proportion as India versus the other States.[5]

Rightly or wrongly, India's neighbours feel themselves threatened by the bigger power center and accuse it of "hegemonistic designs."[6] Relations between India and its four smaller neighbours (Pakistan, Bangladesh, Nepal, and Sri Lanka) have been marked by continuing tensions that have varied in intensity at different times. In the case of Pakistan, besides the lingering Kashmir dispute, this hostility has led to three wars that climaxed in the dismemberment of Pakistan in 1971.[7]

Although India helped in the emergence of Bangladesh, it has not been able to solve all their disputes, such as, their maritime borders dispute, and India's problem of immigrants from its eastern neighbour. With Sri Lanka, the ethnic issue of the Tamil minority community in that country has remained an irritant. Even landlocked Nepal is unhappy with India about hindrance to its trade with the rest of the world and India's reluctance to accept Nepal as a "zone of peace." India is blamed by its neighbours for all their political conflicts, for using "strong-arm tactics," and for "bullying and intimidating" its smaller neighbours in its ruthless pursuit of becoming "the dominant power of South Asia, an eminent power of Asia and a potential global power, perhaps even a mini-super power."[8] Justifiably or not, inter-State relations in the region, ever since independence, have been "characterized by a state of flux, distortions, endemic tensions, mutual distrust, bilateral discords, and occasional hostilities."[9]

India's Expanding Claims

It is important to examine the impact of the recent developments in the law of the sea on South Asia. It is interesting to note that all the newly-independent South Asian States, in tune with the time, have tried to take the maximum benefit of current turmoil in the sea law and extend their national jurisdictions. Thus, as early as March 1956, India extended its territorial sea from the traditional three-mile limit of British India to six miles,[10] and within a few months, in December 1956, adopted a twelve-mile contiguous zone for

[5] See Mohammad Iqbal, "SAARC: The Urge for Cooperation in South Asia," *Regional Studies* vol. IV, no. 4 (Islamabad: Autumn 1986), p. 49.

[6] See A.I. Akram, "Security of Small States: Implications for South Asia," *Regional Studies*, vol III, n. 3 (Islamabad: Summer 1985), p. 8; hereafter cited as "Security".

[7] See also A.I. Akram, "India and Pakistan: A Glorious Future," *Regional Studies*, vol. II, n. 3 (Islamabad: Spring 1984), p. 34.

[8] See Akram, "Security," p. 8.

[9] Iftekharuzzaman, "Bangladesh and SAARC: Reflections on the Region and Motivations for Cooperation," in Ahmad and Kalam, *BFR*, p. 79.

[10] See *Gazette of India, Extraordinary*, Part II, Section 3, n. 81, March 22, 1956.

purposes of security, customs, and sanitary regulations.[11] The Maritime Zones Act of 1976 extended its territorial sea to twelve miles and also extended contiguous zone of India to twenty-four nautical miles for the purposes of its security, immigration, sanitation, customs and other fiscal matters.[12]

Occupying a central position in the Indian Ocean, with a continental coastline extending to 5700 kilometers (km.), and having about 1200 islands and islets (668 in the Bay of Bengal, including the Andaman and Nicobar archipelagos and 508 in the Arabian Sea, including the Lakshadweep group of islands), lying on one of the most important international maritime routes of the Indian Ocean, India added many prime maritime routes and several areas to its sovereign jurisdiction. It is also important to note the richness of these marine areas in natural resources, both living and non-living. In fact, India's continental shelf and margin run into vast expanses of the sea surrounding its mainland and islands. It has about 131,800 square nautical miles (sq.nm.).[13] In the Bay of Bengal the seabed is covered by thick piles of sediments, the thickness of which varies between 10 and 16 km. in the north to between 6 and 8 km. in the middle. In the southern part of the Bay of Bengal, the thickness of sediments tapers from 3 km. to 1 km. It is estimated that nearly 40 percent of the total sediments present in the Indian Ocean are to be found in the Arabian Sea and the Bay of Bengal. The continental shelf area in the Arabian Sea is said to extend to about 150 nm. from the coast south-westward of the Gulf of Bombay. The embayment of the North Arabian Sea has sediments of eight km. thickness towards the deep sea. The foot of the continental slope in the Bay of Bengal is at an average distance of 50 nm.[14] All these areas are potentially rich in oil and gas. India's interest in securing exclusive jurisdiction over these lucrative areas of the continental shelf would be obvious.

India's first formal claim to the continental shelf was made by a Presidential Proclamation on August 30, 1955, whereby it claimed "full and exclusive sovereign rights over the seabed and subsoil of the continental shelf adjoining its territory and beyond its territorial waters."[15] The legal limits of the continental shelf was defined on November 24, 1959 in terms of the 1958 UN Convention on the Continental Shelf as extending to a depth of 200

[11] Presidential Proclamation of 3 December 1956 in UN Doc., A/Conf 19/5.

[12] The Parliament passed the Territorial Waters, Continental Shelf, Exclusive Economic Zone and other Maritime Zones Act in 1976. See Myron Nordquist, S. Houston Lay, Kenneth R. Simmonds, *New Directions in the Law of the Sea*, vol. V (London, Oceana Publications, 1986), p. 306. Hereafter cited as New Directions.

[13] U.S. Dept. of State, Office of the Geographer, *Limits in the Seas*, no. 46, August 12, 1972.

[14] See Rama Puri, *India and National Jurisdiction in the Sea* (New Delhi, 1985), p. 135. Hereafter cited as India and Nat. Jur.

[15] *Gazette of India Extraordinary* (New Delhi), Part II, Section 3, quoted in Rama Puri India and Nat. Jur., p. 121.

meters or beyond to "where the depth of the superjacent water admits of the exploitation of the natural resources of the areas."[16] After the International Court of Justice defined continental shelf as the "natural prolongation of the land territory of a State into and under the sea" in the *North Sea Continental Shelf* Cases,[17] and in accordance with the general trend, India redefined, in the 1976 Maritime Zone Act, its continental shelf as extending "throughout the natural prolongation of its land territory to the outer edge of the continental margin or to a distance of two hundred nautical miles from the baseline...where the outer edge of the continental margin does not extend up to that distance."[18]

Further, in accordance with the consensus emerging in the Third Law of the Sea Conference, India declared in the 1976 Maritime Zone Act an exclusive economic zone (EEZ) extending to two hundred nm. in which it would have, *inter alia*, "sovereign rights for the purpose of exploration, exploitation, conservative and management of the natural resources, both living and non-living, as well as for producing energy from tides, winds and currents."[19]

It is important to note that India's claims in regard to its maritime jurisdictions were not merely endorsed by the UN Convention on the Law of the Sea (UNCLOS) concluded in 1982, but the latter accepted even wider limits of continental shelf, extending in some cases to 350 nm. or 100 nm. beyond the 2500 meter isobath (Article 76, (5, 7)). India has been a great beneficiary according to these provisions of the 1982 Convention especially because of its large coastline and wide continental shelf. It has gained at least 587,600 sq.nm. of real estate within its sovereign jurisdiction as part of its EEZ for the exploration and exploitation of its natural resources, both living and non-living. It has already found its continental shelf rich in oil and gas resources and is producing almost 19 million tons of crude oil from its offshore oil field.[20] Besides the Bombay offshore region, where the majority of resources lie, India has discovered oil in Godavari, Krishna and Palk Bay basins and gas in Andaman offshore. Its current strategy is aimed at building self reliance in offshore exploration and development. India has also begun construction of highly sophisticated and technologically complex drillships at its yard in Vishakapatnam with Japanese collaboration. Further, even with their outdated methods and outmoded gear, Indian fishermen catch nearly 18 million metric tons of fish from India's economic zone.[21]

[16] See Rama Puri, *India and Nat. Jur.*, p. 121.

[17] *ICJ Reports* (1969), p. 22.

[18] Nordquist, *New Directions,* Article 6(1), p. 308.

[19] Ibid., Article 7(1), Maritime Zones Act, p. 310.

[20] See Puri, India and Nat. Jur., p. 135.

[21] See Ted L. McDorman, "Extended Jurisdiction and Ocean Resource Conflict in the Indian Ocean," *International Journal of Estuarine and Coastal Law*, 3 (1988): 234. Hereafter cited as "Ext. Jur. and Ocean Resource Conflict."

It is also pertinent to mention that by a resolution (Resolution II) adopted by the UNCLOS III, India, along with France, Japan, and Soviet Union, was recognized as a "pioneer investor" in Seabed exploratory activities for the recovery of polymetallic nodules from the ocean. The pioneer investor status was subject to the fulfillment of two conditions. One, that it be a signatory to the Convention, which all these States were; and two, that such a "State or state enterprise or natural or juridical person has expended, before 1 January 1983, an amount equivalent to at least $30 million (U.S.)...in pioneer activities and has expended no less than 10 percent of that amount in location, survey and evaluation of the area." Pioneer activities were described in the resolution to include:

(i) any at-sea observation and evaluation activity which has as its objective the establishment and documentation of the nature, shape, concentration, location and grade of polymetallic nodules and of the environmental, technical and other appropriate factors which must be taken into account before exploitation.
(ii) the recovery from the Area of polymetallic nodules with a view to the designing, fabricating and testing of equipment which is intended to be used in the exploitation of polymetallic nodules.

To have achieved some measure of expertise to be recognized as a "pioneer investor" and being the first developing country to acquire a high level of technological excellence in the related fields of science and technology was no mean achievement for a poor country like India. It may also be noted that India was the first country to be registered as a "pioneer investor" by the Preparatory Commission in 1987 for conducting exploratory activities for deep seabed mining in 150,000 km. of the Indian Ocean.[22] Whether seabed exploitation at the present stage is economically feasible or not, and whether India will be able to exploit these metallic resources in the near future or it fails to do so, are not important issues here. There is little doubt, however, that it has made a marked change in the image of India, especially among its neighbours.[23]

Pakistan's Extended Limits

Already a subject of jealousy and fear amongst its neighbours in South Asia because of its size and resources, the vast maritime extensions by India, this

[22] See H.N. Siddique and P.S. Rao, "Exploration for Polymetallic Nodules in the Indian Ocean," Ocean Development and International Law Journal 19 (1988), pp. 323-35. See also S.P. Jagota, "Recent Developments in the Law of the Sea," *Ocean Yearbook 7* (Chicago: The University of Chicago Press, 1989), pp. 65 ff.

[23] See Institute of Regional Study, Islamabad, "The Law of the Sea: Its Impacts on Inter-State Relations in South Asia, *Spotlight on Regional Affairs*, VII (May-June 1988), pp. 5-8, 10-16.

"giant" among them, have further exacerbated their feelings. Thus Pakistan, less than one-fourth of its size in land area, has a small coastline of 440 miles, and even the extension of maritime zones to include 12 miles of territorial sea, 200 miles of EEZ, and continental shelf, extending to the end of the continental margin under UNCLOS and as claimed by Pakistan under its Territorial Waters and Maritime Zones Act of 1976, though helpful, is not much compared to India.[24] Pakistan has nearly 9200 sq.nm. enclosed within its EEZ, out of which 1700 sq.nm. lies within its 200-meter isobath. But so far the exploration for oil and gas in its waters have not been very encouraging.

Declaring the Rann of Kutch, a marsh land between the Indian State of Gujarat and Pakistan's Province of Sind and potentially an oil-rich area, as a "land-locked sea" or a "boundary lake," Pakistan sought to take part of the area from India in the 1960s.[25] But when the use of force did not succeed in the settlement of the dispute, the matter was submitted to an international arbitration tribunal which awarded more than ninety percent of the disputed area to India.[26] Frustrated and angry, Pakistan has not so far demarcated its maritime boundary with India. But since the area is not expected to yield oil and gas, nobody seems to be in a hurry to demarcate the boundary.

Bangladesh and Its Unusual Claims

Bangladesh, as is well known, emerged as an independent State after the Indo-Pakistan War of 1971 and owes much to India for its independence and escape from Pakistan's clutches. It was not long, however, before it found itself entangled with India on various issues of vital interests to its economy and well-being. Some of these crucial issues related to maritime boundaries between the two neighbours and sharing of water of numerous (fifty-two) rivers that flow to Bangladesh through India.

Surrounded by India on the north, west, and east, it also shares a border with Burma in the east. To the south lies its deeply indented concave coastline in the Bay of Bengal, which is said to be "unstable, broken and irregular."[27] Bangladesh is a land of mighty rivers (Ganges, Brahmputra, and Meghna, and their innumerable tributaries) that flow from the high Himalayas, through

[24] Pakistan earlier claimed seabed extending to 100 fathoms contour and signed the Continental Shelf Convention though it did not ratify it. In 1966, Pakistan claimed 12 miles of exclusive fishing zone and 100 km. of conservation zone. See M. Habibur Rahman, "Delineation of Maritime Boundaries," *Asian Survey* 24 (December 1986), pp. 1307. Hereafter cited as "Delineation."

[25] See *The Kutch-Sind Border Question* (New Delhi: Indian Society of International Law, 1965).

[26] See R.P. Anand, "The Kutch Award," in R.P. Anand, *Studies in International Adjudication* (New Delhi, 1968).

[27] See Rahman, n. 24, p. 1306.

Nepal and India, and carry down to the Bay a colossal discharge of silt. This, together with heavy monsoon rainfall, cyclonic storms, and tidal surges, contributes to a continuous process of erosion and shoaling both on land and in the sea on the mouths of rivers. The presence of deltas and islands off the coast of Bangladesh in the Bay adds further complications in the delimitation of its maritime zones.[28]

Classisfied by the UN as one of the least developed countries of the world,[29] Bangladesh has hardly any mineral resources and depends largely on agriculture and fishing to feed its teeming millions and for its meager foreign exchange.[30] Until its independence, as part of Pakistan, Bangladesh claimed the same jurisdictions over its coastal zones as Pakistan. After its emergence as an independent State, Bangladesh enacted, in February 1974, its own Territorial Waters and Maritime Zones Act under which it declared, on April 12, 1976, a 12 nm. territorial sea, 200 miles of EEZ, and a continental shelf, extending to the outer limits of the continental margin.[31] A serious dispute arose, however, between Bangladesh and its neighbours, India and Burma, about delimitation of their overlapping maritime boundaries. As we mentioned, the great rivers of the Ganges (called Padma in Bangladesh), Jamuna, and Meghna carry an enormous amount of silt that they deposit in the ocean, making the seaward slope extremely gentle in the Bengal Basin. The effect of geological features and climatic condition on Bangladesh's coastal regions have led to the following characteristics:

(1) The estuary of Bangladesh is such that no stable water line or demarcation of landward and seaward area exists.
(2) The continual process of alluvian and sedimentation forms mudbanks, and the area is so shallow as to be non-navigable by other than small boats.
(3) The navigable channels through the aforesaid banks are continuously changing their course and require soundings to establish their demarcation.

These geomorphological considerations necessitated, according to Bangladesh, "depth-method baselines" rather than "normal baselines" or "straight baselines" for delimitation of its territorial sea, as envisaged in Article 4 of the 1958 Territorial Sea Convention. It, therefore, suggested an amendment to Article 4 of the Territorial Sea Convention that would permit delineation of baseline by the depth method, i.e., geograpic coordinates at specific depths of the coastal waters linked by straight lines to demarcate

[28] Ibid.

[29] Vide UN General Assembly Resolution 3487 (XXX).

[30] See Rahman, n. 24, p 1306.

[31] See Bangladesh's Territorial Waters and Maritime Zones Act, 1974 and announcement about maritime zones, Myron Nordquist, S. Houston Lay, Kenneth R. Simmonds, "New Directions," p. 201 II.

effectively the landward and seaward areas.[32] At the Caracas session of UNCLOS III, it proposed the following amendment to Article 6(2) of the Revised Single Negotiating Text:

> Where because of the presence of a delta and other natural conditions, the waters adjacent to the coasts are marked by continual fluvial erosion and sedimentation creating a highly unstable baseline, the baseline may be delimited by a straight line or a series of straight lines connecting appropriate points of such adjacent waters.[33]

Bangladesh's amendment was not accepted. To meet Bangladesh's specific situation, however, at least to some extent, Article 7(2) of the 1982 Convention provided:

> Where because of the presence of a delta and other natural conditions the coastline is highly unstable, the appropriate points may be selected along the furthest seaward extent of the low-water line and, notwithstanding subsequent regression of the low-water line, the straight baselines shall remain effective until changed by the coastal State in accordance with this Convention.

Disappointed because Article 7(2) did not meet what it wanted, in 1974 Bangladesh proclaimed a set of straight baselines drawn on the basis of a depth method, taking into account the geological and topographical peculiarities of its coastline. Measuring 221 nm., the baseline joins 8 fixed points at 10 fathoms depth, which at some places puts the baseline as much as 50 miles from the shore. Thus, although it has a coastline of only 310 miles, it has enclosed 6200 sq nm. of coastal areas and continental shelf within its internal waters[34] through its 'floating' baselines. Moreover, since none of the 8 points defining the baseline is anchored to the coast anywhere, it is technically possible to enter and sail into the internal waters of Bangladesh without crossing its straight baseline. It is not surprising that both India and Burma have rejected Bangladesh's claim[35] and it has not received the approval of any country so far.[36] Clearly, Bangladesh's straight baselines do not fulfill

[32] See Rahman, "Delineation," p. 1311.

[33] See R. Platzoeder, *The Third United Nations Conference on the Law of the Sea: Documents,* vol. IV (Dobbs Ferry, New York: Oceana Publications, Inc., 1983), pp. 389 ff.

[34] See Manjula Shyam, "Extended Maritime Jurisdiction and its Impact on South Asia," *Ocean Development and International Law,* 10 (1981-82), p. 102; hereafter cited as "Extended Jurisdiction." See also Rahman, "Delineation," pp. 1312-13.

[35] See Shyam, "Extended Jurisdiction," p. 102. It is interesting to note that Vietnam is the only country that supported Bangladesh's claim because, it is said, it was in a similar situation. See Sally McDonald and Victor Prescott, "Baselines along Unstable Coast: An Interpretation of Article 7(2)," *Ocean Yearbook 8* (Chicago: The University of Chicago Press, 1990), p. 74. Hereafter cited as "Baselines."

[36] See J.R. V. Prescott, *The Maritime Political Boundaries of the World* (London: Methuen & Co., Ltd., 1985), pp. 163-66; hereafter cited as Maritime Boundaries. See also McDonald and Prescott, "Baselines," p. 83.

the limitations for straight baselines laid down in paragraph 3 of Article 7, which provide that:

> The drawing of straight baselines must not depart to any appreciable extent from the general direction of the coast, and the sea areas lying within the lines must be sufficiently closely linked to the land domain to be subject to the regime of internal waters.

The Ganges-Brahmputra Delta of the Bay of Bengal located at the combined mouths of the Ganges and Brahmputra rivers is a promising, petroleum-rich area in which both Bangladesh and India are interested. The delimitation of this area is a subject of dispute between these two neighbouring countries. While India would like the area to be divided on the basis of an equidistance line, Bangladesh, because of its concave coastline, would find itself at a disadvantaged position if the equidistance method is used. The dispute between them surfaced when Petro-Bangla, a government-controlled corporation, signed production-sharing contracts for conducting seismic surveys and exploratory drilling with six companies in 1974. The block that was awarded to Ashland was disputed by India which lodged a formal protest to Bangladesh against granting exploratory rights in an area which, under the equidistance principle, would fall within the Indian EEZ.[37]

The dispute was further complicated by the emergence or formation in 1970, after cyclonic activity, of a new island in the Bay of Bengal, in the estuary of the Haribhanga River on the border between the two countries, known as New Moore Island or Purbasha in India and South Talpatty island in Bangladesh. It is a U-shaped formation with an approximate area of two square miles (sq.m.), lying 5 nm. from the coast of Bangladesh and 2 nm. off the coast of India. India claims the island on the grounds that the flow of the Haribhanga River (which forms the boundary between the two countries) is to the east of the island, which, therefore, lies on the natural prolongation of the Indian territory. Bangladesh contests this claims and asserts that the river flows to the west of the island and cannot be said to be on the natural prolongation of the Indian territory. In any case, India has claimed the island since 1971 as lying within its territorial sea and, after its discovery and occupation, it notified immediately the U.S. Naval Oceanographic Office and the British Admiralty. Maintaining an effective occupation by conducting frequent surveys, although the island is not inhabited, India has prevented all attempts by Bangladesh, especially in 1981, to land on the island to hoist its flag. The island is of great importance for Bangladesh since, if the island falls to India, any line of equidistance that takes account of the island would erode the area claimed by Bangladesh.[38]

[37] Shyam, "Extended Jurisdiction," pp. 100-101.

[38] See Prescott, *Maritime Boundaries*, p. 176. Recently it was reported that the disputed New Moore or South Talpatty Island was getting smaller and gradually

Besides its maritime boundary with India's mainland, Bangladesh's boundary with Andaman and Nicobar Islands, on the one hand, and its boundaries with Burma and Sri Lanka, on the other, need to be delineated. Whether India and Bangladesh would be willing to make concessions to each other depends upon other aspects of their relationship. The dispute over the sharing of river waters, the construction of Farakka barrage, the exchange of small land enclaves on the Indo-Bangladesh border, and the treatment of non-Muslim minorities in Bangladesh have soured the relations between the two countries.

Sri Lanks and its Limited Expansion

Sri Lanka is a small island State in the South of India with a small coastline of 650 nm. Although it has an area of 150,000 sq.nm. of EEZ, its continental shelf is not very wide. In fact the average distance at which 200-meter isobath occurs off the coast of Sri Lanka is not more than 20 nm. The total area within the 200 meter isobath is about 7,800 sq.nm. Sri Lanka brought it to the attention of UNCLOS III that in its case the foot of the continental slope and the 2,500 meter isobath were very close to its coast and a very large proportion of the sedimentary rock of the continental margin of Sri Lanka was beneath the rise. The application of the rule adopted in Article 76 of the Convention, therefore, limiting the outer edge of the continental margin according to the thickness of sedimentary rocks or 60 miles from the foot of the continental slope, according to Sri Lanka, would deny it more than half of its margin, which would otherwise belong to it, since the continental margin consists of the shelf, slope, and the rise. It, therefore, requested the conference to agree, on grounds of equity, to an exceptional method of delimitation, taking into account the special characteristics of its continental margin.[39] The Conference partially agreed to it and permitted Sri Lanka to establish the outer edge of its continental fixed points defined by latitude and longitude, at each of which the thickness of sedimentary rock was not less than one kilometer.[40] How far this method of delimitation of continental shelf will help Sri Lanka, it is difficult to say. But it seems that although geomorphologically, Sri Lanka has a very wide continental rise, legally its continent shelf will not extend beyond 200 miles from the baseline.[41] A lot of exploratory activities have been started off Sri Lanka's coast.

---

facing extinction following consistent wave action and other natural calamities of the Bay of Bengal. See *The Hindu* (Madras: December 26, 1989).

[39] See UN Doc. A/Conf 62/1.51 and NG 6/5; also Puri, *India and Nat. Jur.*, p. 142.

[40] See Annex II to the 1982 Convention.

[41] See Bernard Oxman, "The Third United Nations Conference on the Law of the Sea: The Eighth Session (1979)," *American Journal of International Law* 74 (January 1980), pp. 23-33. See also Shyam, "Extended Jurisdiction," p. 110.

It is important to mention here that India and Sri Lanka have amicably completed the process of their boundary delimitation in 1977 through three separate agreements. The first agreement, signed in 1974, related to the conflicting claims of the two countries to the Island of Kacchativu, a half-coral, half-sand island, about 3.75 sq.km. in area, lying in the Palk Strait about 12 miles from the nearest Indian coast and 10.5 miles from Sri Lanka. Used for centuries by fishermen from both the countries, the island was for the most part uninhabited except for a chapel which was occasionally used by the faithful, living both in India and Sri Lanka, especially at an annual fair at the Shrine of St. Anthony. Although both the countries claimed the island on historical grounds, neither party could prove an actual display of State activities to the exclusion of the other. The Kacchativu Island became a major obstacle in the boundary agreement and led to a climate of suspicion affecting the entire range of relations between them. By an agreement signed in June 1974, India relinquished its claim over the island but, as a concession to India, the two parties agreed to divide the Palk Strait on the basis of the equidistance principle irrespective of the island. The median line was drawn in the area of the Kacchativu about 11 miles from the nearest point in India and one mile from the island. Indian pilgrims and fishermen were also permitted by the agreement to visit the island without visas as before.[42]

It is important to note that both India and Sri Lanka claim Palk Strait, Palk Bay, and the Gulf of Manaar as historic waters and have included provisions to that effect in their respective Maritime Zones Acts, passed in 1976, following the conclusion of maritime boundary agreements between them.[43] The Palk Bay and the Gulf of Manaar constitute the northern and southern sectors, respectively, of the sea between the mainland of India and Sri Lanka. They are divided by the Island of Rameswaram and a continuous line of coral reefs, called Adam's Bridge, leading to the mainland of Sri Lanka. The Palk Bay is an inlet of Bay of Bengal, measuring about 74 nm. along its north-south axis and 76 nm. along the major east-west axis, and is bordered by the Indian peninsula on the west, Adam's Bridge on the south, and the island of Ceylon on the east. The Gulf of Manaar opens into the Indian Ocean in the south, but is otherwise almost wholly surrounded by land. At its widest point, between point De Galle in Sri Lanka and Kanyakumari in India, the Gulf is about 200 miles. In the north the Gulf is about 17 miles, and from north to south 130 miles.

The Palk Bay and the Gulf of Manaar have been well-known from time immemorial for their pearl and chank fisheries. There is ample historical authority to prove that the sovereigns of both India and Sri Lanka considered themselves as the exclusive owners of the beds of pearl oysters and chanks

[42] See Shyam, "Extended Jurisdiction," pp. 104-105; see also U.S. Dept. of State, "Historic Water Boundary: India-Sri Lanka," *Limits in the Seas, no. 66* (December 12, 1975).

in the Palk Bay and the Gulf of Manaar. The question of historicity of Palk Bay was resolved by a decision of the Madras High Court in 1904 in the case of *Annakumaru Pillai vs. Muthupayalru* (ILR (1904) 27 Madras 551). At that time both India and Sri Lanka were part of the British Empire. The Court decided that Palk Bay was "land locked by His Majesty's dominions for eight-ninths of its circumference (and) effectively occupied for centuries by the inhabitants of the adjacent districts of India and Ceylon, respectively." The Court added that "we do not think that Palk's Bay can be regarded as being in any sense the open sea and therefore outside the territorial jurisdiction of His Majesty." Further, according to the Court, the British occupation had received "the acquiescence of other nations."[44] The Court went on to declare that the Gulf of Manaar was also an "historic bay" and an integral part of the British dominions.[45]

On January 15, 1977, the Government of India, notifying the limits of India's historic waters in Palk Strait, Palk Bay, and the Gulf of Manaar, referred to their status as follows:

> The historic waters of India in the Palk Strait and the Palk Bay area of sea are internal waters of India. The historic waters of India beyond the appropriate baseline referred to in section 3(2) of the Act in the Gulf of Manaar area of sea have the same status as the territorial waters of India.

Sri Lanka issued a similar proclamation in respect of its historical waters in Palk Strait, Palk Bay and the Gulf of Manaar.[46]

The agreement on maritime boundaries was also accompanied by an agreement on fisheries, according to which fishermen from Sri Lanka were allowed to continue fishing at Wadge Bank south of Cape Comorin in India's EEZ for three years until 1979 and were given five years thereafter to phase out their fishing activity in the area.[47] It was agreed that for a period of five years India would provide annually to Sri Lanka, at their request, 2000 tons of fish of a quality and species and at a price to be mutually agreed upon by the two Governments.[48]

[43] See 1974 India-Sri Lanka agreement, and their agreement establishing maritime boundaries in the Gulf of Manaar and the Bay of Bengal, U.S. Department of State, *Limits in the Sea, no. 77* (February 16, 1978).

[44] See *Limits in the Sea,* no. 77, p. 4.

[45] See for an exhaustive discussion of the Palk Bay and the Gulf of Mannar, P. Chandrasekhara Rao, *The New Law of Maritime Zones; With Special Reference to India's Maritime Zones* (New Delhi, 1983), p. 68.

[46] Ibid., p. 75.

[47] See Shyam, "Extended Jurisdiction," p. 105.

[48] See S.P. Jagota, *Maritime Boundary* (Dordrecht: M. Nijhoff, 1985), p. 80.

Maldives' Extraordinary Claims of Jurisdiction in the Sea

The Republic of Maldives consists of about 1000 tiny islands mostly .6 to .8 km. long with a total land area of 298 sq.km.[49] (or 115 sq.m.), out of which only some 204 islands or 20 percent are inhabited by a total population of about 140,000. The island chain stretches some 475 miles in the Indian Ocean with its center point about 400 miles west and a little south of Sri Lanka. It could claim archipelagic status under the 1982 Convention although it has not done so. By its constitution adopted in 1964, the territory of Maldives was defined as the islands, air, and sea surrounding and in between the islands contained within a rectangle formed by meridians and parallels. The rectangle was slightly amended in 1972 and is declared to be within 72 degrees 30 minutes and 30 seconds east and 73 degrees 48 minutes west and the parallels 7 degrees 9 minutes 30 seconds north and 0 degrees 45 minutes 15 seconds south. At no point do these floating baselines of the constitutional rectangle touch any of the territory of Maldives, though the northern and some part of the eastern boundary will be within one nautical mile of some atolls. But on the west and the east, respectively, they pass 52 and 38 nm. from the nearest land.[50] Maldives established its fisheries zone in 1969, territorial sea and fishing zone in 1970, and EEZ in 1976, by declaring limits that were parallel to the constitutional rectangle. While the drawing of such baselines is questionable under customary or conventional international law, India, along with Sri Lanka, negotiated in July 1976 a boundary delimitation agreement with Maldives recognizing each other's maritime zones and laying down a trijunction point (T point) between the three countries. In December 1976, India concluded another agreement with Maldives delimiting the maritime boundary between the two countries in the Arabian Sea. India again recognized Maldives' economic zone limits by this agreement.[51]

Although Maldives' claim to its economic zone around its constitutional rectangle has been more or less ignored so far, in the south, it impinges on the area that would fall in the economic zone of the British Indian Ocean Territory. The area involved is said to about 21600 sq.nm.[52] While Britain has so far ignored the infringement because it is using the Indian Ocean

[49] Some, such as Male, the capital and the only town in the country, are one mile long. Some islands are two or three miles long, but are quite narrow. The largest island in Maldives is Fu Mulaku, which is three-and-one-half by one-and-one-half miles and has a lake in the middle. See Clarence Maloney, *People of the Maldive Islands* (Bombay: Orient Longman, 1980), pp. 1-3.

[50] See Prescott, *Maritime Boundaries*, p. 161.

[51] Dept. of State, "Maritime Boundary: India, Maldives and Maldives' Claimed 'Economic Zone," *Limits in the Sea*, no. 78.

[52] See Prescott, *Maritime Boundaries*, p. 161.

Territory for strategic purposes only, a different situation may arise if Mauritius regained this area as part of its territory to whom it rightfully belongs.

Burma's Claims of Straight Baselines

Despite all its self-imposed isolation in its international relations, Burma has not failed to take advantage of the recent developments in the law of the sea to extend its maritime jurisdictions. On November 15, 1968, Burma proclaimed the use of straight baselines "where it is necessary by reason of the geographical conditions prevailing on the Union of Burma coasts, and for the purpose of safeguarding the vital interests of the inhabitants of the coastal regions...." Slightly amended in 1977, these 826 nm. of straight baselines not only closed the wide Gulf of Martaban with a single baseline extending to 222.3 nm., but joined on the Tanassim coast the Mergui Archipelago by joining outermost points of the outermost islands. Besides long individual baselines, which have made it the longest segment of straight baselines in the world, they enclosed water-to-land at the ratio of 50 to 1 and at one point the baseline was 75 miles from the nearest coast and made a deflection of 14 degrees from the general direction of the coastline.[53] In spite of the presence of a delta, the shallowness of the region,[54] and the instability of the shoreline surrounding the Gulf of Martaban, the legal validity of Burmese baselines is questionable under the 1982 Convention.

Another problem between India and Burma concerned Narcondam Island in the Andaman Sea, owned and occupied by India. A craterless volcano, Narcondam Island has an area of 7 sq.km. that stands 710 meters above sea level and is bounded by cliffs 100 meters in height. If India's claim to give full effect to Narcondam Island in its boundary delimitation is accepted, it will cover part of the continental shelf of the Irrawaddy River Delta. The area concerned would depend on whether the line of equidistance between India and Burma was based on the Burmese coastline or the Burmese baseline closing the Gulf of Martaban. In the first case the area would be 1175 sq.m. and in the second case580 sq.m. India had defied all Burmese claims to Narcondam Island and was determined to defend its sovereignty over the

[53] See Prescott, Maritime Boundaries, p. 166; and Kriangsak Kittichaisaree, *The Law of the Sea and Maritime Boundary Delimitation in South-East Asia* (Singapore: Oxford University Press, 1987), pp. 13-14.

[54] The Gulf is very shallow (between 2 to 5 fathoms deep), because several rivers flow into it, contributing to sediment buildup in the area. Moreover, composed of mud and sand, the mouth of the Rangoon River is very unstable and extends for a distance of about five miles. See Indian Naval Hydrographic Office, Rangoon River to Moubnein (Govt. Printing Office, Map. no. 411, 1985); also U.S. Naval Oceanographic Office, *Rangoon River and Approaches* (Govt. Printing Office, Map. no. 63413, 1978).

island.[55] On December 23, 1986, Burma and India concluded an agreement delimiting their boundaries in the Bay of Bengal and the Andaman Sea. While India's claim to Narcondam Island has been confirmed in the agreement, it says nothing about Burma's unique baselines claims.[56] Earlier, on July 25, 1980, Burma and Thailand signed an agreement delimiting their maritime boundary in the Andaman Sea.[57]

Geographically Disadvantaged States in South Asia: Nepal and Bhutan

These two small South Asian countries are land-locked States dependent on coastal States for their transit passage to use the sea and enjoy its bounties. Unlike several other landlocked States that may have some options in choosing their transit passage through more than one country, e.g., Switzerland and Austria, both Nepal and Bhutan are virtually dependent on India for the exercise of their rights with regard to the sea. Although Nepal also has China as a neighbour to reach the ocean, the topography of the area and high barriers of the Himalayas have made transit route through China almost inaccessible. This dependence on India is not particularly liked by Nepal and Bhutan and it has led sometimes to terrible tensions, especially between Nepal and Bhutan.

Further, although under Article 69 of the 1982 Convention on the Law of the Sea, the landlocked States have a "right to participate, on an equitable basis, in the exploitation of an appropriate part of the surplus of the living resources of the EEZs of the coastal States of the same sub-region or region," this right can be made effective only through an agreement with the coastal State of the region. This again means virtual dependence on India. Although Bangladesh and Pakistan are in the same region, they have only small coastlines and very limited area compared to India's large coastline and vast EEZ area. It will also not be easy for Nepal and Bhutan to use the EEZ of Sri Lanka or Maldives. No wonder both Nepal and Bhutan expressed their disappointment at the provisions concerning the land-locked States in the 1982 Convention. The representative of Nepal said at the concluding session of UNCLOS III:

> The provisions relating to land-locked countries, particularly Part X of the Convention, are of special importance to us. We are not wholly satisfied with regard to the rights of transit of land-locked countries in Article 69 of the Convention. Similarly, provisions relating to the sharing of resources on the

[55] See Prescott, *Maritime Boundaries*, p. 176.

[56] See Ted L. McDorman, "Ext. Jur. and Ocean Resource Conflict," n. 21, p. 217.

[57] U.S. Dept. of State, "Maritime Boundary: Burma-Thailand," *Limits in the Sea*, no. 102 (January 30, 1985).

continental shelf and to the exclusive economic zone do not correspond to our aspirations.[58]

The delegate from Bhutan also expressed his disappointment:

> We also regret that better and more resource-sharing criteria with regard to the continental shelf and the EEZ could not be provided in the Convention. However, it is our hope that in the very near future the problems of land-locked countries will become better understood and that steps will be initiated, especially by the transit States concerned, to alleviate their specific difficulties.[59]

India has seven neighbouring States for the purposes of maritime boundaries, namely, Bangladesh, Burma, Maldives, Pakistan, Sri Lanka, Indonesia, and Thailand. While two States, Bangladesh and Pakistan, are located on the same coast adjacent to India, with the other five States the coasts appear to be opposite. It is interesting to note that while the maritime boundaries between India with all its opposite States have been delimited, boundary negotiations with Bangladesh commenced in October 1974 and have not been concluded so far, and maritime boundary talks with Pakistan have not even begun.

Between 1974 and 1979, India concluded nine agreements with four of its neighbours, namely, Sri Lanka, Maldives, Indonesia and Thailand, and in 1986 delineated its maritime boundaries with Burma. Trilateral agreements fixing trijunctions among India, Sri Lanka and Maldives were concluded in 1976, and among India, Indonesia, and Thailand in 1978. Although no reference was made in these agreements to the applicable principles for drawing the boundaries, and the boundaries were generally described with reference to points whose latitudes and longitudes were indicated in the agreements, the boundaries were drawn, except in two cases, on the basis of median lines between opposite coasts, or, where the boundary extended laterally into the sea, the equidistance line from the adjoining coasts of the two countries. The two exceptions were (1) Palk Bay, where some adjustment in boundary was made because of the Kacchativu Island, and (2) the Andaman Sea between India and Thailand where minor adjustments were thought necessary.

Fishery Resources

With the exception of a few incidents in which fishermen from Tamilnadu in South India were arrested for trespassing in Sri Lanka waters, there have been no fishery disputes in South Asia. This can be attributed to several

[58] Statement by the delegate of Nepal, 191st Meeting, Dec. 1982, para 8, p. 101.

[59] Ibid., paras. 112 and 14, p. 109. See also "The Law of the Sea: Its Impact in Inter-State Relations in South Asia," *Spotlight on Regional Affairs* (Islamabad, May-June 1988), pp. 11 ff.

factors. First, for most of the littoral States of the Indian Ocean, including those in South Asia, the fishery resources are not fully exploited and the government policies are designed to encourage greater efforts in the new extended zones. Less than 22 percent of the potential commercial catch is harvested in the Indian Ocean. Second, the shrimp stocks, highly coveted in the region, are found well within the 200-mile zones. There are no known instances in which significant shrimp stocks migrate through the EEZ of more than one State. Third, in most of the Indian Ocean States, fishing is small-scale, local, or artisanal.[60] Industrial fishing is not unknown, but it is not widespread. But with the advent of the 200-mile EEZ, government policies have been focused upon expanding fish catches for the small-scale local fishermen and encouraging stock assessment and industrial exploitation in the extended zone. This has led to the inevitable conflict between local fishermen, who utilize the resources of the near-shore, and industrial interests, who are supposed to fish in the deeper waters but always seek to exploit resources near shore where fish are usually abundant.[61]

A South Asian country may soon conclude that the best way to exploit the fish stock in the extended EEZ is to sell them to the highest bidder. Under the new fishing regime, several long-distance fishing States have idle fishing capacities as their traditional fishing grounds have been closed off in EEZs. For example, the operation of such vessels off the coast of Pakistan would certainly affect the catch of fishermen in Gujarat. Already it seems that tuna resources are attracting the fishing fleets of nations beyond the Indian Ocean, such as those of Japan, Korea and Taiwan, to come in the Indian Ocean, including South Asia waters. Thus, Pakistan has given some concessions to the South Koreans on a production-sharing basis, and this has led to a considerable amount of poaching in the Indian waters by the South Koreans and the Taiwanese. There are scores of cases where South Koreans and Taiwanese have been caught by the Indian Coastguard. So also Thai vessels have been caught by India, Bangladesh, and Burma. This is also a problem in Sri Lanka and the Maldives, which are incapable of enforcing their restrictions. The Koreans and Taiwanese come in and even conceal their names and numbers so that they cannot be identified and take out enormous amounts of fish without paying their dues.[62] This is one area where collective efforts are called for to control poaching and control the growth of fishing.[63]

[60] See Shyam, "Extended Jurisdiction," pp. 106-107.

[61] See McDorman, "Ext. Jur. and Ocean Resource Conflict," n. 21, p. 213.

[62] See *India, The United States and the Indian Ocean, Report of the Indo-American Task Force on the Indian Ocean* (Washington, D.C.: Carnegie Endowment, 1985), p. 92.

[63] McDorman, "Ext. Jur. and Ocean Resource Conflict," n. 21, p. 214.

A New International Economic Order for Sustainable Development?

Small But Divided World

Although tremendous developments in science and technology, especially in the means of travel and communications, have tied all the peoples of the earth in an unprecedented intimacy of contact, mutuality of vulnerability, and interdependence of welfare, we are still living in a world fragmented into numerous independent States all of which claim to be sovereign and answerable to no one except their own authority. Despite all the denunciations of the doctrine of sovereignty as "unworkable", "misleading" and even "dangerous political dogma," which no longer corresponds with the facts of international life, it remains the very basis of international relations and is accepted as one of its most sacred principles.[1] In the *Eastern Carelia* case,[2] the Permanent Court of International Justice declared the independence of States as "a fundamental principle of international law"[3] and asserted in the *Lotus* case that "restrictions upon the independence of States cannot... be presumed". Reiterated in numerous international arbitral and judicial decisions, sovereignty of States has been enshrined in the Charter of the United Nations which declares in unmistakable terms that "the Organisation is based on the principle of the sovereign equality of all its Members." (Article 2, paragraph 1).[4] Science and technology may have made our planet a small global village absolutely inter-dependent with a common future, but our world is still a divided world with innumerable problems. It is beginning to be realized, however, that we must face our problems in unison if we are not to perish all together.

With the collapse of communism during the last few years and the disintegration of the Soviet Empire and the Soviet Union itself, the cold war, waged relentlessly since the Second World War, has subsided and there is

* Professor of International Law, Jawaharlal Nehru University, New Delhi.

[1] See R.P. Anand, (1987). "Sovereignty of States in International Law", in R.P. Anand, *Confrontation or Cooperation: International Law and the Developing Countries*, New Delhi and Dordrecht, p. 72.

[2] *Eastern Carelia Case* (1923), *PCIJ Series* B, No. 5, p. 27.

[3] *PCIJ Series* A, No. 10, p. 18.

[4] See R.P. Anand, "Sovereign Equality of States in International Law", *Recueil des cours*, vol. 197 (1986-III).

some respite. But the world is still deeply divided. The "great divide" today is between the rich and the poor. As the former Finance Minister of Pakistan, Dr. Mehbood ul Haq pointed out:

> "A poverty curtain has descended right across the face of our world, dividing it materially and philosophically into two different worlds, two separate planets, two unequal humanities – one embarrassingly rich and the other desperately poor. This invisible barrier exists within nations as well as between them, and often provides a unity of thought and purpose to the Third World countries which otherwise have their own economic, political and cultural differences. The struggle to lift this curtain of poverty is certainly the most formidable challenge of our time".[5]

Chasm Between the Rich and the Poor

The ever-widening gap between the developed rich countries of the North and the underdeveloped (courteously called "developing") miserable poor countries of the South has become a cliché. It is no longer a gap, it is a chasm. On one side are about two dozen or so industrialized countries (including the United States, West European community, Canada, Australia, New Zealand and Japan) whose 1.2 billion citizens live in an environment of relative abundance, with per capita income varying between 19,000 to 27,000 US dollars per annum, produce most of the world's manufactured goods, consume most of the world's resources, and enjoy history's highest standard of living. On the other are more than 120 underdeveloped nations – more than 4.5 billion people – which struggle to survive on per capita incomes ranging between 350 and 600 US dollars. In 1990, some 30 developing countries, including some of the populous countries of South Asia, had a per capita income of $ 400 or less, with a median value of about $ 200, almost one hundredth of the per capita income of the most developed countries.[6]

The simple fact is that most people in underdeveloped countries do not have enough to eat. Today, 85 per cent of the world's income goes to 23 per cent of its people – the affluent consumers. By contrast, more than 1 billion people, the absolute poor, survive on less than one dollar a day.[7] It is a bitter truth that one-third to one-half of human beings in these poor countries suffer from hunger or malnutrition. One in three children is malnourished

[5] M. Ul Haq, *The Poverty Curtain: Choices for the Third World,* New York, (1976) p. xv.

[6] *World Economic Survey 1993: Current Trends and Policies in the World Economy* (1993), New York: UN, p. 6.

[7] See S. Postel, "Denial in the Decisive Decade", in *State of the World 1992: A Worldwatch Institute Report on Progress towards a Sustainable Society*, New York, (1992) p. 4.

and 20 to 25 per cent of them die before their fifth birthday. And millions who do not die lead impeded lives because their brains have been damaged and bodies stunted by nutritional deficiencies. About 3 million children die annually from diseases that could be averted by immunization. Some one billion people cannot read or write, and more than 100 million children of primary school age are not in school. This is "absolute poverty" of "marginal" human beings, men and women barely surviving on the margin of life under conditions so degraded by disease, illiteracy, malnutrition, and squalor as to deny them basic human necessities. They are trapped in a "condition of life so degrading as to insult human dignity – and yet a condition of life so common as to be the lot of 40 per cent", some 2.4 billion peoples of the developing countries.[8]

Millions of human beings in the Third World have just no homes. Other millions live in houses or huts in slums and tenements made of corrugated iron sheets, cardboard boxes, or such other easily destructible materials in overcrowded cities. they have no running water and no toilets. These luxuries they cannot afford. Health services are rarely within walking distance, and have to be paid for. Primary education may be available and free but often children are needed for work. There is generally no social security or unemployment pay, and so many people – some 500 million according to some estimates – are without any kind of employment.[9]

On the other hand, with the "blessings" of science and technology, the rich countries have reached a level of prosperity which the previous generations would have found difficult to imagine. In fact it has created the problem of overaffluence. The problems of "overweight society" and "overdevelopment" are as common in our age as those of underdevelopment. The fact that less than 7 per cent of the world's population consumes more than 67 per cent of the world's wealth indicates a voracious appetite for new materials and resources at the cost of the rest of the world. Most of the raw materials and minerals produced in the developing countries go to the industrialized countries. Indeed, never in history has there been so much waste, together with so much destruction of environment, as we have witnessed during the last few decades.[10]

According to René Dumont, "we must not forget that the rich countries are the plunderers of the Third World. They are the ones who 'underpay' for the rare raw materials of the Third World and then squander them".[11] He pointed out that livestock in the rich countries consumed 385 million tons of

[8] See R.S. McNamara, Address to the Board of Governors of the World Bank, Washington, D.C., (1974) p. 2.

[9] T. Hayter, *The Creation of World Poverty*, New Delhi, (1982) p. 18.

[10] See B. Ward, & R. Dubos, *Only One Earth*, London, (1972) p. 23.

[11] Dumont, R., "Population and Cannibals", *Development Forum*, Geneva, vol. 2, No. 7, p. 2.

cereals in 1973, which could have fed two billion Asians, since they consumed their cereals directly and only a small part after transformation into animal products. Thus, said Dumont:

> "The rich white man, with his overconsumption of meat and his lack of generosity for poor people, behaves like a cannibal – an indirect cannibal. By consuming meat, which wastes the grain that could have saved them, last year we ate the children of Sahel, Ethiopia and Bangladesh. And we continue to eat them with undiminished appetite".[12]

Legacy of the Colonial Age

There is a general and widespread feeling, not only in the underdeveloped States but even in Western industrialized countries as well, that the latter are largely responsible for the poverty of the Third World. Thus, explaining his views on the "development of underdevelopment", André Gunder Frank points out.

> "Contemporary underdevelopment is in large part the historical product of past and continuing economic and other relations between satellite underdeveloped and the now developed metropolitan countries".[13]

Walter Rodney also in his *How Europe Underdeveloped Africa* (1972) says:

> "The developed and underdeveloped parts of the present capitalist section of the world have been in continuous contact for four and a half centuries. The contention here is that over that period Africa helped to develop Western Europe in the same proportion as Western Europe helped to underdevelop Africa".[14]

The search for new markets motivated the European countries' expansion all through the nineteenth century and still does so today. After the occupation and control of India and its markets Europe undermined much of the local textile industry in Africa by bringing in textiles from India, thus adding to the destruction of African commerce, mining and industry. These Indian textiles in Africa and also in America, then began to be replaced by textiles from Britain. It is well-known how the British proceeded to destroy the Indian textile industry by eliminating competition from Indian textiles through an elaborated network of restrictions and prohibitive duties. Even within India, taxes effectively discriminated against local cloth. The resulting hardship was great for the Indian weavers. Sir Charles Trevelyan declared to a Parliamentary enquiry in 1840:

> "The population of Dacca has fallen from 150,000 to 30,000 or 40,000 and the jungle and malaria are fast encroaching upon the town... Dacca which used to be

[12] R. Dumont, ibid.

[13] Quoted in T. Hayter, n. 9, p. 38.

[14] Quoted in T. Hayter, ibid.

the Manchester of India, has fallen off from a flourishing town to a very poor and small one".[15]

Not only textiles, but the iron and steel industry were destroyed as well. The duties imposed on Indian exports into Britain were, in spite of the "free trade" policies being promoted at the time, 5 to 25 times higher than the duties that were allowed on British imports into India. The destruction was completed by physical means, where necessary.

There thus began the gradual process of the conversion of the dominated territories into markets for the products of European industry and suppliers of raw material and primary commodities. The theories of free trade and comparative advantage have held powerful sway in the West and are propounded, as a scientific explanation of reality. But Adam Smith and Ricardo, and their "neo-classical" successors, produced their theories on free trade only after the British had established their industrial pre-eminence. In the beginning, they not only destroyed the long-established industries of others, but protected their own from competition. As the economic historian Carlo Cippolo in the *European Culture and European Expansion* (Penguin 1970), remarks:

> "It is fortunate for England that no Indian Ricardo arose to convince the English people that, according to the law of comparative costs, it would be advantageous for them to turn into shepherds and to import from India all the textiles they needed".[16 and 17]

The use of force to open up new markets was common practice. China was forced to open its markets and legalise even the banned opium trade after the Opium war in 1840 when the British fleet attacked China. When towards the end of the nineteenth century, Britain's industrial pre-eminence was threatened by other European powers, they and Britain embarked on another process of colonization, this time mainly in Africa, in order to obtain for themselves protected markets abroad. The struggle for markets led the Europeans to fight among themselves which culminated in the First World War of 1914-18.

The inexorable conversion of the dominated areas in Asia and Africa into markets for European manufactured goods and suppliers of primary commodities and raw materials for European industries undermined not only their previous self-sufficiency in manufactures, but increasingly their ability to feed themselves. Colonies were converted into virtual plantations (or mines) producing one or two crops (or mineral products) for export to Europe for their burgeoning industries.[18]

[15]Quoted in T. Hayter, ibid., p. 48.

[16] See T. Hayter, ibid., pp. 46-49.

[17] Quoted in T. Hayter, ibid., p. 51.

[18] See how introduction of monoculture in various countries of the Third World led to destruction of their economies and ruined their people. T. Hayter, ibid., pp. 53-59.

Continuing Exploitation

One need not dwell in the past only when the Asian-African countries, under colonial domination, had no choice. Unfortunately, the exploitation of the poor countries still continues through subtle and sophisticated means and under an economic order which is merely a continuation of the hated colonial era. Although colonialism has died a natural death, the international framework of the old order has been kept intact by the more pragmatic and self-confident colonial powers. The "white man's burden" in respect of the impoverished, conquered and humiliated natives of the Third World still continues through the developed countries' superiority and dominant voice in the international economic system. The division of labour between developed and underdeveloped countries, imposed in the colonial era, still continues and it is difficult to escape from it. Developed countries, or rather their business interests and transnational corporations, are unwilling to share their technology. Trade secrets are jealously guarded and markets are dominated by companies of the developed countries, and it is difficult for newcomers to enter them. The prices charged for manufactured goods are largely monopoly prices, and in any case they rise steadily over time.

The international monetary system and the international economic institutions, created after the Second World War by the Bretton Woods Agreement amongst the industrialized rich countries, established the basis of progress in the industrial world while completely ignoring the needs and demands of the developing countries. The present international monetary system has been described as "unfair, unequal, unsuitable, uncertain and inconsistent".[19] The poor nations have hardly any participation in the economic decision-making of the world. Their advice is never solicited when the big ten industrialized nations get together to take key decisions on the world's economic future. Their voting strength in the Bretton Woods institutions (World Bank and I.M.F.) is less than one-third of the total; and their numerical majority in the UN General Assembly, as we shall see, has meant no real influence on international economic decisions.[20]

Underdeveloped countries, still producing mainly primary commodities and raw materials for the developed economies, have several problems. The prices for their primary commodities and raw materials fall not only in relative and sometimes in absolute terms, but they fluctuate widely from year to year; their economies are highly dependent on exports and many of them are highly dependent on the export of new, sometimes just one or two, commodities. The fluctuations in commodity prices can be dramatic and are accentuated by speculation in commodity markets in London, outside the control of the underdeveloped countries. In the mid-1970s, for instance, the

[19] See Keutcha (Cameroon), U.N. Doc. A/PV. 2340, 8 September, 1975, pp. 48-50.

[20] M. Ul Haq, n. 5, p. 161.

price of sugar dropped from 64 cents a pound to 6 cents a pound in 18 months. Tanzania's sisal price dropped from 90 pounds to 60 pounds. The Brandt Report, referring to Zambia, pointed out that a boom in copper prices took the price to $ 3034 in April 1974; but it fell to $ 1290 before the end of the year. It may also be remembered that according to the Brandt Report, in the seventies, more than half the developing countries, excluding the oil-exporting countries, got more than half of their export earnings only from one or two commodities. Zambia got 94 per cent from copper; Mauritius 90 per cent from sugar; Cuba 84 per cent from sugar, and Gambia 85 per cent from groundnuts and groundnut oil.[21]

The developed countries have always refused to discuss the problem of raw materials in an integrated scheme because they claim it is in conflict with the system of free enterprise. How "free" the system is can be seen from the fact that while heavy tariffs are levied on industrial goods imported from the developing countries (to discourage their industrialization) low duties are imposed on raw materials imported from these countries. As Dr. Mehbub ul Haq has pointed out, the rich nations are making it increasingly impossible for the "free" international market mechanism to work. The cornerstone of the free market mechanism is based, he points out, on the free movement of labour and capital as well as goods and services so that rewards to factors of production are equalized all over the world. Yet immigration laws in all the rich nations make it impossible for any large-scale movement of unskilled labour in a world-wide search for economic opportunities. Only highly skilled labour is permitted to move on a very restrictive basis which, in the form of "brain drain", helps only the rich nations at the cost of the poor. Not much capital is permitted to cross international boundaries either because of poor countries' sensitivities or rich nations' own needs. Additional barriers have been raised against the free movement of goods and services. For example, over 20 billion dollars in farm subsidies alone are paid to farmers in the rich nations to protect their agriculture, and progressively higher tariffs and quotas are enforced against the simple consumer goods exports of the developing countries. The rich thus are drawing a protective wall around their life styles, telling the poor nations that they can compete neither with their labour nor with their goods.[22]

The UN Commission on Environment and Development (Brundtland Commission), also pointed out in its report, *Our Common Future*, that agriculture

> "production in industrialized countries has usually been highly subsidized and protected from international competition. These subsidies have encouraged the

[21] W. Brandt, *North-South: A Programme for Survival. The Report of the Independent Commission on International Development Issues under the Chairmanship of Willy Brandt*, (1980); also quoted in T. Hayter, n. 9, pp. 68-69.

[22] M. Ul Haq, n. 5, p. 160.

overuse of soil and chemicals, the pollution of water resources and foods with these chemicals and the degradation of the countryside. Much of this effort has produced surpluses and their associated financial burdens. And some of this surplus has been sent at concessional rates to the developing world, where it has undermined the farming policies of recipient nations".[23]

Direct or indirect subsidies, which now cover the entire food cycle, according to the Commission, have become very expensive. In the United States, the cost of farm support had grown from $ 2.7 billion in 1980 to $ 25.8 billion in 1986. In the EEC such costs had risen from $ 6.2 billion in 1976 to $ 21.5 billion in 1986. It is politically more attractive and cheaper to export surpluses – often as food aid – rather than store them. These highly subsidized surpluses depress the international market prices of commodities like sugar and rice and create severe problems for developing countries.[24]

In fact as absolute masters of the market for the purchase of raw materials, the developed countries buy them at the prices they fix. Furthermore, as absolute masters of the market for manufactured goods, they sell them at the prices they desire. The result is that soap, cotton, paper, iron ore, copper, etc. – all raw materials – are bought in the developing countries for the price of a slice of bread and the products come back to them at prices they cannot afford to pay. A banana-exporting country receives only 70 cents out of $ 6.00 which represents the sale price abroad of a box of bananas produced in that country. While the prices of primary products have been historically depressed, the prices of manufactured goods have been constantly buoyant. For more than a quarter of a century before they took control of their product, the oil-producing countries received only one-tenth of each dollar paid by the oil consumers in the industrialized countries that imported oil, while the rest went into the coffers of the monopolistic companies or their governments.[25] This has resulted in what has been called the steady deterioration in terms of trade. Mathematically, the poorest must continue to grow poorer while the rich continue to get richer. There is little wonder that poor, pressured and powerless, the primary producers have been confined to the periphery of international economic relations while the wheels of power and control are turned by the industrialized States operating them at the centre. The constant deterioration in terms of trade led to a decline in the share of the developing countries from 21.3 per cent in 1960 to 17.6 per cent in 1970, while their external debt quadrupled in ten years exceeding 80 billion US dollars.

Since then the economic situation of the developing countries has much

[23] See World Commission on Environment and Development, (chairman Gro Harlem Brundtland) (1987). *Our Common Future*, New York, p. 71.

[24] Ibid., p. 123.

[25] See Al Thani (Qatar) U.N. Doc. A/P.V. 2346, 10 Sept., 1975, pp. 24-25.

worsened. Thus, in 1987 the World Commission on Environment and Development in its report on *Our Common Future* pointed out:

> "Within the last decade, many Sub-Saharan countries have been hit by adverse trends in commodity terms of trade and external shocks such as higher oil prices, fluctuating exchange rates, and higher interest rates. Over the last 10 years, the prices of major commodities such as copper, iron ore, sugar, ground-nuts, rubber, timber and cotton have fallen significantly. In 1985, the terms of trade of Sub-Saharan countries (except oil-exporting countries) were 10 per cent below 1970 levels. In countries eligible for funds from the International Development Association the average fall was well over 20 per cent, with even greater drops in some, including Ethiopia, Liberia, Sierra Leone, Zaire and Zambia".[26]

Developing countries were particularly hit in the 1980s because of stagnation in world trade and falling commodity prices. According to the Brundtland Commission, "between 1980 and 1984, developing countries lost about $ 55 billion in export earnings because of the fall in commodity prices, a blow felt most keenly in Latin America and Africa".[27] Over half of all developing countries actually experienced declining per capita gross domestic product (GDP) in the years 1982-85 and per capita GDP fell, for developing countries as a whole, by around 10 per cent in the 1980s.[28]

What we need is a rational reordering of global priorities and global resources. By far the biggest share of available resources is being diverted to the most unproductive area of human activity: armaments and arsenals. Mankind is spending over a thousand billion dollars every year on the means of its own destruction. This figures out to about two million dollars per minute in perfecting our path to extinction. We need a world order which is more than a dance of death. We need a new world order which helps in saving mankind and fulfilling the human personality. But this is possible only by large-scale disarmament which has become feasible when the world is no longer divided into political groups devoted to ideological wrangling and destruction. But as India's former Prime Minister Rajiv Gandhi said –

> "Disarmament is not only a mechanical process of reducing stockpiles but a mental process of looking upon the world as one family, of promoting international cooperation, of pursuing policies of peaceful co-existence..."[29]

Ever since their political independence in the 1940s and 1950s, the developing countries have been demanding a change in their lives. They have asserted with reason that they could not continue with their hopeless lives; that political independence without economic freedom was of little

[26] *Our Common Future*, n. 23, p. 12.

[27] Ibid., p. 36.

[28] Ibid.

[29] R. Gandhi, "Poverty, Development and Collective Survival", *Development*, (1988), no. 1, p. 9.

consequence; that the developed countries were largely responsible for their misery; that the economic order created after the Second World War was inequitable, unjust and unreasonable; that they must get a new economic order which was more humane and would help them in their development. But all pleadings to change the inequitable economic system, their demands for help, and their appeals for consideration went unheeded and were simply ignored. No State enjoying privileges would be prepared to give them up of its own free will. There was a clear lack of will on the part of the rich countries. The fundamental problems remained the same as during the colonial period: inequality in the terms of trade; stabilization of forces and markets for primary commodities; access to the market of the developed countries; and a generalised system of preference.

Unable to get any concessions from the developed countries, who simply ignored them, by 1960 the developing countries joined hands together to put an end to the present inequitable system that tended to impoverish their entire world. They were sick of being meek and started making their demands more militantly. The "damned of the earth", resigned and submissive until then, changed themselves into confident and revolutionary advocates of a new order learning about themselves and the earth in the course of the struggle. There was nothing fatal, they asserted, about what was modestly called the deterioration in the terms of trade. It was the operation of a deliberate system which was fundamentally bad. To put an end to this situation the international community must evolve a new system which would bring greater justice and equity to international economic relations. It was unjust, they felt, that the prices of manufactured goods fixed by the economic powers should surge ahead while the prices for the primary commodities necessary for the manufacture of those products were maintained at the same level or were even allowed to decline by the same powers. They wanted to take steps to index the prices of the products exported by the developing countries to tie them to the prices of the manufactured and capital goods they must import. They asked for some correlation between the prices of raw materials and those of manufactured goods. The developed countries must also open their markets, they demanded, to the products of the developing countries by doing away with the protectionist barriers which led to decrease of exports by the underdeveloped countries.

In order to put maximum pressure on the rich industrialized countries the United Nations General Assembly, where the turbulent countries of the Third World had come to constitute a solid and virtually unbeatable majority, was used in the 1970s as a forum in the economic campaign of the developing countries. Forming a new consortium – the Group of 77 – containing actually more than 125 members, the poor countries used all the diplomatic pressure they could muster in their struggle for a new deal. They used the popular forum to declare the 1960s as the first UN Development Decade and the 1970s as the second Development Decade; organized the United Nations

Conference on Trade and Development on a regular basis to focus on the needs of the developing countries; established a UN Capital Fund; and formed a Special Committee on Trade Preference. In 1974 and 1975 they called two special sessions (VI and VII) of the General Assembly to discuss their problem of raw materials and do something about it. At these sessions the developing countries spoke boldly, even bluntly, and put their demands very forcefully. They accused the rich countries of the west of wasting energy and minerals, building weapons they did not need, polluting the air and the oceans, eating too much and contributing to the starvation of others. They got two resolutions adopted by the General Assembly (G.A. Resolutions 3201 and 3202 (S-VI) containing the Establishment of the New International Economic Order and the Declaration and Programme of Action. The first resolution proclaimed the "united determination" of the Members of the United Nations "to work urgently for the establishment of a new international economic order", and laid down general principles on which the new economic order should be founded. The second spelt out the programme of action to be carried out for the purpose of achieving the above ideal and for bringing about the maximum possible "economic cooperation and understanding among all States, particularly between developed and developing countries, based on the principle of dignity and sovereign equality".

Charter of Economic Rights and Duties

Dissatisfied with more promises which always remained unfulfilled the developing countries sought to obtain from the developed countries a legally binding commitment to certain economic rights and duties of States of a juridical nature which might help in the development process of all the countries. Despite the doubts and objections of the western industrialized countries about the "advisability, possibility or feasibility of making the rights and duties formulated in a draft Charter legally binding on States", the Charter of Economic Rights and Duties of States was adopted by the General Assembly at its 29th Session on 12 December 1974, by an overwhelming vote of 120 to 6 (Belgium, Denmark, FRG, Luxembourg, U.K. and the U.S.A.), with 10 abstentions.[31 and 32] (G.A. Resolution 3281 (XXIX)). It declared in its preamble that-

"it is a fundamental purpose of this Charter to promote the establishment of the

[30] R.P. Anand, "Towards a New International Economic Order", in R.P. Anand, n. 1, pp. 110-11.

[31] See Report of the Working Group of the Charter of Economic Rights and Duties of States UNCTAD Doc. TD/B/AC.12/1, 6 March 1973, pp. 4-6.

[32] The ten countries which abstained were Austria, Canada, France, Ireland, Israel, Italy, Japan, The Netherlands, Norway and Spain.

new international economic order, based on equity, sovereign equality, interdependence, common interest, and cooperation among all States, irrespective of their domestic and social systems".

Rich Countries Get Irritated and Angry

Whatever the legal authority of this Charter, or political significance of their intense pleadings for a new economic order and a new deal, all that the poor countries received was sympathy for their deplorable conditions, recognition of the fact that it was an interdependent world and needed cooperation to achieve common development goals, and innocuous promises of cooperation provided that the rich countries were not pressurized and the decisions were reached through negotiations and consensus. The impatient poor countries were warned that confrontations – embargoes, cartels, seizures, or even bitter rhetoric – would avail them little. Starving masses were advised to be patient. Otherwise, they were told, "we would enter an age of festering resentment, of increased resort to economic warfare, a hardening of blocs, the undermining of cooperation, the erosion of international institutions, and failed development".[33]

While the General Assembly at its 30th session, on 12 December 1975, reiterated its "determination to strengthen and develop the new international economic order"[34], the developed countries were getting irritated and angry at the increasingly militant demands of the poor and weak States of the Third World and the persistent criticism by the world's mendicants of the role behaviour and life styles of the rich and industrial western powers.[35] All this led to numerous clashes between an increasingly self-confident but needy Third World and a decreasingly responsive industrialized world.

Utter Failure

But despite all this pressure and all the resolutions by the General Assembly and other organs of the United Nations, all efforts by the poor countries to better their lot failed miserably. Instead of getting better their economic condition further deteriorated in the 1970s and even more in the 1980s. In 1980, as the Brundtland commission noted, the total number of poor people not getting enough calories to prevent stunted growth and serious health risks had increased by 14 per cent since 1970 and numbered 340 million in 87 developing countries. The number of people living in slums and shanty

[33] See address by U.S. Secretary of State Henry Kissinger before the VII Special Session of the General Assembly in UN Doc. A/PV. 2327, 1 September 1975, pp. 18-20.

[34] See General Assembly Resolution 3486 (XXX) adopted by 114 votes to 3 (Germany, U.K. and U.S.A.) with 11 abstentions.

[35] See R.P. Anand, n. 30, pp. 118 et seq.

towns, the Commission pointed out, was rising not falling. A growing number lacked access to clean water and sanitation and hence were prey to diseases that arose from this lack.[36]

It was pointed out by some observers that the demand for a new international economic order and the Charter of Economic Rights and Duties was not the "beginning of a new era", as imagined by the "Group of 77". Rather, it was

> "more akin to a summary of postulates, wishes and demands of the developing countries, whose radicalism and disregard for real international relations has delayed, rather than accelerated, the process of change in many matters. This is particularly true of the principle of economic sovereignty".[37]

It was suggested "that the present stagnation, or lack of political interest of States, stems from the attempt at undue acceleration taken up by the developing countries during the decade between UNCTAD I and the adoption of the 'Charter of Rights'" and that "this obvious fiasco should give warning for the future on both political – economic as well as legal planes".[38]

Industrialised countries Richer But Not Better

But along with the deteriorating conditions of the poor in the evershrinking world society, leading to tensions and confrontations between the rich and the poor, as we have seen above, there came a realisation in the late 1960s that while the rich were getting richer by exploiting the poor through an economic system which was a legacy of the colonial age, they were not necessarily getting better. In the process of getting an economically richer life, in their relentless struggle for luxuries, by introducing more and more sophisticated, massive and novel technology in their ever-expanding industrialization, they were destroying the very life-support system of the earth. The environmental consequences of industrialisation and economic development, and the pollution of the air, water and land which give us sustenance was indeed a high price that they had to pay for economic advancement. It came to be widely accepted that environmental pollution was an inescapable by-product of industrial development. Life could only be sustained through a delicate equilibrium between man and nature. Blind to the need of cooperating with nature, the equilibrium seemed to be menaced by the pressure of increasing population, but even more importantly, by the strain of pollution generated by the developing technologies in large-scale industrialization. The vast use of energy and new materials, industrial effluents, urbanization and consumer habits in the developed countries were

[36] *Our Common Future*, n. 23, p. 29.

[37] See J. Makarczyk, *Principles of New International Economic Order: A Study of International Law in the Making*, Dordrecht, (1988), p. 351.

[38] J. Makarczyk, ibid.

leading the industrialized countries on a course which could alter dangerously, if not irreversibly, the natural system of our planet upon which our biological survival depended. Already rivers had "caught fire", lakes and inland seas – the Baltic and the the Mediterranean – were under threat from untreated wastes threatening marine life. The burning of fossil fuel was increasing with unforeseeable consequences for the earth's climate and atmosphere. Even the vast oceans were becoming far more vulnerable to man's polluting activities than had been assumed. With too many poisons, insecticides and fertilizers running into the oceans, vast oil spills and long-life chemicals that were generated into the air or dumped into the sea, the oceans could not remain endless dumping grounds and a perpetual source of freshening winds and currents.[39] With the kind of technology that was coming into use by the industrialized countries – huge tankers with carrying capacities of 500,000 tons of crude oil, large nuclear power plants, toxic stock-piles of nerve gas and biological agents – with increasing possibilities of accidents with far-reaching consequences, some ecologists like Paul Ehrlich warned that everybody – the whole world – might "disappear in cloud of smoke in 20 years". Even if one did not subscribe to such doomsday threats, it was clear that the world could not avoid the possibility or even inevitability of a catastrophe if we did not do something about it.

Global Problem

It was realized that the problem of environmental pollution was a global problem which concerned all States irrespective of their size, stage of development, or ideology. Despite all the political and ideological divisions of the society, it was a small world indeed. There was no escape from the underlying unity and interconnection of the ocean world. The seas and oceans, like the winds above, mingled with each other, cleansed or poisoned each other, passed on each other's burdens, and made a seamless watery web. The sovereign States might proclaim their territorial controls and national independence; but airs brought in the acid rains, oceans carried toxic substances to other shores, and pollution moved from continent to continent. As Frances Cairncross said recently:

> "Nature is no respecter of national boundaries. Across those dotted lines on the globe, winds blow, rivers flow and migrating species walk or fly. The dotted lines may carve up the earth, but the sea and the atmosphere remain open to all, to cherish or plunder. When people in one country harm that bit of the environment

[39] See B. Ward & R. Dubos, *Only One Earth: The Care and Maintenance of a Small Planet*, New York, (1972), pp. xii-xviii, 1-12; See also R.A. Falk, *The Endangered Planet*, New York: Wade Rowland (1972), and *The Plot to Save the World*, Toronto (1972).

they assume to be theirs, many others may suffer too. But, how, and how much, can countries make their neighbours change their ways".[40]

If China or France tested nuclear weapons, the winds blew the fallout to other countries. As the winds and oceans flew round our little planet, China's Strontium–90 was as lethal as that of France, the Soviet Union, or the United States, and not only in their own countries. Thus it was pointed out that the danger of "irresponsible" disposal of radioactive wastes from nuclear energy plants was perhaps more of a threat to the security of other States than was the danger of war and conquest.[41] Yet this is what is already happening. According to recent reports, "Asia is fast turning into waste dump for the west, having received five million tons of such high-tech cargo during the last four years".[42] The rising environmental threat is reminding humanity of both its vulnerability and compulsion for common survival on a fragile planet.

Rising Expectations

But despite all these interdependences – in biosphere and technosphere alike – and realization that we did indeed belong to a single system and our survival depended on the balance and health of the total system, it could not escape the serious attention of all perceptive observers that our small planet Earth was deeply divided. As the UN Secretary-General, U Thant, noted: "Squalid poverty lives side by side with overabundance on our earth. We have reached the moon but we have not reached each other".[43] While the rich countries were risking the health of their people by overconsumption, and endangering the planet by over-industrialization and industrial pollutants, two-thirds of humanity was groaning under the unbearable weight of abject poverty. But that was not all. In the shrinking world society, a growing number of these poor were waking up to the realization of how the people in the rich countries were living. As the image, ways of life and consumer habits of the rich countries, impressive evidence of prosperity, not to say of opulent living, of their peoples, were transmitted to the remotest corners of the world by the transistor, the communication satellites and the world-wide TV, ambitions to imitate them naturally arose awakening new aspirations. This new awareness gave rise to what was called the "revolution of rising expectations". The poor people knew that they did not have to be hungry; they wanted food and shelter; they wanted bicycles, refrigerators, radios,

[40] F. Cairncross, "The Environment: Whose World is it, anyway?" *Economist*, May 30, 1991, p. 5.

[41] See Falk, n. 39, p. 197; Ward and Dubos, n. 39, pp. 202-203.

[42] See S. Lal, "Down with the Dumps", *Times of India*, Feb. 6, 1994, p. 16.

[43] U Thant, quoted in J.L. Hargroves, (ed.) *Law, Institutions and the Global Environment*, Dobbs Ferry, N.Y., (1972), p. 44.

movies, and they wanted them soon. They came to realize that the only way to free themselves from long and humiliating servitude was to achieve the industrial base which was necessary to provide them with adequate fighting capabilities, at least to defend themselves. This was the road adopted in the last century by Japan, and which in the modern age was attracting countries like China, India, Mexico, Brazil and others.

Poor Contribute to the Environmental Degradation

The national leaders in the developing countries, aware of the aspirations of their people, had no choice but to promise them an improving economic future. In their desperate efforts to achieve their goal, "modernize" and develop their economies, and create affluent societies like those in North America and Europe, the side effects were seldom taken into account.[44] It may be noticed that the environmental side effects were even more serious in the less-developed than in the developed countries. Thus, it had been found that nearly every irrigation project in the developing countries had been followed by outbreaks, sometimes disastrous, of waterborne diseases of humans or of animals. Some irrigation projects, like the pervasive system of dams on the Nile, or the modern canal system in West Punjab in Pakistan had induced large-scale geophysical changes which had, in turn, reduced the agricultural potential of the regions.[45] Previously productive lands had been known to have been reduced in fertility or even completely destroyed by poorly managed irrigation systems. Problems of waterlogging, alkalization, cementation of soils and erosion of slopes, had been traced to the use of irrigation in many countries. Nearly every reported instance involving the chemical control of agricultural pests in newly developed agricultural areas had been characterized by serious ecological hazards. Case histories of technological improvements in animal husbandry and fisheries depicted the same picture of unexpected hazard.[46] These ecological failures, it was felt, were not the random accidents of progress but evidence that introduction of new technology into the developing countries had adverse ecological consequences which were seldom taken into consideration.[47]

[44] See O. Soemarwote, "Environmental Quality: Dilemma of Development", in Y.J. Wu & W.A. Clemente, II (eds.) *Environment and or Development in Asia, Hope and Frustration*, Ann Arbor, Michigan, (1972), p. 190.

[45] See B. Commoner, "On the Meaning of Ecological Failures in International Development", in M. Taghi Farvar, & J.P. Milton, (eds.) *The Careless Technology: Ecology and International Development*, Garden City, N.Y., (1972), pp. xxii, 214.

[46] See R.O. Adegbaye, "Environmental Aspects of Agricultural Development: Africa", in D.M. Dworkin, *Environment and Development*, Indianapolis, Indiana, (1976), pp. 2-7.

[47] See B. Commoner, n. 45, pp. xxii-xxiii.

Thus, the poor countries, too occupied in their always unsuccessful attempts merely to survive, were contributing to the ever-growing environmental degradation. But some economists did not hesitate to point out that the developing countries could never hope to achieve the consumption patterns of the developed countries. To raise the living standards of the world's existing population to American levels, the annual world-wide production would have to be increased 75 times, that of copper 100 times, that of lead 100 times, and that of tin 250 times. If a country like India were to use fertilizers at the per capita level of Holland, it would consume one-half of the total world output of fertilizers. Clearly, the parity of the developing countries with the developed ones was not compatible with the existing stocks of natural resources. It was, therefore, suggested by some observers that for the survival of mankind the poor developing countries should remain in a state of underdevelopment because if the evils of industrialization were to reach them life on the planet would be in jeopardy.[48] They were horrified to imagine the risk to human society if more than two-thirds of the "wretched of the earth" were also to try to live like Europeans or Japanese or sought American standards.[49] "The irony of the development is", it was warned, "that to the extent it succeeds, the world situation worsens".[50]

Stockholm conference on Human Environment

In this continuous economic struggle in which the rich countries were trying to maintain and improve their life styles which the poor were trying to imitate and catch up with, environment was neglected and suffered terrible degradation until it was realized that it could no longer be ignored. In 1972 the U.N. Conference on Human Environment was called at Stockholm to take stock of the situation. At Stockholm for the first time several well-meaning environmentally conscious individuals, like Maurice Strong, Barbara Ward and others, brought to the world's attention the seriousness of the problem and the dire need which dictated that the Earth must be cleansed of its foul air and water if the human species was to survive.

But the poor countries reminded the rich nations that while they understood the need to protect the environment, they could not continue, or should not even be expected to continue, to linger in misery. They brought to the attention of the rich countries the distinction between the "pollution of affluence" and the "pollution of poverty" which was recognized by the Conference in its Declaration. It accepted the fact that "while in industrialized

[48] See criticism of such views in J.A. De Araujo Castro, "Environment and Development: The Case of the Developing Countries", in D. Kay, & E.B. Skolnikoff, (eds.) *World Eco-Crises,* Madison, Wisconsin, (1972), pp. 240-241.

[49] Ward & Dubos, n. 39, pp. 11, 118-19.

[50] Falk, n. 39, p. 33. See also R.P. Anand, "Development and Environment: The Case of the Developing Countries", in R.P. Anand, n. 1, pp. 155-58.

countries, environmental problems are generally related to industrialization and technological development", in the poor countries "most of the environmental problems are caused by under-development".[51] Although the developing countries were experiencing, in varying degrees, the environmental problems that arose in the course of growth and some industrialization, and were not unconcerned about the growing menace to the human environment, they were not and could not be convinced of the logic of non-development. The two-thirds of humanity who were barely surviving on the margin of life, could not equal the passionate alarm of the industrialized countries unless environmental issues could be equated with developmental issues. Poverty, they felt, was the greatest source of pollution. As a UN Panel of experts said in its report in 1971, in both the towns and the villages in the Third World,

> "not merely the 'quality of life', but life itself is endangered by poor water, housing, sanitation and nutrition, by sickness and disease, and by natural disasters. These are the problems, no less than those of industrial pollution, that clamour for attention in the context for human environment".[52]

Most of the people in the Third World were acutely aware that there were "two worlds, two planets, two humanities", said Pakistan's Mhabub ul Haq:

> "In your world, there is a concern today about the quality of life; in our world, there is concern about life itself which is threatened by hunger and malnutrition. In your world, there is concern today about the conservation of non-renewable resources... In our world, the anxiety is not about the depletion of resources but about the best distribution and exploitation of these resources, for the benefit of all mankind rather than for the benefit of a few nations. While you are worried about industrial pollution, we are worried about the pollution of poverty, because our problems arise not out of excess of development and technology but because of lack of development and technology and inadequate control over natural phenomena. In the developed countries, you can afford to fuss about the adverse effects of DDT; we have to be concerned about what it means for our crops and for sustaining human lives. You can afford to be concerned about polluted beaches. We have to worry a lot about the fact that less than 10 per cent of the population in the Third World has even drinkable water".[53]

He added that unfortunately "our two worlds, while they touch and meet, they rarely communicate. And it is that process of real communication, real dialogue, that we have to encourage today in case we have to equip ourselves to deal with the problems of this world."[54]

[51] See Declaration of the U.N. Conference on Human Environment, 1972, para. 4.

[52] See *Development and Environment,* Report of a Panel of Experts convened by the Secretary-General of the UN Conference on Human Environment, Fountex, Switzerland, 4-12 June 1971 (known as Fountex Report), UN Doc. A/Conf. 48/10/ Annex 1, pp. 3-4.

[53] Haq, n. 5, p. 82.

[54] Haq, ibid.

At the Stockholm Conference there was a lot of concern expressed by both the developed and the developing countries for the total disregard of the environment by all the countries. For the first time the world became aware of the terrible degradation of the environment which, if it remained unchecked, would lead to the destruction of the whole world. Everybody agreed that protection and improvement of human environment was "a major issue", needed "more prudent care", and "through ignorance and indifference", we could "do massive and irreversible harm to earthly environment on which our life and well-being" depended.[55] The Conference pressed for several actions for the protection of our fragile environment and adopted 26 principles recommending various measures to bring man and his activities in harmony with nature. It was also recognized that poverty must be abated and the poor must be helped if the environment had to be saved (see Principles 8 to 12).

It must be stressed, however, that there was little, if any, real communication between the rich and the poor at Stockholm. It was more or less like a dialogue between the deaf, each harping on their own problems without bothering about what the others had to say. The acceptance of the body of principles, which was not an easy task, consisted of a largely unenforceable set of recommendations which were hortatory in nature and could be generally ignored as soon as the delegates reached home.

Environmental Decline and Response

Vast industrial expansion took place in the developed countries after the Second World War without any regard to the environment, resulting in terrible pollution. This was symbolized by the Los Angeles smog, the proclaimed death of Lake Erie; progressive pollution of the Meuse, Elbe and Rhine; and chemical poisoning in several parts of the United States and Europe. But by the late 1960s, growing awareness and public concern led to action by governments and industry in the industrial countries. Expenditures rose as high as 2 per cent of the G.N.P. in some of the industrial countries after the Stockholm Conference by the late 1970s. The results were mixed but with the cooperation of the industry, during the 1970s a number of industrial countries experienced a significant improvement in environmental quality. There was a considerable roll back in air pollution in many cities and in water pollution in many lakes and rivers. Certain chemicals were controlled.

But despite these achievements, the progress was limited and was confined only to a few industrial countries who were willing and could afford to take preventive measures to reduce, control, and prevent air and water pollution. On the whole, however taking the entire biosphere as one unit, the condition was worsening. The King of Sweden, addressing the opening of the UNCED

[55] See *Declaration of the UN Conference on the Human Environment.*

in 1992, reminded the delegates about the uneven progress following Stockholm's earnest and great promise. He said:

> "There has been great environmental improvement on the local, national and regional levels, while the global threats are more serious than ever".[56]

Fertilizer run-off and sewage discharges into rivers, lakes and coastal waters had increased, with terrible effects on fishing, drinking water, navigation and scenic beauty. As to oceanic pollution, Philip Elmer-Dewitt pointed out:

> "Anyone who has been near the seashore lately... knows that the oceans are a mess littered with plastic and tar balls and rapidly losing fish. But the garbage dumps, the oil spills, the sewage discharges, the drift nets and factory ships are only the most visible problems. The real threats to the oceans, accounting for 70% to 80% of all maritime pollution, are the sediments and contaminants that flow into the seas from land-based sources - topsoil, fertilizers, pesticides and all manner of industrial wastes".[57]

The quality of major rivers had not markedly improved. Industrial countries still suffered from "traditional" forms of air and land pollution. In fact, it came to be realized that sources and causes of pollution were far more diffused, complex and inter-related, and the effects of pollution more widespread, cumulative and chronic than hitherto believed. The incidence of major accidents involving toxic chemicals had grown.[58]

In the meantime, the poor developing countries were making their own contributions. Engrossed in their own problems, the rich did not have time to look at the miseries of the poor nor, in spite of all their rhetoric, did they have an inclination to help them economically. The result was further deterioration in their economic conditions. While in the industrial countries the population growth had been under 1 per cent and in some countries was approaching zero population growth, in the developing countries it had reached 3.7 billion by 1985 and was likely to grow to 6.8 billion by 2025.[59] But besides this population explosion in the developing countries which neutralized all the economic progress they made, and was ticking like a time bomb, deteriorating terms of trade, rising debt-service obligations, stagnating flows of aid, and growing protectionism in the developed market economies, caused severe external payment problems. These economic difficulties led

[56] See quoted in R.K.L. Panjabi, "From Stockholm to Rio: A Comparison of the Declaratory Principles of International Environmental Law", *Denver J. of Int. Law*, vol. 21, (1993), p. 257.

[57] P.E. Dewitt, "Summit to Save the Earth: Rich vs. Poor", *Time*, June 1, 1992, p. 32.

[58] See Brundtland Commission Report, n. 23, pp. 210-212.

[59] Ibid.

to devastating social impacts: malnutrition, hunger and droughts, especially in Africa.[60]

If Africa had an acute debt problem, in Latin America it reached the level of a crisis. In 1985 their debts constituted roughly two-thirds of outstanding loans of banks to developing countries. Real wages fell and growing poverty and deteriorating environmental conditions were visible everywhere in Latin America. Latin American natural resources were being used not for development or to raise living standards, but to meet the financial requirements of the industrialized countries.[61]

Environmental Crises

Poverty, there is no doubt, was "a major cause and effect of global environmental problems" which were becoming all pervading, threatening life on earth.[62] Each year another 6 million hectares of productive dry land was turning into worthless desert. More than 11 million hectares of forest was being destroyed yearly and turned into low-grade farmland unable to support the farmers who settled it. In Europe, acid precipitation was killing forests and lakes and damaging the architectural heritage of nations. The burning of fossil fuels put into the atmosphere carbon dioxide which was causing gradual global warming. The "greenhouse effect" might in a few years increase average global temperatures to shift agricultural production areas, raise sea-level to flood coastal areas and even drown some island States. According to experts in the field, the consequence of this one dramatic alteration of our environment – not including the thousands of other environmental problems we face – may "stand second only to global nuclear war". It may lead to –

> "catastrophic floods and droughts... entire species and regions of plants, forests and animals could be wiped out at rates nearly unprecedented in evolutionary history... the delicate ecological balance of oceanic conditions and biotics could be dramatically upset...; and human mortality could increase catastrophically due to temperature changes and resultant proliferation of disease and malnutrition at rates that would far exceed the speed of scientific advancement and response".[63 and 64]

[60] See ibid., pp. 72-73.

[61] Ibid., pp. 74-75.

[62] Ibid., p. 3.

[63] See S.E. Holly, "Global Warming: Construction and Enforcement of an International Accord", *Stanford Environment Law Journal*, vol.10, (1991), p. 45; D. Magraw, "World Climate Change: Greenhouse Effect", *Proceedings of the American Society of International Law,* 8th Annual Meeting, (1990), pp. 344-45; see also R.M. White, "The Great Climate Debate", ibid., pp. 346-56; E. Brown Weiss, ibid., pp. 356-63.

[64] See R.K.L. Panjabi, "From Stockholm to Rio: A Comparison of the Declaratory Principles of International Environmental Law", *Journal of International Law and Policy*, vol. 21, (1993), p. 2.

Other industrial gases had already depleted the planet's protective ozone shield threatening increase in the number of human and animal cancers and perhaps disrupting the human food chain. Not only was environmental degradation proceeding at an alarming rate but in the 1980s numerous economic-environmental disasters occurred. Food production per capita declined in 94 countries between 1985 and 1989. The drought-triggered environment crisis in Africa killed more than one million people, threatening another 35 million. In 1984, a leakage in a pesticides factory in Bhopal (India) killed more than 2000 people and blinded and injured over 200,000 more. Liquid gas tanks exploded in Mexico City killing 1000 people and leaving thousands more homeless. In 1986, an accident at a nuclear reactor in Chernobyl, USSR, killed at least 25 people and sent radioactive fallout across Europe which, it was estimated, might cause anywhere from 14000 to 475,000 cancer deaths.[65] Agricultural chemicals, solvents and mercury flowed into the River Rhine during a warehouse fire in Switzerland killing millions of fish and threatening drinking water in Germany and the Netherlands.[66]

Our Common Future

These environment crises jolted the world once again and it was decided to call a new Earth Conference in a desperate attempt to save the world. The World Commission on Environment and Development (also called Brundtland Commission) established in 1983 said in its report, Our Common Future, published in 1987, that recent changes –

> "have locked the global economy and global ecology in new ways. We have been in the past concerned about the impacts of economic growth upon the environment. We are now forced to concern ourselves with the impacts of ecological stress – degradation of soils, water regimes, atmosphere and forests – upon our economic prospects. we have in the more recent past been forced to face up to a sharp increase in economic interdependence among nations. Ecology and economy are becoming even more interwoven – locally, regionally, nationally, and globally – into a seamless net of causes and effects".[67]

The Commission went on to say that "life threatening environmental concerns had surfaced" both in the developing world and the rich countries. And yet the poor countries must "operate in a world in which the resources gap between most developing and industrial nations is widening, in which the industrial world dominates in the rule-making of some key international bodies, and in which the industrial world had already used much of the plants' ecological capital. This inequality is the planet's main 'environmental' problem; it is also the main 'development' problem".[68]

[65] Ibid., p. 236.
[66] Brundtland Report, n. 23, p. 3.
[67] Ibid., p. 5.
[68] Ibid., pp. 5-6.

The Commission recommended that the present trends, both in economic and environment fields, must be reversed. While the poor must have at least "sustainable development" to save the environment, the rich must slow down so as not to overheat the environment. Unless the industrialized countries adhered to "sustainable development" even for themselves, it would be difficult to survive. "All nations will have to play a role in changing trends", said the Commission, "and in righting an international economic system that increases rather than decreases inequality, that increases rather than decreases the numbers of poor and hungry". The time had come to "break out of the past patterns" and in fact "security must be sought through change". Indeed, the Commission expressed its unanimous "conviction that the security, well-being, and very survival of the planet depend[ed] on such changes".[69]

Meaning of Sustainable Development

Sustainable development, which became the new slogan at the Rio Conference in 1992, means development that lasts. A basic concern is that those who enjoy the fruits of economic development today may be making future generations worse off by excessively degrading the earth's resources and polluting the earth's environment. According to the World Commission on Environment and Development, "sustainable development was meant to ensure that it meets the needs of the present without compromising the ability of future generations to meet their own needs". Sustainable development, therefore, implied limits "imposed by the present state of technology and social organization on environmental resources and by the ability of the biosphere to absorb effects of human activities". Thus, poverty was not inevitable. The Brundtland Commission was convinced that –

> "Poverty is not only an evil in itself, but *sustainable development* requires meeting the basic needs of all and extending to all the opportunity to fulfill their aspiration for a better life. A world in which poverty is endemic will always be prone to ecological and other catastrophes".[70]

But *sustainable development* also required, according to the Commission, "that those who are more affluent adopt life-styles within the planet's ecological means – in their use of energy for example". Rapidly growing populations can increase the pressure on resources. Sustainable development can only be achieved "if population size and growth are in harmony with the changing production potential of the ecosystem".[71]

Failures to manage the environment and to sustain development threatened to overwhelm all countries. The Commission insisted that "environment and development are not separate challenges; they are inexorably linked.

[69] Ibid., pp. 22-23.
[70] Ibid., p. 8.
[71] Ibid., pp. 8-9.

Development cannot subsist upon a deteriorating environmental resource base; the environment cannot be protected when growth leaves out of account the costs of environmental destruction".[72]

Sustainable development could not ignore and must meet the needs and aspirations of the present without compromising the ability to meet those of the future. Therefore, said the Commission:

> "Far from requiring the cessation of economic growth, it recognizes that the problems of poverty and underdevelopment cannot be solved unless we have a new era of growth in which developing countries play a large role and reap large benefits".[73]

One thing was certain however, according to the Commission. No country could "develop in isolation from others". Long-term sustainable growth would require, therefore, "far-reaching changes to produce trade, capital and technology flows that are more equitable and better synchronized to environmental imperatives".[74]

The Human Development Report of 1993 also insists that it is as important to address the "silent emergencies" of poverty like water pollution, land degradation and environmental diseases, as it is to focus on "loud emergencies" like global warming and ozone depletion, that usually dominate the headlines. While the old motive of fighting the cold war is dead, the new motive must be the war against global poverty because –

> "this is an investment not only in the development of poor nations but in the security of the rich nations. The real threat in the next few decades is that global poverty will begin to travel, without a passport, in many unpleasant forms; drugs, diseases, terrorism, migrations. Poverty anywhere is a threat to prosperity everywhere".[75]

Rio Conference on Environment and Development (UNCED), 1992

The Stockholm Conference had raised public awareness about our ailing planet. The Rio Summit extended this interest worldwide as television and radio carried the message to every corner of the earth. The Stockholm Conference was attended by two heads of government, Indian Prime Minister Indira Gandhi and Swedish Prime Minister Olaf Palme. The Earth Summit at Rio drew more than 100 heads of State and government. Both the seriousness of global environmental problems and general awareness about them increased dramatically, it was correctly noticed, as did "the level of human suffering due to related poverty".[76] During two decades between

[72] Ibid., p. 37.
[73] Ibid., p. 40.
[74] Ibid., p.p. 40-41.
[75] Human Development Report, 1993, pp. 4, 8.
[76] See Panjabi, n. 56, p. 222.

Stockholm and Rio, the population on our crowded planet rose from 3.5 billion to 5.5 billion, 95 per cent of it in poor countries; the earth lost 500 million acres of trees; for the growth of food crops, the world lost 500 million tons of topsoil, an amount equal to the tillable soil of India and France combined; food production declined in 94 countries between 1985 and 1989; at the end of 1991 the debt burden of the developing countries rose to $ 1281 billion. UNICEF estimated that about half a million children in the developing world died in 1988 because "social progress in Third World countries had been stalled or reversed by crushing debts and falling revenues". Clearly, it was pointed out, the South was still subsidizing the high standard of living in the North.[77] Canada's Minister of Environment, Jean Charest, reminded delegates at Rio that in the past "thirty years, income disparities between the North and the South have grown from twenty times to sixty times" and commented that "this trend is simply not sustainable".[78] The North with 25 per cent of the world population, still consumed 70 per cent of the world's energy, 75 per cent of its metals, 85 per cent of its wood.[79] India's former Minister of Environment, Maneka Gandhi, pointed out at Rio that one Western child consumed as much as 125 Eastern children did. She concluded that "nearly all environmental degradation in the East is due to consumption in the West".[80]

Further, the lack of diversity of many developing economies, part of the imperial heritage, still continued unabated. As Ivan Head explained –

> "In the countries of the South... there is in all-too-many instances an overwhelming dependence on a single economic activity. Simply stated, most economic eggs are in one basket.

And to make dependence even more keen, more often than not those eggs assume the form of a single agricultural commodity – coffee, cocoa, sugar, ground-nuts, etc. – or a single mineral – tin, copper, gold, as examples".[81]

Slower growth and world recession had led to a decline in the North in demand for these commodities from the South. As a result, as Ivan Head described it:

> "Should world prices collapses in one of these commodities, or should access to a major market be blocked, the results can be catastrophic. If the bulk of foreign exchange earnings is derived from that product, government income falls, social programmes suffer, all related economic activity (transportation, processing, etc.) stagnates and the country finds itself in desperate circumstances. This is the

[77] See Panjabi, ibid., pp. 233, 238.
[78] Quoted in Panjabi, ibid., p. 239.
[79] See S. Begley, "Is it Apocalypse Now?", *Newsweek*, June 1 1992, p. 36.
[80] Quoted in Begley, ibid., p. 36.
[81] I. Head, *On a Hinge of History*, (1991), p. 46.

reality of an undiversified economy. This is the disadvantage of a seller in a buyer's market".[82]

Rio Conference Adopts Various Instruments

To correct some of these imbalances, to coordinate actions of all States, rich and poor, on various fronts with a view to "establish a new and equitable global partnership", and to cooperate in the achievement of sustainable development for everyone, which had become absolutely essential if the Earth, our only home, had to be saved from the impending, catastrophe, the Rio Conference adopted various instruments trying to elaborate and prescribe general rights and obligations "to meet developmental and environmental needs of the present and future generations".[83] Besides a general Rio Declaration on Environment and Development proclaiming 27 principles for "the further development of international law in the field of sustainable development" (Principle 27), UNCED adopted a Convention on Climate Change, Convention on Biological Diversity, a Statement of Principles on Forests, and Agenda 21, which was more or less a Charter of demands by the developing countries. Agenda 21 became the main forum for North-South wrangling on every imaginable topic, including the spread of deserts, disposal of toxic wastes, and even the protection of women's rights. In the end, all that the delegates could agree was that some of these problems did need to be solved. But what they could not agree was the means to solve them. To bring about meaningful change in most of these areas would require overhauling the way the world does business – from the laws that control international trade to the financial institutions that direct the ebb and flow of capital. That was a task the negotiators were not prepared for and had barely even begun.[84]

Rio Achieves No Progress

If the purpose of the Rio Conference on Environment and Development, attended by more than 100 heads of State and government and thousands of delegates, was to forge a new global partnership between the rich and the poor countries, and to develop a new law of environment and development for the protection of our small planet which is under a serious threat of almost certain doom, it achieved neither. The instruments adopted in Rio were not really binding in law and were couched in such vague and uncertain language that they entailed no legal, political, or even moral obligation. That so much thundering rhetoric accompanied the formulation of declarations never meant to be legally binding both at Stockholm and Rio, merely shows

[82] Ibid.
[83] See P.E. Dewitt, n. 57, p. 37.
[84] See Principle 3 of the Rio Declaration on Environment and Development.

extreme conservativeness, if not insincerity, of the delegates who were more concerned about their "sovereignty" and entrenched "sovereign rights" in a world which is said to have became one (see Principle 2). The differing priorities of the rich developed world for environmentalism, and the poor developing world for development were clearly reflected in the long and bitter debates at Rio which resulted in a rather shoddy "less than inspirational text of Rio Declaration".[85] The proposed Earth Charter led to emotional outbursts, became a "graphic symbol of the North-South divide", and "was converted into a mere pedestrian, rather wordy declaration which the world accepted with somewhat resigned sense of inevitability".[86] The head of the Canadian delegation, Arthur Campeau, described the final declaration as "a document suitable for bureaucrats".[87] Sometimes generously described as "soft law" and widely acclaimed, it really led nowhere. On the other hand, Agenda 21, described as a "750 page document of unsurpassed U.N. verbosity, intended to be the world's programme for sustainable development",[88] is not even likely, according to some observers, "to be read widely or perused by the general public".[89]

Rich-Poor Dichotomy Continues

While the poor countries have been really concerned about their crushing poverty and have continued to compare their miserable lives with the lavish standards in the industrialized countries, the latter have got sick and tired of listening to these comparisons and details of their over-consumption and wastages. Thus the United States, whose consumer society was uppermost in the minds of most poor countries, contemptuously rejected at Rio any condemnation of its affluent way of living. American delegates insisted "over and over that the American life-style is not up for negotiation".[90] This does not mean that the western world is not aware of the frightful implications of its life style which requires more goods than the earth can safely provide and produces more waste than that it can possibly clear away. But the nature of the present economic system depends on creating ever new needs, and the prevailing political arrogance makes any kind of self-restraint unacceptable and rules out effective counter measures.[91] Thus, the United States, itself

[85] See Panjabi, n. 56, p. 221.

[86] Ibid.

[87] Quoted by Panjabi, ibid., p. 221.

[88] Bargain not a Whinge, *Times* (London), June 1 1992, p. 15; quoted in Panjabi, ibid., pp. 2221-222.

[89] Panjabi, ibid.

[90] See P.E. Dewitt, "Summit to Save the Earth: Rich vs. Poor", *Time*, June 1 1992, p. 42.

[91] See S. Lal, n. 42, p. 16.

producing 25 per cent of all CO_2 in the world, steadfastly refused to even consider the proposed cutting of CO_2 emissions to the 1990 levels by the year 2000 – a relatively modest reduction suggested by the European Community – because that would mean a decline in industrial production and loss of jobs.[92] Given that approach of the rich countries, all that the Rio Declaration could say was:

> "To achieve sustainable development and a higher quality of life for all people, States should reduce and eliminate unsustainable patterns of production and consumption..." (Principle 8)

It is all too well-known that the rich countries are not prepared to abandon their privileges. They are more keen to preserve their life styles than to accept disciplines which require a lowering of their irrational levels of consumption of energy, food, paper and a hundred other things. Whatever their leaders say for the record, their deeds speak louder than their words and betray their inability to look at the ecological issues from a global perspective. As we have seen above, the condition of the poor countries – their indebtedness, their terms of trade, their population, their environment – have all deteriorated during the last twenty years. Nationalism still reigns supreme and is the single largest obstacle to international cooperation.

Dumping radio-active and other poisonous waste in the developing countries from the so-called First World – which produces 90 per cent of all hazardous wastes – still continues, increasing the health hazards for millions of poor people by exposing their soil, air, and under-ground water to lethal wastes. Whether this is being done stealthily or with the consent of the Asian-African regimes concerned, often too ashamed to tell their people of what is happening, it is easy for rich countries to sell this policy to their own public on the ground that the fight for a cleaner environment, like charity, begins at home. If the preservation of affluence in the West requires keeping down prices of primary commodities produced by the Third World and jacking up prices of the drugs they need for the use of their impoverished population, the maintenance of a cleaner environment at home should be enough reason for passing on the risks involved in exposure to toxic wastes to those already used to living in squalor.[93] Moreover, as things are, no country, least of all the ones with high-tech weaponary, can be held accountable for disasters which endanger thousands of lives in neighbouring or even remote areas. Russia got away with Chernobyl and dumping nuclear waste in the sea off the coasts of Korea and Japan. France does not feel

[92] See P.E. Dewitt, n. 57, pp. 31-32.

[93] See S. Lal, n. 42, p. 16. There are at least six principles in the Rio Declaration which deal with the concerns of the developing countries. The Stockholm Declaration also referred to their concerns and to the protection of their interests in its Preamble and six of its principles.

constrained for having caused many deaths in remote Pacific islands because of radiation which resulted from its repeated nuclear tests despite widespread protests. Many people may be dying because of eating fish from the seas contaminated by toxic wastes without even being able to name the guilty.[94]

It is well-known that the latest GATT negotiations, such as the Uruguay round, were largely conducted between the United States, the European Economic Community and Japan. The latest GATT agreement (sometimes referred to as the Dunkel draft) is essentially a compromise between them, irrespective of the conditions of the poor and the developing countries. The poor countries are merely dragging along whatever principles might have been recommended at Stockholm and Rio to help them. Thus, though there is a crying need for sharing the world's scientific resources, developing countries have found that access to western technology is neither easy nor cheap. In 1980, eight years after the Stockholm promises, the poor developing countries paid almost two billion dollars in fees and royalties to industrial countries.[95] The importance of proprietary rights is emphasised in industrialized countries because patent protection is said to act as an incentive for the development of new technology. Thus, in 1980 industrialized market economies accounted for 65 per cent of the world total of patents granted world-wide and the Eastern European countries held 29 per cent. Developing countries held a mere 6 per cent of global patents with many of them being granted to non-residents.[96] There might be serious differences between economists as to whether the latest GATT agreement for trade between States may accidentally help India, China, Brazil or Nigeria. But where is the choice for them?

Progress Towards What and Progress for Whom?

As early as 1908, that great perceptive Indian writer, Rabindranath Tagore, raised some doubts about the so-called "progress" towards which we were being dragged along by the prosperous West, which are as relevant today:

> "We have for over a century been dragged by the prosperous West behind its chariot, choked by the dust, deafened by the noise, and over-whelmed by the speed... If we ever ventured to ask, 'progress towards what and progress for whom', it was considered to be peculiarly and ridiculously Oriental to entertain such doubts about the absoluteness of progress".[97]

[94] *Our Common Future*, n. 23, pp. 226-28.

[95] See Panjabi, n. 56, p. 244.

[96] Ibid.

[97] Quoted by G. Axinu, "Sustainable Development Reconsidered", *Development*, Nos. 1-4, p. 120.

As we look at the Western countries and their people continuously struggling to have even more luxurious lives completely disregarding the environmental destruction and progressing towards an uncertain future, and a large number of poor third world countries with their aspiring millions desperately trying to follow them irrespective of the consequences and getting stuck in the thick mire of even more difficult economic and environmental problems, we, as orientals, have those lingering doubts, progress towards what and progress for whom? We have found no answer to these questions.

Index

MIX
Papier aus verantwortungsvollen Quellen
Paper from responsible sources
FSC® C105338

If you have any concerns about our products,
you can contact us on
ProductSafety@springernature.com

In case Publisher is established outside the EU,
the EU authorized representative is:
Springer Nature Customer Service Center GmbH
Europaplatz 3, 69115 Heidelberg, Germany

Printed by Libri Plureos GmbH
in Hamburg, Germany